MW01130670

RECOVERING
IDIOT

© 2015 Ben Casper

PREFACE

I've always lived on the edge. I'm not a leader. I'm not a follower. I've been a bad boy. I've been a good boy. I've never given up. I believe I'll be forgiven because I continue to endure.

NOTE FROM THE EDITOR

Delving into the life and mind of Ben Casper can be a very dangerous thing, but I have heard rumors of this book for years and I confess, I couldn't wait to get my hands on it. Ben doesn't disappoint.

Preserving the integrity of Ben's voice and his wonderful ability to tell a great story without becoming entangled in the chaos of his life became my task as editor. Organization itself is a job of migraine proportions; in the end my approach was to tidy up, dust, and polish, as opposed to completely redecorating. Ultimately, for the sanity of the reader, some of the furniture demanded rearranging, which means this work is not a logical progression from point A to point B. There are plenty of tangents, distractions, and the seemingly unavoidable dive off into the weeds. I hope that the personal narrative which results gives us a true view into how Ben's mind works and how his life moves on a daily basis. I have purposely left much of the original spelling and word usage, i.e., creative misspellings and intentional misuse of words, intact. In doing so, I can almost hear his voice in my head building up steam as he gets to the punch line.

If you do not personally know Ben Casper, you may doubt the authenticity of his words and I promise you that as you read these pages you will shake your head in disbelief. If you are one of the privileged who know the living (for now), breathing Ben Casper, you too will shake your head. It's not because you won't believe him; you just won't believe he is doing it *again*. In fact, I think that I will suggest that any subsequent editions include a catalog of testimonials verifying the truth of Ben's words. Please feel free to submit your name if you wish to be included on that list.

By way of warning if you are easily offended, at all concerned with political correctness, or even with living the letter of the law in general, you might want to seek reading entertainment elsewhere. If you are searching for ideas for reality television shows or information on possible lawsuits, you are holding a gold mine. If you are simply hoping for some quality entertainment, I can promise you that you are in for a real treat. You might want to have a box of tissues handy if side-splitting laughter has that effect on you. I'm not really trying to be funny here, just trying to alert you to the potential dangers involved. Prepare to be perplexed, bewildered, astounded and laugh until the tears flow freely, especially if you are reading aloud.

In closing, I really feel that one thing cannot be overstated, which is perhaps the overriding, undergirding theme of this whole work . . . Michele, you are a wonder!

T. Specht

DEDICATION

To my God who gives me all. No words
are adequate. I thank Thee.

• • •

To my good wife Michele of 37+ years who truly hung
in there. We both agree it has been worth it. I love you,
even if you didn't laugh once while proofreading.

• • •

To my parents Bill and Joan who are gone. I wouldn't
have wanted anyone else. You're the best.

• • •

To my six children, Hauni, Derek, Meg,
Christianne, Will, and Michael who are
living lives better than mine. Keep it up.

• • •

To my siblings and kinfolk., I
apologize. I'm sure I should.

• • •

To my friends. You provided fodder, support,
and usually, forgiveness. Enjoy.

• • •

To me. Without you I wouldn't have any stories.

CONTENTS

INTRODUCTION

One day, back in the 80s after a meeting in La Grande, Oregon, one of my business partners took me to the airport. He was a former pilot and had owned the Ford dealership in La Grande for many years. The wind was howling in 40-50 mph gusts. As I got out of his Blazer, he said, "Now make sure that you take off against the wind."

Since there was no control tower, Claude must have thought I needed someone to tell me in which direction my nose should be pointed and on which runway to take off. It struck me as unnecessary advice and borderline condescension. Since it bugged me a little I said, "Claude, don't tell me what to do. I know which way to take off so you don't need to tell me." For heaven's sake, I'd only wrecked one plane up to that point.

Well, Claude repeated his instructions. I felt like I was getting a lecture I didn't need. I told him that he should have known me well enough by then to know that if someone told me to do something in a particular way, that I would do the opposite just to show them.

If he wanted to verify this, he could call my dad. This is a unique and usually unhealthy trait I picked up as a toddler. If my dad told me to jump, I would say, "No." If he told me not to jump, I would say, "How high?"

Claude kept harping and didn't stop the impromptu flight school discourse so finally I said, "All right, Claude, I'm going to take off with the wind just to show you."

He started swearing at me and my stupidity. I told him thanks for the ride and to be sure to stick around for the sure-to-be-exciting downwind takeoff. I climbed out of Claude's rig, walked across the tarmac, warmed the plane up, and headed for the prohibited runway that had all of a sudden become a challenge I was willing to pursue to the bitter end. It was all Claude's fault.

I have always been a daredevil, but I had no idea how near a fatal accident I was about to brush up against. My extreme confidence was smothering my now totally absent common sense.

The runway was nice and long, about a mile in length. A natural optimist, I didn't consider that there would be any problems because I had so much pavement in front of me. I taxied to the very end of the wrong runway, announced my foolish intentions on the radio, stomped on the brakes, wound the engine up, released the brakes, and let 'er rip.

I kept the flaps off because I didn't want anything impeding my acceleration until I reached flying speed. The wind was pushing me from the back end. This would have been a good thing if we were talking about sailboats, but it's not when you're trying to take off in an airplane.

A short primer for those who don't know a lot about flying:

An airplane must have headwind in order to fly. This "headwind" air speed provides the lift necessary to get and keep the plane in the air. It also provides the pilot the luxury to control the craft. To be safe and effective, an airplane must always take off and land into a headwind. If it is done in a tailwind, the pilot is flirting with major disaster. The runway drastically shortens up with every mile an hour of tailwind. Conversely, the stronger the headwind, the quicker liftoff occurs.

Stalls, spins, and collisions with the ground and other immoveable objects usually occur due to loss of, or not maintaining enough, airspeed. I believe most airplane crashes occur from the root cause of inadequate headwind, or airspeed, and resulting loss of control. Pilot inattention and error, weather conditions, and engine problems can all lead to this juncture.

I started gaining groundspeed quickly, but soon realized I wasn't picking up appreciable and necessary airspeed. The airspeed indicator was still stuck on zero and a quarter of the runway had already passed under my tail. Beads of sweat appeared on my brow and every body orifice I owned began contracting.

Passing the halfway point on the runway, I finally saw the indicator start to move. It showed 10 mph while I was actually tripping along at 60 or 70. The runway was getting shorter in a quick hurry. The airspeed was about half of what the ground speed was. We were screaming over the pavement at a hundred miles an hour. If I had wet my finger and stuck it out the side window, I would have felt a gentle breeze, however, I had no time for an exercise such as this.

My airplane had never gone this fast while still on the ground. It started shaking like the wheels were going to come off and I realized both me and my airship were in uncharted territory. I could see the end of the runway looming larger and larger; every instant seemed to be hammering another nail in the coffin.

I pulled back on the stick and got no response. I wanted to stop this nightmare, but it was much too late. If I tried to abort the takeoff, I would hit the end of the runway at 120 mph. The point of no return was now a long way behind me.

There was a ditch, fence, pasture, and some cows and trees just off the end of the runway I was racing toward. With just a few feet left before the end of the asphalt and the beginning of the cow pies, I jerked full flaps on, pulled the wheel back, and rammed the landing gear into the wheel wells. These actions gave me the only chance of getting off the ground and cleaning up the airplane aerodynamics; they were my singular hope of getting and keeping the plane in the air at this late date.

The Mooney sluggishly rose from ground effect, bouncing up and down with the gusts of wind around us. We finally started to crawl upwards into the air, inch by most welcome inch. The gusty environment bounced us around. I didn't mind the bounces up, but I didn't appreciate the times we dropped.

The rough ride didn't bother me. I was ecstatic I wasn't planted nose first in the far bank of the ditch or in an inverted position trying to pull tree branches out of my pitot tube. There's no question that with the high speed I was traveling, it would have been a fatal wreck.

The next morning I got a call from my partners in La Grande. Claude was livid. He started yelling and cussing me out for my stupidity. I agreed with him. I knew I had made a really naughty decision. I admitted he was right and promised I would never do it again. Do you think that satisfied him? Not a chance. He continued to rant and rave and call me every name in the book. After more than ten minutes of aeronautical abuse, I finally told him to lay off and to get back to the business at hand. I was a little bugged that Claude didn't at least compliment me on my excellent flying skills.

When I think of this experience, I marvel at the ground speed my Mooney and I attained before we finally scratched and clawed our way into the air, inches above the catastrophic danger of cows and ditches just below.

• •

As this book began rattling around in the back of my empty noggin, I realized that I have always liked the sound of the way alcoholics on the mend greet each other at their meetings. So I quickly seized on the title, *Hi, My Name is Ben and I'm a Recovering Alcoholic.* But then I realized I don't have that particular malady. So I decided to call it, *Hi, My Name is Ben and I'm a Recovering Idiot.*

As anyone who knows me will attest, I do have that particular malady. However, if someone is trying to locate this book in a grade school library in a hundred years, that title is too long and refers to me at least three different times. Since I'm feeling the modest need to refer to myself less, I'm just going to call it, *Recovering Idiot.*

The stories that follow are absolutely true, but if any of them land me in court, those particular accounts are absolutely a figment of my imagination.

My thanks to my (usually) good wife Michele, Taneil Specht and Brianne Huwe for their encouragement, editing, proofreading and laughter. It got and kept me going. Another big thanks to Josh Kessie for making this book look like something I didn't do. You did a great job, Josh!

I apologize if the comings and goings of this book drive you nuts. Au contraire, if you like it, please send me, Ben Casper, a cash donation in unmarked bills in a sealed envelope marked *Confidential and Private.* (Michele always gets the mail.)

In spite of what you might think after reading this, I really believe law enforcement is essential to our society and that many good individuals fill its ranks.

I apologize for using the term "I" so many times. It's the story of my life so I, oops sorry, so me has no other choice.

CHAPTER 1

DIRT POOR FARMERS, FILTHY RICH HUNTERS, AND ME

I have been told for decades to write a book about my life. The more time and troubles I wade through, the more I think my advisers are just looking for a little dirt.

Who, besides Bill Clinton, would want all of their dirty laundry put out on the public clothesline? Well, to be honest, I guess I don't mind. It must be something about having the same initials.

So here's the book . . .

Dad and Mom moved to the desolate and deserted desert of the Columbia Basin in Washington State in 1957 with a thousand dollars, a car pulling a homemade trailer holding everything they owned, and big ideas to farm. My folks had bushel loads of desire to make their own way and raise a family in the process. However, the odds were stacked against them. It was a hard life.

In the cold winter of 1957 with few tools, no utilities in place, and nary a neighbor to help, Dad started building a home to house his future posterity. Mom, Dad, and I usually did this at night since Dad had a day job working as a county agent. My sister Teresa was a baby and a little too young to help with the actual construction.

I was two years old at the time and toddled around the place in freezing weather while the folks built the house. I probably wasn't much help. Dad mixed concrete for the foundation by hand and shovel. They illuminated the primitive worksite with the car headlights. Because the temperatures were freezing, the concrete froze before it cured the next morning. I guess they felt they had to get the job done and didn't worry about the finer details.

My future with the capitals "BT" for "Big Trouble" was foretold one cold winter night when I stuck my tongue on the business end of a frozen hammer. The folks got a little concerned when they saw me walking around with a claw hammer hanging out of my mouth.

How to thaw and separate? There was no electricity, heat, or running water. I was screaming and time was of the essence. The only warm substance available was mom's spit so she started hocking loogies toward my connection point with this foreign object until we finally separated. Yuck! She would never have gotten away with that in later years. However, since I never learn, I would probably still be agreeable to sticking my tongue on a frosty hammer if it looked like it needed cleaning.

My earliest memories of life are of living with my poor, sodbuster parents in a desolate, sometimes hot, sometimes cold, windy, sandy, sagebrush sprinkled, cheat grass covered, coyote and snake-infested spot, a mile or two north of the Columbia River in southeastern Washington State. The local shoreline at the Columbia was called Ringold, just a few miles downriver from White Bluffs. White Bluffs is where the Feds kicked farmers and townspeople out in the 40s so they could build the A-Bomb to blow up Hiroshima. This place was and still is home. My life has always been centered in this cradle of agriculture and home of "salt of the earth" farmers.

Starting out, it wasn't a farm. It was blow sand and sagebrush, pretty much a constant dust storm with nary a neighboring farm in sight. The Grand Coulee Dam had been built some eighty miles upstream on the Columbia River and a huge canal system had recently been dug. This brought life-sustaining irrigation water to the Basin and allowed energetic folk like Mom and Dad to get a shaky start as young farmers.

Most of the new settlers were destitute, young couples not unlike the hard scrabble folk living during The Depression and Dust Bowl eras. The majority of them lived in tents, shacks, and other substandard accommodations, with high hopes for better times to come. Many stayed for a few months, or a year or two, and then gave up, returning to their former, and more pleasant, locales and livelihoods that they had previously abandoned. Most came with more resources than my folks, but few had more ambition.

Mom and Dad started out buying forty acres with my dad holding down a job as a county agent, assisting other farmers as they tried to tame the wild ground. He would rise early in the morning to work his own field, go to work for eight or nine hours, and then return in the evening to again work on his farm until late each night. He stayed with his job for just a year and then went full-time as a farmer. I remember watching him through the front window as he left for work in a county-issued pickup each morning, and crying because I wanted to go with him. I was three at the time.

His job included surveying undeveloped land. He staked and flagged it so the new farmers could level the uneven ground to grade. This was absolutely necessary before it could be farmed since it gave the new farmer the ability to get the life-giving water to run down the crop rows to the bottom of the field. I remember him taking me a time or two, a toddler trudging through the hot sand, trying to keep up with his surveying and fast-striding father.

Back then, the area had minimal green vegetation. Most of the ground was a conduit for the scorching sun. In the early years, dust devils or whirlwinds were a constant sight. Spinning sand, tumbleweeds, and other available debris were sucked into the vortex, often rising a half mile into the air. It was always entertaining to watch. Trying to guess which direction the twister would go and watching its minor destruction was fun for us kids.

Nowadays, dust devils are a rarity in the irrigated areas of this tamed desert. I assume this is because there is no longer just hot sand to reflect the heat and stir up the twisters. Green crops abound now and keep the temperatures and topsoil more subdued.

Dad would rise at 4:30 each morning and work at a dead run until 9:00 or later in the evening. He continued at this pace from 1957 until around 1985 when he came down with Multiple Sclerosis. He had to spend the next eighteen years hobbling around, eventually becoming relegated to a wheelchair. The MS years were very hard on him. I wouldn't have had as hard of a time as he did with this debilitating disease since I don't mind sitting around and dreaming up new ideas, usually about how to get out of work.

Speaking of work, Mom was just as much of a worker as Dad. I am still amazed by their accomplishments, love, and example. It has been a great blessing to have been raised in their home.

Things changed in 1958. I remember as a three-year-old sitting on my tricycle outside our house watching a truck coming down the gravel road with a big army barracks loaded on the back. A man stood on the roof with a board and lifted each power line up and over the house-on-wheels as the truck pulled it past, underneath the lines.

We finally had some neighbors and they were only a quarter of a mile away! The Cooks happened to be members of The Church of Jesus Christ of Latter-day Saints, Mormons, as were we. They had a boy my age named Brian who created half of an inseparable duo for double trouble for the next decade or so. We managed to squeeze in an amazing amount of extracurricular activities for two farm boys whose fathers kept the work piled on.

Household luxuries were scarce. We didn't have running water for two years. Mom would hook up a trailer to the back of our tractor every week and drive to the nearest neighboring farmhouse that had running water. The water was used for washing, drinking, cooking, and other essentials. My sisters and I rode on the flatbed trailer carrying the water tank.

Saturday night was bath night. Several pots of water were heated on the stove and then dumped into a tin tub in the front room. My sisters bathed and then I. Next, Mom crawled in and Dad finally finished the cleaning process in the dirty bathwater. We were ready to go to church the next day.

We had to walk several hundred feet to a homemade outhouse every time we needed to "do our business." I remember the sometimes freezing seat and always smelly atmosphere this job entailed.

The Cooks also had an outhouse. Since we were their closest neighbors and were a good quarter of a mile away from their outhouse, Brian's mom Donna had no problem leaving their privy door open that just so happened to face our home and the prevailing wind. She found this greatly diminished the smell factor. Her open-door policy remained in effect until the day she found out that my dad had purchased a new pair of binoculars.

In my early years, my folks were just getting started with their farming career. They had just a couple of small "units" of ground and were struggling with all aspects of eking out a living from the just-inaugurated and newly irrigated desert sand. Isolation, miniscule financing, overwhelming forces of nature, and limited equipment were matched by their unlimited and tenacious desire to work.

• •

One Saturday evening in the fall of 1960, when I was five, a very unusual sight settled upon our humble abode. A caravan of fancy Lincoln Continentals and Cadillacs pulled up in our yard and a large group of men exited. (Little did any of us realize, 21 years later, some of the same group would be witnesses and participants to a farming accident that almost killed me.)

They introduced themselves as bird hunters from Seattle and asked if it might be possible for them to hunt pheasants, ducks, and geese around our farm. My folks soon found out that most of them were originally from Utah and were Mormon.

That memorable evening was the beginning of a long and wonderful friendship. Three brothers formed the core of the group: Monte (ML), Stan, and Eugene Bean. The Bean brothers had grown up in Richfield, Utah, and worked their way north for college and work. Among the others were Dr. Boyd Simmons, Dr. Ben Taylor (a psychiatrist), and Dr. Lynn Whimpey (a dentist).

ML worked for Skaggs Department Stores in Portland, Oregon, in the 50s and worked his way up in the company. He was also called as the first stake president when the Portland Stake was organized. In the Mormon church we have bishops that are responsible for local congregations, called wards, of roughly 300 to 600 members. Stake presidents are responsible for regions that are comprised of six to ten of these wards. Interestingly enough, 64 years later when the Portland stake was absorbed into other stakes in the area and the stake president was released, my youngest brother Bryan happened to be that stake president. There are now seven stakes in the Portland area.

ML was a very successful businessman, owning and operating a chain of several hundred Pay 'N Save drug stores, Ernst Hardware stores, and Malmo nurseries. Since this was before Bill Gates began his reign, ML was the wealthiest man in the state of Washington, and yet, I don't ever remember him talking about his money. I do remember hearing that one year ML was honored with a ticker tape parade in downtown Seattle.

Stan and Eugene owned a chain of Seattle Sporting Goods stores. Their hunting comrades included dentists, psychiatrists, doctors, and other professionals. Most of them were LDS and often attended church with us when they came out to hunt in the fall. After church, Mom and Dad would fix them a nice dinner. They were all genuinely nice guys.

They always showed up on the first Saturday morning of hunting season, which was usually around the first week of October. They brought 'No Hunting' signs that got posted around the boundaries of Dad's and a few other farms, thereby establishing their right to exclusively canvass the territory. Pheasants were plentiful back then. The weather always seemed beautiful. Hunting season started at noon. When the clock struck twelve, gunshots began ringing out for miles around. Being a beautifully-feathered game cock had its disadvantages on those fall days. Everyone usually limited out with three roosters apiece.

Those Saturday afternoons were heaven for yours truly, a little boy they let tag along. After they had tromped through a cornfield with their dogs scaring up birds, they would take a break by their cars, listening to the University of Washington Huskies football games on the radio. Soda pop, chips, and candy were a rare luxury to our family, but a common staple during those Saturdays in October. This yearly experience was a delight to our family. They often brought gifts of food, a shotgun for my dad, footballs, and other items that we never would have seen without "the hunters" showing up. Dad was always working, but I got to tag along and listen to their banter. I loved those episodes.

• •

The only help Dad had for the first few years of farming was Mom and I. My sisters, Teresa and Jill, were enlisted as soon as they were able. Mom would often drive a tractor to cultivate or work the ground and perform many other "man-jobs" around the farm. My parents worked long days. Usually the two of them did the work of three or four regular individuals, which is to say the equivalent of 15 or 20 government workers.

This was the early days of farming in the Columbia Basin with virtually no automation or comforts of home. Scorching sun, blasting wind, massive requirements of long and hard labor, few neighbors in the isolated desert, no infrastructure, and rudimentary housing, were but a few of the daily pressures on these farms. No home could keep the dust out. When settlers awoke in the morning after a windstorm, their pillows would be coated with a thick covering of dirt except where their heads had been. Some of our neighbors lived in tents. It was a hard life.

Dad's second farm, which I now own, consisted of around 100 acres of blow sand. He planted it into hay, which required harvesting four or sometimes five times a year. We had an old mowing machine, which had a long, fast moving serrated knife sticking out a good eight feet behind the tractor on one side. The knife cut and laid the hay down. It was also hard on the legs of mother pheasants protecting their nests if they hesitated a little too long before taking flight. Nowadays, a swather is the farmer's weapon of choice. The swather does triple duty. It cuts the hay and then runs it through a conditioner, which smashes the hay stems, allowing the hay to dry much quicker. Finally, as the newly cut hay exits the swather, it gets channeled into a windrow. Back then, the farmer dropped the hay and then came back several times to rake it into windrows and turn it so it could dry. There was no conditioner to expedite the drying. Finally, after a much longer period of drying than is needed these days with the swather conditioners, the hay would get baled.

In 1958 I was three years old and felt it was high time my motor vehicle driving career began. Mom heard the tractor start up one day. She figured it was my dad going out to work ground, but after looking outside, decided she had an emergency on her hands.

I had started the tractor and after pushing the throttle as far forward as it would go, I sat on the seat and yelled, "I go to Ken Benson's! I go to Ken Benson's!" Ken was our one and only neighbor at that time and I guess I felt like he might be getting lonely. Luckily, I had pushed the throttle forward and not the clutch; otherwise, I might have gone and seen Ken Benson. Mom killed the tractor and probably wanted to kill me.

When I was four, Dad needed someone to drive truck so he could stack bales of hay on the back of it and haul the hay out of the field. Mom had her hands full with my three younger siblings who were at and under the age of three. She had no running water or bathroom and was stuck in the middle of a dust bowl. Dad had just a couple of pieces of land at that time. One was a field full of hay bales with no one but my dad and I to bring them in.

We had an old 2-ton Chevy flatbed truck and a ground-driven circular bale elevator that could be hooked to the side of the truck. As the truck motored forward, the elevator would hoist the bales up the side of the truck so that a person standing on the truck bed or stacked hay could retrieve and stack the 100 pound bales.

Still fresh in my mind is the day I first drove. We drove to the field filled with hay my dad had just baled. He put me in the driver's seat. I stood three and a half feet tall. There was no way I could reach the pedals so I knelt on the seat and peered over the dash to see out the window. The steering wheel was much larger back then. Dad put the truck in gear, let out on the clutch, jumped off the step, hopped on the back of the truck, and away we went. The truck had a hand throttle I could use to speed up or slow down. If I needed to stop I was told to shut the key off. The only thing I had to worry about was turning the big steering wheel and guiding the truck past the bales and into the chute so the elevator could catch and scoop them up to Dad.

As was the case with most farm kids of that era, I was driving tractors and trucks on a regular basis by the time I hit first grade. It was necessary back then as there was so much work to do and the finances of the times usually didn't allow the luxury of hired help. The modern, heavy-handed regulations and sticky-fingered revenue collecting appetite of the government hadn't entered our free enterprise system yet. If it had, everyone would have gone broke. One of the major benefits to the family farm was that the kids could help with the overwhelming workload. The farmer's offspring could pitch in without Big Brother's intervention. In other words, we worked our butts off. I didn't like it much then, but I am glad now that I had the experience.

To those who say I'm exaggerating the government's dominance, read on. The year this book was finished (2015) my sister Teresa and her husband Bret were harvesting apples on their farm just like every other year. Over 400 bins of their crop had been picked and sent to the apple packing facility. Each bin holds 1,000 lbs of apples.

I drove up to their orchard one morning. I talked to Bret while stuffing my pockets with apples every time he looked the other way. This exercise usually occurs every fall and Bret has become accustomed to looking the other way whenever I show up.

A few minutes after I said goodbye to Bret and drove away with my load of fruit, two ladies drove past Bret in the bin yard adjacent to the orchard. They looked like they were lost. A few minutes later they returned. They informed Bret they had noticed a couple of kids in the orchard. They claimed they saw them putting apples in a bin. This may or may not have happened.

The kids were eight and eleven years old. Their parents were picking apples nearby and have worked for Bret for years. The kids were in the orchard because that's where their parents could keep an eye on them. They were in no danger and causing no trouble. Whether they put an apple or two in a bin is within the realm of possibility. It's something I can see any kid doing. The problem was that these women determined that Bret was paying them.

I know without a doubt that Bret was not paying them. I've been around his farming operation for many years and know for a certainty that he does not hire children.

They then informed Bret they were from the Department of Labor in Seattle, a federal agency. They asked Bret a bunch of questions and the following nightmare ensued. The women claimed that since they saw the kids putting apples in bins, the apples were "hot" and illegally picked. Therefore all the apples that had been picked in that orchard were "hot." Bret's protests fell on deaf (and dumb) ears.

The legalized extortionists contacted the packing house that was ready to run Bret's apples. They slapped a hold on the packer so he could not do a thing with the fruit until the DOL lifted it. Basically, the 400,000 lbs of apples would rot if they couldn't be packed. After picking, the time an apple sits waiting to be packed and shipped makes a big difference in the quality of the fruit.

Next, these "ladies" told Bret that he must sign a form admitting he had hired children. If he did not sign, his apples would never be run and would be junk.

If he wanted his fruit back, he must sign a false admission that he had hired kids and he must then give the DOL a $16,000 cashier's check to pay the fine it handed him.

They told him that they were going to make an example out of him. It did not matter that he had never hired kids. They didn't care. All they wanted to do was hold him hostage for their resumes and egos until he met their blackmail demands.

They also told him his records for the last few years were going to be audited. Who knows how that will go considering the caliber of the people running the system? To those who take for granted that our government is a warm and fuzzy friend and the bureaucrats wielding power are simply serving the citizenry, I submit you are naïve at best.

This little activity could potentially ruin Bret and Teresa who have farmed for the last 25 years. The fact that it could even happen gives great credence to those who want to retain control of their firearms not only to protect their lives and property, but also to keep the government at bay.

• •

Just before Christmas when I was four years old, my Grandpa Riggs told me a story about a little boy who wanted a pony for Christmas. Like the boy in the story, I also wanted a pony. Grandpa told me that on Christmas morning when the boy put his hand in his stocking, all that was in his hand when he pulled it out was horse manure. The little boy looked at it for a minute and then said, "It looks like the pony got away."

So on Christmas morning when I got up, my grandpa steered me toward my stocking. He was more excited than I was for me to stick my hand in the stocking to discover its contents. I jammed my hand and arm down the big sock. When I pulled it out, I was clutching a big gob of horse manure, just like the little boy in the story. However, I had a little different reaction. I instinctively threw the green, smelly substance as fast and as hard as I could to get away from it.

Grandpa howled with laughter. My folks were mortified and jumped on my case. Green horse crap was scattered on the ceiling, walls and floor of our humble abode. The only one who was happy was Grandpa.

After they got the mess cleaned up and my grandpa calmed down, they took me outside and showed me a Shetland pony tied to the fence. I guess he didn't get away after all.

We had the pony for several years, but he was more trouble than he was worth. He was "corral bossy," which meant that at any moment while you were riding him, if he got a notion, he would turn and start running for the corral (his home) as fast as his stubby little legs could go. Once we arrived in the vicinity of the corral, he wouldn't slow until he got right to the fence. He would then lurch to a sudden stop, kind of like he had hit a brick wall.

I had little control over the stubborn animal while riding him, which immediately downgraded to absolutely no control once he got into his "homeward bound" mode. Whenever he decreased his momentum at the fence, my momentum seemingly increased and continued forward until terra firma or a fence plank halted my progress. My initial love for "Sandy" decreased in direct relation to the number of times he helped me dismount at the Not-So-OK Corral.

I quit riding him. He got out of the corral one day and happened upon some grain that was stored in a small shed. The horse then made a pig of himself. He foundered (excess consumption of grain causing horses' hooves to grow out of control) and soon was useless. Dad got rid of him. Soon after his departure, I went to kindergarten. Sandy probably helped hold my schoolwork together whenever we pulled out the Elmer's glue.

● ●

I was eight in September of 1963. President John F. Kennedy came to town. He was invited to dedicate a nuclear reactor out on the Hanford Atomic Energy Range, which was just across the Columbia River from our farm. The dedication site was probably 10 miles away from our home as the crow flies.

Unfortunately there were no crows big enough to haul our entire family to the engagement. There was also no bridge in the area, so we had to drive some 60 miles to get to the site via the Tri-Cities. I remember it was very hot and there were a bunch of people attending (37,000). We hung around in a large crowd, hot, sweating, and waiting to see the President. He was late, but finally arrived in a helicopter. It was an exciting day for our family in spite of the heat and all the traffic and waiting. Eight weeks later he was assassinated.

● ●

When I was ten, Dad asked me to take our 730 John Deere tractor and head over to one of our farms about six miles away from the home place. He said he would be along shortly in the pickup.

The old 730 was a two-cylinder gas machine with long vertical hand controls for the throttle and clutch rising up from the floor to the right of the steering wheel. It was your typical Johnny Popper as the old John Deere tractors are affectionately called. I loved that tractor. Dad bought it new around 1960 and I felt fortunate enough to find it later in life and buy it from a guy who had restored it.

I headed for the farm at top speed, which was 15 miles an hour. After traveling for three miles and reaching the top of a large hill, I approached an intersection where I had to make a right turn. Being a mature ten-year-old and loving a challenge, as I got closer to the turn I decided I would see if I could take the 90-degree corner at top speed.

As I went into the turn I realized I had neglected to factor in a change in road conditions. If it had continued, the pavement I was turning off of would have allowed me to turn at high speed and still stick to the desired route without much trouble. However, the gravel road I was turning onto became like unto an ice skating rink, even though it was a hot summer day.

The tractor started sliding sideways as soon as we hit the gravel. It slid toward the outside of the turn like an astronaut's centrifuge, skidding off the road and into the deep barrow pit as I frantically turned the steering wheel righter and righter. I had my hands full. I couldn't slow down or stop because I was 110% occupied with the steering wheel and couldn't grab the clutch or gas handles. There were no foot controls for the gas and clutch on this baby! Having no seat belt left me hanging on for dear life by clutching the steering wheel and trying to steer at the same time while bouncing through the off-road terrain.

A three inch by eight foot, square, solid metal tool bar was hooked on the back of the tractor, sticking ten feet across and poking out two feet on each side of the speeding green machine. Krrack!! As Johnny Popper and I slid into the barrow pit at full speed, I heard the outstretched tool bar strike and snap off the stop sign post as it passed my nine o'clock position.

Even though the stop sign was for traffic coming the other way, for the first time in my young life, I really wanted to obey it. Johnny didn't. So we did it his way and continued bouncing along the side of the road at full speed. I had the front wheels cranked to the right as far as they would go and yet the tractor wouldn't turn back up on the road. The wheels were sliding, unable to turn the tractor as the momentum, the slope we were on, and the relatively slick dirt and gravel, kept the tractor off the road. Finally, the tires grabbed and we shot back up on the desired surface.

My speed was still maxed out, however, and before I could take action to get things settled down, we shot across the road and ended up in the exact same configuration and motion. The only difference was we were now on the other side of the road in the opposite gutter and trying to turn left instead of right. Krrack!! Up until that moment there had been a "SLOW, CURVES AHEAD" sign standing erect on the opposing side of the road from the stop sign location. This was no longer the case. In less than 10 seconds, I had taken out two signs and installed some new ruts in the off-road gutters. Finally, I was able to reach up and pull the clutch back, hit the 2 foot-pedal brakes and stop my ride.

I needed a break. I deserved a rest. I had single-handedly stopped a renegade John Deere. I had adrenaline pumping and was totally aware that I had just avoided a major problem, namely my death. I still had a minor problem. Two county warning signs were toast and my dad was going to show up at any moment. I jumped off the tractor and ran a 50-yard dash back to the fallen stop sign. The four by four wooden post had sheared off right at ground level. It lay comatose.

I was able to raise the stop sign back up to a vertical stance by wrapping both my arms around it, holding it against my body, and grunting repeatedly as I righted the sign. After finally getting the red part pointing heavenward, I was able to lift the entire assembly up a few inches and set it back down on the splintered base. It was critical that I matched the top splinters that were on the bottom of the post I was clutching with the bottom splinters that were on the top of the anchored post in the ground.

At this point, I began moving the post around until I had it perfectly balanced. I stepped back, amazed at the good luck I was finally experiencing. That baby was balanced and holding. The red octagon stood in its full majesty, ready to stop anybody that came its way. The splintered tongue and groove repair job and balancing act had turned a potentially disastrous "father sees broken sign spectacle and kills kid" into a miraculous healing act that would show up Oral Roberts at a staged leprosy revival.

The only signs of the break were the splinters at the base. I hurriedly scooped dirt and gravel around the post and soon had a nice little mound covering the injury. It didn't lend any additional support, but made the scene look authentic and untouched.

"I just might make it," I said to myself.

So far there was no sign of Dad. I raced back to the "Curves Ahead" sign and began replicating the previous repair. This one was harder to balance. As I worked, I kept looking over my shoulder for Dad to come around the bend. I had barely finished teaching the sucker to stand on its own when I saw Dad coming over the rise of the hill in his pickup.

"Am I going to pull this off?" I wondered, as I stepped back and admired my work while still keeping a hand on it for stability's sake.

As he approached and began making the right turn to head my way, Lady Luck picked a most inopportune time to run out on me. The stop sign decided it was time to return to its prone position. My dad is the only person in the entire world who has had a stop sign drop dead, right in front of him. I'm sure he was bewildered. His confusion was compounded as I relinquished my stability-lending stance and let go of the second sign. A lumberjack would have yelled, "Timber!" I whispered, "Oh crap." My dad pulled up and jumped out of his pickup. "What in the heck is going on?"

I explained the situation, putting my driving skills in the best light possible. Dad didn't buy it. We declared the signs deceased and went back to farming. I had to listen to tractor-driving safety tips the rest of the day.

• •

Speaking of the 730 tractor, early one morning I headed out to move sprinklers. I was 11 and driving the 730 while a teenage kid who was working for us rode on one of the fenders just above the rear tires. We were going down the road at full throttle with my cocker spaniel Prince running along on our right side. A car was coming the other way and just as it went past, Prince darted to his left to chase the car. He ran in front of the right rear tire and it rolled over him. The tractor bumped up and down as Prince rolled yelping off into the barrow pit.

I was devastated. He was dead. I moved several sprinkler lines that morning in tears. When Dad showed up to help me finish the last sprinkler line, he could see I was upset. After we finished moving water, he took me in the pickup to where Prince lay in the weeds. We picked him up and laid him in the back of the pickup. Our one-pickup funeral procession then took him down and buried him in the soil bank at the bottom of what is now my farm. Little did I know that a few years later, a tractor would roll over me in the same way, except with the left rear tire.

CHAPTER 2

SEVERAL FIRST TASTES
AND A FEW MUSINGS

Growing up in the 1960s and 70s was an adventure, at least in the neck of woods that I was raised in. Actually, the only woods that were around my growing up years consisted of sagebrush sprinkled in with a few willow branches and lathes from the woodshed, often used on my backside. I was raised in a home full of love, hard work, and good examples, although there was a touch too much "touch" when it came to corporeal attitude adjustments.

When my folks started their parenting years, one of my grandfathers advised them not to spare the rod or the child would be spoiled. This was a mistake with my free spirit. The physical efforts at corrective maneuvers just made me want to be a little freer. I was the first of nine kids, and therefore, the prototypical experimental model. I started out at a very early age developing the attitude that if my dad wanted me to do one thing, I would do just the opposite. I struggle with this Johnny Reb thinking process to this very day.

This narrative is my life. Of those who read, some will express righteous, and therefore probably self-righteous, indignation. A few saintly souls will honestly be offended and ashamed that they know me. The rest of the readership has probably had a few of the same struggles, albeit not near the volume, frequency, quality, or quantity. A few will laugh. Some will even relate. If this narrative provides help, hope, or other positive perspectives for readers, I will be happy. My work and life are not a total waste.

Most will read and think, "You wouldn't catch me doing that!" "What an idiot!" or "His poor wife!" A few will muse, "When is he going to die?" One or two will say, "Been there, done that."

Liability concerns require me at this point to warn the reader that they are not to attempt these stunts at home. Acts were performed by a quasi-semi-professional, though admittedly recovering idiot.

I constantly have trouble staying on task, but have always loved heading off into the unknown frontiers of new ideas. Years ago, I watched a show called "Nightshift" with Michael Keaton and Henry Winkler. In one scene, I think it was Keaton who admits he has no talent or anything else to offer except ideas. He was an "Idea Man". He didn't have much in the way of substance to offer but, Boy! Was he excited!

I immediately realized that that's me to a T. Ideas. No Fear. No Hesitation. Just Ideas.

Stay up all night dreaming up ideas and spend all day trying to make them happen. Stay away from the nuts and bolts and details. Use a broad brush. Utilize the day to work and the night to dream. Out with the old; in with the new. Leave the unfinished and often heavily invested-in old dreams behind and work on the more expensive and exciting new idea of the moment.

Don't get the wrong idea. I do work from time to time. And once in a while, I might focus on a detail or two. But I still like to dream.

Being bipolar has helped fill the story hopper. I made, and still manage to make, major and minor mistakes daily. I took chances. My life was up and down, back and forth, high and low, warm and fuzzy and all together at times, but more often than not laying on life's hard, cold floor in little pieces.

A few years ago, I took a seminar designed to improve personal performance. The instructor mentioned that, previously, his father had been going downhill fast with a fatal ailment. Hospice workers came in and helped care for him in his last months of life. The instructor was so grateful and impressed with the care the hospice workers provided his father that he began doing hospice work himself, in a gesture to pay back some of the service his family received.

As he performed this charitable work, he noticed one very striking aspect. A great majority of the people he cared for that were dying had a singular comment and wish. Their greatest regret was that they hadn't taken more chances, opportunities, and risks in their lives. I will never have that regret. Risky Business Boulevard and Take-A-Chance Turnpike are the two main roads I've always traveled.

I sincerely hope no one will think they can tempt fate or bypass common sense as I have. It may appear I got away scot-free, without any problems, after taking so many risks. To the contrary, I've heaped plenty of problems upon myself from various wacky escapades. I just haven't been killed or locked up yet. But life is short; I still might die someday.

I don't claim to have never sinned. I've made more mistakes than your average human "bean". I don't claim a spot in heaven. However, I do hope for one. Maybe I can slip in the backdoor and hide in the balcony. Actually I really don't believe it's going to work that way. Lip service means little.

Since early on, I have harbored the hope that something great is going to happen that will completely change my life and its direction. Who hasn't? That new direction will lead straight to heaven and lots of money and fame. I'll have no more debt. My spouse will start doing everything I think she should. No more mistakes, bills, doubts, dirty deals, sickness, money worries, temptations, kid problems. The reality is, I know in my heart that something like that is not going to happen in the next day or two, and most likely never will occur—especially the part about the wife. I think I hope for it because I, like everyone else, need a pleasant pipe dream to keep me going on those really bad days.

I've done some good and I've done some bad. I've had great times and endured some absolutely horrible periods of hell on Earth. Who hasn't? I know there are worse folk than I out there and I know there are better. Except for those times after I have just finished dealing with a real snake, I usually subscribe to the adage that "the best of us are not that much better than the worst of us, and the worst of us are not that much worse than the best of us."

I often fail. Judge not. To forgive is divine. Read, shake your head, and be glad you ain't me.

In the beginning of my full-time, moneymaking years, I had no assets. Almost 40 years later and I'm not much better off. In the interim I've lost at least half a million on wacky investments and business ventures. Another seven hundred thousand was lost in money that people owed me, but neglected to pay.

It is an absolute miracle that with all of my knuckleheaded decisions I have not gone bankrupt. So far I have been able to pay my bills and keep my wife in bonbons and my kids in diapers. I attribute it to crazy luck, staying up all night drumming up solutions, hard work, fast-talking, and paying my tithing. I pay the Lord what He asks and He gives me a little extra help whenever I get into a serious jam. I wouldn't consider not paying my tithing. I am sincerely convinced I get much more out of the tithing deal than if I didn't pay. If I kept the ten percent, I'd be on my own. Since I pay a tenth, I've got the greatest partner I could possibly ask for.

I've had to sell my program to many different bankers in order to keep the bearings greased and wheels turning to pay the proverbial Paul. I've been kicked out of most of those same banks after a year or two of paper-thin operating successes, the tires falling off the previous year's budget projections, and my constant venturing into new adventures. I've always miraculously been able to repay Peter by finding and borrowing from a new Paul.

Monetarily, I would have been much more successful had I stuck to just one or two of the more promising projects. But I like new ideas. So I took on about everything that came my way or entered into my vastly open, seemingly empty, and fairly non-discriminating mind. Some of these get-rich-quick schemes wasted years of my life. Some of them cost me a lot of up-front borrowed cash.

The upside? I wasn't burdened with boring forethought or worry for extended periods of time as to whether I should jump in. However, my poor wife and I have been financially dogged with the results of a lot of poor decision-making as I've forged ahead through the years. My wife has always complained that living with me is never boring.

• •

Through the years, I've been intrigued by the burning of tires. There is a bundle of energy packed into each black, round balloon that keeps cargo and people of the world rolling to their next destination. I think this attraction began early in my youth.

In our early years my buddy Brian and I became infatuated with the squeal, struggle-to-grip, and visual effects generated when loads of power are poured into the four little footprints most vehicles use on the bottom of their tires to stay connected to the asphalt.

After spending years of our adolescence practicing with standard transmissions and gravel roads, we graduated into teen hood, automatic transmissions, and black pavement. We soon discovered ways to make our folks' late 60s and early 70s era station wagons put out the same sights and smells found on the ground floor of a Saturday night drag strip.

I think we were in ninth grade at the time of one memorable attempted burnout. Brian's mom had driven us home from a wrestling match in Ritzville we'd both participated in. She was in a hurry to get home so we stopped at their house. She got out and told Brian to drive me home. I lived a couple of miles away from Cook's and since we'd been driving around our parents' farms since we were four, this was no big deal.

However, once we got out on the main road, a big deal materialized. Brian offered to show me how powerful their new hemi-powered Dodge Polaris station wagon was. I'm sure I said, "Sounds like fun!"

That poor Dodge. We were just getting started on that car. You'll hear about additional pains we inflicted on it in later pages.

It was dark and was probably around 10:00 pm. Brian stopped the car after we had traveled a mile from the Cook's house. He shifted the tranny into neutral and revved the engine. I don't mean he tacked a few hundred RPMs on. I mean, he put his foot, ankle, and gas pedal through the floor. The motor immediately began screaming like a banshee! Even I, the wild child that I was, immediately lost all faith that we would experience a pleasant burnout that evening. I was no mechanic, but I had an overwhelming feeling in my inner being that it would end in disaster. I decided to tell him that maybe he should ease the pedal off the metal just a bit.

"Brian, I think that's a hair too much throttle," I called out. He didn't hear a thing. His ears were focused on the exciting engine roar, while his eyes proudly watched the tachometer spin around in its second revolution.

I screamed, "Hey, Cook!" But it was too late.

At the height of the revs, way past what the Dodge engineers envisioned when they originally put a pencil to the power train performance specs, Brian pulled the gearshift down into the "D" position. On a normal day,

"D" stood for "Drive". On this particular night, "D" stood for "Dumb" or "Demolish", or both.

There was an ultra-loud *"BANG"* and smoke filled the cockpit. If I remember correctly, the engine died. Motorless silence and loads of smoke filled the area around the car. We both knew this racecar was done for the night. Specifically, we weren't sure just what the problem was, but deep in our hearts we knew a cataclysmic event had just transpired and we were smack dab in the middle of it. We walked back to Cook's in the wintry dark to see if they had another rig that could take me home, a rig that would move when shifted into "D."

As we walked, even though it was a cold evening in November, we had time to thaw and cook up a scenario for the Cooks' car. I remembered that we had passed a dead dog on the road just before we had attempted our dragster impersonation. It was a conveniently placed excuse for us (but not for the dog). We delivered a tall tale to Brian's dad, Vern, that we had stopped to check out the dead canine and saw car lights coming up behind us.

"So what were we to do?" we humbly asked Brian's dad. It was obvious. We did the same thing that any other innocent and careful, young men would do. We jumped back in the car, in a hurry to get moving and accelerate out of the way of the approaching, albeit imaginary, car. Brian shifted back into the truth zone by stating that when we went to take off, the car just quit.

Vern took the car into a repair shop the next morning. We heard later that the mechanic who fixed the drive train said that with the damage that was done, he figured the only way it could have happened was for someone to be driving 60 mph down the road and then shift the car into reverse.

We assured Vern that the car was definitely never shifted into "R."

• •

Life for me as a kid almost ended in death. Many times. When I was five, my dad had an irrigation pond on the farm that I now own. This was in 1960 when farms were just getting developed and there weren't many people out in the "blocks." (The blocks were large areas of land containing future farms, mapped out for identification purposes.)

The farmers that were sparsely scattered around the countryside didn't have much. A few had irrigation ponds, a reservoir for the irrigation pumps to draw water from. Even though we were poor, we had a pond!

The kids in the area considered this dirty, algae-filled, pollywog-infested pond a luxurious resort for cooling off in the summertime. Most of them were older than I so I felt great excitement one hot afternoon when my dad dropped my sister Teresa and I off at the pond. He went back to working on the farm, oblivious to the danger around the corner. I remember neighbors like the Cooks and the Goodsels were there with a few others. Most were several years older than I.

To me, most of the Cooks appeared to be Olympic-caliber swimmers. They even had webbed toes grown together for better water traction, built-in flippers. I was jealous! Brian was no exception; he could swim like a fish. I couldn't swim or even dog paddle.

Everyone was in the water or lounging around on the pond bank. Brian took off swimming across the pond and I felt I had to be out there with him, just in case he got into trouble. I found a wooden fence post lying nearby. I pulled it into the water, lay on my stomach on top of it and paddled out to the middle of the pond. I enjoyed the newfound sensation of floating out there with the big boys. There was no realization of the danger involved.

All of a sudden the laws of physics, most of them previously unknown to me, kicked in. The heavy weight, which was me on the top of the log, met up with the factors of gravity, weight and balance, water viscosity, and who knows what else. The post rolled over. Instead of the continued enjoyment of basking on the top layer of the warm water coupled with the even warmer sunshine, I encountered my first brush with the Grim Reaper. My enabler and makeshift flotation device, the fence post, turned traitor and was holding me under water. I was like a wrestler on his back with no clue how to keep from getting pinned.

This was a whole new experience for me. A half a century later, I can still hear the quiet, yet deafening roar of the drowning water and see the light green hue of the underwater tomb. I didn't know what to do. I let go of the log and hung suspended underwater in the middle of the pond. Even as a little boy, I knew I was dead or at least in big trouble.

I had no idea how to swim, and therefore had no options from which to choose. I was stuck. The only thing I could think of to do was pray and so I did. Thank goodness my parents were churchgoers! Immediately inspiration came, and not a moment too soon. The idea came to me I should push the water up with my hands, which would propel me to the bottom. I did this and soon was standing in mud about eight feet underwater. My lungs were bursting. I kept pumping with my arms to keep my feet on the slippery bottom while slowly and carefully walking out of the pond. I was out of oxygen and poised to drown.

By the time I reached the glorious air above the water, I was done. A few more seconds would have found me taking my first and last breath of H2O. If I hadn't been able to hold my breath that long, or if I hadn't been inspired by the good Spirit to do exactly what I did, I would have drowned with no one around the wiser. I lay on the bank for a long time, just gasping for air and feeling very lucky. No one at the pond had missed me, but I know that I was watched over and guided. My parents didn't hear about this experience until I was nineteen and leaving on my mission.

CHAPTER 3

DOUBLE THE TROUBLE

In our single-digit years, Brian and I were together daily. Each of our fathers had farm shops where they worked on machinery. We watched them weld many times, repairing equipment. We were cautioned not to watch the arc as the brilliant light would hurt our eyes. Since we had caught glimpses of the flash with no resulting damage, we thought the warnings were a little overdone. I might add here that the damage to eyes from welding is greatly multiplied if the welding is done at night or in a dark atmosphere. The pupils are dilated and allow much more of the damaging welding flash into the eye.

One Saturday evening, Brian and I decided to try our hand at welding. We were nine or ten years old. Each shop had only one welding helmet, which meant only one pair of eyes at a time were going to get zapped. We were at my dad's shop that night and I remember that we would trade the helmet periodically. We found that welding was actually quite simple. Turn the welder on, hook up the ground clamp to make a connection with whatever you wanted to weld and then stick the welding lead and rod next to the metal. A tremendous arc would occur and the metal joints would be instantly super-heated and welded together. This was pretty exciting stuff for two little boys. We were doing a man's job without having so much as a single minute's worth of instruction from an adult. We weren't really familiar with the finer points of welding so we often saw the arc with our naked eyes. It didn't hurt; just blinded you for a minute.

The only problem was that one of us got his eyes fried that eve. In this particular instance, it was Brian. The pain that accompanies welding flash does not occur immediately. It usually waits until the victim is tucked comfortably into bed and has a few hours of sleep under his belt. Then, BANGO! The eyes are cooked. They want to wake you up and tell you all about it.

The victim wakes up with a gunnysack full of sand in both eyes. For those who have not experienced the sensation, it is an absolute killer! There is nothing that can be done to stop the pain. If you get up and turn the light on, the dreadful discomfort multiplies.

In the old days, we went to church at the grade school in Mesa. The morning after our welding venture happened to be Sunday, and therefore, required our physical attendance at church. When I walked into our Sunday school class and saw Brian, I immediately burst into laughter. He looked funny and out-of-place. He was wearing dark sunglasses, looking similar to a very young Tom Cruise on a *Risky Business* poster. I had never seen anyone wear dark sunglasses to church, especially a grade-schooler.

He was not a happy camper. He was also not a happy welder. His eyes were killing him. He had been up all night with excruciating pain. He looked like he was trying to be a Hollywood movie star with the shades on. I thought it was hilarious, only because I had not yet tasted the fruit of that particular malady. I must not have caught the rays that particular time, but I have many times since.

Not long after this, since I had escaped the pain, I did a little welding on my own. As a beginner, it takes some practice to get the arc started and keep it going so one can weld. The old welding helmets contained a lens of very dark glass, which makes it impossible to see where you are welding until you get the arc started. Since it was hard to see where the rod was through the lens, the problem was solved by popping the helmet up and watching the rod as I navigated it toward the, as yet, unwelded parts.

Sure enough, I woke up with sand in the eyes. I went in and told my folks what had happened. They scolded me for using the welder and sent me back to bed. It was one of the more miserable nights of my life. The next morning Mom called the eye doctor and took me to town. Even though there was school that day, there was no way I could go. I couldn't stand to open either eye. She had to lead me wherever I walked.

I was in sixth grade at the time. When my mother led me into the doctor's office, I learned that a girl in my class was there also. Her attendance at the eye doctor was not near as glamorous as mine. She didn't have welder's flash, she was simply in there for an eye exam. She also happened to be my current crush at the time. I remember feeling excited that she was there, but also disappointed that I couldn't see her.

The doctor gave me medicine and some dark plastic glasses, but it didn't help. I suffered through the day. Quite a few times since, I've gotten flashed, even as an adult. Often, the eyes take the brunt of the welder's work. It's just part of the job, especially if one is as careless and intent on getting the job done as I.

• •

At age 11, I wanted a gun. I knew a real gun was out of the question, but I felt I was ready to move up from the sidearm I was packing (a squirt gun) so I settled on a high caliber BB gun. My folks were struggling financially so I could see it was up to me if I was going to get an upgrade. Thumbing through a *Boy's Life* magazine one day, I saw an ad informing me that I could gain ownership of a BB gun if I would just sell some Christmas cards.

What a deal! I ordered their sample pack and waited. Eventually I got the sample cards and order forms. I struck out on my bicycle, cruising gravel roads on a hot August day to remind my neighbors that Christmas was coming. My neighbors were few and far between, but most were kind enough to listen to me and a few even placed orders.

I ended up four miles from home and made my last sale. I turned the bike around and headed for home. Besides being an excellent shot with my squirt gun, I had also honed my skills as a bicyclist. As I pedaled down the gravel road, I found it easier to ride with no hands. I was not only packing my squirt gun, but also sales boxes, sample Christmas cards, and order forms.

Having both hands and arms available to carry everything was helpful and doable. I considered myself a master at "Look Ma, no hands!" Soon I was riding no-hands down a steep hill on a gravel road with the sales materials filling the space between my arms.

It was about that time I noticed two girls, a little younger than me, watching me race down the gravel slope. They were standing at the end of their driveway at the edge of the road, halfway down the hill. This presented a perfect opportunity to show these younger female acquaintances what a great bike rider I was, along with my important position as a salesman, complete with all the impressive sales tools I had in my arms.

Instead of putting one of my upper extremities back on the handlebars and conservatively and safely coasting down the grade, I decided I would really impress the blondes. I started pedaling as fast as I could. I whizzed by the girls, enjoying the thought that they had probably never seen someone ride down this hill at this speed, especially in the no-hands mode!

All of a sudden, the handlebars started shaking. I couldn't do anything about it as my hands were wrapped around the cards instead of the handlebars. The shaking got worse, and in a few seconds, the front wheel made a 90-degree turn on its own which made for a very effective brake. The bike stopped. My cards and I did not.

On the way over, my left thigh hit the handlebars. I bent the steel bar and then continued flying downhill until I touched down, well, more like crashed down, on my hands and knees. I didn't immediately stop, but continued skidding down the hill with skin battling gravel until I slid to a halt. All four contact points were scraped and full of dirt and sharp little rocks. Blood was flowing and my thigh was killing me. I wanted to lie down on the hot, sun-baked, arrowhead-infested road and die.

Instead, the girls were watching so I had to do the manly thing. I postponed crying for my mommy and compensated by moaning and groaning under my breath. I got to my feet and hobbled around gathering up my Christmas card samples. I clutched them to my thumping chest with one hand, caught a glance of the girls who were enthralled by my spectacle, and crawled on the bike to continue the trip home.

It was murder. My left leg didn't work. I had to push down on the right pedal with my good leg, hook my foot under the bottom of the pedal, and pull it back up to complete the revolution. This was how I covered the remaining four miles home on that hot, pain-filled day. I could only hold on to the handlebar with one bloody hand which cut my leverage/power ratio significantly. My thigh had done a number on my handlebar, it was noticeably bent. I moaned every foot of the way. I realized then that sales work is harder than it looks.

My mom took me to the doctor the next day. He said I was not to do any exercises or running for a few months. I had a big blood clot on the thigh and he said it would calcify and leave a large, hard deposit if I exercised that leg. A few years later, I would do even more major damage to that same thigh and femur, also while riding a bike.

I did sell enough Christmas cards to win a BB gun. One night I stayed over at my friend Scot's place. We were bored so we went outside after dark and decided to have a BB gun fight. We were not thinking straight that night. We hid behind farm equipment in his dad's yard and started shooting. This was long before paintball games and we wore no protective equipment. The BB's were plinking and whizzing all around us. Periodically, one of us would score a direct hit and the other would scream in pain. It's a wonder that an eye didn't get put out.

Another evening after school when we were in fifth grade, Brian asked if he could hold my BB gun. I gave it to him, he cocked it, aimed it back at me, and told me to stand up against the wall of my dad's shed. He said he was going to shoot me if I didn't do as he said. I did as instructed and yet, several times, he shot me anyway, quickly recocking and forcing me to stay where I was. He thought it was great fun holding me at bay and aiming at my zipper. It was a miserable experience getting shot with my own gun, bought with the hard labor of Christmas card sales, especially when you threw in the bike wreck.

• •

One night a few years later, found Scot McGary and I hiking down and setting up camp at the Washington State Fish Hatchery at Ringold on the Columbia River. The next morning we grabbed our poles and walked over to the large hatchery pond. We threw our lines out and hundreds of fish started fighting over who could swallow our hooks first. We pulled fish out at will.

This fun frenzy went on for a few minutes until we heard a vehicle coming. We started running for cover, but realized we were caught red-handed. The local game warden was patrolling in his pickup and watched us as we loped off the pond bank. It wouldn't have been so bad if we didn't have his fish hanging and swinging at the end of both of our lines.

We were surprised he let us go. He must have known we were local boys and a few missing fish weren't going to hurt the hatchery output. These days, I'm sure we would have been charged with numerous state and federal felony offenses. Our poles would have been confiscated and we would probably have been sent to Guantanamo Bay. It's a given that we would not have enjoyed fish for lunch like we did back then.

• •

And then there were the motorcycles. Motorcycles were a necessary part of doing farm work, changing sprinklers, and moving around on the farm in an efficient and economical manner. One day when we were about 11, Brian and I were riding our fathers' Honda Trail 90s around the ditch banks and farm roads in our valley. We found a jump, consisting of a dirt mound running across the road, and initiated a contest to find out who could stay airborne the longest. We approached the jump faster and flew farther each time. I finally got tired of the competition and decided I would ice the win.

I retreated back a good quarter of a mile from the jump. I took off and went up through the gears of the Trail 90. Approaching the jump, I flew past Brian. I could hear him yell, "Casper, you're going to kill yourself!" I rolled on to the jump at about 30 mph and took off for the wild blue yonder just after settling into the realization that I had gone a little too far and much too fast this time. When I finally came down, my bike-not-made-for-jumps and I bounced hard and took off again. The next time I landed I was completely out of control. The bike and I rolled and slid through the dirt and finally came to a stop.

I was banged up a little. Brian figured I was dead. The bike had kicked up a tremendous amount of dust and it took a while before he could even find me. Evil Knievel's Snake River jump would have looked subpar when compared to this flight, mainly because of all of the dust. No major damage, but another high speed memory.

This was the first of many motorcycle adventures. Brian and I canvassed the countryside as fast and as often as we could on our bikes. Hill climbing was our love. Many times we would tackle a hill only to get halfway up, wheelie over, and crash back down. After school or work we were often found down in the Ringold area, climbing the giant white clay bluffs, steeply rising hundreds of feet above the banks of the Columbia River.

• •

Throughout high school, I attended early morning seminary. This was a religious instructional class that the LDS Church provided for the youth members. I learned a lot of important principles those four years in seminary. It was a sacrifice to attend early in the morning, but I'm glad I did it.

I didn't miss a chance to mess around, however. One morning, a testimony meeting with all the classes was scheduled in the chapel. There were about thirty kids and two teachers in attendance.

Scot Haws and I decided we would have a little fun. We were sophomores. Before anyone else came in, we crawled up into a loft in the front of the chapel where the large organ speaker was located. It made a fairly comfortable seat so we sat and watched as the proceedings began. Because there were so many kids, we weren't missed. We could see through the material covering the loft, but the people sitting in the pews down below couldn't see us.

In the middle of the meeting, for reasons still unfathomable to me, Scot decided he wanted to get down. I told him "NO!" He started climbing down anyway. The room below us was filled with shelves of sheet music and books. He was a klutz and began knocking books to the floor and making a big ruckus. The meeting ground to a halt. The head instructor, Lois Haws (who was also Scot's mother), demanded in an unnecessarily loud voice, "Who's in there?"

Scot opened the door and slithered out. I was sensing my options were rapidly diminishing as to what I should do.

"Is anybody else in there?" she demanded. I crawled down with much less noise than the previous oaf and sheepishly sat down among the glares of adults and snickers of the other kids.

I don't think either of us shared our testimonies of the gospel that day.

CHAPTER 4

GUILTY BY ASSOCIATION

My father grew up in Heber Valley, Utah. Mom's early years were spent in Kansas before her family moved to Eugene, Oregon. We usually visited our grandparents in Oregon and Utah yearly. Trips to Utah back in those days took 14 or 15 hours and we made it that fast only because we never stopped to eat. Mom always packed a lunch. We traveled through every little town along the way. Today it takes 10 hours on the interstate and that includes stopping and buying lunch along the way.

When we traveled to Utah we arrived late in the evening. Coming into Salt Lake, we would see the Mormon Temple, lit up and spectacular. Mom and Dad were married there, as well as Michele and I years later. The temple is now pretty much blocked from view by all the high buildings around it.

Just before we could see the temple, we would see several refineries along the highway. Each of them had a tall stack with a big flame on top. One night as we drove into Salt Lake, my dad said, "Look at the flame, kids. That flame burns all the time. It never goes out." Just then, the flame went out.

Over the next 40 or 50 years, we got a lot of mileage teasing Dad about that.

• •

When I was in sixth grade, our cousins came up from Eugene, Oregon, to visit. My younger brother Brad and cousin David were in the area by our well house trying to build a boat out of old Army surplus ammunition boxes. It was getting dark when I happened upon them. I figured I would offer to help and asked them if they wanted some light. They said, "Sure."

After rounding up some tin cans out of the trash barrel, I filled a bucket with gasoline from the farm fuel tank. After filling the cans with gas, I spread them around the boat construction worksite. Next, I struck up a flamer and lit them. Poof! One after another, the cans flamed on. The flames danced on the top of the gasoline, flickered out of the top of the can, and provided the needed illumination for the work crew.

After a few minutes, the wind picked up and was hindering the flames. I went over to the large haystack by our corral and drug some 100 pound hay bales over. I placed them as a wind-break between the makeshift torches and the ever increasing breeze. This was a wise move as the flames returned to normal. But the wisdom and tame flames lasted only a few more minutes.

Another problem soon surfaced. As the flames burned, the gas heated up and soon began boiling. The fuel boiled over the top of the cans and began spreading out across the ground. The hay bales were in close proximity to the cans. The bales soon caught on fire.

This was a big emergency in the boatyard! I ran over to the well house, grabbed a hose, turned the water on and started spraying the burning bales. Soon I had the fires out. I knew if my dad found out I would be a deceased fireman. I decided to return the bales back where I had found them. I drug them to the haystack and placed them with the burned sides hidden snugly up against the stack. The evidence was now hidden. I threw the cans in the garbage.

I felt pretty good and mentally patted myself on the back. I'd had several problems crop up and had managed to solve them all. However, we no longer had any light so we went in the house. About a half hour later, someone started banging on our back door. It opened and one of our neighbors started yelling, "Did you know your haystack's on fire?!"

My heart sank. I wasn't sure what had happened, but I was sure that I was part of the problem. We ran out and sure enough, there was a huge fireball in the same place where there had been a large haystack a half hour earlier. Neighbors were pulling into the yard to help. The fire was visible for miles. Dad was running around trying to find water hoses and other solutions to this disaster.

As he ran by me he yelled, "Were you out there smoking again?" I gave a meek response sprinkled with indignation and innocence, indicating that his guess was incorrect. I was also a little peeved that he had made the false and unwarranted accusation in front of all the neighbors, including and especially, Bishop Cook.

They managed to save some of the hay but most of it was lost. It also burned some of the corrals and hay mangers, which can still be seen today, almost 50 years later. They eventually got the fire under control and part of my punishment was to stay out there the entire night and make sure it didn't get out of control again. There was plenty of firelight available to anyone, for the rest of that night, who wanted to build boats out of ammunition boxes.

• •

I would like to thank the local school district for providing a lifetime's worth of entertainment through my junior high and high school years. This was during the late 60s and early 70s. We rode the school bus for an hour and a half in the morning and an equal term again in the evening. The entire trip was filled with laughter and excitement as we entertained each other during the long commute. It was a place where we had minimal supervision and maximum latitude of expression. Some youngsters did homework, but my circle of friends did not include any of the studying type. However, we did learn a lot during these bus rides.

In today's world, the bus driver would have been censured for yanking on our hair and yelling at us. Also, the teacher giving the paddling would definitely have been thrown in the clink for child abuse and gotten sued by the parents. In today's world, many parents insist that their child is an innocent bystander, berating the other parents for what their "delinquent hellion did to our innocent child." Back then, the parents just figured the kid probably had it coming. They were usually correct.

At school, when we did get caught and disciplined, we usually knew we earned it. Even if we acted irresponsibly, we usually accepted responsibility. For punishment we often received hacks. ("Bend over and grab your ankles!" And then you got WHACKED with a large wooden paddle.)

• •

Our bus driver was Max. He drove me to and from school from the time I entered kindergarten until I got out of high school. He was a short little man who knew hundreds of homespun poems by heart. I loved the guy! He owned a big peach orchard down by the river. He would drive the bus and us to school each morning, do plumbing work in the little town of Connell throughout the day, and then haul us home in the evening. He stood about four feet ten inches tall. He had two inch by four inch wooden blocks wired to each of the clutch, brake, and gas pedals so that his feet could reach them. He spent more time looking in the mirror trying to catch us at whatever we were up to than he did watching the road. He would yell instructions, reprimands, and threats at us without pausing to breathe. Often he would run out of air, but kept yelling. There would be no sound, but his mouth would still be moving. We thought this was great fun. It's lucky he didn't pass out from lack of oxygen.

Spit wads were often the weapon of choice. Not only would we hit each other, but at times the wads were directed at Max if we felt he deserved them. It became a contest. He constantly glared in his mirror to catch the "shooter," while we would see who could score a bull's eye without getting caught.

Countless were the opportunities that arose for recreation. I don't believe we ever turned one down. Often we would get turned in and be required to have our parents visit with the driver or the school principal. Once in a while we would get kicked off the bus and have to find another way to school for a week or two. I remember walking several miles each morning and night to a different bus route area because Max wouldn't let me on his bus.

In eighth grade we had an especially memorable experience. At that time, in my circle of friends, we each owned a chrome cigarette lighter. It was the "in" thing to have. You didn't have to smoke to be cool; you just had to have a lighter. We would grasp the lighter between our thumb and middle and forefingers. We would then snap our fingers off the top of the lighter and catch the base of it with our fingers and thumb. If we were successful, the top would pivot away from the lighter and a pleasant clicking sound would occur. This was all done with one hand. This maneuver took a little practice, but once mastered, made us feel like we were professional lighter openers.

One afternoon after school, those of us who were in the seventh and eighth grades got on the bus at the old junior high. We then rode across town to the high school to pick the big kids up. My buddies and I were in the back of the bus. Scot McGary was in the left rear corner and Brian Cook and I were sitting in the seat directly in front of him.

For some reason, Scot was trying to fill a balloon with gas from a butane lighter refill canister. As the high schoolers were getting on at the front of the bus, he accidentally snapped off the top of the gas canister. An instant hiss sounded and began enriching the atmosphere. He yelled, "What should I do?"

Brian happened to have his lighter in his hand. He turned around and said, "Here, let me light it!" Scot yelled, "NO! NO! NO!!!!!!!" his voice a rapidly rising crescendo. He then began the up-to-then impossible feat of frantically climbing up the curved backside of the bus with his own backside. However, it was a little too late for evacuating. The play was in motion. Apparently Brian didn't hear Scot screaming, "NO!"

Click.

The air around us exploded with flames. It lasted just a couple of seconds but hung around long enough to singe our hair and eyebrows. Actually, a couple of seconds is all any good explosion takes.

It also provided the oncoming high school students with a panoramic view of the back end of their very own school bus totally engulfed in flames. They started screaming and exiting en masse via the stampede method. The canister remained on fire. It rolled around on the floor spewing flames for a few seconds and then went out. I would guess a good four minutes elapsed before the commotion settled down and Max was able to find his extinguisher, get past all of the evacuating high schoolers, and arrive at the back of the bus. As volunteer but not-sworn-in firefighters, we had everything under control long before he arrived.

We had everyone sworn to secrecy before Max's arrival. Max didn't get to use his fire extinguisher which I think kind of ticked him off. His interrogation as to the identity of the perpetrators was fruitless (although he did have some mighty strong and correct suspicions).

The next morning Max reported the incident to the school. We were led in, one by one, to the principal's office and thoroughly interrogated. Scot Haws was also included in the mix even though he rode a different bus to an entirely different part of the county. He had nothing to do with the explosion. He lived a good ten miles away from the rest of us. He had been included in the investigation because he was one of our friends. They suspected he was guilty by association. The poor guy didn't have a chance.

When the vice principal, Mr. Johnson, finally narrowed down the troublemakers, he assigned the number of hacks each person was going to get. I felt very fortunate because, by this time, they had bought my story, ascertained my innocence, and allowed me to go back to class. Brian was informed that he was going to get three hacks for detonating the gaseous vapors. McGary was informed he would get a couple of hacks for providing the explosive mixture. Haws was also informed that he was going to get a couple of hacks.

I might mention at this point that these hacks hurt in a big way. Each hack would take your breath away and bring tears to your eyes, no matter how tough you were. Red were the wide welts you would sport between your knees and your rear cheeks.

Haws was shocked. He protested that he was innocent. "What am I getting hacked for? I wasn't even there!"

Mr. Johnson paused, searching for a reason, and while shaking the paddle at him directly under his nose, responded, "Well...well...you've got..." He thought and thought. Somewhere in these pauses he must have realized Haws had done nothing wrong, however, he was mad and also knew he needed to keep the upper hand. "You've got...a bad attitude!" All the kids laughed except the innocent one. He got hacked with the rest.

• •

As the summer approached each year, the weather would turn hot. This brought out the water balloons. Of course, these were strictly forbidden, but nevertheless fully utilized, becoming more prevalent as each day rolled by. Summer vacation was approaching and water fights were the order of the day. Air conditioners were the grownups' way to fight the heat. Water balloons were our weapons of choice to fight other kids.

As the last days of school arrived, Max would look through each student's carry-on baggage to verify that there was no water contraband. Max was every bit as efficient as your everyday, garden-variety Homeland Security baggage screener of today and, in addition to that, Max had a personality.

While this exercise was going on in the front of the bus, kids still outside the bus handed boxes and duffel bags filled with balloons to kids inside the back of the bus through the windows. For every water balloon Max confiscated at the front, 15 or 20 were shoveled in the back. This procedure in and of itself was great fun. I imagine Max would figure he had done a great job until the balloons started flying. He probably stayed awake at night wondering how that many balloons had slipped by him.

By the time a couple of miles had passed under Max's tires, several inches of water would be sloshing about on the entire floor of the bus. Whenever the bus turned, the water would rush to the side of the bus opposite the turn. Everyone inside the bus was soaked, including Max. Once in a while, if we came up on a road construction crew or went past a car stopped at a stop sign, it and anything else within range would get pelted. I remember a guy on a road construction crew waving to the nice kids on the bus, only to get nailed in the chest with a water balloon. The busload of kids roared as the bus left him in the dust. I think McGary threw that particular cooling device.

If and when I ever get to heaven, I'm going to find Max, apologize, and then see if he wants to have a celestial water balloon fight.

CHAPTER 5

I DECIDE TO TAKE THE SUMMER OFF

When I was 13, I had a major event happen that had a lasting impact on my life. Many people come into contact with Mormon missionaries at one time or another during their sojourn on earth. Most of these contacts are brief, and yet, many times lives are changed from these contacts. My life was also changed in a big way by meeting the Mormon elders on this particular day and way.

On June 1, 1968, the elders and I came in contact, although in a slightly different manner than one usually might meet the missionaries. School had just gotten out for the summer the day before. My brother and sisters and I had been entertaining ourselves that day by racing our bicycles around the driveway that surrounded our home, yard, and garden. Part of this course led out to the county road for a couple hundred feet and then back on the driveway to the start/finish line. I would guess the entire length was 700 to 800 feet. We had an old clock in the shed to time ourselves.

On this particular Saturday evening, I was getting ready to make a run. Mom called us in for dinner and I've been told I yelled back, "Okay, I just want to go around one more time." I took off for a life-changing rendezvous with the missionaries, one that wasn't in their appointment book. It wasn't in mine either.

Out where our driveway met the graveled county road there were two tall poplar trees planted on each side of the drive. A line of trees also ran parallel with the county road, in line with the poplar tree on the west side, effectively obscuring the line of sight to the road for anyone on the driveway.

I guess we had never considered the possibility that someone might dare to drive on part of our racecourse, even if it were the county road. Therefore, as we tried to beat the fastest time up to that point, we didn't come to a complete stop and look both ways before venturing out of the driveway. In fact, we had the pedal to the metal through the entire length of our little course. Big mistake. A cop looking for stop sign violators would have had a grand time giving us tickets on that particular Friday and Saturday.

In a hurry to obey the dinner bell and to set a world speed record for the Juniper Road circuit, I came barreling around the turn at 15-20 miles an hour. The Mormon elders were living a half mile down the road at Cook's old barracks. They were probably going 30 mph when we met, head on.

I don't remember a thing. My sister Jill heard the collision and ran into the house screaming. The elders didn't see me. They just heard a crash. After they got stopped, they ran back and gave me a Priesthood blessing.

My dad hurried out to where I lay, looked at me, and went back to the house. After the car hit me, the force had thrown me back 35 feet (no exaggeration) in the direction I had just come from. This was not good for my race time. This was not good for me or any of my limbs, including the one on top of my neck. For those not familiar with how far 35 feet is, in my mind it is exactly three and a half times the length of a football field (embellished just a tad).

Dad told Mom I was dead. She fainted.

My forehead had a major contusion on it protruding three inches out. Foamy blood was coming out of my mouth. I was lying on my back and my left femur had a compound fracture. The leg was twisted around so my toes were in the gravel (I wasn't wearing shoes). I had some other broken bones and injuries, but my head and leg were the serious ones.

When Mom came to, the family picked her up off the floor. She walked out to the road with my dad and when she saw me not breathing, she knelt down and started coaxing me to breathe. Eventually, I began gasping for air. One of the kids ran down to Cooks to give them the news. Dad and Grandpa Riggs found a sheet of plywood and loaded me on it. They called the ambulance, but had no idea when it was going to get there so they put me in the station wagon. My folks and our neighbor/bishop, Vern Cook, headed for town.

After they had driven at least eight miles, the ambulance caught up with them. The ambulance service at this time was all-volunteer. It consisted of farmers and fertilizer salesmen who were willing to haul casualties into town, kind of a scoop and run operation.

The ambulance driver was John Hargraves, a big, excitable guy who took one look at me and went crazy. He was looking at the bone that was sticking out of my leg and torn pants. "We've gotta cut it off right now!" he yelled. He neglected to mention that he was talking about my pant leg.

My five foot, two inch mother thought he was going to cut my leg off. She jumped in front of the six foot plus, 250-pounder and prepared to fight. "You are not going to cut it off!" she exclaimed. Vern told me later that even though the situation was very serious, he couldn't help but laugh at the big misunderstanding.

They got me to the hospital. I was in a coma. A few days later I started thrashing around and they had to tie my arms and good leg to the bed. The bad leg was locked up in traction. A nurse got too close at one point and I hit her, giving her a black eye.

Elder Kane, the poor missionary who was driving, had been scheduled to go home a couple days after the wreck. He was a wreck. I heard after he returned home to Florida that he had a nervous breakdown.

Five or six days later, I started coming around. Keith Barber, my stake president, stopped in and visited. He asked me if I knew who he was. I said, "Yes, you're Dwight David Eisenhower."

The first thing I remember was on June 6th. I saw a newspaper lying on the bed stand in front of me with the headline that Robert F. Kennedy had been shot and killed. Around this time, I also remember my mom at my bedside, talking to me and being very relieved that I was talking back.

I spent a month in traction, flat on my back. It was miserable. At the end of the month, they wheeled me to a room where they proceeded to put a body cast on me. It covered my chest, trunk and stomach and enclosed my entire left leg to my toes.

There was a metal pin that they had driven through my left knee bone right after the wreck. Throughout the month, there were weights hanging on a pulley pulling on both sides of that pin and thus the knee. I spent some time each day of that month wondering how they were going to get that pin out after I was done with the traction phase. I was sure they would knock me out or at least give me a local anesthetic.

No such luck. On the much anticipated day of getting out of traction and into a body cast, Dr. Pettee pulled out a pair of pliers, positioned himself so he could push against my leg while he pulled and yanked on the pin with the pliers. I was aghast! It hurt as he twisted and tugged! Finally, he pulled it hard enough that it slid out.

The next day I was able to leave the hospital. I had become good friends with the nurses. After arriving home that night I cried because I missed them.

The next couple of months, July and August, were hell. Every day I stewed in that bloody cast. It was hot. I was on crutches, lugging around a 100 pound cement enclosure; at least it seemed like that. I threatened several times to anyone who would listen that I was going to cut the cast off.

At one point I crutched myself out to the shed, retrieved a hacksaw, and started sawing. My sisters started crying. My folks soon got wind of the medical procedure going on out on the driveway and put a quick stop to it. The hot summer nights found me lying in bed with major itches up and down my sweaty body. I learned to stretch out a hanger, stick it inside my cast, and push it down past my chest and stomach. I could then scratch my leg, sometimes going clear down to my ankle and foot with the hanger.

One day during this miserable period I was standing outside, leaning on my crutches. I was lighting firecrackers to make the time go by faster. All of a sudden I lost my balance and began falling backwards. Since I couldn't bend my leg or torso, I realized I better just hang on for the ride. I wrapped my arms around the cast on my chest and tilted my head forward so I wouldn't smack it on impact. After I hit terra firma, I found my cast had cracked completely around my midsection. We took a trip back to the doctor for repairs.

There was a great, wonderful, and memorable day in August of that year. I don't know which day it was; I just remember how amazing it felt when they finally sawed the cast off. I felt like I could fly, even though I was still on crutches. That night, after three months, I was able to take a bath. Getting clean after three months of traction and hot, summer sweat soaked into a body cast was the best feeling ever! I still remember sitting in that tub, enjoying being immersed in the warm water and peeling large sections of dead skin off my bad leg, just like a snake sheds its skin. That singular experience might be the reason why I still prefer baths over showers.

The leg looked shriveled and malnourished. It took a year to get over the limp, but eventually I was able to participate in athletics and other physical activities. Since that accident, and bolstered by subsequent injuries, I've always appreciated the blessing of being able to walk and run. The wide scar that wrapped around my thigh stayed numb for years. I still get major charley horses or cramps, after a hard day, in the hamstring muscle that was torn when the broken femur bone cut through.

After the accident I would often get a sharp, agonizing pain in the front of my head for 20 or 30 seconds. This continued for decades, but doesn't happen much anymore. Frontal lobe injuries can affect judgment and personality characteristics. I am of the opinion, and use the excuse, that many of my crazy decisions and actions after the accident may have been influenced, to one degree or another, by the smack my forehead took on the grill of the elders' car. I don't have an excuse as to what caused these problems before the wreck.

Many are the times I have been in the doghouse with parents, wife, teachers, principals, wife, friends, bankers, wife, bill collectors, government officials, wife, church leaders, lawyers, wife, cops, judges, Les Schwab management, and wife. I am sometimes asked why in the world I did this or that. I never had an answer. Now I do. Well, maybe it's more of an excuse. Frontal lobe head injury: convenient, non-arguable, sympathy-evoking, and maybe even true.

• •

In 1965, the Bean group, or "hunters" as we called them, invited us to go to Ilwaco, located at the mouth of the Columbia, to go deep-sea fishing with them. Several of our neighbors were also invited. For some reason, I was the only kid who got to go.

They chartered three boats as there were probably 30 or 40 "hunters" and "farmers" going. My parents went on a different boat than I did. I was on the boat with my grandparents. ML was also on our boat.

ML was a longtime sportsman. He regularly fished and hunted, even going on several safaris in Africa. Many years later he donated the funds and many stuffed animal specimens to build the Monte L Bean Life Science Museum at Brigham Young University in Provo, Utah.

We fished through the morning. Our skipper was a young, tanned buck that thought he knew it all. I was standing by ML and he was showing me how to let my line out and reel it in. The skipper came up and started giving ML instructions on how to fish. ML was a tall, mustachioed, very dignified, and deep-voiced individual. He looked at the skipper and said, "Son, you don't need to tell me how to fish. I was fishing long before you were in diapers." As a ten-year-old and just barely out of diapers myself, I got a kick out of that.

Everyone on our boat caught fish. It was great. The day wore on. I caught two 15 or 20 pound salmon. I really wanted to catch my limit of three. All of a sudden, a big lunker hit my line. I fought and reeled for at least 30 minutes. We both were exhausted by the time we met up at the side of the boat. Just as the deck hand reached out to net him, he chewed through the line and got away.

Everybody agreed that it was the biggest fish anyone had caught on our boat. They said it was at least a 30 pound King. I was greatly disappointed, but I was glad it was over. I was tired!

I had just gotten my hook baited and my line out again when the skipper said to reel in; we were done for the day. As I started reeling in, I got another bite. This was another winner! I could tell by the way he was trying to pull the exhausted little ten-year-old out of the boat.

I was determined not to lose him. Everyone on board was excited that I had hooked another big one, except for maybe the homesick captain. I fought and reeled and struggled as another 30 minutes ticked by. Eventually I got him up to the boat. We landed Mr. King without a problem. I was worn out. After we got back to the docks, he weighed in at 32 pounds. I weighed in at just a few ounces more.

We went out several more years after that. In August of 1968, ML invited my folks and me to spend a couple of days fishing with him and his wife on their new yacht, the Lady B. His wife's name was Birdie. I was still on crutches as this was the summer of my head-on crash with the missionaries from three months earlier.

His boat was a beauty. Everything was either chrome or painted gleaming white. It was the biggest boat anchored at Ilwaco. ML had to make special docking arrangements as the facilities in the harbor didn't have a slip big enough for it. ML had a retired Navy skipper hired full-time to pilot the boat. When we started the journey from the ocean back to port after the first day, the skipper motioned for me to hobble up and sit at the controls. There were many shiny gauges and switches, but the heart of the controls was the big chrome steering wheel and the two throttles for the motors.

It had two large diesel motors and props that powered the boat. It went fast enough that ML told us he had pulled his grandkids on water skis. I thought I had died and gone to heaven as I steered and throttled the Lady B back to port.

We went fishing for two days. The first day was sunny and nice; we caught lots of fish. The second day was bleak and rainy, but turned out to be more memorable than the first. Later in the morning, the ocean started getting choppy enough that we couldn't continue fishing. We headed in. When we got to the bar, where the Columbia meets the ocean, it got worse.

As we motored through the big swells, we saw a small boat (about 17 feet long) racing through the water. We all started making comments about how those people were nuts. Just as the speeding boat passed by us on our left side, it hit a big wave and its front end flipped over. The boat assumed an upside down position heading the opposite direction. I've never seen anything like that except when unlimited hydroplanes decide they would rather fly than skim the water. Soon, one guy popped up at the side of the capsized boat and then another. I'm sure they were cold, scared, and disoriented.

Our skipper, being the experienced Navy guy, immediately got on the radio and called the Coast Guard, giving them the coordinates of our location. They said they would have a cutter out there ASAP.

We waited for the rescue craft about five minutes. We finally saw it coming and the entertainment continued. As the cutter sped toward us, we could see a couple of sailors up on the deck, stripping their clothes off and donning wet suits.

As the rescue boat reached the capsized craft, the frogmen dove off the relatively high cutter deck into the sea. They swam to the boat, grabbed one guy and assisted him over to their ship. The deck was so high that they had to lift him up from the water and the crew from the cutter leaned down to grab his outstretched hands. The frogmen then swam back and looked like they were trying to get the second guy to leave the boat. He wouldn't go. We couldn't figure out what the problem was. All of a sudden, the frogmen started diving under the overturned boat. We realized there must be someone still under the boat.

I figured whoever was under there was a goner. The boat had been upside down for at least ten minutes at that point. After a few dives, the frogmen grabbed the guy and forced him to go with them to the cutter. We could tell he was upset and didn't want to leave.

The cutter quickly motored its way to the front end of the boat. The crew threw a rope and lashed it to the cutter while the frogmen tied the other end to the front of the bellied-up boat. Everyone was moving fast. As soon as the swimmers could grab hold, the cutter took off, pulling the boat in tow.

The boat flipped upright immediately. The divers crawled in and began working at something that was hidden from our view. Soon, they pulled a young girl out but, just as they did, the boat rolled over again. They swam the girl to the cutter and lifted her up to outstretched arms. We could see that she was alive and functioning. I felt it was a miracle, seeing as she had been underwater for so long. She must have been strapped in the boat, but able to find an air pocket to breathe in during those long minutes.

The drama wasn't over. The divers swam back to the boat and the cutter took off once again. Again, the boat flipped up and the divers crawled back inside. There must be another one! We were shocked and worried that maybe this one had drowned.

He hadn't. A little kid was unbuckled and the divers hustled him to the cutter. We were incredulous at what we had just witnessed. The cutter took off, pulling the no-longer-speeding craft behind it towards the port. The captain of the cutter called our skipper and thanked him for the excellent directions and help he had given. Even though the fishing was lousy that day, we all felt great. We had observed an exciting rescue with no fatalities.

After the fishing trip we went up to Seattle and stayed with the Simmons for a day or two. One of the Simmons girls was named Debbie. She was a year older than I and cute, blond, vivacious . . .the cheerleader type. An older Seattle cheerleader hanging with a young, wet-behind-the-ears farm boy on crutches from Basin City. It didn't get any better than that in my book. She was way out of my league.

We went to where the Seattle World's Fair was held in the 60s and rode the Ferris wheel most of the day. I was dizzy by the time we left for home, but wasn't sure if it was from the circular heights of the wheel or the attentive blonde. Regardless, it was a good dizzy.

I'd had a horrible summer that year, but the fishing trip and riding the Ferris wheel with kind Debbie helped me finish on a high note.

Forty-seven years later, I attended the funeral of my mission president's wife in Salt Lake. Just before it started, in walked Debbie Simmons. How random is that? And she actually remembered and brought up the Ferris wheel experience.

Years after the fishing experience, in the late 70s, my folks got an invitation from ML to attend a dinner and the dedication of the ML Bean Life Science Museum at BYU. They couldn't make it, but forwarded the tickets to me. This was during the time I was operating my tire store in Utah. It was a grand affair and I got to spend a few minutes afterward with ML. I have always treasured the relationships and experiences I had with the Beans and their companions.

• •

When I was in second grade we were given an Iowa Basic Skills test. When we got the results back, I was made out to be somewhat of a brain. I scored in the top percentiles, but didn't recognize the promise and opportunities that could be mine if I focused and studied. So I didn't.

Fourth grade brought a loser of a teacher. He used jump ropes to tie kids in their desks. He regularly took groups of boys outside the classroom and told us that we were all going to end up in the penitentiary. The guy was a loser. I developed a bad taste in my mouth for education and authority.

Fifth grade brought a teacher that swung a mean pointer. He called it his "hot wire." If he caught you doing something that he deemed unacceptable, he swung that rod around and caught you in the back of the legs. It was brutal. I wanted to scream and cry when it connected. Kind of like the old days in the woodshed.

Sixth grade introduced me to the world of hacks. Scot McGary and I left the classroom a little early one day and our teacher determined that misdeed was worthy of a hack. It was my first of many until I got out of high school. I went to Ricks College the year I graduated from high school and Brigham Young University in Provo after my mission. I don't recall ever getting a hack at either college. I was pleasantly surprised, but can't say I really missed them.

I think I was doomed after grade school, at least in an educational sense. Through grade school, I loved reading. I read continuously. I read when I was supposed to be doing chores. I read in class with my preferred book tucked tightly inside my school book, giving the teacher the appearance that I was toeing the line.

After my run-in with the car and resulting head injury, things seemed to get worse. I've since read that head injuries can cause manic-depression, ADD, bad judgment, and other such maladies. Whatever the source,

71

I picked up some peculiar behavior quirks along the way, as the astute reader will soon ascertain.

CHAPTER 6

IT SEEMED LIKE A GOOD IDEA

The summer after my bike wreck (1969), I was visited by Brian one night. He had taken his folks' car out the night before and cruised to a neighboring town about 20 miles away. This was new territory for me, but after thinking about it for one or two seconds I realized it might broaden my horizons and make me a little more popular with the girls if I, too, started stealing cars. A minor problem that went largely unconsidered initially is that we were only 14 years old and still two years away from driver's licenses. However, we had been driving on the farm for years and felt more than qualified to utilize some of the blacktop that our parents had been paying taxes on.

The next six months were a contest to see who could outdo the other, resulting in a series of misadventures and possible misdemeanors, perhaps even a felony or two. Danger and close calls kept us entertained and constantly switching first place for bragging rights. We would sneak out of our houses at night and push our folks' car down the road until we could start it without interrupting their slumber. I probably went on these midnight adventures a good ten times with unusual happenings, crazy experiences, and close calls on every trip.

We would usually travel to Connell since that's where we went to school. Each time we looked up girls. These brazen exercises accomplished two purposes. We thought we were pretty macho with all the excursions we were taking and wanted the girls to be aware of this fact. The other reason we knocked on their doors was that we needed witnesses to verify our trips to anyone at school who might doubt our claims.

We had several other buddies who went with us from time to time. They could always count on excitement if they dared climb into the various rigs we utilized. One night found McGary and me sneaking out of a Wednesday night church meeting called MIA (Mutual Improvement Association) and heading for town. This particular night we were having our own MIA (Meatheads In Action). We always drove as fast as the particular vehicle we were in would go, which was usually at least 100 miles an hour. This night found us in my folks' blue Ford station wagon with the pedal to the metal.

We approached a turnoff, but I was lost in thought and wasn't slowing down. I was probably thinking about the girl we were going to see that night and how impressed she was going to be when she saw us pull up in her yard in a station wagon that probably had steam or smoke wafting out from underneath the hood.

In the middle of my reverie, Scot yelled, "Aren't you going to turn?!!" A few years later, he would be yelling similar words to me in an even more dangerous predicament. I snapped out of my girl-crazy trance, hit the brakes, and turned the wheel. The car started sliding sideways. I am still in awe, decades later, that the poor Ford didn't roll. There must have been some loose gravel at that intersection allowing the tires to slide a bit, or a couple of MIA guardian angels pushing down on the side of the car that was trying to roll.

We slid hundreds of feet with the driver's door in the lead, finally skidding to a stop. I looked out my side window and the stop sign post was looking huge. It stood approximately three inches from the car door and five inches from my nose. A few more millimeters and the car would have had a smashed side, a red flag to dear old Dad. We continued to town and visited Robin, a girl from our class.

After a few minutes of our flesh and blood appearance to the cute girl at the door, we drove back to MIA. We arrived before it was over and just waited in the bathroom until the classes dismissed. Then we went out and rode home in the blue Ford station wagon that was already all warmed up.

I asked Mom if I could drive. She said I was too young.

• •

Another eve, Brian, one of the Scots, and I left in the same car. A few minutes after takeoff, the headlights started blinking on and off. I think the headlight switch was going out. Did this deter us? Nay. We continued on to Highway 17, drove eight miles on that highway with our lights still going on and off, oftentimes traveling a minute or more in the dark. Thank goodness for the white stripes in the middle of the road and a full moon.

Turning on to Highway 260, we blinked our way to Connell. If we had happened upon an officer who was on the lookout for suspicious activity such as blinking headlights, we would have been cuffed and stuffed immediately. The seriousness of our situation was swallowed up by our stupidity and the excitement of the moment.

Once there, the three of us got out and started walking around town to see if any girls were still up. By this time it was probably 11:30 pm. The lights were on in one house and I was elected to knock and see if Diane was home. I had to knock several times and finally her dad came to the door. He was not happy. I asked if Diane was home and he tore into me. "She's in bed! What do you need her for? Do you know what time it is? What's your name?"

I was taken aback by all the questions. Being the polite lad I was, I answered, "Ben Casper." I could hear the faint, incredulous snickers of my friends in the bushes. They were astonished I had given up my real name. He asked if my dad was Bill Casper. I answered in the affirmative. "Does he know you're out this late?" I answered in the negative.

He then informed me he was going to call my dad and notify him of my whereabouts. I stuck my tail between my legs and exited. Diane informed me the next day that she had been awake and had heard the confrontational discussion. As soon as I left, she came out and lectured her dad on the finer points of correctly entertaining guests, even 14-year-olds who arrive late at night.

She also informed him he was not going to call my dad. I guess he then stuck his tail between his legs and hung up the phone. I loved Diane for years for this act of kindness. We headed home with our cop-beckoning, blinking headlights and made it without further incident.

• •

My dad had a Chevy pickup that he had just put a rebuilt engine in. It had a Holley four barrel carburetor which sucked the fuel, but gave welcome acceleration for a farm pickup. I took off one evening by myself and headed for the big city. After completing my rounds in town, I headed back. I kept the low-geared truck at full throttle. With about 15 miles left to go, all of a sudden a horrendous racket started. The banging was terrible and I was sure there was no way I would make it home. However, it wasn't quite so unbearable if I kept the engine at an idle. So I idled down the highway for the next hour or so until I arrived home. I felt bad about screwing up my dad's new motor, but had the faint hope that if I let it sit for a day or two without running it might heal itself.

A couple of nights later at the dinner table my dad expressed discouragement at the fact that his new engine was bad. He figured he must have done something wrong when he put it in because it was making a terrible noise. He later tore the motor apart and discovered it had a broken piston. Sorry, Dad. I'm still amazed the truck got me home that night.

• •

One Friday night my parents went to a party in town. I hadn't had an adrenaline fix for a day or two so I called my buddy, Dan, and asked if he wanted to make a trip to Pasco. He was game, but we really didn't have a rig because the pickup had a terrible knock in the engine and my folks had taken the car. I didn't want to take the tractor as it would have taken at least two days to make the trip. Dad had just bought a brand new Chevy 2-ton truck to haul sugar beets. It was a nice machine, but a little bigger than what we needed. We took it anyway.

Truckin' down the highway, we had a slight tailwind which enabled me to get our ground speed up to 85 mph. It was dark and there wasn't another rig on the road. Or so we thought. All of a sudden, directly in front of us, was an over-loaded-with-spuds 10-wheeler truck with its lights off!

I didn't see it until we were a few feet from it, probably a second away from impact. It was parked sideways in the road, completely blocking off our path. I had no time to react. In fact, I often wonder if I even did react. I honestly think one of my guardian angels stepped in and helped out at this particular moment.

One way or another, the steering wheel got jerked to the right and we flew off the road at 85 mph. We bounced along through weeds and rough terrain while I struggled to regain control. The next instant we smacked into a berm leading up to a side road that intersected with the main road.

The front tires of the truck hit the berm and lofted the truck skyward. The impact was so great that I thought the front axle had been torn off. The rear wheels then hit the rise and the truck was air born. We flew through the dark and eventually landed for just a sliver of a second. The truck bounced up again, landed, and continued its path in the gutter. I was finally able to get the brakes engaged and make the madness stop. I shut the ignition off and we sat there, both of us in a cold sweat and speechless.

I remember thinking that if I were big and strong like Brian's brother, Kent, I would go back and knock the driver of that spud truck around, at least show him how to turn his truck lights on. But being the little kid I was, I stayed in the truck. I'm sure the driver of the spud truck was wondering what had just flown past him and where he might find some clean underwear.

Dan and I sat in the cab for a good ten minutes, having lost the ability to speak. We finally were able to communicate with monosyllables like "crap" and "dang". A few more minutes found our confidence returning. Soon we decided to continue our trip to town. I maneuvered the truck back up on the road and proceeded, albeit a bit slower.

Coming into Pasco, I decided I'd better check the truck out just to make sure nothing had been damaged after our takeoff and landing. Jumping out and walking to the rear of the new, but used truck, I discovered we had no taillights. We engaged a few previously unused brain cells, thought carefully, then wisely turned around and headed home. The very lucky 10-wheeler was long gone by the time we made our way back to the incident location. Chevrolet must have built a good truck that year as that particular truck ran for many years after, hauling thousands of loads of spuds and beets.

• •

These experiences weren't slowing us down. In fact, I think our confidence was growing. Our next adventure found us climbing out of the bathroom window at church during another MIA meeting and taking off in Brian's dad's new car, you know, the one that had an even newer driveline in it.

Unbeknownst to us, the car had had a flat tire on the left rear earlier in the day and the tire had been left at a repair shop. The spare that was now mounted on the car was half flat, but we were unaware of this minor problem as we headed off into the high-speed night.

Brian was driving, I was in the middle of the front bench seat, and Dan was on the right. The car was soon up to our normal speed of 110 mph, but something just wasn't right. It was swerving all over the road, however, that didn't slow Brian down. He was enjoying the new driving challenge that the low-pressured tire was providing. We proceeded a few miles and went past the foster home of a fellow juvenile delinquent friend of ours. Brian honked the horn as we screamed by.

We raced for another mile and all of a sudden heard a big bang that was accompanied by a major loss of control. We swerved and swayed back and forth, but the 14-year-old driving veteran was able to keep it on the road. He finally got the thing stopped just before we arrived at a bridge and 40-foot wide canal full of water. We got out and looked around. The left rear tire was completely gone. The wheel was smoking with the smell of burnt rubber and was also ruined. No problem, we thought. We'll just change the tire and head back before they discover we are MIA from MIA. Rummaging through the back, we found an empty hole where the spare should have been.

At that point, we started feeling like we were in a bit of trouble. We went over our options and then walked back to our friend's foster home and knocked on the door. Leonard Marble lived across the road. (You'll hear more about Leonard later and understand why we didn't knock on his door.) The owner of the home was a farmer named Henry. He came to the door and asked what we wanted. We said we had a flat tire up the road and needed a spare. He asked if that was us that had gone by with our horn honking a few minutes earlier. We sheepishly admitted to the affirmative. He then asked, "How fast were you going? It sounded like you were going 150 mph as the horn went....." He then made a sound like a horn going by at 150 mph. Brian stated he thought our speed was around 50, but I think the gentleman knew better and was a little closer to the correct speed estimation.

He didn't have a spare, but agreed to take us back to the church. We got back just as the meeting was finishing. We played dumb while Brian's dad (who was still the bishop) called the State Patrol to report his new car was missing.

The next morning Vern (Bishop Cook) showed up to take us to early morning seminary in the lost (but now found), car. He had never driven us to seminary before so I sensed this was a special occasion. I could tell he was not happy as he drove us to the church in Basin City. No one said a word. Usually the radio played as we traveled. I guess the circumstances on this unique day required that the radio remain off. As the kids started getting out, the bishop said he wanted Brian, Dan and I to stay in the car. He then asked where I had been during Mutual the night before. I wasn't sure what to say and finally settled on our prearranged Wednesday night alibi. "I was in the bathroom." It must have sounded unconvincing and even dumb; especially since when he asked Dan and Brian where they were, they left me and my excuse to hang and just told him they couldn't account for their whereabouts.

Vern told Dan and I that we were to tell our parents about this problem that very night or he would. We agonized all day, but got off easier than expected that evening. I think it was because we told our moms instead of our dads. We promised that it would never happen again. It didn't. For awhile.

We stayed out of trouble until a good six months had rolled by.

● ●

In April of 1970, Brian's folks took off for General Conference, a church conference in Salt Lake. He and I got together and decided to take a ride for old time's sake. We decided on the first Friday night in April to meet at my dad's spud shed at 11:00 pm. Unfortunately, I fell asleep while waiting for my parents to go to bed. When I awoke the next morning, I realized I had missed our appointment. Brian was tougher than I, and I was a little afraid that he was going to use me for a punching bag because I stood him up.

I didn't see him that Saturday but did see him the next day at church. He wasn't happy that I had kept him waiting for three hours, but we decided to try it again that very night. We met as planned around 11:00 pm and headed for town. The neighbor's dogs had been bothering Cooks' cows so Brian brought his .22 rifle in case he saw one of the dogs. We headed straight for the Tri-Cities and forgot about the dog. We aimlessly drove around town for an hour or so.

We stopped at our favorite radio station KALE, but the door was locked. I distinctly remember listening to KALE as we drove around town that night. "American Woman" and "Bridge Over Troubled Waters" were two of the songs that were played. Little did we know that we would be heading for a bridge over troubled waters before we wrapped things up for the evening.

We drove into Kennewick and past a couple of cops that were parked on Columbia Drive, which spooked us. We turned off into a fenced-in store lot called Art Carpenter's Army Surplus. We chilled in the dark for fifteen minutes in case the cops were looking for us.

Back on the road, we ended up in a deserted Albertson's parking lot, near what is now Lampson Field. We decided we could use a little extra change so Brian got out and shot the phone booth next to the store with the .22 he'd intended for the neighbor's dog. The shot was very loud and made me want to exit the area immediately. Brian exclaimed, "Casper, there's a cop!"

"Yeah, right," I said, knowing that he was just trying to scare me. But when he jumped in the car and I saw the look on his face, the realization arrived that this was no false alarm. Looking to the right rear, I saw the potential troublemaker/peace officer stopped at an intersection behind us. Brian started the car up, took off, and soon was on a street that appeared deserted. It was around 1:30 in the morning by this time.

Our luck didn't hold. Somehow the cop found us and stayed right on our tail. Each second brought a stronger realization of just how much trouble we were in. It was a whole new world, full of scary realities.

We had been living in a fantasyland. That fantasyland had pulled up stakes and left us in the lurch just after Brian shot that phone booth. We suddenly began realizing we had gone way too far. We were scared out of our minds.

The cop followed us for a good mile and then turned on his lights. Brian yelled, "What should we do?" I yelled back, "Let's get the heck out of here!" (or similar phraseology). He hit the gas and the chase was on along with the officer's siren. Since it had been a slow Sunday night, when the cop started following us, he radioed his buds concerning our suspicious vehicle.

He later said that he never heard the gunshot, but just saw us sitting in an empty parking lot and wondered if we needed help. Cops from five jurisdictions were en route to help their partner in case he needed them. All this radio chatter was done before he even tried to stop us.

The inside of our car was lit up by the spotlight he had trained on us, not to mention all the red and blue lights that were materializing and flashing around us. We were madly skidding around the streets with cop cars in close pursuit behind us. Brian turned down a side street and realized an officer had parked his car sideways across the street blocking our path. The officer was out with his flashlight and gun pointed at us. Brian tried to turn around and ended up just about hitting him. He thought we were trying to run him over. He ran around to my side of the car and pointed his gun at my face just outside my window.

I had had enough. "We gotta stop!" I whimpered.

"We've gone too far now!" Brian responded. Since he was in the driver's seat, I had a feeling we would be moving on. I was also sure that more excitement was coming our way. We peeled back up the street and out onto Highway 395.

Sirens, amplified by red and blue lights, appeared wherever I looked. We were scared out of our fairly empty minds! Brian turned the car right, racing toward home. The gunman and his innocent passenger were now headed for the Blue Bridge over the Columbia River. We were homeward bound, or so I hoped.

I don't know if it was good luck or bad luck that we didn't make it to the bridge. We found out later that there were four cop cars parked sideways across the Blue Bridge with the officers waiting on the bridge walkway with shotguns. A total of 18 cop cars were involved in the pursuit.

Back to the chase: The highway went down a long hill from the Kennewick Highlands. Brian took full advantage of the hill to build up some steam. I believe we were in the neighborhood of 120-130 miles per hour by the time we reached the bottom of the slope where the road started curving toward a couple of overpasses, the bridge, and the river. Reaching the bottom of the hill, Brian stomped on the brakes, as we were going way too fast to negotiate the curve. The car started sliding. We quickly lost control and, after skidding some 600 feet, flew off the 395 overpass on to Columbia Avenue below. I remember the seemingly eternal screeching of tires followed by complete blackness, liftoff, and then a terrible crash.

The next thing I remember was the great pain in my head, right arm and side. My side of the car was caved in. The side impact caused all my injuries. If I had had my seatbelt on I have no doubt I would have been killed. Instead, I was thrown across the car onto Brian's side. In a matter of seconds, my head wound had soaked us both with blood. I was lying on top of Brian and I remember him saying, "Come on! Let's get out of here!" I moaned that I couldn't. He threw me into the back seat.

I was bleeding badly out of the top of my head and having a hard time breathing. My right side had been hammered by the caved-in door on the passenger side. I vaguely remember kicking the side window out. My next memory was standing on the hood of the car, passing out, and then standing on the street. A cop came up, put his gun against my back, and told me to hold it right there. I passed out at that point.

They caught Brian and stuck him in the back of a police car. They tried to stop the bleeding on my head. The cops were afraid I was going to die. They told Brian that if I did they were going to charge him with homicide. Brian told me later that if I would have died, he was going to tell the cops that I was driving. I had no problem with that since Brian had been doing some bodacious driving that I wouldn't have minded getting credit for.

Decades later, my wife and I were passed by a speeding Idaho State Patrol car on the freeway as we drove through Boise. A few miles later we passed him and a lady cop who were pulled over behind a van. Their guns were drawn and they were yelling at the guy in the van. Just as we passed he was getting out of the van with his hands in the air. I told my wife I hadn't seen anything like that for a long time. She asked when. I said, "Probably back in '70 when the cops pulled their guns on Brian and I under the overpass in Kennewick." We both laughed.

Two Hurt In Chase And Crash

A 15-year-old Basin City youth is hospitalized and a Mesa friend, also 15, is in juvenile home after a Sunday night ride ended in a crash at the Highway 12 cloverleaf near Kennewick.

Driver Brian Cook, Star Route, Mesa, was charged by Kennewick police with reckless driving and no operator's license. Police charged he took a 1969 station wagon without permission of its owner about 11:40 p.m.

Passenger Ben Casper, Basin City, was reported today in stable condition and still under observation at Kennewick General Hospital.

Police said a squad car approached the stationwagon containing the two youths while it was parked with its lights off near a supermarket. The car raced away, heading up Kennewick Avenue to Angus Village and around back streets. It then headed toward Pasco on Highway 14, going out of control and crashing off the Highway 12 cloverleaf, police said.

Pasco Complaints

• •

Meanwhile, back at the overpass . . . the ambulance was delayed by a train and the cops were stressed that it hadn't gotten there yet. They were pretty worried about getting me to the hospital before I bled out. I was hurting and feeling absolutely terrible about the whole mess. I kept apologizing to the cops about how sorry I was that I had caused such trouble. I remember agonizing about how bad I felt about letting all the people down in Basin City.

The ambulance finally arrived. They hauled me to the hospital and Dr. DeBit, our family doctor, met me there. It was 2:00 am by the time Ralph DeBit started stitching me up.

The doc told me that he was going to have to call my parents. I asked him if we could do it another time, but he claimed there was no time like the present. He picked up a phone and demanded the number.

I finally gave it to him. Mom was not happy when Dr. DeBit interrupted her sleep. He told her that he was with me in the hospital. She told him he was mistaken. "Ben is sleeping downstairs."

He handed the phone to me and she acted surprised to hear my voice. I had to tell her what had happened. She then said, "You left without our permission, didn't you?" I thought that was pretty apparent and remember being a little put out with her question. By the time we got off the phone, she had asked that question at least five more times. I remember getting really irritated with the redundancy. She told me they would be in to see me the next morning. We hung up and then she had my dad go downstairs and make sure I wasn't in bed. I guess maybe she thought Doc DeBit and I were playing a practical joke on them.

The hospital bed I slept in was probably a little more comfortable than the cot that Brian had to sleep on in the Fred English Juvenile Home. After a few days of vegetating in the clink, he scrawled the title of a Joe South song on his cell wall, "Don't it Make You Want to Go Home?" I thought that was not only brilliant, but also pretty funny.

Years afterwards, when I would see a flashing light, even a blinker on a car, my heart would race and I would start feeling physically sick. That night was very traumatic. We didn't take any more joy rides in stolen vehicles, but I don't think we slowed down much either after we started driving again. (Cooks got another new car and a few months later, a neighbor spotted Brian driving it 100 miles an hour past his house. He chased Brian down and asked him what in the heck he was doing? Brian said he had just washed the car and was now drying it off.)

After the wreck, I was in the hospital for a few days recuperating and one of my high school teachers came in to visit. Because I have a competitive streak in me, I was in the middle of a one-man contest to see how full I could get my urinal before the nurses noticed it.

I had the thing just about full (probably a good half gallon) when Mrs. Clary walked in to visit. I was trying to inconspicuously pull the urinal out from under the sheet to hang it up on the side rail of the bed when it lost its balance. There was a big splash and the plastic jug bounced around on the floor. Nurses and mops were summoned, a major hazardous waste spill-containment procedure instituted, and every time I saw my teacher for the next couple months, she would start laughing hysterically at the memory.

My folks were more understanding than I thought they would be. I've since realized it was because I had brought home such wonderful grades a day or two before the accident. Mom and Dad had planned to fly me to Seattle to visit my friend, Bob Simmons. In my adolescent mind, the trip was geared more to the tune of going on some more Ferris wheel rides with his sister, Debbie. Even after the wreck, they told me they were still going to let me take the trip because I had done so well in school. Their state of mind remained intact until after my mom signed up for Parent-Teacher Conferences and visited my teachers at the high school the day after I arrived home.

The scene was something like this: "Well, Mrs. Casper, what are we going to do about your son?" "What do you mean? He's doing much better than he used to. He was getting D's and F's, but he got an A from you on this last report card!" She received this same reception from the next six teachers she visited.

In a moment of desperation, while riding home on Max's bus, I had changed all of my F's to A's and all of my D's to B's. If my school had had a class in deceptive scholastic skills, I would have gotten an A without having to change anything.

The trip to Seattle was immediately called off. No plane trip. No Bob. No Ferris wheel. That last one really disappointed me. The accident had instantly taken on a more sinister slant in my parent's narrow and prejudiced point of view. My perceived integrity and wisdom immediately took a back seat and my deceit and stupidity were now on full display. The next period of house arrest and probation took forever to pass. I still drove fast, but at least I refrained from riding in stolen cars.

CHAPTER 7

THE ATHLETE IN ME

In eighth grade, I took track in the spring. A couple of years before, I had won the district wide elementary school 50-yard dash and considered myself pretty quick. However, the 50-yard victory occurred before I had the wreck with the missionaries.

A couple of weeks into my eighth grade track season, I went to the doctor to get my leg looked at because of the accident. He informed my mom and me that my leg had quit growing. The compound fracture of the femur had messed up something that caused the leg to stop growing. My left leg was three inches shorter than my right leg. He scheduled me for surgery.

Right about this time I discovered guitars. I wanted one in the worst way, but things were pretty tight at home and I was told that if I wanted an ax, I would have to pay for it myself. I saved up my money and finally reached the point where I could afford a cheap acoustic. The evening that my folks took me into the hospital for the following morning's operation, we stopped at Griggs Department Store, and I bought the guitar. I remember it as if it had happened yesterday. It was strange and magical. I loved the sound and imagined possibilities it offered.

I wanted to take it to the hospital with me, but the folks said no. I guess the hospital was probably not the best place for a beginner to start learning how to rock out.

The nurses gave me a sedative that night to relax me and help me get to sleep. I think they gave me a little too much as I started hallucinating. Wild colors and strange objects flew by me for a time until I finally dropped off to sleep.

The next morning they wheeled me down to the operating room. I was feeling like I was in a friendly and comfortable place since I had spent a month of my life in that hospital the year before.

They told me they were going to put me out. I didn't believe that they had that power. I decided I was going to grit my teeth and hold onto my consciousness for a long time. They told me to count. I think I got to two.

When I started waking up, the hospital had lost all semblances of friendliness and comfort. I was nauseous and throwing up. I was hungry, yet couldn't hold anything down. Even worse, my knee was killing me. They had taken a perfectly good knee and chopped into it from both sides.

After a couple of very unpleasant days in the hospital, they sent me home with my knee wrapped in an ace bandage. The knee was still hurting, but I wanted to get back to school. The first day back taught me that I should have taken a little more time to recuperate. It throbbed and pounded. I couldn't take it and crutched my way into the office for some relief.

Mrs. Wilson, the kind office secretary that I was good friends with, put me on the sick bed. I elevated my leg up until it was higher than the rest of me. This was the only way I could get relief. If it was lower, the blood pressure on the cut-up knee brought excruciating pain.

After I got home that night, I bagged any thoughts of going back to school for a few days. Soon after, I discovered that if I wrapped the ace bandage tightly around my knee, the pain diminished. Therefore, if a little tension was good, a lot was better.

The knee was greatly swollen and had every color of the rainbow. It was red and green and purple and yellow and blue. It was ugly.

About that time, Dr. Boyd Simmons (one of the "hunters") from Seattle and Salmon, Idaho, visited us. When I showed him my knee and explained my "tight bandage" solution to the pain, he informed me I was asking for bigger problems. By tightening the bandage around the knee, I was creating a tourniquet, cutting off the blood flow to the rest of the leg. He said if I wrapped the whole leg tightly instead of just at the knee, I would accomplish the relief I wanted without cutting off the blood supply. It worked and I greatly appreciated his help.

● ●

I took football my freshman year. I like sports and competition, but I didn't like the hits incurred in blocks and tackles. My legs had already taken a beating so I was a little gun shy. I spent most of my time on the bench. One game, we were getting hammered. Toward the end of the game the coach sent me in as a defensive halfback. On the first play, the opposing quarterback threw the ball to the kid I was defending. I dove in, grabbed the interception and ran up field. After 10 or 15 yards I got hit and went down. The ball ended up sandwiched between my stomach and the ground.

I couldn't breath. The wind was knocked out of me. The rest of the team cheered for the interception and drug me off the field. I lay in the grass for a few minutes and finally got my breathing back to normal. About that time, the other team got the ball back.

The coach asked me if I felt like going back in. I said, "Sure."

The first play from scrimmage was identical to the prior one. I caught another interception, however, when I got tackled I kept the ball away from my breathing apparatus. We went home in defeat as a team, but I reveled in the two plays I had been involved in.

The next week, I skipped the game. I have no idea why. The following day, the other kids told me that when the coach was picking the starting lineup, for the first time that year, he chose me because of my prior game performance. I was AWOL. Another missed opportunity. It was a recurring theme in the story of my life. It's like I was afraid of success.

Toward the end of the season, Mr. Richardson, the varsity coach, traveled with us to a game in Royal City. I still wasn't playing much, but I was quite familiar with Richardson as I ended up taking Algebra 1 from him for three years and still didn't pass.

At one point in the game, the JV coach put me in on a kickoff return team. The kick was short and ended up in my hands. I did my best to avoid tacklers, but eventually was brought down. When I ran off the field, several of my friends came over and said that when I caught the ball and started running, OUR Coach Richardson started yelling to the opposing team to "Get him! Smear him! Take him out!"

He must have not liked my homework the night before.

● ●

Richardson was also the head basketball coach. One day in Algebra class we entered into a discussion as to which one of us would prevail in a foot race. We ended up betting five or ten dollars (which was a lot of money in those days) on the outcome and arranged the contest for that evening in the gym during his basketball practice. I showed up at the appointed hour and we agreed to race from one end of the gym to the other end and back again.

The race began with all his basketball players, who were upperclassmen, standing around watching. I pulled out ahead and had a commanding lead at the turnaround point at the far side of the gym. However, on my way back, his players formed a gauntlet type obstacle course and I spent a lot of my time dodging Richardson supporters and getting pummeled and tripped. I still managed to finish first, but I don't remember if I ever got paid.

Speaking of bets, when I was a sophomore I was on the track team. I had high hopes of breaking through the 11 second time barrier for the 100 yard dash. I set my sights on running 10.9 seconds. I figured that for added incentive I would broadcast my goal among my teammates, which would add pressure and motivation for me. I thought this little move would be a good thing.

Some of the upperclassmen didn't think I could do it. I did. So we bet. In my mind, this was even more motivation. I bet enough that I couldn't afford not to accomplish my goal. I had the whole season to produce and mentally I was licking my chops for the day when I broke the barrier.

The bets were for five or ten dollars a person. I could earn a buck and a half an hour working for my dad. I bet a total of 60 dollars. I just knew by the end of track season, I was going to be a wealthy man.

It didn't happen. Race after race I ran my best. The fastest time I posted was 11.1 seconds at a meet in Pasco. By the end of the season I had accepted the fact that I was a failure and in massive debt. At this time in my life I was unaware of the bankruptcy law of the land that could have allowed me to skate away from my obligations and creditors.

So I scrimped and saved and worked and earned. I paid off all my debts except for one. I had bet Ross Montierth $10. He was a couple years older than I and we grew up in the church together. When I rounded up the money to pay him he declined saying he appreciated me stepping up, but he didn't want my money. It was an act that I have always remembered and appreciated.

I loved to run as a kid. In spite of all the broken bones and torn ligaments, I was a hair on the fast side, but not near as fast as Don Mitchell, Ross Montierth, Daryl Stoker, Greg Gibson, Terry Bailie, Ron Winn. . . I could go on and on. You get the idea. I wasn't really that fast. In fact, I felt like it was a miracle I could even walk or breathe after all the close calls I had experienced.

After my mission, I took a track class at BYU. I was noticeably faster than in high school. My fastest time running the 100 was 10.5 seconds. And I reached that time without placing a single bet.

• •

About this same time in high school, I had another experience that made quite an impression on me. During a class break one morning, we were walking up to A Building for our next class. I was walking with Glen Chapman when another kid named Alvin Adams started giving him a hard time. I told Alvin to knock it off. He asked if I was going to make him knock it off. Without a second of forethought I answered in the affirmative. Alvin said, "Let's go."

We walked toward the far end of A Building where there were no teachers around. By the time we walked out of the building, word had quickly spread and there was a large contingent of onlookers. I had never been in a fist fight before so I decided it would be best not to place bets on the outcome. I put up my fists like I had seen boxers do on TV and began dancing around with Alvin.

Let me tell you about Alvin. He was living at the Bailie Memorial Youth Ranch up above Basin City. Loen Bailie had built a large complex of homes for "juvenile delinquents." There were a lot of kids living there that had run afoul of the law. Most came from the Seattle area. Most were street smart and had been in plenty of fight training situations before they arrived at the Youth Ranch.

A good three seconds elapsed before I realized that standing up for Glen Chapman had been a valiant act, but not very wise or healthy. I didn't have my hands up far enough to protect my jaw and it got clobbered. I saw stars and down I went with a bloody lip. There were a bunch of ooh's and aah's from the crowd which signaled to me that Alvin and I were putting on a good show and they wanted more. I found my way to my feet and put my dukes up again. Once again, I didn't put them high enough.

BAM! I went back down on the grass, seeing more stars as I dropped. By this time I was starting to realize that I had made a major mistake. As much as I disliked school, I would have much preferred peacefully sitting in a classroom setting. I was hurt and bleeding. I could even feel a couple of loose teeth in my mouth that had been nice and secure 60 seconds earlier. But the crowd wanted more.

My pride stood me back up. Alvin put me back down. For the third time. I wondered how much more of this I was going to have to take before the school bell rang to signal an end to the fight.

Just as I staggered back up, an upperclassman named Greg Mauseth stepped in and said he'd seen enough. I had admired Greg in the past. At this moment, I fell in love with him. The crowd broke up and I walked to the restroom to fix my hair. My face was a mess. I don't think Glen ever thanked me.

When I went home that night, my folks asked me what in the heck had happened to my mouth. I told them I was getting a drink from a water fountain and Allen Olberding had accidently hit my head. My mouth had gotten all cut up from hitting the water nozzle. They bought it.

• •

Speaking of Greg Mauseth, a few years ago I hauled a large and heavy trailer load of scrap steel to town. It was in the winter and the roads were treacherous with slick ice and a good foot of snow. It was not a good day to venture out, but you know how I love a good challenge.

I drove 10 miles and decided I had better stop at Merrill's Corner for gas since my pickup was running on fumes. I filled up and drove toward town. 15 miles down the road I remembered that the scrap yard required ID when they paid for scrap metal to try to keep thieves at bay. I reached for my pocket to make sure I had my wallet. It wasn't there! I instantly remembered I had laid it on the gas dispenser at Merrill's Corner.

I did not want to turn my load around and drive clear back up the road. It was very possible that the next gas customer to follow me at Mr. Quik's had already acquired the billfold. I was upset. I pulled off the road and wondered what I should do.

My phone rang. It was my wife. She informed me that Greg Mauseth had called her and told her he found my wallet. He left it at the counter at Mr. Quik's; another reason to love Greg.

I headed for town. I told my sad story to the guy at the scrap yard. He allowed me to dump my scrap without ID. I picked up my wallet on my way home. All in all, it was a good day. Much better than the day I had when Greg stopped the fight.

• •

As a sophomore, I decided to wrestle. I actually won a few matches and one night at practice had a challenge match for team placing with Scot Haws. I was ahead going into the second period and was on the bottom in the referee's position. At the whistle, I stood up and started wrenching my way free. Scot threw his arms around my torso, wrapped his left leg around my lower left leg and sat back. As we went down I experienced terrible pain. My left knee had been dislocated and the cartilage torn.

As I writhed around on the mat, the coaches grabbed me and popped my knee back in place. The only problem was that the torn cartilage was now trapped tightly inside the joint. I hobbled to the dressing room, forfeiting the match.

My parents didn't want to take me to the doctor. It seemed to them that I was constantly getting hurt. They thought maybe I had just sprained it and would recover shortly.

I didn't. The cartilage was torn and trapped. My leg was frozen in a partially bent configuration and I had an obvious limp. After a couple of weeks of hobbling around, they took me to the doctor.

Dr. Pettee stuck me in traction in the hospital for a few days and when that didn't work, he operated. Now, both my knees were loose and screwed up.

• •

The next year, I didn't wrestle on the team. I was a little skittish about my knees. The school had an intramural wrestling tournament, open to everyone who wasn't on the wrestling team. The competitions were held in the gym every day during lunch hour. I entered and, in one of the matches, got paired up with Bob Franklin. Bob was one of the top students in our class, an officer in student government, and a jock on the football and basketball teams.

I knew I didn't stand a chance. I was none of the above. He knew it too.

When I walked into the locker room to change, he was already there, talking big about what he was going to do to me. When I materialized, he asked me which round I preferred to get pinned in: the first, second, or third?

I didn't really know so I told him he would have to decide. He laughed and continued carrying on. I knew he was going to beat me, but I thought he was going a little overboard with his braggadocio.

We wrestled. It was a tough match and I wasn't that bad. He wasn't that good. I beat him fair and square.

He was mad. At the end of the match, when the opponents usually shake hands and the winner's hand is raised, he refused to shake my hand and stormed out. I was tired, shocked, and feeling a little better about myself.

I walked into the locker room and he was already in the shower bawling like a baby, carrying on about how wrong it all was. I tried to console him, but he ignored me. He dressed quickly and stormed out.

I got dressed and headed out of the locker room. Once outside, I looked over and noticed Bob was sitting alone on a bench by the Ag Shop, his head in his hands. I felt bad for the poor wrestler and walked over to console him. I actually liked the guy, even if he was a little cocky.

When I got to him, I could hear him sob, over and over, "Anybody but Casper, anybody but Casper." I didn't say anything. I walked away, wondering what was so bad about me.

CHAPTER 8

BOY BAND WANNABE

They say girls love athletes and musicians so being the very logical person that I am, I figured I would excel in both. I practiced the guitar and picked up a few basics while recovering from my surgery in eighth grade. In my freshman year, our high school had an assembly one afternoon. A rock and roll band performed and I was enthralled and hooked. This was the first live electric band I had ever heard. It must have been on a Friday because that night the same band played at our church Youth Conference at Pasco High School.

I remember the excited feelings I had as I watched them play their tunes. The organ and guitars and drums were something I wanted to be a part of. I went home and practiced some more. It was kind of a letdown playing my cheap acoustic with essentially no skills on the picking end.

In the summer between my freshman and sophomore years, I saved up my money. One day Mom took me to town where I bought a Harmony electric guitar and Ampeg amplifier. I was on the road now! Soon after, I found out that Nolan Empey had an electric bass. We got together and started jamming on three chord songs, mostly Credence Clearwater Revival tunes.

It didn't take too long before another friend, Kevin Jenks, became our drummer and we were the beginnings of an actual rock n' roll band. We practiced and got a few songs down. As quickly as I could, I spent my savings on cheap microphones, a Montgomery Ward's organ, a tambourine, and other odds and ends. We couldn't be a real band unless we had the tools. Back then, I figured the more equipment you had, the better you would sound. I was never really much of a musician, but I was really good at spending money to acquire equipment. My folks, Dad especially, were not happy with my new vocation.

Our first performance was playing a few songs at an early morning church seminary party we had. The night before, we assembled at my

97

house and practiced our numbers. We played "I'm a Believer," "Who'll Stop the Rain," and "Down on the Corner." I was so excited for the next morning's performance I couldn't sleep. After everyone else had retired to sleep, I was still up, pacing around our equipment and wondering what the actual experience of performing was going to be like. I wanted everything to be just right.

The next morning, we hauled our stuff to the church and set our equipment up. Since we needed someone to play keyboards, my sister Teresa had been recruited and she played along with us. When we set up on the stage of the church gym, we discovered there were different colored stage lights that we could turn on for ambience. It was all new and magical to me.

We played primitively, but were happy with our performance. Our group was a novelty and everyone liked us. Since we were the only game in town, we were the best band they had.

• •

During the spring of '73 when I was living away from home, I was playing in the last concert of my high school career. I accompanied the school choir and also the select choral group called the C-Notes on the guitar and organ. I had done a lot of preparation and was looking forward to the night. A nice Hammond organ had been brought in from a local music store that I was going to play.

My dad had never been to an athletic event during my schooling. He had never been to a school concert that I had played at. My mom had attended, but he had been too busy with work and church. I must admit that this bothered me. This night was the night I was going to show him my stuff.

When I got to the school that night, I began getting my paraphernalia together. I had a hard time trying to find my music. I spent an hour looking for my folder without luck. I was getting frantic. I enlisted the help of a few friends and we turned the music room inside out, to no avail. Finally, about ten minutes before the event was to start, I forlornly walked up to the stage where the band was tuning up. I walked over to where Nolan was sitting and asked him if he had any idea where my folder was. He laughed and said, "Yeah, I took it home tonight."

I wanted to kill him. It was my folder. I had a lot of music in it, some from our band. We had a gig the following night at Pasco High for a youth conference. He must have thought he was helping me out. I had no time for the 50-minute round trip to Nolan's to grab the music.

It was a very bad night. The music teacher, Mr. Bergren, was a little bugged at the Nolan-instituted downgrade his groups were experiencing. He told me to get up and sing with the groups since I couldn't play. Singing was the last thing I felt like doing.

After the performance, my mom found me and told me she wanted me to go home with her that night. To get where I was staying out at Warr's, I had to drive through 15 miles of deserted "badlands" and tricky curves. I am positive, with my state of mind that evening, I would have sped and wrecked on the way home. Thanks, Mom.

In August of 1973, just before I was to leave to go to Ricks College, our band played one last gig. It was an opening youth social for the kids at our church. We decided we were going to play outside under the lights on the ball field for a dance. We usually would get paid a hundred bucks or more for dances, but since this was our last hurrah and for the home crowd, we did it pro bono.

It was a very hot day and we arrived late in the afternoon to set up. Kevin and I were always trying to get each other's goat and I walked into the perfect setup right after I arrived. He was unloading his drums and happened to be in the trunk of his parent's green Plymouth. He must have been trying to find a drumstick under the spare tire. Whatever he was looking for didn't attract my attention.

What did get my attention was the fact that he was completely in the trunk. I reached up, grabbed the trunk lid and slammed it shut. Those of us standing around got a big kick out of it. It was hilarious that Kevin had allowed himself to get locked inside his own trunk!

I leaned over and asked Kevin how he was doing. In reply he said, "Casper, I've got the keys in my pocket!"

All of a sudden, I got a little concerned. How were we going to get him out? Mustering up a little bravado, I told him to just hang on, we would figure something out. I walked around to the back seat and examined the situation from that point of view. Back then, cars were built a little more solid and heavy. The seat had a stout frame around it and it didn't look like we were going to access Kevin from the back seat. I started thinking that maybe we were going to have to drive up to Jenks' and retrieve another set of keys.

I walked back to the rear of the car and started talking to Kevin. Then, terror struck my heart. I could hear Kevin in a weak voice, panting and choking and saying, "I can't breathe." All the fun evaporated in the hot August air. I had visions of Kevin dying of asphyxiation or heat stroke at my hands. The moment of hilarity was gone.

I wanted him to stay conscious. "Hang on, I'll get you out!" I yelled. I started running back and forth between the back of the car and the back seat, reefing on anything I could get my fingers under. Finally I decided that the most logical thing to do would be to access an airway behind the rear seat. Kevin continued weakly choking.

A gallon jug could not have contained the adrenalin I was pumping. I was scared and feeling stupid and frantic. I grabbed the seat frame and started reefing on it. I jerked and tugged. The heavy frame wouldn't budge. My resolve to save Kevin was unwavering. Eventually I was able to start bending the seat. Normally, this feat could not have been accomplished, however, in these circumstances I figured it was the bent seat and Kevin's dad a little miffed on the one hand or Kevin in the cemetery and me in the penitentiary on the other.

I finally got it bent enough that I could squeeze my hand past the frame, push aside the material and trunk covering, and make an airway so Kevin could breathe. At this point, I could hear him gasping and just knew he was ready to succumb.

"Breathe, Kevin, breathe!" I yelled. "Put your face up here and breathe!"

I held the trunk covering back and waited for him to grab some fresh air. Instead, what I saw turned my emotions upside down once again. I saw two fingers lightly dangling some keys back and forth. There was no more gasping, but suddenly I could hear Kevin chuckling from inside the trunk.

I was relieved, exhausted, and ticked off. I quit bending the seat and walked away. I had expended every ounce of energy I had in trying to keep him alive and here he was, getting a kick out of my emergency. Someone finally got the keys and let him out. The way I felt as I lay on the grass, he could have stayed in that trunk and rotted.

• •

Kevin Jenks—what a guy! He was a year younger than I. He and five of his brothers each took first place wrestling at state. Some did it several times. He was an athletic star and yet, kind of a klutz. Many were the times that he would end up in funny predicaments. He was constantly slipping and falling even though I know he had great balance because of his athletic accomplishments.

Following are a couple of stories that he denies happened, but I swear are true. I'll never forget them. I won't even embellish them.

One winter day during the time we were in high school, we came home on the bus. There was a lot of snow on the ground and the roads were icy. We pulled up to Jenks' house and Max, our bus driver, opened the door for the Jenks clan to get off. Jay and Julie exited, but Kevin decided to be funny and take his sweet time. He slowly sauntered down the aisle from the back of the bus to the front. There were several cars and a truck heading the opposite direction, stopped and waiting for the Jenks to cross the road.

Kevin finally made it off the bus after Max yelled at him to hurry up. Then he meandered over to their mail and paper box and retrieved their newspaper. He was taking his time and enjoying the attention.

All of a sudden, as he turned to cross the road, he started slipping and sliding. His feet went out from underneath him and he fell. He tried to get up and fell again. Everyone on the bus started laughing. The people facing us in the cars and truck were laughing. He couldn't get up. His school books were scattered on the roadway. His newspaper had become unfolded and was spread out on the road in several different sections. It was one of the funniest things I've ever seen. His face was getting redder by the second.

Finally, he was able to assemble his books and newspaper, stand up, and make his way across the road. The newspaper was not folded up like it had been a minute before, but was grasped in the form of a big ball of sheets in Kevin's arms, along with his books. The traffic began moving again and the busload of kids, minus the Jenks, laughed all the way home.

• •

Another time, Scot McGary and I went to Kevin's house after school. Before we could do whatever it was that we had planned, Kevin had to do his chores which included feeding his dad's cows. We got in their pickup and drove to the haystack to load up.

We stacked a bunch of hay bales in the bed of the pickup and proceeded to the field where the cows were. Our job was to throw the flakes of hay off for the hungry livestock. The bales were probably four rows high in the pickup bed. Scot and I got on top of the stack to begin throwing the hay off while Kevin drove through the field.

He decided to have a little fun with us so he started jerking the pickup back and forth by giving it the gas and then stomping on the brake. We were lurching back and forth, doing our best to stay on top of the stack and feed the hay. I'm sure we fell off once or twice, and I know I made a personal commitment that Kevin would pay for his monkey business after we finished.

When we finally fed all the hay, we ran up to the cab of the truck and tried to open the door, but Kevin had it locked. The only thing we could do was to jump in the back while he drove home.

After we pulled into their yard, Kevin stopped the pickup, jumped out, and began running away from us. I jumped out of the back and looked down for a rock in the driveway. Instead, the only thing I saw was a fairly fresh cow pie on the ground. I picked it up and could see that it was still fairly moisturized, green, and heavy. I knew that there was no way I could throw that stinky ball and have it stay together after launching.

Kevin, by this time, was quite a ways off. He and we knew that he was out of range for us to throw anything at him. He was running away from us, but had his head turned back toward us, laughing at our inability to pay him back. Nevertheless, in spite of the obvious futility of my desire for revenge, I leaned back and threw the pie as hard as I could.

It started flying. Scot and I stood there marveling at its ability to stay in one piece. Soon we were marveling at my ability to chuck manure accurately. It sailed toward Kevin and his laughing, open mouth. Whoosh! The entire ball smacked him just below his nose and just above his chin. Most of the fecal matter lodged inside his mouth and he instantly realized that the tables had turned. He stopped laughing.

He leaned over and started trying to discharge the heavy load he had just acquired. Scot and I started laughing. We were incredulous. We were dying. We couldn't stop.

Kevin couldn't stop spitting. After he got the majority of the crap out of his mouth, he started walking back toward us and the house. He had a great urgency to get to some water and do some flushing. The closer he got, the funnier he looked. There was a big green ring around the outside of his mouth.

I don't remember him ever trying to bounce me off of a pickup bed again.

• •

One summer eve McGary and I were over at a party for the kids in our church group. We were there on our motorcycles. Scot had a girlfriend and there was another girl that I was interested in. We eventually talked them into taking a ride with us on the bikes. We motored down the road and eventually ended up at a big pile of gravel the county had stockpiled. My memory is that this gravel pile was 25 feet high or more.

We got the idea that the girls would think it was romantic if we all climbed up it and watched the sun set. So we did. After climbing to just below the crest of the rock, we sat down and made ourselves comfortable.

A few minutes after we arrived, we could hear some drunk, Hispanic men in the distance carrying on. We couldn't see them since it was getting dark, however they must have been able to see us against the backdrop of rock. All of a sudden, bullets started whizzing around us and striking the gravel, mixed immediately thereafter with the sound of gunshots.

You've never seen kids jump and run up and over the side of a gravel pile as fast as we did that night. The shots were close enough that they could have just as easily hit us as not. We jumped on the bikes and sped off. It kind of ruined the romance of the evening.

CHAPTER 9

HAND LINES, WHEEL LINES, OTHER LINES

Growing up on the farm under the guidance of my father meant working much of the time when we weren't in school. We farmed a thousand acres of irrigated ground consisting of various row crops and alfalfa hay. Today, automatic pivot irrigation systems water the fields. Push a couple of buttons and you're done. In the 60s and 70s we used wheel lines, hand lines, and siphon tubes, which required changing at least every twelve hours.

Let's talk about hand lines, since they were the hardest. Each sprinkler line normally contained around 30 pipe. If you changed five hand lines every morning and night, it was not uncommon to walk ten miles a day just to "move water." Over ten thousand pounds of pipe would be carried in that scenario. There were obstacles such as muddy fields, tall and thick crops to be walked through, the burning sun, very hot sun-baked pipe, mosquitoes, ice covered pipes and crops, and water logged pipes; the list gets long when you talk about the negatives of changing sprinklers.

Moving hand lines was a constant job. If a field's boundaries weren't straight and square, wheel lines didn't work on it. Farming a thousand acres of mostly odd-shaped fields meant that we changed a lot more hand lines than wheel lines. Moving thirty to forty, or more, forty foot long pipe weighing thirty-five pounds each (if you let all the water drain out) and walking them sixty feet and then back again constituted moving a sprinkler line. Back and forth, bending over to unhook, picking up the pipe, walking sixty feet, and then trying to hook one pipe end into another required strength and skill. Miles of walking through mud, large sugar beet leaves, hay, potato vines, and other crops was also included in each session of "moving water." Changing each sprinkler line usually required walking more than 5,000 feet.

We changed sprinklers every morning and night, and sometimes more often, if the crop required it. It was hard work and it was monotonous. We changed hundreds of pipes every shift, usually beginning around five o'clock every morning for two or three hours, and then again that night. The watering season usually lasted from late March into October. In the early and late months of watering, the morning shift found us moving sprinklers in a thick coating of ice brought on by the water and cold temperatures.

Dad would usually go out and move a few hand lines and then come in and rouse us to help with the rest of the pipe to be moved. At 5:30 each morning, I dreaded the sound of him opening the garage door and tromping down the wooden stairs to get us up. How I wanted to stay in bed! It was kind of like the prisoner in his cell hearing the hangman tromping down into the dungeon to get him and take him to the gallows. I'm sure the hangee and I had the same feelings. The only problem is, I had it worse. It didn't happen just one time. This exercise lasted from March until October, every morning, for many years. I felt a little like Bill Murray did in the movie, *Groundhog Day*.

With all these years of practice, we became expert at unhooking, carrying, balancing, and rehooking the pipe. Often the line of pipes you had just shut off would remain filled with water. Unhooking each pipe would involve manhandling a pipe that weighed a hundred and fifty pounds until you could lift it and get the water to drain. When empty, the pipes weighed a more manageable 35 pounds.

Usually you would have a heavy stream of water going through the newly moved line of pipes so they would remain stable while you hooked up the pipe you were carrying. If you didn't get the end of the pipe properly positioned and correctly hooked quickly, the pipe would fill up and be too heavy to continue lifting.

It was an art. If the pipe didn't get hooked correctly, after the line became pressurized with 40-60 psi, it would blow apart and much more time and work would be involved to get the job done right.

The king of all sprinkler movers was my dad. He did it constantly. For many years he changed hundreds of pipe a day, every day through the season. He walked (actually, it was always a half-run) an average of fifteen miles a day just moving sprinklers. That's around 4,000 miles per season. He kept up this pace from before 1960 through the mid 80s. He covered approximately 100,000 miles of back and forth walking while moving a 35-pound pipe. That's walking around the earth four times! He moved somewhere in the neighborhood of three million sprinkler pipe.

I know these claims sound wild and unbelievable. They aren't. Neighbors, hired men, and our family saw it happen. In the hours between sprinkler changing, all the other farm work took place. The guy was absolutely driven. And I had to be his first-born, which meant that I moved a few pipe myself.

Hand lines are a thing of the past. Farmers today, unless they were here back then, don't have a clue what it was like.

• •

Mormons celebrate their pioneer ancestors' arrival in the Salt Lake valley on the 24th of July. Every year we have a big celebration on that day. A few years ago, both of our Basin City wards got together down at the Basin City Park for the annual party. One of the activities they had was a sprinkler pipe moving contest.

My brother Brent was put in charge. He rounded up enough pipe for two, ten-pipe, sprinkler lines. He had a clipboard and stopwatch and timed two contestants at a time as they moved the sprinkler lines and then ran back to the starting point. It was interesting to watch, but I had no interest in competing. Most of the contestants were half my age, lighter in weight, and in much better shape.

At one point, Mike Rowley, five years younger than I, raced his teenage son. He won and ended up with the fastest time up to that point. As he walked back to where his proud family was picnicking on the lawn and congratulating him, I watched him get a big grin on his face and say, "Well, I've still got it!"

The races continued. Finally, Brent came out looking for guys who hadn't competed yet. Scot Haws, also an old sprinkler pipe moving aficionado and I were sitting on the lawn, not the least bit interested in working up a sweat and reliving the days of our youth. We were enjoying the picnic and all I felt like lifting was a spoon or fork. Brent coaxed and begged, and finally, we decided to give it a try.

Brent said, "Go," and started the clock. I ran as fast as a fat man can and moved pipe. The years of balancing and unhooking and hooking while in constant motion were ingrained in my being. I smoothly completed the job. I was worn out and gasping for air by the time I got back to the starting point, beating Scot by a length of pipe or two. Brent announced my time. Of all the men and boys who had raced, I had the fastest time.

Later that evening, a young buck raced a second time and beat my time by one second. Just as I was getting ready to leave for home, Mike came up and said, "Ben, did you really do it in that time?" I said yes, but I could tell he didn't believe me.

A few years later, on a Boy Scout campout with our sons, I put up a tent with Mike. As we worked, I asked him if he remembered the sprinkler race. He did.

"I got the feeling you didn't believe I did it that fast," I said.

"I didn't," he answered.

"You still don't?" I asked.

"Well, I do now," he replied.

I asked him why he finally believed it. He answered that when we had my dad's funeral, one of the subjects we covered was all the pipe we had moved in the 60s, 70s, and 80s. He said it was then that he realized that I probably did move them that fast. Up until that point, I think he thought Brent and I had a brotherly cheating thing going on at the pioneer celebration.

• •

Wheel lines are comprised of 40 foot long aluminum pipe, four inches in diameter, with six foot metal wheels attached to the center of each pipe. A motor and transmission with four outrigger wheels rolled the pipe which made the entire line of wheeled pipes roll across the field.

After a twelve hour set of the sprinkler line watering the sixty foot by quarter mile swath of crop, we would shut the water off and disconnect the first pipe from the main line. We would allow the pipes to drain, walk to the motorized mover in the middle of the approximately twelve hundred foot long line, and roll the wheel line three revolutions, or sixty feet. Each end of the line needed to be rolled and straightened so the sprinkler heads were all straight up and then the first pipe hooked back up to the mainline and turned on.

One summer I was helping another hired man named Bob Muleberger move each section of wheel line to a different field. This usually never happened as the wheel lines normally stayed in one field. They were too much of a hassle to move. We would disconnect each pipe and then lift the heavy aluminum pipe and steel wheel into the back of a pickup. Because the wheels were so large, we could only carry two pipes per load.

We arrived at the new field and began unfastening our load. One end of the pipe was extended out, well past the front of the pickup. The other end stuck out 10 feet or more behind the tailgate. We had already moved many pipes. On this particular move, I was standing on the ground behind the pickup holding on to and steadying the back end of the pipe. Bob was standing in the pickup and rolled the six foot wheel over the side of the pickup. It dropped straight to the ground. When the wheel hit the ground, my end of the pipe bounced in an equal and opposite reaction upward. Thanks, Mr. Newton.

My chin happened to be in the reactive area of the high-velocity pipe end. Bob later told me that when the pipe hit my chin, I initiated and completed a 270-degree backwards flip and landed on my stomach. This was the first and last time I've ever done a backward flip without a trampoline. Several minutes later, I regained consciousness and woke up spitting blood and chips of teeth. The next day, I visited the dentist. And then went back to moving more wheel lines.

• •

I wasn't the only one who experienced pain while doing farm work. One day I was driving the pickup alongside a fence line. My dad was pulling fence rods and electric fence insulators out of the ground and throwing them in the back of the pickup. I started the pickup moving forward before my dad was out of the way and the right rear tire ran over his foot. He started yelling. I assumed I was still on his foot so I hit the brakes, jammed the transmission in reverse and backed up. Back over his foot I traveled again. This caused more yelling on his part.

• •

I loved to listen to rock and roll on the radio. My dad loved to listen to silence on the radio. Often he would get in the pickup after I had been listening to the radio. He would turn the key on to start the motor and the music of the day would begin emanating from the speaker. This bugged him in a big way. He would hurriedly reach up and turn the volume knob toward what he assumed was the off direction. In reality, he cranked the volume clear up. Rock would blare out of the speaker just the way I thought it was supposed to. I loved it, but only for a second.

His intolerance of my music would instantly multiply and he would finally get the radio knob going toward the off position. This same musical experience occurred on many occasions. It was always entertaining.

• •

When I was young, my dad had a couple of grain bins to store corn and wheat in. When he emptied the bins, it was always tough getting the last of the grain out of the bin. Therefore, he hooked one end of a cable onto a piece of plywood and would hook the other end up to a tractor. I was relegated to pull the plywood back to the far end of the inside of the bin. He would then drive the tractor forward, pulling the plywood toward the door and "sweeping" the grain out of the bin. The grain would flow onto an open elevator with chained metal slats that performed like a conveyor belt to carry the grain from the bottom of the bin up the elevator into the back of a semi-truck. The elevator was powered by hooking it up to a second tractor's power take-off shaft, or PTO, which would spin at a rate of several hundred revolutions per minute, powering the upward movement of the grain elevator.

This process was repeated numerous times until all the grain was cleaned out of the bin and loaded into the truck. I would take my shoes off while working in the bin so that the corn wouldn't go down my shoes.

The operation was stopped for a few minutes one time so something could be fixed. I looked out the door of the bin and wondered how full the semi was that we were filling. I couldn't see in the truck so I thought I would walk up the elevator and take a gander. With my bare feet, I gingerly walked up the incline of the elevator and stood at the top, looking down into the bed of the truck.

My dad finished his repair and yelled, "Come on down, Ben. Let's get going." I immediately started walking down the flat elevator bed toward the bin we were emptying. Dad must have really been focused on getting the grain bin dumped because right after he called me to come down, he got on the tractor powering the elevator and started it up. The chains and slats sprang into action and I could see I was in trouble. I was standing on an elevator that had metal panels going up while I was trying to walk down in my bare feet.

Several guys yelled at my dad to stop the tractor. He had forgotten all about me, two seconds after telling me to come down. I could see that these slats were moving fast and were going to tear my feet up in an instant. I had no choice but to jump off the elevator. I was standing a good 10 feet off the ground at that point.

I jumped, barefoot, and landed on the gravel driveway. I wasn't real thrilled about being forgotten about so quickly by my own flesh and blood, but was glad I had no broken bones or missing phalanges. I got back in the bin before my dad got the tractor started again.

• •

On August 10, 1972, our family was seated in the dining room eating lunch. One of us happened to notice a fireball in the sky, streaking south to north. It was one of the most unusual things I've ever seen in my life.

It looked huge and was passing at a high rate of speed to the east of us. I don't know if the thing was 30 miles away or 300 miles away; it was hard to tell. However, I do know that we jumped up and ran out on the deck and watched it travel. It was moving in a parallel line to the horizon, not an arc. It didn't lose altitude and was very visible in an otherwise clear blue sky. It stayed visible for at least sixty seconds. Thousands of people from Utah to Canada saw it. It was a once in a lifetime experience.

• •

The next couple of years were fairly uneventful although there were a lot of struggles on the home front. I was playing in a band and wanted my hair a foot or two longer than permitted by my folks. We had some knock-down, drag-out fights. In retrospect, I understand why Mom and Dad stood their ground. Every rebellious move I wanted to make took me a little further away from their values. They wanted me to stay conservative, righteous, and religious. They felt that if I let myself go with the ways of the world, I would not end up in a good place. Back then, I thought they were just trying to keep me from having a good time. Now, I appreciate their efforts and count myself lucky that they stuck to their guns.

• •

In the spring of my senior year, I'd had enough of my dad and I know he felt full, too. Scot McGary had moved up on the hill and was working for a farmer, Glen Warr. I wanted the same experience so I checked out of my home base and moved up to a little bungalow that Scot and I shared with a couple of other farm hands. My parents were not happy about my decision, but I was 18 and finally free!

I needed wheels and made a deal to buy a '65 Mustang from a fellow classmate. Again, my parents were not happy. We worked hard. Glen was hard to please. We were kids.

One Saturday morning, Glen and Scot decided to go to a church ball tournament. I wanted to stay home and work. Glen asked me if I had ever planted alfalfa. I said no. He asked me if I had ever planted wheat. I said yes. He said the jobs were very similar. He told me where the field was he wanted seeded and where the seed was. And then he was gone.

A grain drill has a large section of bins positioned across it that seeds are dumped into for planting. Large sized seeds such as wheat, barley, and oats are intended for these bins. A much smaller section of bins are located in front of the large bins. These bins hold much smaller seeds such as alfalfa. I was not fully aware of the smaller bins. Do you see where I'm going with this story?

I pulled the grain drill up to the bags of alfalfa seed, loaded up the large bins with the small seeds, and headed for the field. I used almost the entire pallet of hay seed before I got the big bins filled. I had never done this before so everything still seemed okay.

I dropped the planting discs in the ground and began planting. I made a pass down the field and part of the way back. "I better stop and check and make sure everything is looking alright," I thought. I jumped off the tractor and happily walked back and lifted up the bin cover. The entire load of seed was gone! I had no idea what was wrong, but I knew something definitely was. I stopped for the day.

When Glen got home that night and heard my story, he was not happy. The large seed feeders in the wheat drill planted the tiny alfalfa seeds hundreds, maybe thousands of times faster than the normal rate. From that point on, Glen was a lot grouchier.

He didn't fire me, but I left a few days later and returned home. My dad offered to compensate him for the seed after he heard about it, but Glen declined.

• •

About this same time I had a crush on a girl named Cindy Eppich (Mackay) who had agreed to go with me to the senior party after graduation. (You'll read more about her later.) I looked upon this planned event as a much more important and monumental event than my graduation. When I stopped by a mutual friend's home to pick her up, she informed me she wasn't going. I cajoled and griped and asked and sweet-talked and at last pleaded, but she was bolted to the floor. This refusal took me by surprise and threw me a little off my game. I finally tucked my tail between my legs and retreated to my car. My younger sister, Jill, and Scot McGary were in the back seat. My sister was giving Scot the cold shoulder, but at least he had a shoulder. I had nothing.

Neither one of us was having much success that night. The memorable graduation night we had hoped for was not taking place. I jumped in, shoved the car in gear, and tore out of the driveway. Turning on the main road, I put the gas pedal down and retreated to my inner sanctum of feeling sorry for myself. The car was barreling down Sheffield Road doing a hundred, when all of a sudden Scot leaned forward and screamed, "Aren't you going to stop?!"

I snapped out of my trance and could see that we were in trouble. We were barreling along at breakneck speed, a few hundred feet away from an intersection with Glade Road, which was the major thoroughfare. Two cars were converging in the night toward the same intersection we were. We were headed for the mother of all T-Bones!

I hit the brakes and the tires started skidding on the pavement. I could see both cars in front of me had their brakes locked up too. I could also see that there was no way we were going to get stopped in time to avoid a collision. I took my foot off the brake and hit the gas. We roared through the intersection doing about 80 miles an hour. Headlights were drilling us from both sides as we sped through the stop sign. It was a very close call.

Sheffield Road was gravel after passing Glade, which was lucky for me. As we flew down the road, the car kicked up a big cloud of dust behind us. One of the cars we almost hit was now chasing us. They were back in the distance however, because we had a running head start and they had to drive much slower because of all the dust we were kicking up. I drove a couple of miles down this gravel road as fast as I could. After reaching another intersection, I shut off the headlights, and turned left.

I idled up the road so that I didn't stir up any dust that would give away the direction we had turned. We had crept up the road a half a mile when the chase car got to the intersection and stopped. He sat there for a couple of minutes looking at his three possible pursuit routes and trying to decide which way we had gone.

Finally he went straight ahead, which was a great relief to me. We continued our escape by driving in the moonlight with no lights on. The smell of fear was in my nostrils for days after. I could not believe how close we came to having a major loss of life.

A day or so later one of my buddies from Othello named Digs, who I talked to at my graduation and who also had just graduated, rolled a jeep over himself and threw several of his friends out. The friends were okay, but he died.

The morning of his funeral, my dad asked me to pick up some sprinkler pipe down in the bottom of a canyon on our farm just above the bluffs of the Columbia River. I took one of our tractors and a pipe trailer down into the draw and soon was in another precarious spot.

I ended up boxed in, headed downhill, and on top of wet and slick "Ringold clay". The factor that penciled in the most dangerous part of this experience was that the tractor was a John Deere 520 tricycle machine. It had one wheel for steering on the front. This made the tractor far less stable than a conventional 4-wheeled tractor. It was always looking for an incline to tip over and roll to the bottom on.

The smart thing would have been to leave the tractor and walk home. The clay would have dried out sooner or later and then the tractor could have been driven out.

Not for me. I hate not finishing a job, especially if it involves challenge or risk. I unhooked the pipe trailer, got back in the seat, and started easing the tractor down the steep incline, inch by inch. Soon I was out of the wet area. The tractor wheels were sliding on the top layer of dry clay. I was standing on both brakes and death gripping the steering wheel, trying to keep the front tires pointed at an angle up one side of the draw to keep the 520 green machine from sliding down and going out of control. I was very worried about the angle of the tractor as I was afraid it was going to tip over at any time.

I had a lot of experience driving farm equipment in hazardous conditions, but never anything like this. With all these concerns, I was a basket case. The chances of going over the bluffs of the Columbia River with a tricycle tractor and getting to the bottom in one piece were astronomically small, similar to the brain I used to get myself in this predicament.

After more than two hours of inching down the steep hillside and finally reaching level ground again, I was totally exhausted. I had to drive around to a back road and take the long way home. It was another four miles, but I didn't mind; the road was level and wonderfully relaxing after what I had just been through.

Then I went to the funeral.

Several years later I happened to mention at the dinner table that I had gone down the bluffs on the 520. My dad got extremely upset and made me promise that I would never do anything like that again. I don't remember if I agreed or not.

CHAPTER 10

I DECIDE WHAT I WANT TO BE WHEN I GROW UP

The fall of '73 found me entering Ricks College, a two-year LDS College in Rexburg, Idaho. I had played in the high school stage band and also our high school rock band. Without much thought, I decided I would major in music. It was much harder than I expected, but I worked hard and learned a lot. Most importantly, I didn't flunk out. My study habits changed dramatically at Ricks.

• •

After a few telephone calls while still at home in Basin City, my mom and I found an apartment that was probably the only one left with a vacancy. It was called "Leif, the Lucky House." It was an old house and turned out to be the only remaining place at Ricks that was considered to be "unapproved housing" for the college. All other facilities were under Ricks College control.

Nine guys stayed there. It was, perhaps, a little crazier place than most abodes in Rexburg. I remember walking through the front door one afternoon and a knife thudding into the door next to my head as I entered. Some of the roomies were having a contest to see who could throw a knife at the wall and get it to stick.

We all cooked on our own. I secured a cupboard and, in order to cut down on missing food, I bought a bicycle lock and locked up the cupboard handles when I wasn't there. It worked until Haws, my hungry buddy from Basin City, stopped by to visit at a time when I was up on campus practicing piano. He found some tools and dismantled the hinges on the cupboard and helped himself. I was more than a little dismayed when I returned.

One of my roommates was a guy named Jon Muceus. We instantly took a liking to each other and hung around together. He was from Pittsburg, California, and took some commercial art classes. Quite a few nights that semester found him looking for sales ideas or slogans or logos for the next day's homework. I had an active imagination and provided most of the ideas for his class work.

Jon and I had some interesting times. On one of the first Sunday mornings in Rexburg, we were sitting in a classroom full of young men. I was parked in the first row with Jon sitting in the seat behind me. Back when I had hair, I had a very tender head. If someone pulled my hair, tears came immediately to my eyes and my reaction could be quite volatile. When my hair got pulled, I usually took on the persona of an axe murderer. Jon reached up in the middle of the church lesson and pulled my hair above the nape of my neck.

Without time to think, and in front of the whole class, I swung my arm around and connected my fist into his jaw, managing to get it somewhat slowed down just before impact. Jon and more than a few others in the class, including myself, were shocked at my instantaneous response. It was a reaction, just like blinking your eyes when something flies at your face. Kind of like Jon's eyes probably blinked right before I actually connected with his jaw. I apologized to him later and we both ended up thinking it was pretty funny. I don't remember him ever pulling my hair again.

One night we heard that the year before, a couple of kids had put soap in a large decorative water fountain at a bank downtown. They had gotten kicked out of school for the stunt. We had the same chance-taking personalities and headed for downtown late one night. We generated a bunch of bubbles, but were sneaky enough that we didn't get caught.

Toward the end of that semester, a dean from the school had all the guys from our "house" come to his office. He informed us that if we wanted to stay enrolled at Ricks, we would have to move into "approved housing." I didn't care because I had just decided I would go on a mission the next semester.

However, some of my roommates were a little more bothered. They argued and ranted and raved and made a scene and said that Ricks had no reason or authority for doing that. The dean then brought out the big guns. He opened a file and started reading instances of school rules that had been broken. I guess the school had recruited spies from the "approved" houses around us. He listed dates when the lights in our house were on all night and when girls were there when they weren't supposed to be. When I returned to the location after my mission, the house was gone and a big apartment complex that I'm sure was "approved housing" covered its former location.

• •

Some three years later, after my mission, I attended BYU in Provo, Utah. I had gotten together with some guys and put a band together. We rented a room to practice and keep our equipment in. It was in the back of Galaxy Music, a music store downtown.

One night we took a break from practicing and I walked outside into the dark alley to cool off. Some guys were walking toward me and just as they passed, I turned and looked as one of the guys walking past did the same.

"Jon?" I asked. "Ben?" he responded.

We had a great reunion. He was living in Logan, a city about 125 miles away. We were both shocked that we would meet up again under such weird circumstances.

Another three years passed by. I was operating a little tire store in Orem, which is the city just north of Provo. One day I watched a van truck circle the block several times. The third time around, I could tell that this guy was lost so I started walking out to help him just as he pulled in and got out to ask directions. It was Jon! We both were shocked once again and experienced another nice reunion. I lost touch with him after that.

Twenty-five years later I was at a local basketball game in Connell, Washington. My friend, Nolan, was telling a story and said something about Jon Muceus. I said, "WHO? You're not talking about Jon Muceus from Pittsburg, California?"

It was the same. Jon was Nolan's wife's cousin. We were both stunned. All these years and we had no clue about the mutual friend. I found out

Jon had married a daughter of the Miller Meat dynasty in Logan, Utah. I determined to hook up with him the next time I went to Utah.

A few months later Nolan informed me that Jon had died riding his Harley around Park City, Utah. I miss him even though we only spent a few months together many years ago. We were kindred spirits.

• •

At the time I attended Ricks, I was convinced that I wanted to be a musician so I majored in music. One of the teachers told our class that something like 95% of the kids who started out majoring in music would wash out. I gritted my teeth and committed that I would stick with the music program. I ended up being in the majority.

However, it wasn't because I continued my nonexistent study habits of high school. I worked hard in college. I learned music theory and all about Humanities. I took piano lessons and climbed several flights of stairs every day in one of the old historic buildings on campus to practice the piano. There were numerous practice rooms on the top floor. I could stop playing at any time and hear music and scales from the other rooms. I played guitar in the jazz band and was enlisted to play guitar in the orchestra for the school's production of *No, No, Nanette*.

I took the standard beginning music major classes and passed with decent grades that semester. It was the first time in my life that I had worked at my schooling.

While at Ricks College, I decided to go on a mission. One might ask why in the heck I would go out and live an austere lifestyle in the prime time of my life? I was into girls and rock and roll at this point. Those two forces were major interests. There were no other attractions at the time that could hold a candle to the allure of females and the magic of music. In fact, in my mind, each romantic force complemented and led me to the other, back and forth, a wonderful conundrum.

With my insecure personality, any time I could round up some positive feedback from a chick I felt much better about life and myself. Playing music helped bring in the girls, which greatly boosted the self esteem. Also, the romantic, melodic situations and solutions posed by the pop music of the day helped me relate to the world and salved my struggles in life.

Many youth have been, and are still, influenced and manipulated to form their lives around the music of the day. I was no exception. I now understand that this is a shallow interest that holds no true answers to the puzzles of life. However, I still like music from the 60s and 70s.

So why, just as I was getting away from the confines of parental control and starting to really enjoy the freedom of getting out on my own, would I decide to go on a Mormon mission? I knew that there would be no dating and a strict "arms length" proximity to girls. There would be very limited contact with my friends and family, lots of hard work, and a strict, self-disciplined lifestyle for two, long years. (Two years back then seemed like eternity. Today, with many years under my belt, two years is more like two minutes.) On top of it all, the only financial help the Church provided was a plane ticket home *if* the mission was completed honorably.

The answer is that I was aware of my situation. I knew I needed the growth and experience that a mission would provide. I had seen many boys older than I leave home as insecure and immature teens and return in two years changed men. They had a confidence and knowledge of God that placed them light years ahead of many of those who hadn't taken the missionary route. I could see that returned missionaries had many experiences in those two years that were impossible to attain without the service. They were impressive and I wanted that.

I also believed that God wanted me to go. I understood that this time would be dedicated to Him. I understood that I would be serving others and that the scriptures taught that when we lose ourselves in the service of others, we find ourselves. Heaven knows I needed to find myself.

During my Ricks College experience, I rubbed shoulders with returned missionaries and got a high concentration of religious and spiritual input. It was an enlightening time and brought me to the point of making the decision to go on a mission.

I called home that semester and told my folks. I guess I had been a little negative about serving a mission while I was in high school. They were very happy that I had turned the corner. Maybe I would make something out of my life after all! Maybe I would pull myself out of the loser bracket. As I look back, I am so glad I went. I would have missed out on many experiences and relationships if I had stayed home. This was the one time in my life when I was unencumbered and able to serve the Lord full-time.

• •

I turned 19 in the spring of 1974, I had reached the eligible missionary age, and I got ready to leave. I believed that this mission would be a turning point in my life. It was. I learned the truth of *The Book of Mormon* scripture that teaches "when ye are in the service of your fellow beings, ye are only in the service of your God." I searched for and found answers for my life that are essential for following and knowing God. I accomplished many things in that two-year period that would not have happened otherwise.

No other distractions like schooling, jobs, and social activities were present. Priceless experiences and associations were formed. The biggest mistake of my life would have been made if I had bypassed that opportunity and challenge. It was hard to go. It was hard to serve. It was hard to come home. This experience and my marriage were the two most important events of my life. I thank God, my parents, and all who supported and made this possible for me.

I won't mention much about my mission. I kept journals and ended up with over 730 pages of daily experiences. Each day was spent knocking on doors from 9:30 in the morning until 9:30 at night. A couple of hours each morning were spent studying. We were involved in trying to help others. Most didn't want help, but we found some that did. Those people and the experiences I had with them made my mission a special time in my life.

That winter of preparation in 1973-74 was memorable. I helped my dad feed several hundred head of cows, along with other jobs on the farm. There was a lot of snow on the ground which always complicates the feeding process. The fall before, when I was at school at Ricks, Dad had a hard time getting the last cutting of hay put up. He had gotten a large farm unit of 160 acres baled, but it started raining immediately afterwards. The hay couldn't be stacked while wet or the stack would catch fire. It never dried so it never got stacked. Then the snow came.

Every day in January and February of '74 I would get in the Harobed (bale stacker) and head for the big field. I've heard the guy who invented the Harobed named it after his daughter, Deborah. He just spelled her name backwards. Thus it became the Harobed. After he got the big check from New Holland for the patent, he drank himself to death.

It was cold. The Harobed had a cab, but it wasn't insulated, had no heat, and many drafts. It was made for summertime use. The driver's seat was hung several feet out in front of the front wheels. When you turned a corner, you often were hanging out over the edge of the road or suspended above a ditch. It was a large, motorized, funny looking machine that would pick the bale off the ground and move it over several different mechanized tables until it was part of a stack of hay totaling about ninety 110 pound bales.

It took a lot of coordination to manage the driving and stacking. It was even more complicated at this time because of the slick terrain I was traversing, namely snow. A Harobed seems to get stuck more easily than a normal vehicle, especially when it doesn't have a heavy load on it. Therefore, I had to keep the speed and momentum up as I loaded the hay.

We had a radio mounted in the cab. I still have strong memories of hitting those hay bales at 10 mph, watching the snow lying on the hay explode upon impact with the Harobed, stacking the hay up on the machine, freezing my buns, and listening to the radio cranked up. Two of the hits I remember were Maria Muldaur singing "Midnight at the Oasis" and MFSB doing "The Sounds of Philadelphia," also known as TSOP. Later, on my mission in Pennsylvania, I found out a good friend I had in Philly named Art had done some home improvements for a guy in MFSB. It must have been a family band as the acronym stood for "Mother, Father, Sister, Brother."

During this time, one day I was on the top of a haystack with two of our hired men, throwing bales off. The stack was 12 feet tall. I stepped back a little too far and went off the stack. I fell headfirst and landed on my head and shoulder. To this day I can't understand why that didn't kill me or break my neck. Twelve feet is a little too far to do a head plant. The hired men were scared to death as they watched me plummet. I was dazed, but crawled back on top of the stack after a few minutes of recovery. I attribute this non-injury incident to the fact that I was soon to be in the Lord's service.

• •

I received my call in March of 1974 to serve in the Pennsylvania, Harrisburg mission. My mission president would be Hugh W. Pinnock. It turned out that President Pinnock was a great example and influential teacher in my life. It was a wonderful experience to serve under this man! He was in charge of a hundred and some young men (imagine keeping all these kids focused and out of trouble!), a few young women, and some older couples. His family was there with him and his service was not for two, but for three years.

He had been a successful insurance salesman in Salt Lake City and dropped everything when the Church called him on a mission. He had a young family and was in his forties when called to Pennsylvania. As a young man, he had served a two-year mission in Colorado. It amazes me that every year, several hundred successful men get a surprise phone call, drop whatever they're doing, and take their families somewhere in the world to serve the Lord for three years. Presently 85,000 young people are serving missions.

• •

Just a personal aside concerning Mormon missions: Young men serve two years and young women serve a year and a half. My dad served in Baghdad, Arizona. My brothers served in Denmark, Fort Worth, Texas (Spanish speaking), and Japan. Two of my sisters served in San Diego, California (Spanish speaking) and Brazil. My wife served in France and Switzerland. Our sons served in Japan, North Carolina, and Brazil. Each of these missions involved great sacrifice and great experiences. None of us regret the effort.

• •

After a very concentrated, but rewarding week in the mission home in Salt Lake, I flew to Pennsylvania with eight other elders, all 19-year-old young men. We landed in Harrisburg and were picked up by some other elders. They explained that President Pinnock wasn't there because he was in Philadelphia at a trial.

A few months earlier, a longhaired dude parked at a stoplight in Philly noticed that some shorthaired dudes (missionaries) were laughing in the car directly in front of his. He assumed they were laughing at him. They actually weren't even aware of him, but he took offense and at the next light jumped out, ran up to their car, and started yelling at them to come out and fight. They weren't interested and took off when the light turned green.

He became enraged and started bumping their car with his. After several bumps he finally hit them so hard that their car went out of control on the turnpike and went into the opposing lanes, colliding head-on with a van. It killed three of the four missionaries. The court ended up slapping the guy's hands while three lives were lost for an imagined offense. I later met the elder who survived. He continued to serve after this horrible incident.

We stayed in the mission home the night we arrived in Harrisburg and the next morning met with our new President. He assigned each of us different areas throughout the state. I was assigned to Altoona. I was loaded on a bus and ended up sitting with a girl who was going to Penn State in the neighboring town of State College. I told her all about the Church before she got off. That was my new job.

Just as the bus pulled into the Altoona depot, I noticed that I had a sign language card in my shirt pocket. A deaf and dumb guy had given it to me in exchange for a donation in the Chicago airport the day before. I saw an opportunity to pull a prank, and yet, as a new "greenie" missionary, I wondered if a prank would be appropriate. Being a greenie actually enhanced the prank as the guys who picked me up had no idea I would have the guts to pull one over on them.

I got off the bus and saw a young elder (Elder Buckley) and an older man (Brother Miller) who turned out to be the "branch correlator" or local Church member assigned to help the missionaries in that area. They said hi to me, but I just looked back at them, handed them the card, and smiled.

I'll never forget the surprised looks they gave as they alternately looked at the card, at me, at each other, and then back at the card. No one from the mission office had told them a deaf elder was coming. They didn't know what to say. Neither knew sign language. I acted like I was ready to go to work even though I couldn't hear or speak. I energetically grabbed my suitcases and stood there, looking expectantly at them and waiting to follow them to the car. They finally snapped out of their surprised state and headed for the car, still speechless.

After arriving at Brother Miller's car, I decided that maybe I had crossed the line. I said, "Hey guys, I'm not really deaf." I got two more amazed looks and then they burst into laughter. Most greenies they had dealt with were shy, scared, and not disposed to use practical jokes as an introduction. They couldn't believe a greenie had taken them. I was relieved they weren't mad.

My companion hadn't arrived yet. He was coming in on a bus that night from Philadelphia with Elder Buckley's companion. I soon realized I was in a trap. The guys I had just met up with were in love with my prank. They said we were going home for lunch and that I just had to do the same trick with Brother Miller's wife. I was starting to get a little uncomfortable, but decided I'd better keep the natives happy.

When we got to the Miller home, the guys did all the introducing of me to Brother Miller's wife. They gave her my card. I just stood there and smiled. In a few minutes, they started making a few jokes at my expense. They expounded on the difficulties my new companion was going to have in dealing with this deaf and DUMB greenie. Sister Miller started getting offended, which made it even more delightful for the guys. I felt uneasy, but glad that I had been accepted so quickly. After 10 or 15 minutes of this light abuse they let her in on the secret. She finally laughed in a relieved sort of way.

That evening they insisted that I do the same thing with the two arriving elders. As they stepped off the bus, I stayed back while the two who were in the know talked to the two who were out of the loop. My new companion was a stern and serious fellow who was totally blindsided by this development. He had never trained a greenie before and was shocked at the additional demands that this handicap was going to place on his work. He couldn't understand why the mission office hadn't warned him.

We piled into Brother Miller's old Chevy and headed for a hamburger joint to get something to eat. I sat in the front with the two jokesters on each side of me. They expounded on the problems my companion was going to have and threw in a few jokes about me. I sat there staring straight ahead, acting completely oblivious to the situation and conversation occurring on each side of my head. The guys in back were getting mad. They thought the comments were bordering on rudeness. I was feeling a little nervous, laughing on the inside, but playing deaf and dumb on the outside. I just hoped my companion would find his sense of humor once the truth came out.

We arrived at the drive-in. Everyone went to the bathroom except me. I sat there and wondered what I should do about this situation. The first guy out was my companion, Elder Clawson. He took a seat in the bench directly across from me and gazed intently into my eyes. He had a determined look of "No matter what trials we will face, we are going to succeed!" It had gone far enough. I said, "Hey, I gotta tell you; I'm not deaf and dumb." He looked more amazed than the guys had earlier that day. He didn't laugh, but finally decided it was funny after the other guys came out and discovered I had let the secret out.

A couple days later, President Pinnock stopped by and we had a barbeque at the Miller's. The other elders launched into the story. I was scared to death I was going to be in trouble. President Pinnock thought it was funny, much to my relief.

CHAPTER 11

QUIXOTIC

One summer eve, while driving home from a chick flick, I mentioned to my wife that I had enjoyed the romantic aspects of the movie we had just seen. Somehow we got into an argument as to who was the most "romantic," her or I. She was dead set on the fact that she was far more romantic than I, and I was just as sure that it was me who was the Don Juan Casanova Casper.

Now, how would a couple in this conundrum determine the correct answer to such a question? I will admit, the woman is usually the romantic. But in our situation, I was quite sure the roles were reversed. I was ready to fight on this one. She had the common sense. I was the dreamer. We remained cemented in our foxholes until arriving home.

I walked in the door, over to the bookcase, and grabbed Noah Webster's Dictionary and proceeded to read: "Romantic: not sensible about practical matters; unrealistic; as quixotic as a restoration of medieval knighthood; a romantic disregard for money; a wild-eyed dream of a world state [syn: quixotic, wild-eyed] n 1: a soulful or amorous idealist."

I set the book down, drew a deep breath and with a dramatic and romantic flourish said, "I rest my case." She immediately capitulated.

I have always spent a fair amount of time in mental la la land. The same tendency that allows me to be creative and come up with ideas and dreams that may or may not make sense also makes me a romantic. Since I was a toddler, I dreamt of having a marriage partner someday that would make everything better. It became an escape mechanism to forget the rough reality of the moment. Beginning in kindergarten and following with grade school, junior high, high school, and afterwards, romantic thoughts and scenarios haunted my world. In the real world, I chased girls and a few chased me, but never did anything turn out like in my daydreams.

That is, until I went to college after my mission. At the end of August, 1976, I checked into my new apartment in Provo, Utah. My sister, Jill, who had just checked in to the same apartment complex, stopped by my place. She had run into a girl that she had known the year before while attending college in Rexburg, Idaho. The girl's name was Terri and she was living in the same apartments as my two sisters and I. She said she was going to send her over.

Jill told Terri to stop by and meet me that first night. She came by. She was nice looking and acted like she enjoyed life. She was full of smiles and before she left I was hooked. She worked for the Dean of Fine Arts at BYU. Before the week was out, I was spending a lot of time in the Fine Arts building even though I had no classes there. All of a sudden, I was getting very interested in Humanities, even though that wasn't my current major. In retrospect, my major at that time was finding my other half. I soon was on a first name basis with the Dean of the college, Lael Woodbury, Terri's boss.

When I get focused on something, whether it is girls or fine arts, it's pretty hard to get me off the path. We started dating immediately and by the time October rolled around I figured my life was complete.

I was committed. She wasn't as sure, but grudgingly admitted she loved me and so agreed to the plan. We decided to get married in December. We went out and bought a ring. Life was great. For about two days.

The second night after our first, but not only, engagement, we went to a Chuck Mangione concert. Just before we left for the concert she gave me the word that the deal was off. My entire life had led up to this pivotal moment. I was committed, in fact, set in concrete, and now I was finding out that she was skating out of my la la land and I didn't have a pair of skates. Chuck Mangione plays a great flugelhorn, but I still remember how off-key he was that night. In fact, his whole band stunk. I could not understand why the crowd kept clapping and cheering.

We sat together. The night was deathly black. It was over. I cancelled my check for the ring and pathetically returned it the next business day.

A couple of days later, we were back together. She was just as willing as I to keep it going. It turned into an on-again, off-again relationship. Somewhere along the line, probably 48 hours after I met her, I had become 100% committed to her and was unable to shut it off and shake loose.

Her folks had been divorced and I got the feeling that their situation had made her unsure of the whole marriage thing.

Also, looking back, I know that she still wanted to play the field and yet didn't want to lose the comfort of having a boy-toy. The whole fall semester was topsy-turvy. We were destined to never be apart during that time. We always ran into each other. We couldn't get away from the situation. We would agree to split up and then we would agree that we couldn't live without each other. It was misery and joy, hell and heaven, her and I. We often mused that ours was the greatest love story of all time.

I had started out that first semester on academic probation because of my high school scholastic prowess. I studied hard and did well enough that they let me off probation at the end of the semester. However, I was so mentally screwed up by the daily romantic situations that I ended up dropping out of BYU halfway through the next semester.

The tuition money I paid was gone and I moved out of the apartment complex so I could get away from her. A few days later, we were back together. I was a loser. I had never prepared myself for a letdown of this nature. During that spring, we managed to get engaged again. I hoped that this time it would stick. I decided to go home to Washington to work that summer. There was no reason to stay in Provo. I had finally accomplished what I had set out to do. We would get married in the fall.

Life was starting to turn around. I bought her another ring. She flew up to see me during the summer and was still committed. She was lots of fun and her smile made me think things were okay. They weren't.

One Sunday in June, my mom was talking on the phone to one of my sisters in Utah. After they finished, she wanted to talk to me. "Did you know that Terri has taken her ring off and is going out with guys?" she asked. I went numb. Then I went berserk. Then I went for a drive. One of the fastest drives of my life, and I've had some fast ones. I did not know how to handle the contortions this woman was putting me through.

I knew that I should stay in Washington because I had a good job. I was working for Kim Haws with my buddies Scot McGary and Scot Haws. Kim had invented an asparagus harvester and was in the middle of manufacturing it. However, I knew that I had to see this girl. She was all I could think about. So for the next couple of months, after work on Friday afternoons, I would head for Utah. It was a long round trip of about 1300 miles and I would usually arrive there after midnight.

I remember at least one time showing up at her apartment and her being out on a date. She knew I was coming and while I waited in my car on the street she was putting the moves on some guy. Looking back, I can't believe I put up with that kind of abuse. When she finally got home, they went inside for an extended length of time. Finally, I used a pay phone across the street from her apartment and called. I told her to get rid of him and she said okay. Ten or fifteen minutes clicked by. I called again. Finally he left. I was a desperado heading for a nervous breakdown.

These trips from Washington to Utah were nightmares. I got three speeding tickets in one weekend. I would drive back on Sunday night and barely make it in time for work, dead tired, dazed, and confused.

Finally I couldn't take it anymore. I moved back to Utah. It was the summer of 1977. I was broke. I had manically borrowed a lot of money over the previous year to buy band equipment and rings. Bills were due. I couldn't find a job as it was "school's out" summertime in a student-infested college town. Job Service was no help. I finally realized nobody was going to help me and I needed to make something happen on my own.

I ended up driving up into the more affluent neighborhood in Provo called Indian Hills. Twenty-two years of age and here I was, playing like a ten-year-old, knocking on doors and asking people if I could weed their gardens. It was humbling. It was a rough summer. This was a time when I should have been preparing for my life's work and yet I was out trimming shrubs and dumping grass clippings.

• •

One summer morning, one of my roommates was sick. He had been working out by Utah Lake for a farmer named Morris Clegg. He didn't feel like going and asked me if I wanted to take his place. I jumped at the chance, even if it was only for a day.

I showed up for work. I could tell immediately that Morris didn't like the idea of a newcomer working on his farm. I think he had had a lot of college kids come out and work for him that didn't have a clue about the farm life. I'm sure each of them was more trouble than they were worth. He figured I was one of them. He grudgingly agreed to let me stay and work the day, but made it clear that I was done after that night. Everything went okay throughout the day until evening came.

Morris told me to get on a tractor and bale some hay in a field. I jumped on and started baling. After I had baled for a bit, I noticed that the baler was starting to kick out broken bales. I immediately stopped, since once a baler starts breaking bales it doesn't fix itself. If you keep going, all you have is a field full of useless, broken bales and a bunch of baling wire strung along the way.

Then I noticed Morris at the top of the field, waving his arms and yelling at me to stop and not proceed. He was far away and I couldn't hear him. He started half walking, half running to get down to where I was before I did any more damage.

The baler was a John Deere, the same type that we had on the farm in Washington. I crawled underneath it and saw what the problem was. Five minutes later I had rethreaded the wire, jumped back on the tractor, and taken off.

Now after you've fixed the problem with a baler, it will spit out a couple more broken bales before returning to tight bales. Therefore, as soon as Morris saw more broken bales emerging, he got mad and really started swinging his arms at me to stop. Then a good bale appeared. And then another.

His frown turned into a smile. In his mind, he had just witnessed a miracle. He walked up to the tractor and climbed on.

"I need a good man here," he said. "You want a full time job?" Boy, did I ever! I worked the rest of that summer and fall for him.

Morris was a great guy. He had been a bachelor into his forties. He had a good friend who farmed and ran a dairy. His friend was married and had eight kids. One day, his good friend and his hired man were up on a silo. One of them got a whiff of the fumes that emanate from stored silage and fell down into the oxygen-depleted pile. He was immediately rendered unconscious. The other jumped down and was also immediately impaired. They both died.

Morris soon was married to the widow and took over a husband's and father's role of taking care of a bunch of kids and a wife. It was a tragedy, but ended up working out as well as it could have. They had me in for lunch every day and we even took cat naps before we went back out to work.

One day we were putting up silage. I was assigned to climb up on top of the silo and take care of the needed work there. There would be spells of 10 or 15 minutes between truckloads. I noticed a couple of Morris' kids over behind the dairy, helping themselves to a patch of grapes. I was a little hungry. So after an empty truck left, I climbed down and made my way toward the grapes.

There was a large cement buttress and a big empty slab of ground between me and the grapes. I stood on the cement and jumped down on the dirt to continue my trek.

The only problem was that it wasn't dirt. It was a thin, dry crust resembling dirt covering a large pond of liquid manure from the dairy. I was standing on concrete one second and in the next second was up to my chin in stinky, green, overpowering slime from the rear ends of a hundred milk cows.

It was unbelievable! I couldn't help but laugh at the crazy situation I was in. I couldn't climb back out where I had jumped in. I had to slowly wade through 20 or 30 feet of crap before I reached the shore. I was lucky it wasn't over my head or I might have drowned in the slime.

I walked back to the dairy, leaving a pungent green trail. It stunk much worse than normal manure. I grabbed a water hose and began spraying myself off. It was a long process. In the middle of my cleansing, Morris and a couple of his hired men showed up. They took one look at me and started laughing uncontrollably. They couldn't believe someone would dive into their manure lagoon.

I never did get the stink out of my apparel. Even though I couldn't afford it at the time, I ended up throwing the entire day's ensemble of clothes and shoes in the garbage. I never did get any grapes.

● ●

Morris had a brother named Von. Von owned a service station at the corner of Geneva Road and Center Street in Orem. He also owned an old house and 2-bay tire store located a couple hundred feet behind the service station. It was here that all the tire work was done for the service station.

As the summer and farm work were drawing to an end, Morris told me that Von was looking for someone to run his tire shop. I immediately went down and applied. Von was interested, but he already had another guy thinking about the job. This guy's name was Steve Erickson. He had worked for Von before his mission and had just returned.

Steve worked for a few days doing tires and then decided he wanted to work at the station. Von called and offered me the job. I jumped at the opportunity, never to weed gardens for hire again.

On my first day at the tire store Steve hung around for a half hour and taught me a few basics about working on tires. Then I was on my own. I loved it. Since it was a one-man shop, I had to do everything while I had absolutely no experience with any of it. I would spend the next three years of my life fixing tires and running a business.

At first I would spend hours working on a job that later would take me ten minutes. I ran, literally, all day long. Most of the pickup and truck tires back then were split rims. They were dangerous and hard to change. Much easier to change drop center tires and wheels gradually became the standard in the years to come, but at that time it was mostly all split rims.

Split rim wheels were used on many pickups and most trucks up until about 1980. They were very hard to break down and change. They consisted of one or two snap rings, or split rings, that were supposed to lodge into one side of the wheel and lock up when you applied air pressure to the tire. Often the rings became deformed from the abuse they endured from dismounting and mounting as the tire was changed.

They were dangerous. Older rings were even worse and were known as widow makers. When air pressure was applied, usually between 45 and 90 psi, if the ring wasn't in place correctly, it would fly off at a very high velocity. There are many tire workers and bystanders who have been killed by split rims. Some stores used metal cages to contain the wheel in case it exploded. I didn't have one. A guy named Ed, who worked at Von's service station, had seen a fellow student who was sitting on a just-repaired truck tire get fatally blown through the roof in their high school automotive shop.

As I changed tires, there were quite a few times that I could see a wheel was suspect. It was scary. Twice I had rings fly off. I was out of the way, but I remember being awed by the force of the explosions.

Drop center tubeless tires replaced split rims. This brought another problem. It was often hard to get the tire to begin inflating as there was no tube in it. Since then, air blasters and other tools assist the inflation process, however, back then it was often a real trick to air the tire up.

Someone told me about starting fluid. It became my tool of necessity. The tire would be laid on the floor and a can of ether sprayed into the void of the tire. You would then stand back and throw a lit match toward the sidewall of the tire. The match would ignite the fumes and explode. There would be a loud bang, the tire would inflate to the wheel, and air would have to be applied immediately to the valve stem. If you didn't get the air going right away, the tire would decompress and lose the seal.

It was an interesting and scary process. Fire and a loud explosion and sometimes even a bouncing tire were involved. Spectators who hadn't seen the process before were very surprised when you lit their tire on fire and it exploded. I've performed this process hundreds of times and have had the hair on my arms and head singed more than once.

When I started, Von told me to keep track of all the sales and expenses. He proposed that I would get a base wage, we would deduct all the expenses, and if there was a profit, we would split it.

Soon I noticed Von was bringing people by to look at the shop. He was trying to sell it. I worked as hard as possible, keeping track of every penny that came and went. After three months of this, I had racked up a nice little profit. I arranged to meet Von at his house one night. I brought all the numbers and showed Von what had transpired. I was devastated when he informed me that he wasn't going to split anything with me after all. The knowledge and experience that he was so benevolently sharing with me was my bonus.

I was ticked. The next morning I informed him that he would rent me the shop with an option to buy or I was quitting, even though I didn't have a dime. We kicked it around for a day or two and Presto! I was the proud operator and soon-to-be-owner of a tire store, inventory, equipment, and an old house attached to the side of it. It was all on contract to him. For the next three years, I made monthly payments on a contract for 60 or 70 thousand dollars. I had no experience, no operating capital besides the inventory in the shop, and no business experience. But I had enthusiasm.

I gradually learned the business by attending the school of hard knocks fulltime and overtime. It was tough. It was a one man band. When I was tired or sick, I still had to work. There were no other employees or backup plan if I couldn't make it. My books were a mess. I did well just to get my statements mailed out at the end of each month.

• •

My first brush with an inspector came in 1977 when I applied for a business license for my new tire store, Ben's Geneva Tire. It was located across the road from the Geneva Steel plant in Orem, Utah. I didn't have two cents to my name and had no clue how to run a business, let alone how to change a tire. Two inspectors with unneeded hard hats showed up and began telling me things that they wanted me to do. Their requirements seemed senseless and trivial to me, like they were looking for a problem so they could write it down on their clipboards.

Finally, their inspection ground to a halt when they said I had to have some kind of a backflow valve on a water faucet or they wouldn't issue me a permit. When I asked them how much it would cost, they said it was something like 60 or 70 dollars. I didn't have that kind of money! I was floored! I asked them why I had to have it and they said because I had a hose hooked on it. I walked over, unscrewed the garden hose, and dropped it on the floor.

"Now do I have to have it?" I asked. They mumbled in the negative and continued looking for more problems to stop my initiative. I had just saved myself 60 bucks which was a lot of money back then. It was also my first lesson in dealing with inspectors.

The State of Utah audited me one time. The auditor showed up and asked to see a bunch of figures and reports that were nigh impossible to produce given the mess that I had. I invited him into the old house and he could immediately see the disarray. He gave me a list of things that I needed to come up with for his return in a few weeks and then hurriedly left. He never came back.

• •

I hustled business whenever possible. There were farms, businesses, the Geneva Steel administration building across the street, and residential areas towards town. I picked up new customers continually. Since I started out with nothing except the inventory on hand and had no other financing, I was always in a cash flow pinch. After busting tires all day, I found it hard to do the collections and book work. It was a major load getting the bills paid every month.

One day I had an opportunity to sell a set of eight truck tires. The only catch was that I had to mount them for the customer at 2:00 am. I was in his shop early the next morning, swinging the tire hammer and reefing on the tire irons. About halfway through the job, as I was standing on a tire and breaking it down with the 12-pound tire hammer, someone came through the door at the other end of the shop. It was one of the workers showing up to work.

He disrupted my rhythm and concentration. The next swing of my tire hammer missed. It didn't hit between the steel rim and tire but rather smacked straight into that bone that protrudes out from the inside of my ankle.

Tire hammers are not your run-of-the-mill standard hammer. They have a narrow, wedge-like piece that leads the way when swung. This allows the wedge to lodge when swung between the tire bead and rim. This also allows the wedge to inflict horrific pain whenever it makes contact with a body part.

I went down, gasping and grasping my foot. My sock was soon soaked with blood. It hurt. I wanted to quit, but I had no choice other than to finish the job. There were still three tires left to change. I hobbled through the job for another couple of hours in terrible pain.

I finally finished and made my way home and then to the doctor. I didn't open the shop that day and sported a major limp through the next few weeks.

• •

And still there was Terri. I remember a couple of times during this two-year trial period when I came close to having a nervous breakdown. She was driving me nuts. I've experienced many a tumultuous time, but these times were the worst. One morning I was sitting outside Terri's apartment in my '74 Dodge Charger SE, waiting for the girl of my dreams who had turned into a nightmare, and my head began spinning. My hands started shaking and I felt like my brain was held in place by a few rubber bands. Several of those bands were stretched to the breaking point and I could actually hear a few of them beginning to pop. I've never experienced this kind of sensation before or since, even though I've had a lot of very stressful times. It gave me empathy for those who do end up breaking down with mental stresses and illness. I should have heeded the warning and bailed. But I didn't.

One week she called me and said she had to give a talk in church. She was very nervous about it so I dropped by and helped her put some thoughts together. I pretty much wrote the talk for her and she was very grateful. So grateful in fact, that she invited me to come to her Church meeting the next Sunday to listen to my words. I went and enjoyed the service. That is until she finished her talk and walked off the stand to sit in the congregation. I had saved a seat for her, but she, and my talk, walked over and sat down by another guy. I left as soon as the meeting was over.

We went up and down and back and forth for two emotional, taxing, fantastic, long, and lonely years. One night she invited me over for a party and then ignored me while putting the moves on another dude that caught her eye that particular night. Most of the experiences of that time have thankfully faded into oblivion. World's greatest love story? Ha! Without a doubt it was the most torturous two years of my life.

CHAPTER 12

MODUS OPERANDI

In the winter of 1977 I moved out of Provo and into the old house that was attached to the tire shop. It was a beater, but suited me just fine. One of my roommates from Provo named Darrell Brown came out to visit me one night. I had just finished work and was sitting in the tub cleaning up. I heard a knock on the door and after wrapping a towel around me, I opened the door. It was Darrell. I invited him in and got him a chair. He sat in the hallway and we talked about our plans for the future. He was a nice guy. Recently I discovered he has been the president of KSL, the Salt Lake NBC affiliate, and is now the president of Bonneville International.

The house had a large living room that was perfect for a rock and roll band practice room. So I looked around and recruited some musicians. They were all students at BYU.

Julie Larson was our female vocalist. Her voice sounded a lot like Linda Ronstadt. We did a few Ronstadt tunes like "Tumbling Dice," "Poor Pitiful Me," "Blue Bayou," and "When Will I be Loved?" I think Julie ended up teaching school. She's been singing the last few years with the Mo Tab (Mormon Tabernacle Choir).

Bill Bollard was our lead singer and rhythm guitarist. After graduation he became an attorney in Southern California and gained notoriety by defending several people who ran into legal trouble in Mexico. He was featured on an hour-long 20/20 program, and after defending Dog the Bounty Hunter, was on Larry King and other news programs. He later served as a mission president in Mexico. Mike Reynolds played bass. He also ended up in Southern California as an accountant.

And then there was our drummer, Randall Edwards. He was a slightly overweight guy who was hilarious. Just before he joined our band he ran as a vice presidential candidate for the ASB position at BYU. His running mate was a guy named Erickson. These two nutty guys turned the 25,000 students and faculty at BYU upside down. Their platform was crazy. They said, if elected, they would distribute the coveted football game tickets by throwing the tickets out of an airplane. They would convert all the drinking fountains at the school so they dispensed Kool-aid instead of water. They would require the teachers and other faculty to park in parking lots on the west side of Utah Lake. The west side of Utah Lake happened to be across the lake from BYU, a good 25 miles from campus.

They packed wooden boxes to the center of campus, stood on them, and made their campaign speeches with megaphones to anyone who would listen, which added up to a lot of people. The students thought it was hilarious. The administration was going nuts. They were mortified that these guys might possibly become the chief ASB officers.

The primaries were held and Erickson-Edwards won by a landslide, the largest in BYU history! Dallin H. Oaks was the president of BYU. I'm sure he slept very little during this period.

Oaks and other leaders at the Y held an emergency meeting and invited (or required) the attendance of Randall and his running mate. The outcome of the meeting was that the two partners withdrew their candidacy. The students were very disappointed and wondered what type of coercion was used at the meeting.

• •

One night we played at a dance at the Springville Art Museum. I had never met Randall's running mate. He was at the dance that night. I talked to him for a minute between one of our sets. He volunteered that he had an egg in his pocket. He pulled it out and sure enough, there was an egg with some string tied around it. I don't remember what he said the reason was for it. I just remember being awestruck at the situation, especially when he started pulling on the string that was attached to the egg. It kept coming and coming. He must have had a mile's worth of string in his pocket. Maybe it was good that President Oaks convinced them not to run.

We played for a dance at a church in Salt Lake one evening. When we started playing, we noticed a guy was walking around the gym looking at an electronic gadget. After a song or two, he came up to us and told us that he was in charge and he had a decibel-meter to make sure we weren't playing too loud. I had played at a lot of dances and had never run into a decibel-meter guy before.

He struck me as not a real fun kind of guy, one who was probably not there to enjoy some rock and roll. For the rest of the night he paced the floor and stared at the meter. Several times he motioned or came up and told us to turn it down.

Eventually we got around to playing the one song that Randall sang lead on. It was "Play That Funky Music." We began playing the opening bars with the guitars playing the distinctive and driving bass line. Next, the lead vocal was supposed to enter with a loud and high-pitched "Heeeyyyy!"

Randall entered at the correct time. He even had the right pitch. The only problems were that his mike was turned up too high, he yelled the "Heeeeyyy!" way too loud, and the microphone was too close to his mouth. The result was that the beginning of his vocal arrangement was deafening. Even though we in the band were veteran rock and rollers and were used to loud noise, we were shocked. The windows in the building shook and nearly shattered, all from Randall's vocal entrance.

We knew we were in trouble. I looked down at the meter-reader on the dance floor and he was holding the box with both hands, staring at it, and shaking violently. He was intently and incredulously watching the needle peg out in the red.

Next, he began a sprint towards us. He raced past those of us who were standing at the front of the stage, tripped through the cords and amplifiers, and made a beeline toward Randall. We were still playing. Randall was banging away on the drums, singing, and oblivious to what was about to happen. I don't think he was aware of the abnormally high volume of his beginning vocal assault.

The dashing authority figure reached Randall's vicinity and grabbed him by the throat with both hands while Randall kept drumming with a slightly surprised look on his face. I'm not sure what happened to the decibel-meter. The man started shaking Randall's neck and head and yelled several times, "We don't play like that here!" He was mad. I don't think he was into funky music either.

Needless to say, we all backed off the volume on the rest of that song, especially Randall. It was probably the meekest and tamest version of

"Play That Funky Music, White Boy" that has ever been played on planet Earth.

I think Randall is now an attorney for the city of Bountiful, Utah.

● ●

Steve (Scots' brother) and Debbie McGary had thrown in the towel farming in Basin City and needed a place to stay while Steve went back to school. Steve had worked for my dad while in high school so I got to know him well. They had a couple of little kids and were as broke as I was.

They moved in and helped with my rent payment, but they had to put up with my band practicing in the evening. Steve eventually got his doctorate and became a dean at BYU-Idaho.

The next August (1978), I visited my former mission president, Hugh Pinnock. As we conversed, I related the unromantic situation I was in with Terri. He looked at me and said, "Do you know what I would do if someone wasted two years of MY life? I would never speak to them again!" I looked back at him and realized he was right.

I drove back to Provo, called her up, and said adios. We had done this many times in the past and failed. The partings and reconciliations had become addicting. The separations were pretty sad and yet the reunions were pretty sweet. We couldn't stay away from each other. She probably snickered on the inside at me, her little fool, as she bid goodbye on the outside. Little did she know that this time I was making a final, desperate move of permanent separation.

I had moved to Provo two years earlier because I wanted to get married, move back to Basin City, and settle down. Seven-hundred-thirty days later, I was anything but settled down. I was tired of the dating game and yet, I was now going to have to start all over.

September, October and November of 1978 found me deeply focused on becoming unsingle. I was familiar with the saying that a goal unwritten is only a wish. I was sick of wishing so I began compiling a list of every girl I knew that might fit the bill. I was on another mission. My primary aim was to get hitched so I could return to Washington, farm with my dad, and start raising a family. I had no other goals.

Every day found me taking girls to lunch and dinner, inviting them to our band practices and performances, going out on dates, going to firesides, and whatever else came along. I did this while still running the tire shop. Many fast and furious prenuptial advances were doomed for one reason or another. After a date or two, girls would all of a sudden be too busy to talk to me on the phone. A few wouldn't return my calls. Some returned the advances, but there wouldn't be any fireworks on my end so I didn't return their calls. I remember times I would show up for a blind date arranged by friends and immediately begin trying to figure out the fastest, easiest, and cheapest way to end the night of torture.

I invited a former roommate of Terri's out to my house one night to listen to our band practice. After we finished, everyone left and this nice looking blond and I started talking. She was a dental hygienist and was making good money. Her dad was a dentist from California and she seemed very well-heeled. For some reason, she started talking about all the nice things she wanted out of life. As she went on, I could see that I would never be able to take care of such a high maintenance female. I kept agreeably saying "uh-huh," but inside my spirit was vigorously shaking its head, no.

As we talked, she started probing as to where I was in the romance department. She knew all the history about her old roommate and me. I told her I had finally had enough and was moving on. My schedule book happened to be on the table. About that time, she noticed her name on the page with a lot of other girls, many of whom had their names crossed off because of lack of compatibility.

She asked what the list was all about so I just gave her the facts. I was taking names and then crossing them out when things didn't go well. Her name had no lines through it and her persona was letting me know that she was glad it wasn't crossed off. I think she was sick of the dating game also, and if she had a list, my name might have been on it.

Finally she left for the night. I could see there was no future in this financially draining filly. I crossed her name off.

The next morning she called me. I was surprised because, in my mind and on my list, we were done. However, she was not aware of the latest list alterations. "Let's do lunch today!" She was kicking it into high gear. I was taken aback, but not wanting to be rude, agreed.

Lunch time rolled around and we met at the Village Inn. She was bright and vivacious and after ordering we talked about nothing. Having an appointment immediately after, I had brought along my schedule book. All of a sudden, she reached across the table and grabbed it. I got a little concerned.

That concern escalated immensely when she began thumbing through the pages until she hit my chick list. She noticed that her name was crossed off, only a few hours after heading the list. She immediately began crying and sobbing and took a ten minute trip to the ladies room. Finally she returned.

"Why?" she asked. "Why did you cross my name off?" I was kind, but honest, and told her I knew there was no way I would be able to keep her supplied with her basic needs. She cried; I gulped lunch down and left as soon as politely possible. I'm pretty sure I paid for lunch before I left.

• •

A tire customer of mine had a girl working for him as a receptionist. Her name was Mary. She was very nice, always smiling. Her smiling so much and being so dang positive almost made me a little uncomfortable. I had become acquainted with her through my work. One day she mentioned that her car was in the shop.

Once in a while I liked being generous and this was one of those times. I had a Mustang and told her she could use it for a week or two. She couldn't believe I would loan out my car, but it was no big deal to me.

Thanksgiving was coming on. After she brought my car back, she invited me to go home with her for turkey day to Malad, Idaho. I didn't have any strong feelings for her, but also didn't have anything else going for Thanksgiving so I agreed. I had to work until the night before Thanksgiving so she left earlier and I drove up after work that night. Her dad was a doctor and owned a ranch outside of town. Her family was very nice and made me feel at home.

The next day we visited and had Thanksgiving dinner. After dinner, around 2:00 in the afternoon, I started feeling very strongly that I needed to head back to my home in Orem. Mary was looking forward to us having a good time for the next few days, but all of a sudden I felt I must go. She had been expecting me to stay the whole weekend and was very disappointed that I was eating and running. I felt bad as I drove away. In a few short hours I would understand why I had this prompting.

I got home in the early evening and walked into a nasty surprise. By this time, the McGary family had moved out and I had three Navaho kids from Ganado, Arizona, living with me. They informed me that someone had broken into the house the night before. I glanced at the room where all of our band gear was supposed to be and it was empty. I went into shock. I owned most of the equipment, but there was also some gear that the other band members owned. It was all gone! Someone had cleaned me out.

I immediately suspected the Native Americans, but after questioning them thoroughly, I started thinking, "Injun no steal 'em."

I was in trouble. We had dances booked through New Year's with no instruments to play. I owed lots of money on items that were no longer in my possession. My house had been invaded. I was one mad and sad hombre.

When my roommates discovered the theft the night before, they immediately called the cops. I headed up to the Orem police station to see what kind of progress they were making. This would mark the first of many experiences I've had with law enforcement; this was one of them that slightly tainted my respect for the Men in Blue.

I was sadly disappointed when I arrived at the counter. They weren't doing a thing and told me to get lost. They said that because this was the Thanksgiving weekend, they wouldn't get anyone to even start investigating it until the next Monday. That was five days away! I had visions of my amps, guitars, synthesizer, PA system, and all the other goodies on a truck, heading out of state, maybe even to Mexico.

I told them their timeline was unacceptable. They treated me like a little kid and told me to mind my own business. They were the professionals and I was meddling. I asked if they had found any fingerprints or evidence in my house the night before and they said they had found one blue glove.

"Can I see it?" I asked. The officer reluctantly left and returned with the glove. The cops found it in the room where the instruments and equipment had been the night before. I had never seen the glove before that moment and knew it belonged to the culprits. The officer told me they would get back to me next week and that they would take care of the investigation.

It was now officially none of my business. I was bugged. I knew that every hour that went by signified that there was less chance that I would get the stuff back. I had a vivid vision of a truck going down the freeway, heading out of state, full of my equipment. I tried to explain my vision to the cop. He told me to leave. I left frustrated and mad.

I couldn't sleep. I drove around my neighborhood and visited anybody that I thought might have driven by the night before and possibly seen something. After all my possible contacts had turned their lights off for the evening, I began aimlessly driving.

I was depressed to say the least. I felt instrumentally raped and it was not a pleasant feeling. I had no idea where to start looking for these jerks. In addition, I had no help from law enforcement. They had let me know in no uncertain terms that they were the professionals and I was to stay out of their business. I knew that before the five day "cop and turkey holiday" was over, my stuff would be dismantled, separated, and sold for pennies on the dollar.

I drove around all night. I tried to sleep with no success. I drove down into Provo and parked outside Terri's house. I hadn't seen her for three months. I needed a friend. Terri would be a welcome respite even if it was two o'clock in the morning. Surprising myself, I didn't get out of the car. I sat there for a while thinking and then left, miserably and aimlessly cruising on. I knew I would be greeted with open arms, but I stuck to my resolve to avoid contact.

The next day was Friday. Like the cops' place of business, my tire shop wasn't open because of the holiday. I continued my quest. I talked to everyone I knew in the vicinity. I spoke separately to two 16-year-old kids, one of whom had worked for me in the past. I asked them where they had been Wednesday night. They both claimed to have been with each other and yet, as I pressed them individually with specific questions, their stories didn't exactly jive. It wasn't a big deal, but I filed it away in the back of my head for the cops, since they were the professionals.

I was depressed, tired, ticked, and unrelenting. I filled in for the absent police all day. The cops could have learned a few things if they had been with me, such as: "Police work can actually be done on holidays and without stopping by the doughnut shop every two hours."

As evening rolled around and it grew dark, I knew I should probably quit. I had been on this quest for over 24 hours straight. I decided to head home. As I rolled past a farmer's dairy, I aimlessly turned into his driveway in a "might as well try it" sort of mode. The farmer, Kay Holdaway, was a good tire customer of mine, and even though I knew that he probably hadn't been by my place the night of the break-in, talking to him couldn't hurt.

He was out by his barn talking to his son and another kid. I could tell by their conversation that the kids were heading out on the town and he was trying to ascertain their intentions. It seemed their conversation went on for a long time and I finally decided I would leave and catch him the next day. It was dark and yet, as I walked by the rear window of the car they were in, I saw an unusual item in the back seat. Without asking permission, I opened the door and grabbed it. It was a glove. Holding it up in the light, I saw that it was blue.

"Can I borrow this? My hand is cold." They didn't have a clue that the other glove was in the hands of the professionals and said, "Sure." I remember feeling a glow. I was hot on the trail. My many hours of work over the Thanksgiving holiday had paid off. I was the professional. The turkey, gravy, and stuffing satiated cops in their cozy, warm houses were really the amateurs.

I drove directly to the police station. When I walked in, the same constables gave me the same looks, only worse, as they had the night before. I could see it in their eyes, "Oh no! Not him again."

My old buddy walked up to the counter with a very disgusted look on his face. I slapped the glove down on the counter. "Could I see that glove again?" He looked at me in disbelief. He didn't say a word. He turned and walked back toward the evidence room. Soon he returned. It was a match. They were speechless. They couldn't believe I had done their work. I detected a bit of embarrassment on the professionals' faces.

A complete change in attitude followed. Disdain turned to awe and respect. They courteously asked for my story and then opened the door for me as we walked out to a squad car. We drove down to Kay's house, and within an hour, I was looking at my equipment. Three teenagers had hidden it out in an old barn. The cops and Kay made his son and the other kids involved (that I had previously interrogated) haul all the stuff back to my house. I sat on the couch and watched them haul it back in to the practice room. They were embarrassed and red-faced. I slept well that night. I'm sure the cops remained on vacation.

• •

We played all the gigs we had that winter, thanks to some wonderful police work by a non-professional. I never told Mary that it was lucky I left right after turkey dinner. In fact, I don't know if I ever saw her again.

That Saturday night, since I had just solved an important case and now had time for some more gallivanting; I took the next girl out on my list. I think her name was Joanie. I had been given some gift certificates from Raynal Pearson, my tire supplier. We had steak and lobster at the Salt Lake Hilton. Raynal owned the Hilton, along with Embassy Suites, Travel Lodge, and Pearson Tire.

The next day after I got home from church, I called Joanie up to see if she wanted to go to a fireside at BYU that night. Her roommate told me she had gone skiing. I crossed her off my list. A Sabbath skiing wife was not what I was looking for.

The next name on my list was a Michele Allred. Some mutual friends of Michele's and mine had decided that I should take her out. The matchmaker was Phyllis Clyde, the wife of Norman Clyde, one of the brothers who owned Geneva Rock, a large cement and construction company in Salt Lake and Utah Valley. His brother Hal just happened to be my bishop in the singles ward I had been in. I had taken Norman and Phyllis' daughter out a couple of years before when I was taking a hiatus from Terri.

I dialed Michele's number and introduced myself. The blind date with Michele ended up working out. I didn't have the urge to turn and run as soon as she opened the door, and I guess she didn't either. We went to the fireside and I could see that she was a much better person than yours truly. I knew I needed that in a mate.

I focused. I decided to put the moves on and make or break her. I found ways to see her every night that week. The next Monday, being the impulsive guy that I am, I showed up at the end of the day at the bank where she worked. I was tired, dirty, and greasy from a hard day in the tire shop.

I explained briefly my situation and then asked her to marry me. She was absolutely floored. Knowing her personality now, I can't believe she even entertained the idea back then. However, we had both been through several engagements and were tired of the dating game.

In the previous week, I had ascertained that she was a quality person and would make a great mother. I ended up being right on both those counts.

After she picked herself up off the asphalt, she asked me if she could have a little time to think things over. Not only was she working, but she was in school at BYU. Finals were ready to start and she wanted to wait to give me a decision after the semester was over. I was ready to move on if she wasn't interested and told her so. I said I would give her two weeks. If she said no, I would cross her off my schedule book and get back to the dating grind. She agreed.

The night after I issued my ultimatum to Michele, my phone rang. It was Terri. She wanted to see me. I hadn't heard from her in almost four months. I still had very strong feelings for her. It had been all I could do to stay away from her entangling web.

I went to her place that night. She was sad, as was I. She told me how she had missed me and eventually got to the punch line. She wanted to get married. To me, no less!

For two years I had wanted nothing other than to hear her say that. She had never been the instigator like she was on this night. And now, I had a proposal hanging out there for another girl! I told her I would marry her in a New York minute, but I had just extended an offer to another.

For some reason, I felt it was very important that I stick to my word and proposal to Michele. We would just have to wait and see what happened. I was not going to leave Michele in the lurch like Terri had left me, even though I'd only known Michele a week. Terri agreed to wait, but added that she feared I was gone. It turned out she was right.

I drove to Washington a few days before Christmas. Michele flew in to the Pendleton airport on Christmas night. My folks, my little sister, Lisa, and I picked her up. I was on pins and needles all the way home, wondering what her answer would be. I was torn. If it was yes, I got Michele. If it was no, I got Terri.

After arriving, everybody went to bed except us. I asked her what she had decided. She pulled out a Christmas present. I tore the wrapping off and saw it was a family journal with the names "Ben and Michele Casper" embossed on the front. There was no turning back.

CHAPTER 13

MY MICHELE

So we got married. A negative charge hooking up with a positive charge usually creates a permanent attraction. Many times we have blown this basic electrical concept out of the water.

I was raised on the farm. She was a city native. I'm a little bit crazy. She's more on the serious side. Let's just say the last 37+ years have been a real adjustment period. The first 20 years of our marriage, she wanted out. Because of our kids, our religion, and our temple marriage, I resisted. I must admit, there were times I entertained the notion of divorce, but when it came right down to it, I insisted that we keep things together. After 20 years of regular, major, traumatic episodes, she began to tell me that she was glad I kept us together. We still struggle, but if historical precedents continue we'll stay an item.

I have watched many families break up into tatters. I have counseled with a few and have noticed how each partner is usually embedded in their own private trench, lobbing nasty attacks at their partner. It becomes a habit. Most of the time, at least one of them is guilty of serious sin. Offensive attacks, defensive strategies, and a permanent hopeless outlook is usually present. Each thinks they are right. No one can convince them they should keep trying.

I am so aware of this mindset. I used to have it. I am so grateful we kept trying. I'm glad we kept seeking counsel, listening, and following. It was so hard and yet we finally won. We got on the same side. We forgave. We have the same team jerseys. We both try, every day. My greatest accomplishment in life has been to stay married. We came so close to making a permanent mess. Now we are one and life is much sweeter.

When I got married, my wife and I weren't real familiar with each other. In fact, we were complete strangers. Fireworks and feeble and sporadic attempts at conflict resolution were constant themes between us.

We really didn't have any trouble until, oh, five minutes after we walked out of the temple on our wedding day. I don't know about her, but by that evening after our reception I knew I had made a big mistake. To tell the truth, I was still in love with Terri. After we got to the honeymoon suite I sat in the bathroom, locked the door, and cried. (Say, isn't that the woman's job?)

Time and all eternity, which is the Mormons' view of marriage vows made in the temple, started looking pretty dang long.

The drama continued. The first few months were filled with adjustments. One afternoon we had a little spat and she decided she was going to run away. She stormed out the door and started walking eastward up Center Street in Orem toward I-15. I yelled at her several times to come back without any luck.

Finally, I jogged up the street after her. After catching her, I cajoled and coaxed for a bit without success. Exasperated and tired of arguing in front of the Center Street traffic crowd, I picked her up, threw her over my shoulder, and marched back down the street to the house. Remember, this is a 25-year-old pregnant woman.

Then, once again, just like a few months earlier, I carried her across the threshold.

One day that summer Michele's mom and dad came out and counseled with us. Her dad was talking to me and made the comment: "Michele is a very serious person." That statement struck me like a bolt of lightning. In my haste to get married I had not taken time to observe this basic personality trait. I realized that perhaps it was one of the big differences we had and it was not going to go away.

● ●

Michele was going to school and I was running the little one-man tire store in Orem. On one of the first Monday mornings after our marriage, she got up and left for school. She came back in the house after a minute and said the battery was dead in our '74 Mustang. I was in a hurry, as usual, and told her to go back outside and I would pull around and give her a jump-start. I got in my old 1-ton tire service truck and pulled out onto the street.

After making a quick U-turn, I headed right for the front end of the car. When I pushed on the brake pedal to slow down, I realized I had absolutely no brakes. The fluid must have leaked out over the weekend. I was probably going 15 miles an hour when the front end of MY pickup impacted with the front end of MY car.

Luckily, my wife wasn't standing between the rigs or it would have been a major tragedy. It became a minor tragedy as my Mustang's tires skidded back a good 10 or 15 feet. I got out and could see broken headlights and grill parts. I was not happy. Running your rig into someone else's rig is bad enough, but running your own rig into your other own rig is much worse.

I started using a few choice words that my wife had never heard before, or so I thought. She immediately put her hands to her face and ran in the house. I knew I was in big trouble. I figured she was probably in the house calling a divorce attorney who specialized in potty language as I stood outside yelling apologies. I decided I'd better go on in and face the music.

When I came through the door, she was standing there laughing her head off. She had put her hands over her face because she didn't want me to see her laughing. I was greatly relieved that she wasn't mad at me, but still felt a bit peeved that my two main assets had depreciated as rapidly as they had in the previous five minutes.

● ●

A year after I was married, my Grandpa Casper died in Heber City, Utah. This was the place my dad had grown up. It is a beautiful valley in the shadow of Mt. Timpanogos. My folks came down for the funeral. During their visit they left my little brothers, Brent and Bryan, to stay with me while they attended to other business. Brent was ten and Bryan, eight. They hung around the shop while I worked.

A trucker had left a flatbed trailer at my store with a load of steel on it. It had a flat tire I was repairing. I was breaking the tire down with a heavy tire hammer. As I walked my way around on top of the tire and wheel, swinging the hammer, I discovered, in a very hard way, that I had laid the tire down a little too close to the back of the trailer. The hammer came down, impacted the just-manufactured, thick steel plates that were loaded on the trailer, and bounced back toward my noggin. The hammer slammed into the top of my head, knocking me to the concrete floor. I was down and out cold.

The boys ran into the house, yelling at Michele to come. I regained my senses about the time she meandered out. She saw me lying there and said, "Oh, Ben, what are you doing down on the floor?" She thought I was trying to be a kidder.

Then she saw the blood. It was flowing profusely. It took me a few minutes to regain my composure and stand back up. She wanted to rush me to the hospital, but I had a tire to fix. I got back up and returned to the repair process, having to wipe the blood out of my eyes periodically so I could see. I moved the tire back from the trailer a bit more before I began pounding on it again. I remember several customers coming in and not being able to understand why I was fixing a tire when I should have been on my way to the hospital.

I finally got the job done, closed the shop doors, and headed for the doc. After he stitched up a big gash on the top of my head, I went back to work.

• •

My new wife was not familiar with the wild and crazy world of tire store owners/farmers. She was raised in the city. She had worked at a bank where everything was clean and calm. Her dad was a violin player for the Utah Symphony and a music teacher at the high school in Spanish Fork. She was in for a few surprises.

Soon after we were married, I needed to go next door to the Boise Cascade lumberyard to buy some boards. Michele wanted to play the interested wife so she tagged along, which I appreciated. She sat in the pickup while I began loading the two-by-sixes.

I think I was trying to impress her with my speed. I got a little too carried away and an eight foot piece of two-by-six sailed past its intended stacking place, through the back window of the pickup, and barely missed her head. Welcome to my world, Michele!

One day when there were no customers around, I went into the house for lunch. Our kitchen and dining area were adjacent to the back door, which led directly into the tire shop. We were in the middle of lunch when I heard a rig pull up outside. I went out and met the customer. He dropped off a flat tire that he said he would leave and pick up later that day. He asked if I had a piece of chalk so he could write his name on the tire. I gave him the chalk and headed back in the house to finish my lunch.

I had a funny feeling that I ought to check on this new and valued customer. I peeked through the curtains of the back door and saw him trying to shove one of my half inch drive air guns down his pants. That set me off. My air gun in his pants? No way!

I ran out and confronted the guy just as he was getting into his pickup. I yelled at him to get out of the rig and give me my gun back. After a weak denial, he relented and started unbuckling his pants to get the gun. We were verbally sparring at the top of our lungs. I finally obtained the newly-defiled gun and told him to leave. He said, "Fine! I'm going to get my tire, too." As an afterthought and an attempt to save face he added, "You probably couldn't fix it anyway."

I went back in to finish lunch. Michele was visibly upset. She acted like she had never experienced a confrontation like that before. In my way of thinking, this was mild compared to events that had already transpired and would yet occur down our road, the very long and winding road.

The year we got married, I started having trouble with the septic tank backing up. I don't remember now what the deal was, but Von had some kind of responsibility for the problem. Perhaps it was hooked into the service station septic or he had promised to take care of it. I just don't remember. I do remember complaining to him several times about it without results.

Before we got married, I promised Michele's mom that I would take care of the problem in the near future. Nolan and Jennifer Empey came down and stayed at my house when we got married. Nolan was my best man along with Kevin Jenks. I guess the night before the big wedding, Jennifer was in the tub and the piping decided it was time for a burp. It got a little ugly. Sorry, Jen.

Soon after the wedding, my new mother-in-law was escalating her negative vibes toward me because I hadn't yet hooked up to the city sewer system. There was a very large hookup fee involved and I didn't feel like

I could afford it. I complained to Von and this time he offered a different solution. "Don't flush any toilet paper," he said. "Put it in your garbage."

I couldn't believe it. He was actually serious. He thought the solution to the nonfunctioning septic tank was to wipe with toilet paper and then throw it in the garbage basket for all to see and smell until the trash got dumped! I forked over the dough to the city sewer district.

My wife lasted in the house for just over a year. It was located directly behind a service station and next to a busy street. Surrounding us was a Boise Cascade lumberyard with a chain link fence. Fifty feet from our bedroom was a railroad crossing with the train rumbling through and blowing its horn every hour or so. Dust and rust from the huge Geneva Steel complex across the street was constantly present. We had no neighbors. Businesses surrounded us. Mice were in abundance.

I reluctantly followed her out to Springville where we lived in her folks' basement apartment for the remainder of our time in Utah.

Michele became pregnant a month or two after we were married. She attended BYU in the fall with the baby expected in December. One night in December, we picked up my cousin Taig at the airport in Salt Lake. He had flown in to enter the LDS Missionary Training Center the next morning. He was going to Japan on his mission. We invited him to stay the night with us and took him out to eat at a Japanese restaurant before heading home. Michele went into labor while we were eating.

It was the 27th of December, windy, and the temp was down around zero. Taig attempted to sleep on the couch while Michele's black cat crawled up and down the curtains above Taig's head and ran across his body all night long.

Michele was miserable and couldn't sleep. I had just installed a wood stove a few days before so she wanted me to build a fire. I got the fire going good just before the wind blew the smoke back down the chimney and into the house.

I had no choice but to open all the doors to get some fresh air in so we could breathe. This little exercise brought the temperature far below what it was before I started the fire. Never one to give up, I built another fire with the same results. We cycled through the night in this manner, interspersed with several fruitless trips to the hospital. Taig, like us, didn't sleep much that night. We delivered him bleary-eyed to the Missionary Training Center the next morning. Michele delivered Hauni twenty hours later.

CHAPTER 14

THE FARM BECKONS ME

I was ready to go home to Washington. I went to Utah to find a wife. I had reached that marker. Now I was ready for home.

However I was saddled with a tire store. I began trying to peddle it. I had several buyers who expressed interest and then vanished. This went on for months. I started getting depressed. I talked to Von one day and he said, "You really do want to leave, don't you?" Von and everybody else in the area thought that since I had done well at the shop, I would be crazy to leave.

I assured him that I wanted to go back to the farm.

He said that maybe he could arrange it. A couple of days later he returned with a proposal. I would give him the property back. He would cancel the rest of the note I owed him. He would pay me for the inventory and equipment. I got nothing for my equity. I agreed.

Later he told me the amount he would pay me. It was a drastic discount from what I had paid for it. It was fifty cents on the dollar for $50,000 of inventory at wholesale cost. He was taking me to the cleaners, but I was motivated to leave. My dad needed me. A day later, he reduced the payoff even further with another discount at what he was going to pay me. He had me over a barrel and was well aware of it.

By the time I left, he owed me a paltry ten thousand dollars and would start paying me every month for the next 5 years. I got three months of payments and then nothing.

I'm still glad I left.

• •

A year after we moved to Washington, we visited Michele's folks in Utah. There were several "friends" in Utah Valley who still owed me money from my tire business the year before. One of them had a very common name, something like John Smith. He was a contractor and active member of the church. I had charged to him thinking I could trust him, but he wouldn't pay.

His bill was $1,700. We were broke and could use the cash. I didn't know where he lived, but I knew his dad and he (we'll call his dad Johnny) were developing and constructing homes by the Provo River. I knew the general area of where he lived. I also knew I would have to take extraordinary steps if I was going to collect.

I scouted around his neighborhood. An elderly lady was in her front yard watering her flowers. I got out of my car, walked over, and complimented her on her nice flowers. Then I asked her if she knew John Smith. Not only did she know John Smith, but she was his grandmother! I complimented her on her flowers again and then asked who her bishop was. I figured John had the same bishop. She gave me his name and I left.

I found a phone booth, looked the bishop up, and drove to his home. I explained the situation to him and asked if John was in his ward. He answered that he was. I then emphasized how John was completely unresponsive to me and my collection efforts. He said that he would talk to John the next day at church and then call me.

The next afternoon the phone rang. It was the bishop. He told me to come over; he had a check. I drove to his home and he gave me a check for $1700. The check was from the ward (church) account. I protested that I couldn't take the church's money. The good bishop said that John promised him that he had money coming in the next week and he would pay the ward back. He insisted I take it. I left happy. I hope he paid it back.

Fast forward 35 years. We were visiting my oldest daughter, Hauni, in Orem. Her son Max had a soccer game one day. We went to the game and while sitting on the grass I met one of Hauni's friends. We talked for a bit and since I had known a few people in Utah Valley back in the day, I asked her who her dad was. (Now remember, Utah Valley has 600,000 people.) She said he was a contractor. I asked what his name was. She said it was

John Smith. I was a little surprised so I asked if his dad's name was Johnny Smith. It was. Both of us were shocked.

She started questioning me about him. I didn't want to tell her of my experience, but she kept pressing me so I did. I tried to sugar coat it and put a good spin on it. It seemed to me from our conversation that he might have done some of the same kind of stuff to her. How I met up with John Smith's daughter 35 years later on a soccer field is beyond me.

• •

Shortly after the move back to Washington, I was asked to be the Boy Scout counselor for the Safe Driving Merit Badge. I could barely conceal my smile. It was kind of like the quintessential fox guarding the hen house. I was shocked, but accepted the assignment. I once again promised myself that with this new responsibility, I would slow down to extend my life (and any others who might be within a nautical mile of me). I might even stop and smell the roses once in a while, especially if the rose bush was next to a stop sign.

In the 20 some years since I was given this Scout assignment, I have had no young men ask me to help them get their safe driving award. They must not understand the wealth of knowledge that they are missing out on. Or their parents were aware of history, and therefore, located a different merit badge counselor.

• •

I started working for my dad on the farm. We were farming a thousand acres with very little help. Dad worked like a crazy man and expected everyone around him to do the same. During this period, he was growing lots of field corn. The guy who owned the local corn drying and grain facility in Basin City was doing well. Because Dad had so much grain going in, he felt like he ought to get a discount for all the grain he was bringing in for drying and handling. His bill was substantial. The gentleman wouldn't budge so Dad decided to build his own facility. Little did I know how much this facility would impact my life 35 years later.

We built the grain bins the first winter I was back working for him. It was cold and nasty, working outdoors pouring concrete and shoving thousands of bolts through grain bin panels and cinching them up. The weather never kept us indoors no matter how cold it got.

One morning I was drilling holes in a panel to bolt an access door on. The large electric drill I was using had been dropped sometime before and had a sizeable hole in the casing. The cooling fan in the motor was visible and close to the users thumb as it spun thousands of RPMs. We all tried to be careful and stay out of its swath as we used it.

On this particular morning, I forgot. The rigid blade ground off the tip of my left thumb. It was painful and ugly. Even my dad agreed I needed to take the day off. I went home, took some pain medicine, doctored the injury, and watched TV as the Iranian hostages were released and Reagan was inaugurated. A good portion of the top of my thumb was missing. Interestingly it filled back in, but is still numb to the touch.

Soon I was back to work. One day we began erecting the elevator leg. It was a large framework of heavy tubes that would eventually reach 95 feet in the air. Each section of the leg stood 10 feet tall and probably weighed 500 pounds or more.

We rented a crane truck to erect the leg. It was expensive to rent. Dad wanted to get the entire leg up in one day so we didn't have to pay another day's rent. He had slipped and taken a header into the bottom of the pit the day before and hurt his shoulder and ribs. I was elected to run the crane.

It wasn't too bad as we assembled, raised, and bolted each section, one on top of the other. Dad was hurting. All he could do was watch which was pretty tough for a guy that was used to being the driving force of his operation.

The construction was precarious. It took four guys to position and bolt down the sections. As we got to the top of the leg, our hired men would cling to the metal structure while trying to manhandle the heavy assemblies that I was trying to lift into place for them. It was nerve-racking and unsafe—and that means something coming from me. An OSHA inspector would have had a field day. There were no safety harnesses as they kept climbing and hanging on for dear life.

The next to the last section was finally bolted into place. The top of the crane was 85 feet high, fully extended. I had it as high as it could go and yet we still had one more piece to lift up and bolt on. The last section, which included a walkway of expanded metal, when in place, would be 95 feet high.

I lifted the heavy section. We had four guys at the top of the leg, struggling to lift and maneuver the monster into place. Their bodies were intertwined with the framework as they lifted, levered, and did everything they could to get it in place. It was one of the hairiest situations I've ever seen. And I was on the ground at the controls, responsible for the movements of the crane. A wrong touch at any time could have sent several men to their deaths.

Dad was helpless. Finally he couldn't take it anymore. He walked around behind a grain bin and sat down and waited. I'm sure he was praying. That was one of the few times before he got MS that I've seen him helpless. We finally got it secured and the men climbed down.

• •

Dad sent me to town the next spring to buy a motorcycle. I needed transportation as I moved sprinklers and did other farm work. Motorcycles were very handy as there were lots of sprinkler lines on the farm that needed to be changed at least twice a day. Bikes could handle rough terrain and they didn't require a road. They left a very narrow footprint as we traveled through the fields, thereby doing much less damage to the crops than a vehicle would have.

I went with Dad's instructions as to how much he wanted me to spend on the bike. The only guideline he gave me was to spend something like 800 or 1,000 dollars. I think he had in mind that I would buy a new, smaller trail bike like a 125cc. As I perused through the motorcycle shops, I found a used Yamaha 500 TT single cylinder 4-stroke "thumper." I don't know if they called it a 500 because of the 500 cubic centimeter engine, the 500 pounds it weighed, or the fact that it would go 500 miles per hour down the ditch road.

I am lucky that I lived through that period with no major wrecks. It was a big and powerful bike for that era and was also unusually heavy. A couple of years later, it tipped over and broke my foot at a most inconvenient time.

When I brought the bike home my dad about choked. Looking back now, I understand his reaction. Back then, however, I couldn't see it as I was in hog heaven. Fortunately I didn't kill myself riding it. I rode it hard and fast for several years. I was 25 or 26, married, had three kids, and drove it like an irresponsible madman with no helmet. Many primitive ditch roads that could be handled at a safe speed of 30 mph would find me consistently riding at 60 or 70 mph on my way to change sprinklers.

One day I was working in a field a couple of miles away from our house. The big bike quit on me and I had to walk home. The bike was too heavy to try to load in the back of my pickup so I decided to get my wife to pull me and the bike home behind the pickup. She was a city girl and very uncomfortable with being asked to do anything of a farming or mechanical nature. Towing a motorcycle behind a pickup fit into that category, but I had no idea she was as inept at towing motorcycles as she turned out to be. I was desperate to get it going again so I could get back to work. I pretty much forced her to drive back with me to tow it.

I tied a rope to the back of the pickup and then tied the other end to the front of the bike. I told her to roll the window down and just follow my yelled instructions. I walked back, straddled the bike, and yelled for her to "Go!" She started the pickup moving, but instead of easing gradually forward until the slack in the rope was taken up, she picked up speed. When the slack was taken up, the bike lurched forward, went out of control, and tipped over. Usually I didn't tie the rope to the bike when getting towed, but for some reason I had cinched the rope to the bike on this particular day.

The Yamaha was on its side, scraping along on the big, sharp rocks that covered the ditch road. "Whoa! Whoa!" I yelled. Instead of stopping she accelerated. I was shocked! I started running behind the dying motorcycle, watching it plow up rocks in the road. I found out later that she thought I was yelling, "Go!" every time I yelled, "Whoa!" When she heard, "Go!" she applied a little more pressure to the accelerator.

"Whoa! Whoa! Whoa!" She went faster.

Most people, when they are towing another vehicle, tend to look behind them once in a while to make sure everything is going fine with the rig being towed. Since Michele had never towed nor been towed before, she was not familiar with this basic concept. The little caravan continued down the road with me bringing up the distant rear.

Finally she stopped after realizing that my vocal transmissions were becoming hysterical, faint, and inconsistent with someone merrily riding their scooter down the road behind her. I ran up to the bike and surveyed the damage. Then I proceeded to the pickup and regrettably did a little more damage of the verbal variety.

At the time, I could not believe she could be that dense. Looking back, I now understand that it probably was not her fault. I was operating under the assumption that she should have the same knowledge as a regular farm hand in respect to towing motorcycles. I, thereafter, refrained from requesting her help towing me on motorcycles, airplanes, dead cows, and any other rideable object that had a leather seat. (As she proofread this before publication, she wrote, "Yeah, right!" in this space.)

• •

One thing about me, my resolutions don't last all that long. We did perform several other towing operations after that. She never enjoyed the experiences. One day she called me from town. The car had broken down and she and the kids were stranded. As usual, I was busy and impatiently stopped my work to go rescue her. I didn't know what was wrong with the car so I hooked a chain on the front of it and secured it to the back of my pickup.

I had her get in the car and told her to follow me and try not to let any slack occur in the chain. We drove uneventfully for 10 or 15 miles. I gradually increased the speed as I wanted to get home.

Thinking back while scooting along, I remembered the way she pulled my motorcycle down the road a few years earlier and decided this was a great time to pay her back. We were on Glade Road which is the main thoroughfare from the Tri-Cities out to Basin City. Soon we were moving along at 60 mph which was making her very uncomfortable. Ahead of us was a semi-truck and trailer traveling at about the same speed we were. I didn't feel like slowing down. Since the road was clear for a ways ahead, I accelerated and began passing the truck. She had no choice but to follow.

I knew the new parameters would make her more than a little uncomfortable, but decided that she had no options other than to follow since she was the chainee. I was right. The pass was perhaps unorthodox, but performed without incident. I imagine the truck driver was a little surprised that a vehicle driven by a woman with white knuckles and three little kids passed his road warrior immediately after a beat-up pickup. I remember Michele complaining emphatically after we made it safely home.

I felt we were now even.

• •

Speaking of Michele and stalled vehicles, I had to go to town and bail her out one other time. I was working for my dad then. We didn't have any spare help for the load of work in front of us and the pressure was on each day to get as much done as possible.

Michele took a pleasure trip to town with the three young'uns and ended up over in Richland. Something went wrong with the Nova we had. I don't remember the problem now, but at the time I thought I could fix it. She caught a ride with my sister who happened to be in town. The car was left at a filling station.

I wasn't able to go in and get the car until late afternoon. There was no one with a driver's license around to help me drive it home. Since all the boys in my family had started driving at an early age on the farm, we were pretty competent operators. My little brother, Brent, was helping me at the time so I told him to get in the pickup with me. He was eleven years old and probably still in the four foot height range. He probably wouldn't have made the minimum height requirement to drive the play cars at Disneyland, let alone the interstate freeway I had in mind.

Before we left, I grabbed a pair of sunglasses, a pillow, and a hat. We drove the 45 miles into Richland and before long I fixed the problem on the car. I then proceeded to give Brent a few last minute instructions on city and high-speed freeway driving before we left.

He donned the hat with the visor pulled down low over his face and put the sunglasses on. He then jumped behind the wheel sitting on top of the doubled-up pillow. The pillow made him look a little taller than a normal eleven-year-old. I told him to stay right behind me and to wear a facial expression of experience and confidence. If a cop got behind him he was to pass me and I would hail the cop down and ask for directions, feigning to be a lost tourist.

We pulled out into rush hour traffic. I must admit the adrenaline was flowing. I had no doubt that Brent could handle the job. He was a smart kid and knew how to drive. I was just worried that we might run into the law or the car might break down again.

As we traveled the freeway past Columbia Center Mall, a couple of old ladies passed us on the left. The disguise we had rigged up for Brent must not have worked that well because as they went by me, I could see them looking back at Brent and yakking away at each other. They were mad that this little kid was out driving on their freeway. In retrospect, I'm glad cell phones weren't available back then or those ladies would have been dialing 911 about the time they passed me. We made it home with no problem. I didn't tell our folks about it until many years later. Dad would have killed me.

CHAPTER 15

GUARDIAN ANGELS—DOUBLE TIME AND OVERTIME

In 1980, because of the high interest rates and debt load they were carrying, my parents were struggling to make the payments on the farm. They had put several circle irrigation systems in to upgrade the operation and reduce labor costs. The transition truly meant much less work in irrigating the crops, but added a lot of red ink with the bank.

In spite of the debt, they wanted a cabin at Priest Lake in Idaho. We had camped at the lake in the past and they wanted a place to stay when our family took a vacation. They purchased a very unfinished cabin on the lakefront that was built in the early 1900s and spent many years fixing it up. It's been a wonderful place for the family to enjoy through the years.

One summer Michele and I took our little family up to the cabin, which is about three and a half hours from home. We arrived in the early evening and set about starting a fire and hauling our supplies in. It was quite windy and cool so I had no plans to go swimming that night.

Our third child was Meg. She was five at the time. She was a cute, little girl with long, blonde curls. After we had worked for fifteen minutes getting settled, someone asked where Meg was. In the back of her mind, Michele recalled possibly hearing Meg call for her earlier, but since she was busy she hadn't responded. She soon regretted it.

We started scurrying around, looking and calling. No Meg. We went upstairs and downstairs and then began looking up and down the beach. No Meg. Where was she? The minutes were ticking by and we became frantic. There was no sign of her and I began to worry that she had walked out on one of the docks and fallen in. I ran back and forth along the beach, frightened and scanning the water.

The water was unsettled because of the wind. Waves were crashing against the docks and the beach. It looked cold and uninviting, and yet, I knew I had to jump in and start searching under the docks.

I pulled my shoes off and dove in. I swam under the long docks and had no doubt that I was going to end up finding the submerged blonde locks and body of our daughter. It was an absolutely horrifying experience. Michele and I were praying for divine help.

Michele, Hauni, and Derek continued yelling and searching and some neighbors began helping. One lady jumped in with me and helped search in the water under the docks. Both of us were in our street clothes. I told Michele to call the sheriff's office.

This exercise continued for 45 minutes. It was filled with terror.

At last, Michele heard the phone ring. It was the sheriff's office. The owner of the tavern in Coolin had called them to report that a little girl had wandered in and they were wondering if anyone was missing her.

What a relief we all experienced! Our little girl was alive! I got out of the lake; shivering and grateful for the help everyone had given us, especially the lady that had been helping search in the cold water.

Michele drove down to the bar and picked up Meg. We found out she had gone outside and become disoriented, losing track of which cabin was ours. She yelled for us as she wandered down the beach. After about a quarter mile, she went around a point of land that juts out into the lake and disappeared from sight. That must have been about the time we missed her.

She was scared as she walked, but after arriving at the bar, quickly calmed down because the owners fed her ice cream. I almost wonder if they gave her a mug of beer to chase the ice cream down because of another event.

We attended a community party one evening. As we were sitting at a table eating, we looked over and noticed that little Meg was canvassing the tables and drinking cups of beer that people had left unattended. We immediately began an intervention as soon as we saw it happening. I'm sure this intervention went easier than most.

When I think of our fears about losing Meg, my heart goes out to the many that really have lost a child. I hope I never have to go through the pain of losing one of my kids.

• •

I remember a time we lost another one of our offspring. We were on a vacation in California and were visiting the beach one day. The beach stretched for miles in each direction and was packed with people.

Soon we noticed that Will, our six-year-old, was missing. We hurriedly began scanning the beach in both directions and eventually we saw him walking away from us. He was far off, almost out of sight.

I began walking after him, keeping him in sight. When I finally got close to him, I stayed off to the side so he wouldn't see me. He kept looking back and forth down the shore. I could tell he was worried as he meandered along. Finally I walked up behind him and called his name. His face broke into a relieved smile and he said, "Dad, I was praying that you would find me." It was nice to see that he relied on prayer. It was nice to be an answer to his prayer.

• •

While living in our little house on the hill, we constantly had to be on the lookout that our two oldest kids, Hauni and Derek, didn't find their way out onto the road that ran past our house. There were blind curves going past the house and rigs would zip by traveling 60 or 70 mph. The other side of the road was a steep drop off for several hundred feet.

Derek was two years old and didn't recognize the danger of speeding cars. I built a fence around the lawn that stood between the house and the road, but it couldn't contain him. It was a wire fence standing about four feet tall. Whenever we put him out on the lawn he would cruise over to a certain spot and start scaling the wire barricade. As soon as he got over it he would make a beeline for the road.

I knew that it was just a matter of time before he would become road kill. I tried various ways of teaching him not to do it. Nothing worked. My imagination kicked in and I came up with the perfect solution. I shared with Michele what I was going to do and she immediately protested. As usual, I figured "Father knows best" and proceeded with one of my earliest inventions.

I had an electric fence shock box to keep cattle from venturing outside the fenced fields they were in. It delivered a jumbo electric shock every couple of seconds to any beast or human that dared touch the fence wire. After relocating the fencer to our domestic abode, I strung a wire across the top of the lawn fence. After hooking it up and plugging it in, we let Derek go out on the lawn. He immediately ran over to his favorite spot to scale and started climbing. I stood by him because I knew an electric shock treatment was imminent.

Sure enough, he grabbed the top hotwire and started screaming. He wouldn't, or couldn't, let go. I grabbed him to pull him off the wire and we both started getting zapped. He was screaming at the newly discovered and very unpleasant sensation at hand and I was screaming at him to let go of the confounded thing. Finally he did. We never had trouble with him climbing the fence again. Some people have accused me of child abuse, however this quick and effective teaching solution was exactly what was needed to keep my dear, little son from becoming a grease spot on the asphalt.

In today's world, if Child Protective Services caught wind of this, they would have sent me to the electric chair.

• •

By the fall of 1981 I was getting tired of working for my dad. I had gone from being the owner-manager of my little tire shop in Utah to being a hired peon, working for Dad. He was under a lot of debt and stress at the time, and with both of our hardheaded personalities and the tremendous workload, there was a lot of discontentment. I was working long and hard days, and sometimes nights, with minimal pay, no incentive, and a lack of opportunity for me to make decisions and expand my horizons. I chafed under the workload and perceived oppression.

I called up an old friend from Philadelphia to see about moving my family back there and working for him. I joined the sheriff's reserves. I bought a bunch of Holstein bull calves. I was desperate for a venture of my own.

• •

On October 10, 1981, I was hauling sprinkler pipe out of a large cornfield as a combine harvested the corn. A large group of the hunters, our friends from Seattle, had arrived that morning to hunt pheasants. When a combine is tearing through the corn, it drives a lot of roosters out of the standing corn into the stubble. This group of hunters was cooking up a strategy to get their limit of birds before dark. Two of the men asked me if they could ride on the pipe trailer as I drove the tractor back up to the top of the field. "Sure, hop on," I said.

I put it in gear and we headed up the ditch rider's road. I was in a hurry because I wanted to catch the combine before it started down through the field. I was going to have the driver, Don Mitchell, cut a swath alongside a sprinkler line so that I could pick the pipe up while driving through the stubble.

As I neared the top of the field, I could see that the large combine had already started its way down the rows, but not beside the sprinkler line. I figured I would run down through the field, stop him, have him back up and harvest down the rows next to the hand line. I had the tractor in high gear. As I slowed down, I pulled out on the diesel fuel cut-off knob and the tractor rolled to a stop, or so I thought. I jumped off the tractor, ran around in front of it, and sprinted for the combine.

Just then I heard a terrible sound. The tractor fuel kill switch had sprung back in and the tractor was off and running. The two hunters were sitting on the pipe trailer basket with their loaded 12-gauge shotguns just behind the newly energized and driverless tractor. There was a large irrigation canal next to the road and I knew no matter where the tractor went that it was a dangerous situation for my Seattle friends.

I sprinted back up on the road and ran across in front of the tractor. The hunters were frozen in place. I wasn't. I ran back, just in front of the rear tire of the tractor, and tried to pull out on the fuel kill switch. Big mistake!

I should have jumped on the tractor before I tried to shut it down. Instead, the rear tractor tire hit me and knocked me backwards and down on the road. It then proceeded to run over my feet, legs, groin, stomach, chest and head. By the time it got to my knees, I knew I was in trouble. By the time it got to my chest, I was out of breath. By the time it ran over my head, I had blacked out.

But not for long. As soon as the tire ran over me, the metal cage on the pipe trailer that the hunters were sitting on behind the tractor impacted me and began rolling and tumbling me mercilessly along the ground and rocks. I was conscious, but I could do absolutely nothing about getting out of the situation.

I could hear the guys sitting on the cage saying, "Oh, Ben! Oh, Ben!" They were still frozen in place on the moving trailer. I was getting the daylights beat out of me.

After the driverless tractor decided it'd had enough, it rolled off the edge of the road, high centered on the canal bank, and stalled. The pipe trailer followed the lead of the tractor and decided it'd had enough also and threw me into the canal.

Remember, this was the tenth of October. That water was just a shiver above freezing! I had had just about enough physical abuse for one day. My entire head, body, and extremities were cramped up, battered, bloody, and hurting. I could only move one arm as I tried to keep my head above water and swim my way over to the bank. One of the hunters took off running for Don, the combine operator, to summon help. The other fellow reached down and tried to pull me up. He struggled for a while without success. Finally, I got tired of waiting, decided to forget the numerous points of pain and pulled myself out with his help.

I lay on the road, beat up from head to foot. I had no idea what kind of shape I was in; I just knew I was hurting everywhere and freezing. I was in shock and hypothermia soon began calling. Don, who was driving the combine, after hearing the news, pulled into the corn stubble and started barreling down the field to my house to tell my wife to call the ambulance. As he motored along at full throttle, the rest of the hunters were hunting and walking through the stubble toward us, not knowing the calamity that had just taken place.

As the combine reached the hunters, one of their dogs was loping across the rows of cut cornstalks. The little doggy was no match for the combine that was hell-bent on getting help. One of its big tires rolled over the retriever as the group of pheasanteers watched in horror. The dog didn't come out of its encounter with a rubber tire alive like I just had.

My wife, after being informed of the accident, called the ambulance. She asked Don if I was dead. He told her he didn't know. The local ambulance wasn't up and running so they had to get one from Mesa, the next station over. People began congregating in the meantime and bundled me up to keep some of my body heat intact.

I was miserable, soaked, cold, shaken, shaking, hurting, bruised, and bloody. Finally, after more than an hour since the initial incident, my ride got there and we headed for town.

In the emergency room, a rookie nurse started trying to give me an IV. I was in shock and freezing so all of my blood vessels had contracted back to where they could cozy up next to my bones. She could not find a vein. For 30 or 40 minutes she poked around, in and out, with no luck. I was getting a little hot even though I was still freezing. After all patience left the patient, I told the doctor to get somebody else to run that needle into my arm or forget the IV. A seasoned veteran soon made a connection. Why is it every time I go to the hospital they have rookies learning how to put the IV in?

I was in the hospital several days with bruises from head to toe, a lacerated scalp, and a swollen knee. Over the next few weeks, everything improved except the knee. I had a regular MD for a doctor and he had me come in several times for checkups. Every time he saw the swollen joint, he would diagnose that I must have water on the knee. He would then get out Andre the Giant's biggest syringe, stick a huge needle on the business end of it and stab my knee. Then he would start drawing the "water" out. The only problem was it wasn't water; it was blood. I finally arrived at the conclusion that he was trying to bleed me out like they did in the old days.

After a few sessions of this, he finally admitted he didn't know what was going on and said that I should go see a specialist. I saw my old friend Dr. Pettee the next day. He slammed me on the table, grabbed my knee, gave two swift jerks and said, "Yeah, your ligament's torn. Let's get you in the hospital and operate."

Dr. Pettee was rough, but I liked him. He knew his stuff and didn't mess around. He and his partner, Dr. Fields, worked on me through several knee and elbow operations and at least 20 broken bones, including the compound fractured femur.

• •

I was on crutches and out of commission for the next three months. Dad fed my calves for the first couple of weeks, along with some brothers from the church helping out. I appreciated it, although I'm sure Dad didn't like it. He had been against my calf project from the get-go.

I had originally purchased 50 or 60 head. I borrowed money from the bank to finance the risky operation. Like everyone who raises day-old calves without their mother's milk, I expected to lose a few. I think most guys lose half their baby calves when they raise them like this. Most evenings found a sick, baby calf on the porch just outside our front door. Most mornings found a dead, baby calf on the porch just outside our front door; and a very unhappy wife just inside our front door.

I was hoping I could beat the odds and make some money, however I lost at least half of them. I figured I could still make a little money since, by the time of my accident, they were big enough not to be dying on me. As soon as I could get around on crutches, I took over feeding the calves. At the time I got hurt, the calves were all off the bottle and ranged from 250 pounds to around 500 pounds.

One Sunday morning I got up to feed the herd before church. I hobbled across the yard on my crutches and over to the corral on the other side of the road. Something looked wrong. I crutched closer and started seeing blood everywhere. I immediately felt sick. Calves were lying in the muck, some already dead. My biggest calf just lay there, unable to get up. Its back was broken. A lot of them were bleeding from injuries on their legs, ears, necks, and backs. I lost 16 of them that day. I think I cried for the first time since my wedding night.

All my work was trashed before my eyes. How was I ever going to repay the bank? Who did this?

I missed church that day. A sheriff's deputy came out and took a report. I knew it was either coyotes or dogs. I had no other place to put the live calves, yet I knew that since the attackers had gotten a taste of blood they would probably be back. But when? Being on crutches, I had a very slim chance of stopping them. The future looked bleak.

Two days later, I awoke in the morning and felt something different. The corral was a good 200 feet away and yet I sensed a slight vibration in the floor of the house. It was coming from the corral. I had a full leg cast on and struggled to slide my pants on as fast as possible. I grabbed a crutch and my shotgun and slammed a couple of shells in it.

I quietly went out the door and maneuvered my way to the corral as fast as a one-legged man with a crutch and a 12-gauge double barrel could. I could hear the livestock bawling and running around inside the corral in a panic. All of a sudden, between the corral boards, I saw two dogs chasing calves and having a great time.

I didn't have a good shot so I hobbled over to the corner post. About that time, the dogs heard me and took off. One jumped out of the manger and headed for the far end. I wasn't ready to get a shot off and he disappeared. The next one came out and started running. I got the gun up just as he was going around the far corner. I pulled the trigger and BOOM! Nailed that sucker! Another half a second and he would have been gone. It was a very lucky, long-distance shot.

Eight more calves died from that attack. Oh, and one dog. I had no idea whose dog it was so I loaded it up in my pickup and headed over to my neighbor, Bill Easterday, to see if he could help. He wasn't sure, but he thought it was another neighbor's dog.

This particular neighbor was a little scary. He and his gun had had run-ins with government people and a neighbor or two. I thought, "Oh, boy. I'm probably going to have a tough time trying to get anything out of this guy." Even so, I was upset enough that I determined that I was going to ask him to make me better.

I pulled into his yard and he came out greeting me warmly, probably because he could see I was a cripple at the moment. I greeted him by name and then asked him to look in the back of my pickup. He looked at his dead dog and asked what happened. I told him the story. He apologized and said he would get in touch with his insurance agent. I felt greatly relieved. I ended up getting a fair price for the damages and was able to pay the bank loan off.

I still had a dozen steers left and continued to feed them. As they got bigger, I built electric fences and tried to keep them in. For those who aren't familiar with animal intelligence quotients, Holstein steers are the dumbest of all animals.

First of all, they are mad because they've been made steers. They walk through fences. They are hard to herd. They aren't built to be a beef animal in the first place. They are tall and bony and just don't put good meat on their bones like a good Hereford will. Holstein cows are great milk producers. They do well in dairies. The downside to Holsteins is that you can't milk the males, therefore, they are the poor man's beef bovine. Dairy operators sell their bull calves for pennies on the dollar when compared to a Holstein heifer.

As an example of how dumb these animals are . . . one winter my brother, Brad, was pasturing some of his cows in a field above my dad's house. On a cold morning my mom walked outside and noticed a cow munching on greenery in her front yard. When she looked closer, she noticed the animal was chowing down on some long, stringy, inorganic matter, namely her electric Christmas lights that happened to be plugged in at the time.

Before she could chase the animal away, a few molars did their job and the cow quickly got turned on to 120 volts. The cow never ate real or fake foliage again. My brother had hamburger for the winter. One of my siblings called the story in and the next day it was retold on Paul Harvey's radio show.

• •

So I had these 1,000+ pound, black and white idiots walking through my fences daily. I had to chase them continually. My knee had healed and I was back in operation.

Neighbors periodically called to tell me my steers were trampling their lawn. Sometimes I chased them on foot. Often I chased them with my motorcycle. Once in a while, they would meander over to the hills below our house where I couldn't get to them. I would drive down the hill on the road and look up at the critters and start yelling. They wouldn't move, even when I honked the horn. I hated climbing hills to chase them so one day I discovered a solution.

I had my shotgun with me and was exasperated enough that I got out and started shooting at them. They were far enough away that I knew I wouldn't seriously hurt them. It worked. When they heard the shots and felt the buckshot peppering their rump roast, they scooted back up the hillside. Herding these exasperating animals with my 12-gauge became my common tool of choice. I remember several neighbors driving by and shaking their heads while I shot at my own cattle.

• •

The next year I got a small settlement from State Industrial for my torn-up knee from when I was run over by the tractor. I took some of the money and bought some tire equipment so I could open a little tire shop in my garage. I used the rest of the dough to purchase a used ultra light "Easy Riser" airplane.

I had the flying bug. I contacted the president of the Experimental Airplane Association in the Tri-Cities and he referred me to a guy who was selling an "Easy Riser". Both these guys were great people. One of them was a teacher. The other was an engineer who worked out at Hanford. It is a little ironic that they were both very safety conscious and helpful to me. Both were killed in separate air crashes over the next three years.

The Easy Riser was a little scary as it was a biplane wing configuration without an elevator or fuselage. The pilot sat in a harness swing nestled between the two wings. This was directly in front of the snowmobile engine and propeller. He swung his weight forward or back to make the contraption go down or up. I didn't like the idea of no mechanical control for pitch so I ordered a retrofit canard elevator.

In the meantime, I decided to take it out in the neighbor's hay field and taxi it around. My wife and two kids followed in the car to watch. I taxied back and forth a few times and went a little faster each time. On my last run, I pushed the throttle and ground speed envelope a little too far, caught a bit of a headwind, and shot up in the air. I was not prepared for this shocking development. I had been motoring along on the ground one second and before I could say, "I don't wanna be up here!" I was sixty feet in the air.

I was unexpectedly in the middle of a major pickle. I had not intended to be sailing off into the wild blue yonder. Suddenly I wanted to be back down on Mother Earth in the worst way, preferably in one piece.

Instinctively, I cut the power to the engine, which was a mistake. My airspeed dropped, the rig stalled, and I began a kamikaze-style nosedive straight down. I pushed my body back as far as I could in the trapeze seat to try to level out before the crash. This maneuver, combined with the airspeed I had picked up as we dove, allowed the bird to level out, flair, and glide down to the expansive landing strip. It turned into a beautiful landing.

I was one relieved and lucky novice pilot! The engine was mounted right behind me and would have gone right through me if we had continued straight down. There is no doubt I would have been killed. I parked the thing and traded it later for a much safer motorcycle.

CHAPTER 16

TIRE MAN

I had been the headcheese in Utah. Farming with my dad just wasn't working. This was hard to take. I could see that if I didn't leave that year, one of us would be leaving soon after, most likely in a casket.

The spring of 1982 found me on my own. I put a tire machine in my garage which adjoined the cinder block house we lived in. The word spread and I gradually accumulated customers.

I rented 100 acres from Dad and became a tire technician/farmer. Many times I would be out moving sprinklers or running machinery and my pager would go off. A customer with a flat tire had shown up at the house so Michele would call my pager. I would have to drop what I was doing, sprint back to my motorcycle, and hurry back to the "shop" and my waiting customer. I fixed the tire and then rode back out to the job to resume my work. Often, this would require an extra half mile or more of walking on my part to get back to what I was doing before the flat tire page.

Several times I lost my pager in the field. I would have my wife call the number on the phone while I ran to and fro in the alfalfa or lima bean field, straining to hear the beep and locate the pager.

This went on for months and by July I could see that I had to get into a different facility and make the tire business my sole occupation. The only problem was, I had no money.

Loen Bailie, the "Father of Basin City," owned many empty lots in Basin City and wanted people to come in and start businesses. I found a piece of sagebrush sprinkled blow sand that I liked and went to see Loen.

I knew of him, but he didn't know of me. I told him that I had started a little tire business down the road a ways and I would like to move out of there and into a shop in Basin City. Since he owned most of Basin City, I needed to buy some ground from him and also needed money to build a shop. He said I could buy the ground and he would finance that, but it was his policy not to finance anything in Basin City except the land.

I told him there was no other way I could do the deal. Banks wouldn't even talk to me. At the time, my dad was struggling to reduce the debt he had instead of taking on more. I had no equity except a few tire tools and a scary ultra light airplane that I had just had a close call in. Loen was in his eighties so I didn't figure he would take my ultra light as collateral. I also knew Loen was my only hope.

So I asked him to stop by and check out my little shop and see what I had accomplished over the last few months. He agreed, but again stipulated that he did not loan out money. I guess I thought since his name was Loen, pronounced 'loan,' he would be open to lending. Not so much.

Two days later he pulled into my yard. I showed him my meager tools, sparse inventory, and accounts receivable and sales records. I think he was impressed even though things were mighty primitive. He said he would think about it.

A few days later he called me up and we made a deal on the land. He also agreed to loan me $25,000 to build a building. We finished building the tire store in September and immediately launched into fixing and selling tires.

• •

A week or two after finishing the store, my family and friends decided to have a surprise party for me to celebrate the occasion. Some friends of ours concocted a ruse to get us to the party without my knowledge. They invited us to go with them to town and have dinner. They were running a little late so I called their house to make sure it was still on. They had left, but their babysitter said, "They're not here; they went to a surprise party for Ben Casper."

I thanked her for the information and hung up. They picked us up a few minutes later and said they wanted to check out my new shop on the way to town. I was all too happy to oblige. The shop was dark and deserted as we got there. I unlocked the door and yelled, "Surprise!" and turned on the lights. There was a shop load of slightly disappointed and, yes, surprised faces.

Loen Bailie was one of the partygoers. He was old and frail. During the party, I was standing by the new alignment pit, shooting the bull with some of my friends. It was a concrete-walled hole that dropped down from the shop floor about three feet. Out of the corner of my eye, I saw Loen step back into the drop-off. I reached out and grabbed him and probably saved myself a big lawsuit. I'm sure there would have been a major injury if I hadn't caught him.

Loen may have been the founder of Basin City, and quite wealthy, but he was also as cheap and headstrong as they come. I found out that he was in the habit of buying his tires in Pasco and always insisted on Michelins. Michelin was not one of the lines that I carried.

One day I noticed, as I went into the local restaurant, that his car needed tires. Like any good salesman, I reminded him that I was in the tire business, in his town no less, and that I'd like to sell him some new tires.

He said he only bought Michelins. I told him I would get some Michelins and let him know when we had them. He said that would work for him. I went to a lot of trouble rounding up the special tires and a day or two later saw his Cadillac parked at the hardware store. "I'll just swing in there and let him know I've got his tires," I thought.

I pulled up next to his car and got out of my pickup. Just as I was slamming my door, I beheld that he had already gone to Pasco and had my competitor slap new Michelins on his rig. I was so shocked that I forgot to pull my hand away from the door as it slammed shut on my thumb.

I had to reach over with my other hand and open the door back up to retrieve my digit. It was smashed and spurting blood. I was in pain and shock; pain from the finger and shock from the realization that Loen had no loyalty and really didn't give a hoot that a new Basin City business could use his support.

I crawled back in my truck, holding my hand out the window so the hemorrhaging finger wouldn't bloody it up. I then retreated up the street to look for some first-aid supplies in my Loen Bailie-financed shop that contained a new set of unsold Michelins.

• •

One day in October, a month after I opened the tire store, I was up on the farm moving sprinklers and straightening a wheel line. My 500 Yamaha was parked behind me and the kick stand started sinking in the sand, unbeknownst to me.

The big, heavy bike fell. I felt a major pain on the top of my foot and realized the handlebar had smashed into my foot, protected only by a thin, rubber boot. I crawled a half a mile to my pickup and headed for the doctor. It was broken. The doctor put it in a cast and told me not to walk on it.

I had very little help at the tire store and was getting more business every day. It was harvest time and a lot of spud trucks were coming in with flat tires. This was in the days when most truck tires were mounted on those dangerous split rims. I spent the entire fall hopping around my shop on one leg, flapping my Plaster of Paris-casted foot in the air, and fixing truck tires. I think of that time as very hard, even nigh impossible, to do the work I did. But I also look at it as very fulfilling since I was in a critical situation and had no choice other than to get the job done. I got the job done and I sold the bike. I also quit farming for a while.

• •

During my farming experience I used an old beater, Chevy pickup when the motorcycle was inadequate to haul stuff. I left the pickup outside the tire shop one night and returned the next morning to find it stolen.

In order to run the tire store, I had to have a truck. I picked up the phone and bought my first new vehicle ever, a ¼-ton Chevy pickup. An hour or so later I bummed a ride up to the Spokane auto dealer with a tire salesman I knew. After the paperwork, I proudly drove the shiny new ride off the lot. I was already way over my head with debts from starting my tire business, but I needed wheels.

A few days later, I got up one morning and headed to work. I have a bad habit of not clearing my windshield of ice and snow before driving. I'm always in too much of a hurry. A friend of mine in town who owns a

186

printing business calls me Ben Hur...ry. I'm constantly feeling pressed to get to my next gig and I know that eventually the defroster will get rid of the ice. Besides, it makes the trip less boring.

I went to work, traversing the half-mile to my shop in my brand new pickup. It was a frosty morning. A light-emitting, yet sight-constricting sheet of ice covered the windshield. There was a clear spot over toward the bottom right side of the windshield. If I looked about 80 degrees to the right of the steering wheel, I could see a little bit of the barrow pit on the side of the road. I pulled up to the stop sign between my home and the tire store and manually rolled down the side windows to check for traffic. A school bus had just gone by before I reached the intersection.

I looked both ways, rolled the windows up, and took a left, struggling to keep my new pickup in proper position on the road in relation to the visible right side gutter. I accelerated to approximately 35 mph and continued looking through the little ice-free zone in the right corner of the glass.

All of a sudden, I remembered the school bus that had passed by me earlier and was now somewhere in the frosty glaze ahead of me. A nano-second later, I remembered the railroad tracks that were invisible at the time, but still very much also in front of me. I quickly added two and two together and realized that since school buses stop at railroad crossings, I might have a major yellow problem on my hands.

I stomped on the binders with both feet. The truck started skidding on the frosty road and soon I could see my opaque windshield turning colors from a frosty white to a bright school bus yellow.

Crash! I immediately came to a halt.

I opened my door but it didn't open like the door on a brand new pickup should. It made a buckling, groaning noise. I had to push hard with both hands in order to get it to swing out far enough so I could get out. My brand new, red and white Chevrolet had its nose and eyeballs buried under the big, black bumper of the school bus.

The lady bus driver soon arrived from the cockpit of the bus to the scene of the accident. We surveyed the damage and concluded that, yes, I was an idiot. I got someone to push me off the road as the engine compartment was smashed in. We waited for the State Patrol to materialize.

The cop arrived and took our statements. The bus wasn't hurt in the least. It left. The patrolman proceeded to hand me a ticket for driving with impaired vision, or not being very smart . . . something like that. The ticket was fairly substantial, but I knew I had it coming. We stood around and shot the bull for a few minutes and I happened to mention that I was a reserve deputy with the county.

He got a look of shock and regret on his face. "Oh, no! Why didn't you tell me that before I wrote the ticket out? I wouldn't have written you up if I'd known that." I told him that my deputy position had already gotten me out of a lot of tickets and that I deserved this one. He still felt bad and I started to wish that I had told him before the citation. We both would have felt better about the situation.

I took the pickup in to a friend of mine who owned a body shop. It was on the verge of being totaled, but he talked the insurance company into letting him fix it. I picked it up a week or two later. It was back in pristine condition.

That night I got a call from Ken, an employee of a good friend and customer, J Wood, to fix a couple of truck tires that had blown out down by Pasco. The ten-wheeler truck was overloaded with spuds and it was imperative that I get the tires fixed before the night got cold and the potatoes froze. I was excited about the sale that this situation had created, but I had a slight problem. The beater service truck I was using had just lost its engine.

I told Ken that the only way I could do the job was if we towed my service truck to the job with my new pickup that had just gotten back from being rebuilt after the bus wreck. He said that was fine so we hooked up and took off on the 20-mile trip. The heavy service truck, loaded with a compressor, supplies, and tools, made my new pickup work hard, but we made it. The last few miles were a little troubling, however. The new pickup started jerking and surging. By the time we arrived at the scene of the flats, it would barely run.

I started the compressor on the service truck and got the two tires changed. J showed up and helped with the job. It was eleven o'clock before we finished. I told him that my new "tow" truck wasn't running right and that there was probably no way that it would pull my other truck back to the shop. After a bit of discussion, I drove the sputtering new pickup out into a field off the road so it wouldn't get vandalized. We chained the service truck up behind J's pickup. I jumped in the truck and J and Kendall started towing me up the road toward Basin City.

At that time, we were young and stupid. J must have wanted to get home so we were soon speeding along the road at 75 or 80 miles an hour, just as fast as his truck could go with the load hanging on behind it. Since my motor wouldn't run and he was directly in front of me, I decided to shut my headlights off to conserve my battery. The road ahead was deserted. I also figured that my headlights might be bothering J in his rearview mirrors. Besides, all I needed to do was to watch and follow J's taillights.

We were clipping along when I shut the lights off. A few seconds later, J decided he wanted to be like me and shut his lights off. I yelled, "What in the heck are you doing?" Of course, he couldn't hear me. We were tearing down the road in complete darkness. I couldn't see the road because his truck was in the way so I just concentrated on following the dark shape of his vehicle directly in front of me. All he had for reference was the white-dotted line, illuminated by the moonlight, in the middle of the road. I didn't even have that! Exhilarating. Crazy. Idiotic.

If there had been any reason he would have needed to hit his brakes, he wouldn't have seen it. If he had hit his brakes, my equipment-loaded, momentum-laden truck would have rammed right into his, as we had a meager ten-foot chain separating us. After about five miles of this activity, J turned his lights back on and we eventually got home.

The next day I took my recently remodeled pickup back to the auto body shop. A canister containing charcoal for the emission system had ruptured in the bus crash. After that was replaced, the truck ran fine.

• •

The first full calendar year of me being a business tycoon in Basin City brought lots of surprises. I built the initial steel building on the cheap, without insulation. That first winter brought temperatures down to the single digits and we froze. A good half inch of frost formed on the inside of the building. It was a major job keeping the air lines and air tools from icing up. I think it was colder indoors than out.

Through that year, I felt like I needed to expand my markets. I had, rather have, a type-A personality. "A" stood for Aggressive. It did not stand for

Astute. I put in a line of sprinkler boots and tennis shoes. Since I had to make trips to the Tri-Cities every day for parts, I advertised a service called "Pak-A-Part" in which, for a small fee, I would pick up parts for the local farmers. I don't think I ever hauled a single part for anyone.

I sold whatever I thought would make a buck. I found an outlet where I could buy big air compressors for a good price. I sold several. One day I got an order. I drove into town to pick it up. It was a tall, vertical unit, standing over six feet high, and weighed a good 350 pounds. It had an 80-gallon tank, a 5 hp motor, and a 2-stage compressor. The compressor and motor were mounted on top of the tank, which made the thing extremely top heavy.

As I've gone through life, I've often taken chances and challenges just to see if I could succeed at the seemingly impossible task I happened to be attempting at the time. This was one of those times. The compressor was housed in a wooden crate and looked like a fine piece of machinery. I had neglected to bring any tie-down straps with me. I instantly accepted the self-induced challenge to see if I could drive the 25 miles to Basin City, balancing the compressor without buckling the thing down.

I carefully wove my way out of town, gingerly steering and cautiously moving down the road. Once I hit the straightaway on Glade Road I picked up speed and decided I could relax. There was no question I was going to make it. The compressor was new and shiny and expensive. I took numerous admiring peeks at it in my rear-view mirror, enjoying the experience of selling the machine and making a quick three hundred bucks.

The last peek I took in my mirror while in this euphoric state gave me a nasty bit of visual information. I was cruising along at 55 mph and the crated bundle must have decided there was just too much headwind. Without my permission, it decided to jump ship and exit out of the vehicle. I helplessly watched it topple back over the tailgate and explode on the pavement. The wooden crate was reduced to hundreds of small pieces of firewood kindling. The compressor was packing major momentum and I watched as it rolled and skidded amid countless sparks along the asphalt.

I was heartsick. I knew that the quick bucks I had been planning on making had now turned into a negative number. I turned around and drove back. The compressor was still lying in the road. I put my flashers on and spent the next fifteen minutes of my sorry life gathering firewood off the road and directing traffic around the disaster. Too late in the day, I realized that buying a strap would have been Astute!

A couple of good Samaritans stopped. With much effort, we were able to manhandle the heavy piece of now scrap iron back into the pickup. I left it in a prone position, much like a casket sits in a hearse. In fact, as I mourned the loss, I felt like I was in a one-car funeral procession all the way home.

I arrived back at the shop in the late afternoon. Ross Montierth is a friend I've had had since I was three years old. He had been reluctant to buy tires from me because, like Loen Bailie, he had always bought Michelins in the past. Being very familiar with my history, he was a little wary of buying anything from me. It just so happened that on this particular afternoon he decided to give me a shot. He owned a Volvo and had just picked it up from a shop in town after a fresh paint job. It looked beautiful. It needed tires. Going against his better judgment, he brought it to me.

I instructed my helpers to put the tires on the car and to be very careful about not touching the paint or doing anything that might mar its finish. Ross and I have always enjoyed talking to each other. We retired to the office and I started regaling him with my experience of losing the compressor on the road. Ten minutes later, in mid-sentence, our conversation was interrupted by the sound of commotion, much screaming, and, as a finale, a loud crash. Full of concern, we dashed out to see what the problem was.

I had just acquired new tire racking and, a day earlier, had bolted the lengths together. Unfortunately, I must have gotten sidetracked before I got all the bolts tight. Many tires had been placed earlier that day on the 4-tier, eight foot high rack that stood adjacent to the service bay Ross's car was in.

The rack must have decided it wanted a closer look at the new paint job. At this most inopportune moment, the weight of the tires and the loose connection points combined to bring the entire load over and down, directly on Ross's car. We jumped in and began pulling tires and racking off the vehicle. Luckily, only a few scratches were inflicted, but I remember that Ross got a free set of tires that day.

• •

You may remember the three foot deep pit that I kept Loen Bailie from falling into. I had ramps for vehicles to drive on to get front end alignments. Lupe Garza worked for me as an alignment tech and mechanic. One day I was in the office and, very similarly to the Montierth episode, heard a scream and commotion in the shop. I ran out and saw a yellow Cadillac El Dorado with its front end and tires down in the pit. I ran over and saw the bumper and grill pressing against Lupe, smashing him against the alignment machine. Lupe was in a lot of pain. I was afraid he had severe internal injuries.

A good customer Ted Tschirky was in the shop and offered to get his pickup to try to pull the El Dorado back. I grabbed a chain and hooked up to Ted's pickup as soon as he backed in. I then yelled for him to take off. As soon as Ted was able to pull the heavy car back a few inches away from Lupe, he crumpled to the floor. We called the ambulance and prayed he would be okay. The ambulance soon hauled him away.

We then reconstructed the accident scene. Most of the cars in the early 80s were rear wheel drive. When they were jacked up and alignments were performed, they didn't move as the rear wheels were in gear or "park" and the emergency brake engaged. The El Dorado was a strange creature back then. It was front wheel drive. When Lupe air-jacked up the front wheels and began reefing on the front end parts to check them, the back wheels were free to roll. And so they did.

The car rolled forward, Lupe screamed, and the jacks catapulted the car past the ramps down into the pit. Lupe was crushed. Fortunately, the nose of the Caddy ended up an inch below Lupe's sternum, compressing his stomach, but providing a flexible area of his body to take the impact and pressure of the car. If it had been any higher, bones would have been broken and serious injuries resulted. Fortunately, Lupe was back to work the next day.

CHAPTER 17

VENTURES, CAPTURES, FRANCHISES

J Wood and I decided to open up a video rental business in the office section of my store. At that time, VHS and Beta were competing varieties and we had to stock both types of tapes. We had a couple of rental VCRs and stayed fairly busy.

Unfortunately, a few undesirables wanted part of the action. By the end of that year (1984), my shop had been broken into four times. I was upset to the max. I was just barely getting started and was getting violated on a regular basis. Tapes, VCRs, car batteries, tires, tools, and other items were getting ripped off. I didn't have insurance for theft at the time and these break-ins were really doing a number on me and my bank account.

The fourth time was toward the end of December. An office window was smashed in to gain access. When I saw it the next morning, I knew it was the same window I had fixed once before. I taped some cardboard in the broken glass area and made a vow that I was going to catch the culprits. I figured they would be back again so why go to the trouble of replacing the window?

Every night for the next two weeks I lay in the back office on the hard floor in a sleeping bag. I had a shotgun, a 357 magnum, a pair of handcuffs, and a PR-24 (a police billy club that stands for "Public Relations 24 hours"). I had amassed my little arsenal during my time serving as a deputy in the sheriff's reserve.

My new schedule required that I work the day shift exhausted from the night before. When night came and I curled up on the hard floor, every little noise I heard kept me on edge. Each car that drove by on the street outside made me wonder if it contained the guy who would soon be breaking in. I got very little sleep each night. By the time each morning rolled around, I was in a progressively worse mood and looking forward all the more to confronting my persecutor.

I had a great fear that I was becoming so tired that someone was going to break in and I would sleep through the entire event. If that happened, they might find me asleep and use my own weapons against me. Therefore I locked both doors that led into the back office in order to slow the culprits down before they found me.

Two long weeks rolled by. It was fourteen nights of hell, but I was determined to get the perp. Finally, my expected guest returned. I was awakened out of a dead sleep by the crash of the remaining glass being knocked out of the window and landing on the office floor.

The room I was in was completely dark. I carefully slithered out of my sleeping bag, felt around, and grabbed a couple of weapons. I didn't want to make any noise and was afraid to unlock the door as the noise might scare him off.

He tried the knob on the front office door for a while. Then I heard him walk around and try the other door leading into the office from the shop. He got more aggressive as time went by. He cycled back and forth between the doors at least five times. Finally, he found a screwdriver and began trying to pry the door loose. He was doing some damage and I figured enough was enough.

I reached out and turned the lock. He wrenched on the door again and Presto . . . the door opened! I'm sure he was pleasantly surprised. However his glee turned to terror as I materialized in the darkness and stuck the double-barreled 12-gauge shotgun toward him. He turned around and started beating feet in retreat. I followed right behind him, yelling at him to stop or I was going to blow his head off.

By the time he reached the window, he could see his options were very limited and he had better stop before the buckshot started flying. I commanded him in a very frustrated and finger-on-the-trigger voice to lie down on the floor. I was out of my head with exhaustion and anger. I gave him a few swift kicks just to let him know I was a little bothered and not just kidding around, and then handcuffed him. He was lying in the broken glass from the window and ended up bleeding from a few places, either from the glass or my punting practice.

I put the gun to his head and told him I was going to take him out in the sagebrush, shoot him, and bury him. Nobody was ever going to know that he had been around. The dude was scared. He offered a couple of promises that I'm sure were honest and heartfelt, such as, if I let him go he would never come back. I declined.

I wanted to know where my property was from the previous heist. I knew it was 100% likely that he was the one who had taken several thousand dollars worth of stuff from the last shoplifting and I wanted it back. It took very little persuasion on my part for him to confess to the previous theft and tell me where the loot was located. It was in Burbank, a town some thirty miles to the south; he even gave me the exact address.

I figured I should call my video partner J since some of the loot was half his. It was around 1:00 in the morning. I called J and got him out of bed. He made the trip down to Basin City in record time. He came running into the office looking like a wild man from a comic book. He had thrown some sweat pants on with the legs tucked into his tall, cowboy boots. He was carrying a deer rifle with a scope on it. He was ready for action. I laughed and told him he probably wouldn't need the scope for this close of a target.

I indicated that I wanted to take him down to Burbank right then and get my stuff back. J was not quite as sure about that course of action and tried to get me to hold off. The thief, I'll call him Jose, lay on the floor and listened as we discussed our options.

After a thorough examination of the situation, we decided to call another close neighbor, Steve Price, to help us make the decision. We got Steve out of bed and he came down and we debated some more. After another spell, we got Nolan Empey out of bed and he came down. My friends thought I should call the cops. I figured if the cops got involved, I would never get my property back.

Finally they persevered and eventually a deputy showed up. I went out and, without telling him any details of what was going on inside the shop, asked him if he could get a search warrant if I had information as to where my stolen property had ended up. He said sure; no problem. For some reason I didn't believe him, but since my friends and enemy inside the office were hoping I'd get the cops involved, I invited him in.

We turned Jose over to the cop, much to his relief. The broken glass and blood on the floor made the crime scene look worse than it actually was. The event quickly spread through the community and everyone seemed to be supportive of my neighborhood crime watch program. Wally Bradley, the sheriff at the time, never even attempted to get a search warrant to retrieve my stuff. Instead, he sent a deputy out to take a statement from me as they were contemplating charging me with assault.

• •

A couple years later, I found out Jose was working for Courtney Calaway, a customer and friend of mine. Courtney knew what had happened. Together we decided to see what Jose would do when he was given an assignment to bring one of Courtney's trucks up to my shop to get worked on. Courtney told him several different times to take trucks up, but Jose always found an excuse not to.

Finally, Courtney called me one day and told me that Jose was heading my way with a truck. A few minutes later a truck pulled in and parked in a far corner of the parking lot. Jose didn't get out. He sat in the truck with his head down, looking at the floorboards. Courtney pulled in to pick him up a few minutes later. After Courtney had parked, he walked over and started talking to me. Jose got out of the truck and ran at a full sprint across the parking lot and jumped in the passenger side of Courtney's pickup. He began looking at the floorboards again. We got a good laugh out of Jose's ignominious return to the scene of his crimes.

• •

In the early years of my tire store, I worked and ran pretty hard and thought my crew should do the same. I felt a lot of financial pressure and pushed the crew to maximize their output. Since I had always worked for my dad or been on my own, I wasn't familiar with paid vacations, Saturdays off, 15-minute breaks, overtime pay, or all the other benefits that state-mandated private businesses must offer.

I had one employee named Randy who was from Oklahoma, had a drawl and, in my estimation, moved a little too slow sometimes. He smoked and often snuck in a smoke break when I wasn't looking. One day the phone rang and his wife asked for him. I was busy and a little peeved at the work interruption. I ran around the shop looking for Randy. He was nowhere to be found.

Finally, I ran out the back door. He was facing toward me but looking down, standing next to a storage van. He was having a smoke break and was also in the middle of a restroom break, if you know what I mean.

I yelled, "Randy, phone!" He looked up, shocked. He didn't know what to put away first, the cigarette or the bathroom utensil. His hands were jumping around and he was completely discombobulated. By the time he got things under control, his hands, some of his clothing, and his cigarette were wet. It was a pretty funny scene. That was one time that I didn't say something to him about the downside of taking a smoke break. I was too busy laughing.

• •

About a year after I built my shop in Basin City, a friend of mine named Vaughn Morgan approached me about putting a tire store in at Merrill's Corner, a very small hamlet about eight miles away from my store in Basin City. I was born with a large amount of guts and no brains. I decided to partner up with him. We ran it for a year and it failed miserably. It was a terrible location and too close to my store in Basin City. Halfway through the endeavor Vaughn could see it wasn't going to work and he wanted to bail out. I let him and took the entire loss. I'm continually amazed at my lack of business acumen.

Vaughn was a gentleman farmer and always on the lookout for a way to make a buck. He was a nice guy and always dressed up real spiffy, cowboy style. He often stopped by my store to see what was happening.

One afternoon I was working on some tractor tires that a farmer had bought at an auction. They were tires that were used in sugar cane fields in the south. They had a very deep lug pattern on them and were filled with some type of lead mud that was very heavy. It was nasty stuff.

Normally we filled farm tires with a calcium chloride mix, which is another vicious liquid that won't freeze and is used to provide weight in the rear tires for extra traction.

These leaded mud tires were a whole different ball game. I couldn't pump them. The farmer wanted the mud out. That's why he dropped them off. I was scratching my head trying to figure out a solution about the time

Vaughn stopped by. He had real nice clothes on, complete with a white cowboy hat. He stood around and gabbed as I worked.

I got an idea to pressure up the tire and see if I could blow the mud out from the added pressure. I aired the tire up to 30 or 40 psi and unscrewed the valve stem. All at once, the stem blew and mud shot out. Vaughn just happened to be standing in the path of the escaping mud propellant.

The brown oozing mud covered him from his leather cowboy boots to his white Stetson. His face was unrecognizable, but I could tell he had a look of shock on it. I burst out laughing. He was speechless. I tried to clean him up, but the stuff didn't want to come off. He left. He'd had enough action for one day.

• •

After I had been in business a couple of years, I began to notice a Les Schwab Tire pickup coming through town every day. Les Schwab was a guy who started a tire store in Prineville, Oregon, in the early 1950s. His first store had one bay, one employee, and one outhouse behind the store for its bathroom. He was a newspaperman who wanted an opportunity to get out on his own. He borrowed some money from his brother-in-law and went to work.

He had a great business plan. He soon began expanding, instituting unique customer service ideas and sharing half of each store's profits with that particular store's employees. This made a huge impact on the motivation of the store crew. It expanded rapidly through small-town farming and logging communities in Oregon and Washington.

Eventually, Les decided to try his hand at the large metro markets in Seattle and Portland. No one in the tire business thought he would make it because they figured his type of operation would only work in the small, rural towns. They were wrong. He not only made it, but he made it big. In 2008, there were over 400 tire stores pumping out around a billion dollars or two per year in sales. When a tire manufacturer wants to find a buyer who has the cash to buy hundreds of thousands of tires in one shot, they call Les Schwab.

At the time I started seeing the Schwab pickup around Basin City, there were around 150 Les Schwab stores throughout the Northwest. They were, and are, the major tire competition in whatever town they occupy. Branded companies, like Goodyear or Bridgestone-Firestone, feel good if they have 5% of a market share. In the towns that Les Schwab occupied, the Schwab store usually enjoyed 50-90% of the market. They were a real anomaly in the tire world.

The majority of Schwab stores are company owned, however, they also have a member dealer program. Member dealers operate their stores just like the company stores. They buy at the same price, honor the same warranties, look the same, and follow the same programs.

The guy cruising through my town was Don McClure, a Les Schwab member dealer. He owned a store in Pasco and had just opened another store in Connell, neighboring towns approximately 20 miles away from Basin City. McClure was a big shot in Pasco. He was on the Port Commission and several other high profile committees. Me? I was nothing except intimidated.

I started seeing his service trucks coming through town on a regular basis and saw Basin City tire sales ending up in his pocket, not mine. He would go to the coffee shop in Basin City and have lunch, making sales and telling the locals that he was going to put a Schwab store in Basin City. I knew that soon after he finished his lunch, he was going to eat my lunch.

I was rattled. I wasn't hooked up with a brand. I was just peddling tires I acquired from several wholesale warehouses. I had just gotten established and it looked like I was going to lose everything if things continued in the same direction.

About this time I met a tire salesman from La Grande, Oregon, named John Bozarth. One day he visited me and I told him my problem. "You have GOT to get hooked up with a branded name," he said. "Get with Schwab or Goodyear or somebody. Otherwise, McClure will drive you out." I knew he was right.

I knew that Les Schwab had the complete tire program. I also knew that if they took me on as a member dealer, McClure wouldn't be able to continue his path into Basin City. So I called them. They immediately sent a guy named Jerry Harper up on a jet. He looked at my store, explained their program, and we had a nice talk. He said that he thought they would take me on. I was excited.

As he left the store, in an afterthought, he mentioned that they would have to check with the neighboring managers and member dealers in the area, but was sure there would be no problem. I was instantly mortified. I knew McClure would raise a stink.

Sure enough, Harper called me the next week. "We aren't going to take you on," he said. "I don't know why, but Don McClure is screaming. We aren't going to upset him."

So I hooked up with Kelly Springfield. I hung their signs, bought their tires, and did everything I could to strengthen my business. I started a local newsletter by printing stories about experiences the original settlers of the Basin had endured. I sold advertising for the paper and mailed it out to everyone in the area. Prominent in the advertising was my store. Every time I did a mailing, I made sure I sent Don McClure one. I wanted him to know that I wasn't going down without a fight.

Up to this point the local paper, the *Connell Graphic*, had always had a subscription charge for their weekly edition. Only subscribers got the *Graphic*. Since I was selling advertising to pay my publishing costs, I didn't charge anything for the community to receive my "paper."

After a few months of "competition," the *Graphic* quit charging their subscription fee and began sending the paper to everyone in the local postal codes. This practice of everyone getting the *Graphic* at no charge has carried on since that time.

A year later, I got in my car and headed for Idaho to collect a tire bill from a deadbeat. I got as far as Connell before I had car trouble. I stopped at the Les Schwab store to enlist some help to get it running so I could turn around and limp home.

The manager, Dave Dallas, asked me if I had heard what was going on. I hadn't. He said McClure was doing a lot of goofy things, almost like he was going crazy. He had contacted Prineville and was going to sell his stores to them. Then he wasn't. Then he was. Then he wasn't sure. Then he was just going to sell them one store. Dave said things were really up in the air and Don was acting unusually strange.

This was on a Saturday. The next Monday morning, I called Jerry Harper. He wasn't in. I called him on Tuesday and he answered. He said he had just gotten to work and saw a note on his desk that said Don wanted to sell his stores. He also mentioned that it looked like if they bought Don out, they would take me on as a member dealer. I was excited!

I had ordered some tractor tires previously from Schwab in Pasco that I couldn't get anywhere else. After the phone call that morning with Harper, I got in my truck and headed for town to pick up the tires. I took Kent Mackay with me as he needed to get some sand for their sandblaster. I told him all the developments as we drove in. I was pretty excited and relieved, hoping that I might soon be putting up the Les Schwab sign.

We walked into McClure's Les Schwab store in Pasco to pick up my tires. It was weird. Usually the store was bustling and all the employees were greeting customers, friendly and talkative. Not that day. We got the tires and left. Both of us noticed the odd atmosphere. I mentioned that maybe it had something to do with the conversation that I had had with Jerry Harper an hour earlier. Maybe the employees had just found out they had a new boss.

We drove out to Central Pre-Mix on Road 100 to pick up Kent's sand. We walked into the office and the first thing we heard from the receptionist was, "Did you hear what just happened? Don McClure just shot himself in the head, right out there at the corner!"

We were flabbergasted. I was pretty sure at that point that I was going to become a Les Schwab Member Dealer since Don was no longer going to be around to fight it. It was a memorable morning, unbelievable happenings to say the least!

I became a Les Schwab Member Dealer in the summer of 1986. They had a great organization with everything a tire store needed. I enjoyed the first ten years of the relationship. It became less attractive as time moved on, until I finally got out after twenty long years.

• •

I was always willing to take on risk and debt as a young whippersnapper. I built a car wash, put in gas and diesel cardlock pumps and tanks, farmed, and built a big addition on to my store. I often used salvage metal in my construction to keep costs down.

One winter day I hooked up one of my dad's pipe trailers to the back of my pickup. I headed into town to buy some heavy I-beams for framework on a construction project I was beginning. As I drove into Pasco, I was a little nervous about pulling the farm pipe trailer in town with no lights or license. The trailer was pretty long, over 30 feet in length.

I approached a mini-mart on A Street going about 35 mph. The store was on the left side of the road. A young, Hispanic male was waiting for me to go by, gunning his engine, and ready to peal out as soon as I passed. I could tell that he was looking both ways for traffic and waiting for me to pass. A foreboding thought struck me. He probably didn't see the pipe trailer behind my pickup. This premonition was right on. He took off as I passed, gunned his car across the empty lane, and broadsided the pipe trailer. The back rack of the trailer hit his right front fender and flipped him 90-degrees instantly.

I groaned and pulled over at the next turnout. He limped in behind me. I knew the pipe trailer was okay. Dad built several of them years before and they were heavy duty and indestructible. His Celica was not heavy duty and it was destructible. It was also a mess.

I got out and could see that there were several thousand dollars in damages to his car. He didn't speak English, but I got him to understand that we needed to call the police and report the accident. "No police, no police! Everything okay!" He repeated this several times. I felt bad for the guy. I'm sure he didn't have insurance, but I figured if he didn't want to report it then that was fine with me. I bid him adieu and departed. I'm sure he drove away without gunning his engine.

• •

Speaking of getting broadsided, another experience comes to mind. After I got my paintball field running in the 1990s, I needed to buy some supplies from the Army Surplus store in Richland. I drove over one afternoon about 5:00 pm. I was in the turning lane, ready to turn left into the parking lot after oncoming traffic went by. The sun was on the horizon and making things a little hard to see.

When the traffic cleared, I began my turn. After a split second, I saw a bicyclist steaming toward me with his head down in fine racing form. He was probably going 45 mph and had no clue that a pickup was sideways, directly in front of his direction of travel.

I hit the gas, trying to get past the biker before he connected. Unfortunately, he connected. Everything on his bike and person went past the back of my pickup except his right knee. This was the first indication to this clueless rider that his ride was over. I heard the thump and looked behind me, just in time to see him helicoptering through the air. He landed on the street to my left rear, screaming in pain.

I called an ambulance and then tried to comfort the poor guy. His knee looked trashed. He could not quit screaming. The cops and ambulance showed up and he was taken to the hospital. An officer pulled me aside and began to take my statement. About then, another guy showed up. From his conversation with the officer, I could tell that he, too, was an officer. Here is the gist of what he said.

"I was stopped back at the intersection with a red light. I noticed this guy on a bicycle pedaling down the hill and cruising through his green light at the intersection where I was stopped. He had his head down and was going way too fast. After he passed through the intersection, I saw the pickup and this driver turn in front of him and then try to accelerate out of the way when he saw the bike rider. The guy on the bike was exceeding the speed limit, wasn't watching where he was going, and is totally at fault. The pickup driver is not at fault."

My insurance company told his attorney to pound sand. They told me they were not going to pay a dime since he was totally at fault. His attorney kept bugging them so they finally paid him 30 or 40 grand. I probably would have been in a lot more trouble if that off-duty cop hadn't been present.

• •

In the late 80s, I had another unusual experience with Kent. We were in the Tri-Cities one day doing business. We were traveling down Clearwater Avenue in his black, Ford Bronco. It had big tires on it. We were on the inside lane of the busy street, talking about going to lunch. "Should we take someone to lunch?" "Sure." "Who?" "How about Ferris Naef?" "Okay."

We had just passed Ferris' accounting office. Kent realized he needed to turn off of Clearwater Avenue and turn around in order to see if Ferris wanted lunch. Since I was with him, I guess Kent felt like he needed to cause an accident so I would feel more at home.

He immediately began to turn into the outside lane without looking. I glanced out my open window and down on a little, fresh-off-the-showroom-floor, Geo Metro. "No, Kent!" I yelled. He jerked the wheel back, but it was too late.

The slightly faster moving Geo's left front bumper hit the spinning right front tire of Kent's Bronco. It proceeded to ride up the tire, which flipped the Geo over on its top. This surreal and unstoppable scene was going on right next to my elbow that was hanging out the window.

The little car slid down the street upside down, probably going 40 miles an hour. I could see the driver's head hanging down at asphalt level. It was scary. I'm quite sure the poor guy didn't have any brakes or steering while he was in that particular position. I also noticed he didn't have a helmet on. Finally he slid to a stop. We pulled over and I ran to a shop and told them to call 911.

By the time I got back, the upside down dude was out of the car and right side up. There was a slight scratch on his head from broken glass, but that was his only injury. His suit still looked freshly pressed. His immaculately prepared hair was in place, just like he had combed it that morning, however it was covered with little pieces of broken glass.

His name was Dave Dickerson. He was a piano tuner. We gave him a ride home. He had just purchased the car. Kent got a ticket. Dave got another new car. He picked up a new customer from this incident as my wife has had him tune our piano ever since.

• •

After Don McClure shot himself and Les Schwab set me up as a member dealer, Prineville obtained control of McClure's Connell store and operated it as a company store. A year later, my zone manager contacted me and asked if I wanted to take over its operation. I sure did. I was aggressive. I considered them my competitor.

However, I was stupid for thinking I could succeed where Schwab had failed. They were brilliant in unloading a dead dog on to my plate.

I went to Prineville and met with Phil Wick, the president of Schwab; Tom Friedman, the CFO; and Von Thompson, the credit vice president. Von and I clashed on a regular basis since we never saw matters eye-to-eye over the years. They painted a rosy picture about how I could do so much better than they had in Connell. What a bunch of baloney!

I bought and ran that store for six years. Never once did I make money. When it was all over, I had lost over $150,000. It was a thorn in my side. The Connell second and third generation dry-land farmers supported the old time Grange Co-Op, which also had a tire store. Most of them were stockholders of the Grange. I guess I can't blame them.

I soon found that another segment of the Connell population went to the Tri-Cities to do their shopping. They bought their Les Schwab tires from one of the three stores there and then returned home, relying on my Connell store to do all the Schwab-mandated free flat repairs, free rotations, and costly road-hazard adjustments. Some of these people used my free services, but never bought a tire from me.

Another problem is the store was never well managed. To be honest, I was in charge. I just didn't stay on top of the way the store was operated. I have no one to blame but myself. I was scattered out in various enterprises and the managers didn't seem to have all the tools needed to make it work.

The last problem was that Connell was not big enough to support two tire stores. My Basin City store, in an unincorporated berg without a post office, averaged close to 2 million dollars a year in tire sales. I was in business there for 25 years. My Connell store, in a town with its own city hall, police force, high school, junior high and state penitentiary, never brought in more than $200,000 a year in sales. I closed it down after six years.

The first day I moved in and Schwab moved out, it rained cats and dogs. Inside the store! It was an old building and there were streams of water, literally torrents, running down through the walls, even past the electrical panel. Schwab had known about this, but neglected to tell me.

I knew immediately that the store needed a new roof. It had an old tar-coated flat roof. I have always been of the opinion that any engineer that designs a flat roof should be taken out and roof-tarred and feathered on the roof he just designed. Water runs off of a sloped roof. Water puddles up on a flat roof until eventually it finds a way to worm its way down into the building.

My little brother, Bryan, was working for me at the time. Bryan has since grown up and is now a key R&D guy at Intel, designing their chips. The oldest kid in my father's family is an idiot and the holder of one or two patents. The youngest is a genius and the holder of hundreds of patents. And we were working together back then.

I decided to cobble together a framework and add a sloping tin roof. We set about erecting the roof during the hottest part of the summer. We got the framework completed and most of the tin screwed on. We were working away when, all of a sudden, we heard someone climbing the ladder. A head appeared and then his mouth started moving, announcing that he was the building inspector for the City of Connell. "Do you fellows have a building permit?"

I answered in the negative. He then told us we were going to have to tear down what we had just erected. Bryan is a very calm and intelligent individual. As soon as the inspector went back down the ladder, Bryan whispered to me that he wanted to push the ladder and inspector over backwards off the roof. I restrained him, luckily for Intel. I jumped through the inspector's hoops and we finished the roof. We no longer experienced flooding in the office every time it rained.

• •

Around 1990, the State of Washington built a nice four-lane road, Highway 395, stretching from the Tri-Cities to Ritzville. It was sorely needed. Many people had died over the years on the previous, narrow, two-lane road. The construction company that built the road enlisted our services to keep their scrapers, loaders, and other big earth-moving equipment tires repaired. I went out and bought a boom truck and some other equipment to take care of the giant tires. We did quite a bit of work for them.

Out of the blue, one day I got word that Scarsella, the construction company working on the highway project, had shanghaied one of my guys. They were going to bring their own truck on-site and hire Sotero away from me. I thought it was a bunch of dirty pool, but that's how things work sometimes. On Sotero's last day of working for me, the store got a service call way out in the dry land wheat farm area to work on a combine tire. It was a two-man job. He was one of the guys that went.

Working down on my farm, I started hearing radio chatter about somebody's foot getting caught in a wheel. It didn't sound too serious so I kept doing what I was doing. The radio kept buzzing with the problem. I'd been doing tires for many years and couldn't understand what in the heck they were having problems with. I had never heard of anyone getting their foot stuck in a tire. I just shook my head and chalked it up to incompetence. But as the minutes ticked by I was bothered on an escalating basis.

Soon, they were talking about getting a torch and cutting up a brand-new combine wheel to get this guy's foot out. That took me over the edge. I abandoned my farm work, jumped in my pickup, and headed out for the dry lands 20 miles away.

When I arrived, I found the combine and associated personnel down in the bottom of a gulch. It was Sotero, and he had a brand-new pair of steel-toed work boots on. He had just bought them in anticipation of the new job he would start the next day. He had been kicking the top bead of the tire down over the rim and his steel toe had become lodged between the heavy bead of the tire and the drop-center of the wheel.

I could immediately see that Sotero was in bad shape. He had been standing on top of the tire for the last two hours. He was in terrible pain from the pressure. A farmer and my other employees were using tire irons, wedges, hammers, anything they could think of to try and relieve the pressure and work his foot out. He was in great distress and everyone there felt helpless.

Tom, my manager in Connell, had already gone back to the shop in Connell and was on his way out to the location with a cutting torch. I figured we would need some water to keep his foot cool so I headed to the nearest farmhouse to borrow some buckets of water so the tire and his foot didn't get too hot. Ten minutes later, we all arrived back at the scene.

We fired up the torch and began cutting. We kept pouring water on his foot and thought we were doing a good job. Finally, we had the heavy and expensive rim cut apart. We carried Sotero to my pickup. He was wasted with fatigue and pain. I rushed him to the hospital.

The medical personnel there told him they were going to have to cut his brand-new boot off. He didn't care. One part of me was thinking, "That's what he gets for jumping ship and going to work for Scarsella." The other part of me was feeling very sorry for him. Soon, all of me was feeling sorry for him.

When they cut the boot off, I was shocked. His foot was knotted up with big protrusions sticking out all over. It looked to me like every bone in his foot was broken. I left the hospital thinking that a surgeon had his work cut out for him if he was going to get all those bones back where they were supposed to be.

Unbelievably, it turned out that nothing was broken. His foot had assumed that gnarly shape because it had been under so much pressure and stress. However, when we cut the wheel apart, I was surprised to learn we hadn't kept it cool enough and the heat had cooked his foot. He was in so much pain from the pressure of the wheel and tire that he didn't notice the heat burning his foot. He had to have plastic surgery to repair the damage from the heat. That was a bad day for Sotero. He never did get to work for Scarsella.

CHAPTER 18

I DABBLE IN LAW

In the early 90s, I began noticing that our road hazard tire adjustment costs were skyrocketing. Les Schwab had an advertised free tire replacement program for road hazard damaged tires. Unfortunately for me, the individual store ended up footing the bill when a customer ruined a tire. After a little investigation I found out why we were replacing so many tires. The county road department had discovered that they could buy gravel for a greatly reduced price at a quarry near Connell.

This quarry mined basalt and shipped the rock around the country for railroad ballast. The ballast was large, very sharp, hard, and ideal for laying a base under railroad tracks, however it was absolutely brutal on tires. It worked fine for the railroads since not too many of their trains ran on tires. The county roads were a different story.

The quarry had a large by-product supply of smaller rock that wasn't suitable for the railroads. Somebody got a brilliant idea that the county could buy it cheap. The county road rock purchases and budget would shrink and the road department could spend it elsewhere. Cactus Quarry could get rid of their junk and make some money on the deal. Everybody was a winner, everybody except me.

I told the guys in the two stores to start saving the rocks they were pulling out of tires. The rocks were large, sharp, arrowhead shaped weapons that had no business being on the road. We soon had a large assortment of these costly tire destroyers. Every time a rock came in, I had to furnish a new tire to replace the ruined one. The Les Schwab Road Hazard program was killing me. It was brutal. Our free flat-repair numbers also mushroomed.

A lady in Connell who was the paper carrier and mail lady, stopped in and complained about all the flats she was having. I confidently told her that if she put on Les Schwab's best, the Toyo Z-800, she would have no more problems. She said to go ahead.

The next afternoon she called me from a farmhouse along her delivery route. Three of her new Z-800s were flat, all punctured by the county's new rock. I decided I'd had enough. I called the county road department and complained. They said they would have their insurance rep come out and talk to me. He arrived and did the bureaucratic shuffle and denial, which netted me nothing.

I then asked for an audience with the county commissioners, which included Harold Mathews, Neva Corkrum, and Sue Miller. They listened politely to my story and denied there was anything wrong. They said my problem was simply a cost of doing business. However, so that I would feel better, they said they would check things out with the road department before they made a final decision concerning my request. Then they would get back to me. They got back to me a few days later with a big "Sorry."

Soon after, I asked my lawyer friend Lowell Barber about suing the county. He suggested I do a small claims court maneuver. It wouldn't cost me much to file it and no lawyers would be involved. It sounded like a great idea.

I nosed around and talked to a few county employees. I found out that the road supervisors had been advised not to use the rock in the first place, but went ahead with it anyway. I heard there had been meetings between the road department and the commissioners concerning this issue, yet the commissioners told me they knew nothing about it.

I filed the claim and began spending time in the Columbia Basin College law library researching my case. I studied gravel specs, road hazard liability, and the government's duty concerning public travel. I accumulated customer experience letters and the boxes of all the county-owned arrowheads my stores had extracted. I called the Les Schwab attorney, Dick Borgman, who is now president of Les Schwab. He encouraged me to stand up for my rights and go after the county. I was loaded for bear.

My wife and I filed into the courtroom one morning at about 9:00. There were several cases on the docket and the judge said that he knew the "rock case" was going to take longer so he would try the other cases first. One other guy was suing the county because he claimed a county snowplow had wrecked his car, but I didn't really buy his story. The judge didn't either and gave him nothing. He grumbled and left.

One or two other cases were presented and judgments made. Ten or fifteen minutes had elapsed. Now it was my turn. There were several people still sitting in their seats. As I looked around, I realized they were all county employees. The judge introduced himself and said that he had been called in from out of town because an impartial judge was needed. We then started talking about the rocks.

The county representative stood and introduced himself. He was Todd Ungerecht, a Franklin County deputy prosecutor. I immediately objected. Small claims courts are off-limits to attorneys. The judge said he would let him represent the county anyway. I figured this was an ominous beginning.

We dove in. I presented my evidence. I detailed my experiences and losses. Often when I stated a fact, the road department employees in attendance grunted and made other disagreeable and negative sounds, which indicated to me that they were not there to support me. I outlined the time frame and numbers and laid out the rocks we had collected. I thought I did a dang good job.

After a couple of hours, we took a recess. Lawyer Todd came up to me and started talking. He was really a pretty nice guy. He said that I should go to law school. I took it he was impressed with my case. It was a little late in life for me to start law school so when my son Derek was old enough, I sent him.

We went back into court—my wife and I against the government. Testimony and cross-examination followed until noon when we broke for lunch. Michele and I talked about it while eating. We agreed that there were a lot of strikes against us, but that we had put up a good fight. We had no idea how it would turn out. I personally felt like even if I lost I had kicked a few county posteriors. I was bugged that the commissioners hadn't done the right thing in the first place, and thought that they should have just paid the damages that had been inflicted on me.

We went back to court and the battle continued. All in all, we were in the courtroom arguing this case for over five hours. My damages totaled $10,000. I had two suits, one for the Connell store and one for the Basin City store. Finally, it was time for a verdict.

The judge recapped everything that had ensued during the hearing. He didn't seem to have a problem with anything I had presented. He even observed that during lunch he had looked closely at the rocks I had brought in and could see that they had, indeed, been in tires. Portions of many of the rocks were worn from their contact with the road. I hadn't considered that aspect previously.

Bottom line: The judge rejected one of my suits since he said I could only have one case. I immediately decided I would appeal since two separate businesses had suffered losses. Then he hit the punch line. He found the county had done wrong. He found in my favor 100%. I was elated!

A day or so later, the front page of the *Tri-City Herald* contained an article about me beating the county in court.

The day after the *Tri-City Herald* article, I started getting heat from Les Schwab. Big newspapers in the Pacific Northwest had picked the story up and printed it. Seattle, Eugene, Lewiston, and Portland, among others, had carried it. My take on it was that it was newsworthy because for once a little guy had prevailed against Big Brother.

My zone manager Steve Scott called me and asked why I hadn't talked to anyone from Les Schwab before pursuing my case. I told him I had. I had talked to their attorney, Dick Borgman, and he told me to go for it.

My district manager Jerry Taylor called me up. He said he had just talked to Phil Wick, the president of the company, and they had a big problem. They didn't like their name associated with a suit against the government. They were trying to win government contracts and they perceived that my little problem was going to hinder their progress.

He told me that I may have won the battle, but I was going to lose the war. I was to drop the suit and not take the county's money. He said I was to call the newspaper up and apologize! I was to tell the *Tri-City Herald* that, in the spirit of Christmas, I was dropping the suit; that I was sorry I had brought it and that the county could keep their money. Even though Schwab was telling me to drop the suit, they wouldn't pay my damages either. To tell you the truth, I wasn't feeling the spirit of Christmas at all.

I was devastated. My euphoric high immediately evaporated and a deep depression and anger replaced it. I knew Les Schwab, the man. Les couldn't stand government's stranglehold and idiotic decisions that were constantly being forced upon the citizenry. I knew if he was involved in the day-to-day of the company, he would be congratulating me instead of allowing this type of skullduggery by his employees. However, Les was in

Palm Springs and knew nothing of this travesty and the role his company was playing in it.

I'd had a fairly high opinion of Phil Wick until things like this began occurring. I called him and politely complained about not collecting the money. He said, "Oh, you'll find that it will all turn out for the best. Your customers will appreciate the fact that you dropped the suit." I didn't buy it. I still don't. After thinking about everything for a couple more hours, I called Phil back several times. He wouldn't take my calls.

I made a last ditch effort to salvage something out of the mess. I called two of the commissioners, Neva Corkrum and Sue Miller. I preemptively said I would drop the suit if they would get me a transcript of the court case. They agreed and were glad that I was going to drop the suit. It had given them a black eye.

The paper published my "apology."

That day, several of my customers came in—mad! Phil was wrong. They couldn't believe I had let the county off without paying. They expressed their feelings that, for once, the little guy had won against Big Brother and then I'd let the county off the hook. My customers now looked at me as a turncoat and a gutless idiot. Schwab had me under such a thick blanket I couldn't even tell my customers the true story, but I had to sit there and take their wrath.

To tell the truth, I am still bugged about the whole incident. I had won the battle, but had to surrender afterwards. Les Schwab (the company) had forced me to quash the truth and left me with egg on my face and a hole in my pocketbook. Neva and Sue never followed through with the transcript. After I dropped the suit, they said they couldn't get it. Another lie. This was not the last bit of trouble I would have with dishonest officials. Another problem with Phil Wick would surface a few years later.

• •

One summer day in 1993, I was out on a farm fixing a tractor tire. I got a call on my radio that another problem had cropped up at the Connell store. It was almost a daily occurrence. I was on my third manager there. Customer complaints were the norm. The store had shown losses continuously. I had remodeled the store in an effort to spruce things up with no positive results. Every year, for six years, produced blood-colored red ink on the bottom line. The mixture of my blood, sweat and tears had the same exact same hue. I was always shoveling good money after bad into the joint.

The store was out of control. The employees manipulated the manager on an everyday basis. They were stealing from me right and left. I'd heard through the grapevine that an employee was dealing drugs on the side. I'd had enough.

"Shut the son of a . . . gun down!" I said on the radio. "Lock the doors and drop the key off in Basin City!" I decided that I would let the other guys go and keep the manager. He would work in Basin City.

The Schwab company was very upset at me for closing the store down without notifying them first. The heck with them. They had pawned a loser of a store off on me in the first place. They had only stayed there a year before they bailed. They stabbed me in the back when I got a just judgment in court. They always had a holier-than-thou attitude about my Connell operation. They could do nothing wrong and had all kinds of remote control advice for me.

After shutting it down, I felt a heck of a lot better. In retrospect, I waited far too long. In fact, I never should have ventured there in the first place.

About this time, I was having another big problem in Basin City. We were losing cash almost daily. I didn't know if the crew was swiping it, or the bookkeeper, or what was going on. I rigged up cameras and recorders and alarms to no avail. The hemorrhaging went on for months. We had no success isolating the problem.

• •

One day at work a guy approached me and mentioned that he had heard a particular employee was living high on the hog on my money. I started thinking about it and it gradually dawned on me what had been going on. The guy was coming into the Basin City store after hours to pick up tires that were needed in the Connell store and leaving the necessary paperwork. That was okay. He was then going to the safe, taking money, and leaving no paperwork. That was not okay.

I wasn't positive it had gone down like this, but the more I thought about it, the more likely it seemed. But how was I going to prove it?

The next day, I called him into my office.

"Jake, I know," I said.

Our eyes locked. I sat there and looked at him. He looked at me. Not a word was spoken. We stared quietly at each other for at least ten minutes. It was one of the strangest, ten-minute periods with another person I've ever encountered.

Finally he spoke up, broke down, and began confessing. My bluff had worked. A large burden was lifted off both of our shoulders. He had no idea how much he had stolen. By the time we were done, we came up with an amount of about ten thousand dollars he had pilfered. I really liked the guy. I felt sorry for him.

He stayed on, working for half salary with the other half going toward restoring stolen funds. He paid the majority of it back and then moved on to another job, promising he would continue to pay me. The payments stopped. We had a slight disagreement about it and eventually decided to have another party help us decide the best course of action.

He resisted, but finally said he would pay but would hold a grudge. Our arbitrator stated that holding a grudge was never good.

He told how he had just attended the funeral of a man who had been active in church in town. This man had a son who had played basketball with a church team from Pasco many years previous. The team had won all their games and then came out to Basin City one night. (This was when I was in high school. I may have played in the game, but I don't remember the incident.) I guess the game was close, but the undefeated Pasco team lost due to a ref's call right at the end of the game. The kid was so mad, when he got home that night, he told his dad he was never going to go to church again. He stuck to his promise. Boy, he really showed 'em!

Decades later, at his father's funeral, the guy asked for some time to speak. What do you think he talked about? He went on and on about how his team got screwed by the ref some 40 years previous. A grudge had totally engrossed and ruined this man's life.

CHAPTER 19

BENZCO, INC.

After moving back to Washington in 1980, I stayed in close contact with Kim Haws. I had helped work on his asparagus picker in 1977, between my crazy, weekly, weekend trips to Utah chasing a pipe dream named Terri.

I grew up with Kim's brother Scot. One invention Kim came up with was a clamp-on beeper that attached to the knobs of compressed gas tanks. Workers often forget to shut the valves off at the tank when they complete welding and cutting jobs. It is a very common problem. The waste of expensive gas and the inconvenience of finding an empty tank the next time you need to use it is a real negative. When the valve was opened, via the beeper, an audible beep sounded at periodic intervals to remind the user that the tank valve was still on. It worked great. When the valve was turned off, the beeper shut off.

Kim had an injection mold made, manufactured a batch of them, sold them on a local level, and got mostly positive feedback. It looked like a moneymaker. I wanted to give product development a shot. We made a deal and I bought the patent rights from him.

The beeper, later called the Valve Alarm, would occupy a lot of my time and attention over the next seven or eight years, even though I was involved in the tire store in Basin City and was taking over the one in Connell throughout this period.

I showed my new little "beeper" opportunity to John Bozarth, my Goodyear friend from La Grande, Oregon. He wanted a part of it. We met several times and made a deal. We formed a company, Benzco, Inc. I gave him 40% and kept 60%.

He recruited a retired guy from his hometown who was into developing new products named Claude Hand. Claude had owned the Ford dealership in La Grande for many years, but had recently sold it. Claude was the guy who read me the riot act when I took off with the wind in my airplane.

We decided Claude would be the nuts and bolts guy. He had a lot of building space from his old dealership and we would use that for the office and warehouse. He would get a certain percentage of the sales or profits.

We did a market survey and found that some people felt like the beeper would be annoying. They wanted a flashing light, which would entail a whole different approach to design and engineering. I was a little uncomfortable with this new direction, but Claude seemed to know what he was doing so I acquiesced. Many months were spent with R&D, raising money, talking to potential buyers, and gearing up to produce the product. Claude was instrumental in the work.

John and I raised some money with a limited stock offering. I sold it to several of my friends, all of us thinking we were going to make a lot of money on the deal. Not one cent was to be used by us personally. I had heard many horror stories about guys raising lots of money for a project and then living high on the proceeds while the project died from lack of capital. I did not want this deal to end up in that situation. We raised around $50,000.

In order to produce the molds and parts that were needed to make this new design, Claude needed another $100,000. He had a farmer friend that he had known for years, Russell Elmer. Russell was wealthy and Claude talked him into loaning our company $100,000 with the proceeds to be repaid by Russell getting $1.00 for every unit we sold. There was no collateral offered or taken.

The contacts we made with national welding chains and gas companies indicated that they would be purchasing many hundreds of thousands of units. Russell and Claude figured the loan would be paid back many times over.

It never happened.

• •

Twenty years later, in 2008, I attended a SEMA show in Las Vegas. I think it is the largest automotive show in the world, a huge extravaganza with tens of thousands of exhibitors and spectators. I had just invented the Tire Squire, but since it was too late to get a booth, I made a deal with Tire Service Equipment Co. out of Phoenix to market it. I traveled down to Vegas and spent the week in their show booth. On the last day, an older gentleman walked by and asked me a question about a tire cutter that was in the booth. I explained a few details and noticed he was carrying a large bag. I asked him what he did and he told me he was the money man for a new product.

He was from Sacramento and had traveled to Las Vegas to see if there were any possibilities for his product. In the course of our talk, he mentioned that, years ago, he had done some business in La Grande, Oregon.

I asked him if he knew of a former business partner of mine named Claude Hand. His eyes got wide and he said he had bought a building from Claude. We were both amazed. It got even weirder when he said that during the time he knew Claude, he missed out on investing in a great little invention that fit on compressed gas tanks that Claude worked on.

I was shocked. I told him that I was the president of that company and that even though we worked quite a few years on it, it never took off. I told him he was a lucky man that he missed out on the investment opportunity.

Back then I made many trips down to La Grande, meeting with the two partners, usually traveling in my airplane. We had high hopes and thought we were big wheeler-dealers and were on the edge of falling into some big bucks. Thinking the invention we had procured and were developing was going to pay out big-time, I fed off the excitement of my partners.

Following a meeting one day, after hearing the number of units we were going to sell and the dollars we were going to make, I jumped to conclusions and decided to buy a shiny new red Corvette, straight from the factory. Claude assured me it was a slam-dunk. No chance of failure. He even said he personally would make the payments if things didn't work out. Yeah, right!

We went down to the Chevy dealer in La Grande and had it ordered in five minutes. It was all done in my name, with my funds. However, I made a mistake that wasn't abnormal for me. I didn't tell my wife about it until later. She was not quite as excited about it as I was. In fact, this experience taught me at least one of the kinds of things that could really tick Michele off.

I loved that '88 Vette. It drove nice, looked nice, and got me in a little trouble. Coming home from Spokane one night, I was cruising between 110 and 120 mph. A car tried to pass me just before I got to Ritzville. He was unsuccessful. I turned off at Ritzville and headed for Connell.

Unbeknownst to me, a state patrolman was coming toward us on the highway coming from Seattle. He spotted us racing and zeroed in on me. I didn't know he was behind, and chasing me, or I would have taken it up a couple of notches. I continued cruising down the highway without a clue while the cop was frantically trying to catch up. I think I was averaging around 110 mph. We drove in this mode for about 50 miles, passing cars left and right. He was focused and I was oblivious. He finally caught up and turned his multi-colored lights on.

He told me he thought he had lost me several times. He asked if I had been drinking and then lectured me on the dangers of speeding. In the course of our conversation, I mentioned I had been in the sheriff's reserves and had taken training to drive at high speeds.

He changed his tack slightly and said that he could drive his cruiser safely at high speeds and that I could probably drive my Corvette safely at high speeds, however, many other cars and drivers couldn't operate safely at high speeds and that was the reason for speed limits. I thought, "Hey, maybe I'll just get a warning out of this."

He came back with a reckless driving ticket.

I flew up to Ritzville for the court a few weeks later. They read me my rights. I told the judge that the cop agreed that I could drive my car at high speeds safely. He didn't buy it and gave me a five hundred plus dollar fine. I wrote the check and figured I was done with that episode.

A couple of weeks later, I got a notice in the mail that I had to surrender my driver's license. "What?!" I called the Adams County prosecutor and he said a reckless driving ticket included a mandatory six-month suspension of your license. I wasn't going to go six months without driving. So I prepared my defense.

I went down to the local sheriff's office and talked to a deputy. We read the RCW (Revised Code of Washington) concerning the definition of reckless driving. I called the Adams County prosecutor back up and informed him that I was going to hire a lawyer, spend lots of money, and beat the ticket.

My reasoning: The cop had told me that I was driving safely. I had informed the judge about the cop's comments that I was driving safely, but he apparently wasn't listening. The definition for reckless driving was something like "jeopardizing the safety and lives of others." I didn't believe I was jeopardizing anyone. From the patrolman's comments, he didn't believe I was either.

In court, I was never told that I could lose my license when they read me my rights. The first time the state informed me of that was when they sent me the notice several weeks after court. If I had known that, I would have asked for a postponement and had a lawyer represent me.

The prosecutor said he would look into it and call me back. He said it was going to be a mess to unravel because we had already had court and the judgment had been processed. He called me a few days later and said he had talked to the judge. I think the judge was made aware that he might have a battle on his hands. He told the prosecutor that he had intended to drop the charge at court, but had forgotten to. (I don't think so!) The prosecutor said they were going to drop the license forfeiture, but keep the fine.

I was happy with the outcome. They already had my money. I still had my license.

• •

The Valve Alarm never took off. We went to trade shows. I peddled it door to door. The people who used it liked it. It saved them gas and money. I developed brochures, customer testimonials, store displays—on and on. It never really took off.

We sold something like 10,000 units. The welding and gas companies we had originally contacted realized, somewhere in their market research, a relevant truth. They would sell Valve Alarms one time. However, with the Valve Alarm saving substantial amounts of gas for their customers, dramatic reductions to their gas sales would also occur. By their own estimates, they figured as much as 50%. Gas sales were their bread and butter.

They decided they didn't want anything to do with the Valve Alarm. This was not some wild, conspiratorial rumor often heard about the oil companies squelching gas-saving inventions. It was what they told us.

We paid Russell Elmer as agreed. One dollar for every unit we sold. He had given us $100,000. We sold almost 10,000 units. He got back about $10,000. He came down with cancer in the middle of this period and just about died. A few years later, he reappeared on the horizon and wanted his money. He began nosing around and found out about my new Corvette and the Mooney airplane I had purchased. He was positive I had bought those items with company funds—his funds.

I visited him several times and showed him the books. We accounted for every dollar that came in and went out. In the course of our reviews, I found that John, when things were looking promising, without my knowledge and with Claude's urging, bought himself a country club membership for $600. That was the only Benzco money ever taken by any of the principals. When I discovered that, I was bothered. It gave Russell a little bit of traction for his claims, however, it was very minor considering all the money that had been collected and spent.

Things gradually ground to a halt. We had a bunch of inventory we couldn't sell. Snap-On Tools had promised us a big sale if we bought an expensive insurance policy to cover them for liability. We spent 30 grand for a policy and yet they didn't buy a single unit.

We paid Kim, the inventor, around $85,000 for royalties and the license to manufacture and market it.

In the course of business, we had taken out a line of credit and it was past due. Claude and John were getting a lot of pressure from the bank. It was in Benzco Inc's name, but John and I were personally signed on it. It was over $20,000. I didn't have it and John didn't have it. Eventually I had to personally borrow the money and pay the bill. John didn't pay a thing. He signed over his Benzco stock to me, which was worth nothing. This was the tail end of Benzco's business life.

It's easy to fork money over at the beginning of the enterprise when everything looks hunky dory. It's another thing entirely to shell out money to bail out a dead dog, however that's what I ended up doing.

Russell wouldn't let up. He called me and I went to La Grande and met with him. He and his wife and son-in-law drove up to my house and we spent a day going over the books. His memory was bad. The stuff we had covered previously was forgotten and we had to rehash everything. I felt bad for him, but I had done nothing wrong.

One morning in church, a friend came up to me and said that he had just been to church in Connell. A gentleman had cornered him and asked a lot of character questions about me. It was Russell. He had driven 150 miles to a neighboring church of mine to try to dig up some dirt.

I started getting letters and calls from an attorney's office in Pendleton. Russell was suing me! I spent a lot of time going over the situation with them and finally stopped hearing from them. I think they realized he didn't have a leg to stand on and let him know the status.

Months later, I started hearing from another attorney in La Grande. Russell was trying to sue me again. I contacted a friend of mine, Lowell Barber, an attorney. We had had some lunches together through the course of the enterprise and he was very interested in the Valve Alarm. His father-in-law had invested $10,000 in it years before. I shared the story with him and asked if he would represent me.

We made a trip to La Grande together and met with Russell and his new attorney. We went over the same old facts once again. I never heard from Russell again. I'm sure his new attorney told him the same thing as his old attorney. Benzco had honored the contract. Sales had not been what we had expected, but he was paid for every Valve Alarm we sold. He didn't have a case. Lowell wouldn't give me a bill. I put some new tires on his car in appreciation. He's a great guy.

• •

Some ten years later I got a call from someone in Portland. They had heard about the Valve Alarm and wanted to buy it from me. It just so happened I was in hot water financially with the tire store, as was normal.

The opportunity to perhaps sell the now defunct business was mouth-watering. I was in desperate need of some money to keep going. I was the sole owner of the now broke company and precariously hanging out on the edge of a personal bankruptcy cliff.

The interested party told me that they were especially interested in the four-cavity injection mold we had. The molds were the major part of the deal for them in their mind. I told them they were at Kaso Plastics in Vancouver and I would round them up.

A few years earlier, I had received a letter from Kaso Plastics, the company who had originally produced Benzco's plastic parts. They were scrapping all their inactive customer's molds and told me to contact them if I wanted to keep the molds. I called them and stated I wanted the molds. They had originally cost us around 100 thousand dollars.

At that time I made a 250 mile trip to Vancouver to get the molds. In the course of my conversation with the Kaso representative, I indicated I still had some interest in trying to make the old project sprout new wings and there was a possibility of future changes and use of the molds. The guy said that since there was a possibility of using them, they would hold onto them for me. He assured me that they wouldn't throw them away.

Years later, after receiving word that I had a possible sale for Benzco assets, I called Kaso and told them I needed the molds. They called back and informed me that they had sold them for salvage to a scrap yard.

This was not what they had agreed to do. If I had known they were going to scrap them, I would have brought them back to Basin City. However, they had no record of my visit or request to hold on to them. They told me I was out of luck.

I started going through old records. I didn't know the name of the guy I had talked to at Kaso. I had a rough idea of the time frame, but that was it. I spent several days going through paperwork, phone records, my journal and planners, computer files, and everything else I could think of.

After many hours of searching, I happened upon a notation in an old day planner of a name that I thought might be the guy. I called Kaso and asked for him. Bingo! The girl told me he no longer worked there. I gulped and asked her if she had his phone number. She did.

I called him and he remembered my visit and our conversation. His comment was that Kaso often had a problem with maintaining control over their customer's molds. He said this was not the first time that they had disposed of a valuable mold.

I had also found phone records that showed my calls to them after they had notified me they were going to scrap the mold. My substantiation was limited, but better than nothing.

About this time, I found out that the party in Portland had lost interest in buying Benzco assets. However, they had alerted me to the mold situation that I probably would never have discovered otherwise.

I made an appointment with the manager of Kaso and traveled to Vancouver once again. When I entered his office, I carried several large files of meaningless paperwork I had grabbed out of my office before I left. I figured that it would look impressive and ominous to the Kaso manager. On top of the files were the phone records and notes from my conversation with their former employee. I began the conversation by outlining the facts. I used their former employee's name and referred to my previous trip and visit to pick up the molds. I then picked up the phone records and told him that I had evidence of the calls I had placed asking them to not destroy the molds.

I could tell he was concerned by the facts. I then told him that I had a couple of ideas as to what could be done about our problem.

The first was that Kaso could make me new molds and replace the ones they had lost. I told him the cost would probably run them $120,000 or so. He didn't disagree. I didn't tell him that by this time I had absolutely no use for the molds, as the potential buyer had evaporated. I was hopeful that he didn't choose this option.

The second choice was that Kaso could write me a check for $60,000 and my claims for the molds would go away. It was up to him as to what choice they made.

He told me that he would have to talk to the owners, but he doubted that they would do either. I said if that was the case, I had a lawyer who would be glad to get involved. I was thinking, if push came to shove, I could enlist Lowell's services. The next week, I got a check in the mail for $60,000. It was unexpected and a godsend.

Speaking of godsends, another incident of similar proportions comes to mind. Back in the early 1990s, computers were becoming something many people were acquiring. I bought one and immediately began looking into the possibilities of dabbling in the stock market.

I found a "service" that was in the business of touting penny stocks and speculative companies. The possibilities of making big money fast and paying off some of my debts was intriguing. I looked at their recommendations daily and began tracking a number of stocks. Throughout that year, I bought and sold a lot of stocks. Anxiety, angst, and exhilaration attended my dealings in the market.

My conservative wife was not in favor of me playing the stock market, however, she was a sport. For Christmas that year she bought me a big dartboard with stock symbols written in each section of the board. Six darts were also furnished.

As always, I was operating on borrowed money. I probably ended up breaking about even after all the money had changed hands, except with one particular stock.

The company was called 'Systems of Excellence.' Its ticker symbol was SEXI. It was a company back east that supposedly had new technology in regards to video conferencing. I watched the stock gradually inch up from 20 cents to 50 or 60 cents a share. The "news" from the advisory service was that this was going to be a hot player.

They claimed Johns Hopkins University and their affiliated hospital were instituting it in their organization, as well as the White House, the Pentagon, and other impressive establishments.

I bought a bunch of shares. I bought them somewhere around 60 cents a share and in a week sold at $4.00 a share, netting a little over $10,000 profit. "Not bad for a week's work," I gloated. I told J about it. I think he bought a thousand dollars worth. The stock kept climbing. I got greedy. I bought more than $55,000 worth of SEXI on margin (loaned money) and sat back to watch my new business venture soar.

It tanked. The more it dropped, the more determined I was to hang on until it went back up. I didn't think I could afford to bail out. One afternoon E-Trade called me. They had just discovered that I was sitting on a pile of near worthless stock that had been bought on margin. They sold me out and demanded I cover the bill.

I was so ticked. I couldn't believe they had sold my entire portfolio without my instructions. Didn't they know that was my money? At the time, I wasn't thinking clearly because, in retrospect, it wasn't my money.

In the weeks to follow, I started feeling major heat and had to go to my bank and get a loan for 55 grand to pay E-Trade. I was still mad at E-Trade. I was determined never to do business with them again. "That'll show 'em," I thought.

The stock continued to fall until it got down around a penny a share. The SEC got involved and the principals of the fake company ended up in jail. Systems of Excellence went bankrupt. I had another large, long-term debt tacked to my wallet.

The stock advisory service and SEXI officers were in cahoots together. They actually had no product. They ruined their lives and many of their investor's pocketbooks. Tens of millions were lost.

I spent the next few years trying to keep tabs on these scoundrels, during and after they got out of prison. To be honest, I entertained thoughts of going to Florida and Virginia and breaking a few kneecaps.

Approximately 12 years later, I was talking to J one day and he asked me if I had gotten anything from the SEXI bankruptcy trustee. I hadn't. He said they were notifying shareholders to turn in proof of their losses. There might be some kind of payment if it turned out there was anything left after the attorneys did their thing.

I asked him if he was going to turn any paperwork in for his shares. He said no. It had been too long ago and besides, nothing ever gets disbursed after a bankruptcy. The lawyers end up with whatever is left.

I agreed. I've never recovered money from a customer who has gone bankrupt. You come up with all the paperwork, attend the bankruptcy meetings, get all riled up again, and it's all for naught; another wonderful law that relieves people of responsibility and nails others who don't deserve the hit.

However I had lost 55 grand. I was still bugged enough that I figured I would make an effort. Even if I got back fifty or a hundred bucks, it would make me feel a little better. Maybe I would take J to dinner with the money.

Now I had to round up the actual stock sales sheets. It had been 12 years and I had no idea if any related records even existed. I went upstairs to the loft and began going through old boxes of records. After a couple of hours, I was still empty handed.

Then I had a thought. There was a slight chance that the accountant I had used during that period just might still have them. I called and told them what I was looking for. They assured me they didn't have them. Records that old were no longer around, but they would look.

A few days later I got a call that they had found them. I didn't get too excited. I knew the chances were still next to nil that I would collect anything.

I got on the internet and found information on how and where to send the documentation. I was shocked to find that I was just a couple of days from the deadline of submission. I filled out the pertinent information and on the deadline day, looked for a post office. I was on an overnight scouting trip with my boys when I tracked down the post office in Cle Elum. I slipped the letter in the slot.

Time passed. A year came and went. I didn't hear a thing. Again, I was in a severe cash crunch when I walked out to get the mail one morning. Rifling through the letters, I noticed an envelope from the Systems of Excellence Trustee.

"Cool," I thought. I waited until I was back in the house to open it. I still was planning on a check for a hundred bucks or so.

I opened the envelope and pulled out a check made out to me for $3,000! I started yelling. Michele ran into the kitchen to see what was wrong. I showed her the check. Neither of us could believe it. She went back to what she was doing.

I noticed there was another piece of paper in the envelope. I figured it must be a letter detailing the disbursement. I opened it up and gawked. It was another check! $52,000! I started yelling again.

CHAPTER 20

BURNED

Back in the 1980s, without going into a lot of detail, I had a big problem with the scrap tires that were constantly piling up at my round rubber sales establishment. To get rid of them was prohibitively expensive, although a few mishaps with inadvertent combustion created blazes that, on a few occasions, partially lightened my outside inventory.

One particular year, I asked my neighbor Dale if I could dump a few scrap tires in a ravine on his farm. He said it was no problem so I started hauling tires. It is amazing how fast those things can pile up. After a year or so, there were several thousand "junks" in his ravine.

One morning he pulled into my shop all excited and upset. He had noticed a pickup from some government ecological agency driving around the tires and he was afraid he was going to be in big trouble. He wanted those tires gone.

What was I to do? What I really needed was a tire cannon that would blow truck and tractor tires out of Buster's canyon, preferably an automatic model. Since there probably wasn't such a thing, I borrowed my buddy Vard's boom loader that he used to load hay bales onto trucks with. It had a long boom that hooked and lifted bales so I figured I would try it. Several hours were spent hoisting tires out.

Twelve tires were moved, seven tires were successfully lifted out. At that rate I figured I would finish the job in the year 2525, if man was still alive (YouTube "Zagar and Evans"). In other words, it would be nigh impossible to retrieve them out of the ravine. And what would I do with them after I got them out?

I was feeling a lot of pressure. I drove up to the site at dusk one eve and all of a sudden noticed smoke emanating from the pile. Before I could do anything to reverse the situation, things were out of control. The wind was howling and I began wishing and hoping and praying that the wind would magically dissolve the smoke. No such luck.

The wind fanned the petroleum-based units and within a few minutes I had an unstoppable inferno on my hands. It was in the backcountry of the county, but with the smoke and flames blowing in the wind, it was visible for many miles. A friend who was traveling from Walla Walla 60 miles away said he saw the smoke in the distance and wondered what disaster was occurring in the faraway reaches of his neighborhood.

The fire went on for hours. A few cars came by on the nearest road to see what was happening. I went out and told them everything was okay and under control. I knew if the proper authority got wind of the incident, I could be in a heap of trouble just for being in the proximity of the event. Finally, around midnight, the majority of the episode had exited to the next county and I was still out of jail. The next day or two, the community buzzed with talk of the big fire. I was glad when the conversation turned to other matters.

On Tuesday of the next week, my phone rang at the tire shop. An official from the Department of Ecology identified herself and said that her department had been informed that there had been an unauthorized tire fire the previous week and that I was the one responsible. My heart sank.

She continued by informing me that they were going to do a full-scale investigation on me. They would be visiting the next week to do an audit concerning where all my scrap tires were going. She said her boss would be doing the investigation and would be calling me in a few days for an appointment. His name was Sam Burnham. She bid me an official goodbye. I meekly hung up the phone.

The next six days were pure agony. I had read about situations like this in tire magazines. Tire store owners had been nailed by Big Brother for tire fires. In some cases they had been fined hundreds of thousands of dollars. I had trouble scraping together enough money to pay a speeding ticket so I knew I had a big problem on my hands.

I slept very little. I wrote down every entity and person I could think of that had taken any of my scrap tires. A few farmers had taken them to place around the sprinkler risers in their fields to keep the vegetation down. A few dairy farms had hauled truckloads of tires to use as weights to keep the plastic covers down on their silage piles. I had cut up a few tractor tires, turned them inside out, and sold them as cow feeders.

There were probably a few other rare occasions when people had taken tires. I racked my brain for substantive corroboration. I dutifully documented every name and occasion and could see that when I got the big audit I was going to be woefully short of defensive evidence. I envisioned myself behind jail bars while conferencing with my bankruptcy attorney as to how I was going to pay the big fine.

I was short on sleep. My blood pressure was up. I was hard on my kids. My help at the shop kept a safe distance from me. My wife's patience was tested—all because of Sam Burnham.

The next Sunday after church and lunch, my wife suggested that we go for a nice, peaceful drive and just get away from all the pressure. It sounded good to me. I was frazzled. We drove down the street and Michele suggested we stop at the Mackay's, who were good friends of ours.

I didn't want to. Even though I'm a social guy, socializing at this particular period in my life seemed very unattractive. I just wanted to be left alone. I knew that if we talked to anyone the tire fire subject would be brought up.

Michele insisted so I reluctantly agreed. As we neared their home, I noticed there were a large number of cars parked around the place. I *really* didn't want to stop after seeing all the cars, but she was resolved to stop.

We walked up to the door, knocked, and were ushered in. There was a small horde of people in the house, including many of my friends who lived in the area. My parents were even there. There must have been 20 to 30 people in the house. This was an unusual mix of people who had gotten together on a Sunday afternoon, which is not normally a Mormon party day. I didn't understand what was going on, but just slunk off into a corner to stay out of the limelight and mentally lick my wounds.

People were gabbing about this and that. I just sat there, trying to mentally drum up more places for Auditor Sam to look when he asked me where I was putting all my customer's old tires.

After a few minutes, J stood and took charge of the group. He called my name which put me more at less ease. "Ben, we're glad you stopped by this afternoon. We've got someone here we'd like you to meet." I couldn't imagine who that would be.

"Ben, we'd like you to meet Sam Burnham!"

I looked and Cindy Mackay came around the corner carrying a big cake. The cake had a bunch of black licorice shaped into round objects, which looked a lot like a pile of tires. She must have poured some starting fluid on them and thrown a match to the mix. They were blazing away. It was an awesome little tire fire, if I do say so myself.

It took a few seconds for everything to compute. Then I felt great relief and the desire to kill, both at the same time. She handed the cake to someone just as I took off after her. We ran around the house a couple of times before I got winded and had to quit.

She and Lana Nielson had cooked this little scheme up after they had talked to me during a Cub Scout activity the week before. They realized how vulnerable I was from the situation and decided to have a little fun. They rounded up someone I didn't know to make the call to me and set the prank into motion. I must admit, it was a great stunt. I was greatly relieved that Sam Burnham was not an employee of Ecology. Even though I was off the hook, I informed Cindy that she better watch her back. I wasn't finished with the prank she set in motion.

A year later, Michele was pregnant with Will. I hatched a plan, using Michele as a decoy. I asked Cindy if we could drop our two-year-old daughter, Christianne, off at their place when Michele went into labor and I took her to the hospital. She said that would be great.

A few days later, on a pleasant summer day, I decided it was time for Michele to go into premature labor. I called Cindy and told her Michele was having pains and I would drop Christianne off. I took Chris down and told Cindy that she could just put her out to play in her fenced backyard and then I left.

A half hour later, I drove back down to Mackay's, snuck around to the back of the house, and motioned for Chris and Brooke (Cindy's little girl) to come over and talk to me. I opened the gate and told Chris to come with me. I told Brooke that if she didn't tell her mommy that Chris had gone with me, I would buy her an ice cream cone. She happily nodded that she wouldn't tell.

We made the getaway without any further attention. I took her home and delivered her to Michele. I then made the diagnosis that Michele wasn't in labor after all.

I waited for another half-hour. I grabbed our video camera and stealthily made my way back toward the Mackay residence. Basin City was fairly uninhabited at the time, which made a fine video setting for the scene that was unfolding.

Cindy was hysterically running back and forth between the deep canal full of water and the vast landscape of sagebrush beyond her house. I was far enough away that I could just barely hear her frantically yelling, "Christianne! Christianne!" It was the best.

I hid behind a small shed and shot my video. The video turned out to be pretty interesting, but all you can hear on the audio is someone laughing his head off.

Prior to the initiation of the payback, I had called Cindy's husband Kent and her brothers who work close by and told them of my plan. I told them she would probably be calling, but to ignore her pleas for help. They performed admirably.

Cindy was devastated. She had lost a child. She had frantically called her husband to come and help her search, but he never showed up. She called her brothers to come and help her search but they, too, were no-shows. After an hour of fruitless search and rescue, she finally gave up, resigned to the fact that Christianne was no more.

I snuck back to the gate where I had originally heisted Chris. Cindy was sitting on the back step of her house with her head in her hands. I had the video camera rolling and said in a slightly taunting voice, "Ohhh, Cinnndieeee?"

She looked up and experienced the same emotions that I had the year before in her front room. In her eyes I detected a look of a desire to kill, and yet, great relief. I think I had that same look the year prior.

To this very day, I'm referred to as Sam Burnham once in a while.

When people hear this story they accuse me of being heartless. On the contrary, I put Cindy out of her misery after a measly sixty minutes. Cindy kept me in misery for a whopping one hundred thirty-two hours.

• •

Speaking of Kent and Cindy, there was a post on Facebook recently from their son Brandon. He grew up with my kids in Basin City and became an F-15 fighter pilot in the Air Force, serving in South Korea, Afghanistan, and several bases in the States. I told my wife I want the following story stamped on my headstone. It let me know that, for once, I did something right. It read as follows:

Ben,

My 9-year-old ran his bike into my Bishop's car today and put a dent in it. Tonight when I came home, he sat down and told me about it. As I was explaining what we had to do to fix it, an experience from my childhood came to mind.

To catch the rest of you up:

When Brad Nielson and I were 10 years old, he came over to my house for an afternoon. I took him with me as I drove up the street to rototill the Casper's garden with my little tractor and rototiller. After the garden was tilled, Brad wanted to drive the tractor back to my house. He had logged more time on the seat of a tractor than I had so I didn't think twice about giving him the wheel. I jumped up on the hood and he jumped into the driver's seat. He put it into gear, popped the clutch, and promptly drove it into the side of the Casper's white suburban, leaving a large dent and gouge in the rear fender. It was an awful feeling for a 10-year-old.

After we told Ben, he got an estimate, and a few days later, Brad and I both had to reach into our bank accounts and pull out $600 each to cover the $1,200 repairs. That was a lot of money for a 10-year-old. We went over to Ben's house, gave him the money, and again said we were sorry. As we went to leave, Ben stopped us and then gave our money back to us. He said that he just wanted to see if we would follow through, then thanked us for being honest.

To my knowledge, there's still a white suburban that drives around Basin City with a very large dent in the right, rear fender. I grew up seeing that dent at church & school activities, and all over the community. And every time I saw it, I thought of how grateful I am for a man that would sacrifice his own possessions to help two young boys learn a valuable lesson, and show them mercy in the process.

Ben, you may not have earned yourself a spot in heaven (yet,) but you sure earned yourself a spot in the backseat of my F-15. On my last flight in the Air Force, I've decided that I'm going to sneak up to Basin City, land on a straight road (probably Glade North), let you climb in, and then give you the stick and just watch you fly. I'll do it with a smile because I know you're the kind of guy that will come visit me in jail afterwards.

Thanks again.

Your Friend,
Brandon "Bullet" Mackay

Thanks, Brandon. You made my day. I'd forgotten all about that.

• •

Back to practical jokes. One of the people who attended the Sam Burnham party was Steve Price. Steve is a great guy, like me. Also like me, he tends to get a little excited if things don't go right. I prefer to stay out of his way when his fuse is lit.

One night we attended a nice, formal, church dinner. The Relief Society (women's church organization) had prepared a good dinner with a lot of fancy table trimmings and decorations. There was a gym-full of people in attendance. Positioned in different spots at the various tables were fishbowls as centerpieces with a live goldfish in each one.

During the dinner, I got an idea. I picked up a fishbowl and walked over to the table where Steve was sitting. He was entertaining the diners around him with stories while he was eating. As he talked and ate, I reached in and snared the fish. As Steve looked the other way down the table, I dropped the squirming gold protein pill into his drink of ice water. Everyone on both sides of the table saw the action except Steve. I held my finger to my lips so they wouldn't advise him of the situation.

Shortly thereafter, Steve quit talking and chewing and hoisted his drink to his lips and started sipping. After a few seconds, he stopped and his eyes crossed, focusing on the goldfish that was swimming less than three inches from his parched lips. I felt sorry for the guy and the fish. They were both in a difficult position. Steve wanted to throw the drink down, discover who had polluted his drink, and start throwing punches.

The fish was swimming upstream but losing headway.

Unfortunately for Steve, there were 10 or 15 pairs of eyes focused on him, waiting expectantly for his next move. Therefore, killing me would not have been socially advantageous. So he sat there, cross-eyedly focused on the fish. His hands started to tremble. Snickers were breaking out around the tables. He may have considered sushi, but finally he slowly set his drink and seafood back down. I got the impression he was no longer thirsty. I hurried back to the safety of my own table.

● ●

Our next door neighbor was Lyn Barnett. He owned the local hardware store and I've known him for many years. One day I was working in the garden behind our home and Lyn pulled up in his driveway in a big rush. He left his pickup running, pulled on his emergency brake, and ran into his house. He even left his door open.

I immediately realized that an opportunity existed for a little fun. Then I thought about how I'm always making people mad, so I dismissed the thought. Then I remembered it was April Fool's Day, so I had no choice but to spring into action.

I jumped over our fence, scurried over, and crawled into Lyn's pickup. I lay down on the seat so I could stay out of sight and waited for Lyn to return. Soon I heard his front door slam which was my signal to release the emergency brake. This normally would not be of import since most driveways are level. Unfortunately for Lyn, his driveway is sloped on a fairly steep incline.

As soon as the brake went away, the pickup started to roll. I was hiding out of Lyn's sight. I couldn't see his reaction, but I could hear it. He gasped and yelled and I could hear his feet begin pitter-pattering on the sidewalk in an effort to stop his truck before major damage ensued. With every step he took I heard another gasp of regret and anguish. It made my efforts so worthwhile.

I let the pickup pick up speed for a few more seconds before I pulled on the brake handle and the rig slid to a halt. I rose up off the seat and was rewarded to see the look of alarm on Lyn's face just before it turned to a look of relief, surprise and realization that he had just been had.

Whenever I go out and work in the garden, I enjoy the memory. Lyn has since moved away. I'm not sure why.

CHAPTER 21

ADRENALINE BY APPOINTMENT

We were short of help at the tire store. One evening I got a call that Gene Satake, a local farmer, needed a flat fixed on his tractor. He asked if we could get to it early the next morning. I decided that I would go up and fix it at 5:00 am.

When I arrived in the field the next day, I got a little surprise. The tractor and tire were both a little unusual. I wasn't familiar with the type of tractor and the tire was abnormally wide and heavier-plied than most rear farm tires. I think it might have been a European brand.

I jacked the tractor up and pumped the calcium chloride out of the tire. I began breaking the tire down. This was a tough job because of the uncommon configuration of the tire. Eventually, I broke it down and set about taking the tire off the rim. It was a drop-center rim with a 12-ply tire, complete with an unusually thick bead. To those who aren't familiar with these terms, just accept my word that this job had turned into a beast.

Using three tire irons and having been born with just two arms, I began working on the bead. It was stiff and unyielding. I twisted and reefed and jerked and pulled to no avail. Finally, the only solution I could see to the problem was to hook one iron under the bead and pull it back 180 degrees to the point where I could precariously hook it on the other side of the rim. I eventually completed that portion of the job and then began trying to get another iron started under the bead so I could dismount another small section of it. Right about then, I noticed a few stars exploding in the heavens.

The first tire iron had lost its grip on the other side of the wheel and began an ultra-quick journey toward my head, specifically my left temple. It contacted my noggin right before the stars appeared. They materialized just before I flew backward for an impressive distance. I landed flat on my back in the mud. By the time I hit, I was out cold.

Some time later, I awoke from my beauty sleep not feeling so well. I shakily got to my feet and tried to remember what day it was. Things eventually started coming together. I realized that even though Gene needed his tractor fixed, I was not the man to finish the job on this particular morning. The nearest home and phone belonged to a friend, Bill Odermott. I left the truck and staggered to Bill's.

When Bill answered the door and saw my swollen head, he got a little concerned. I told him I needed to use his phone. He thought I was going to call the ambulance. I assured him we didn't need to do that.

I called one of my guys and explained the situation. A couple of employees came up later and fixed the tire. I called Michele to come and get me. I went home with double vision and a major headache.

After cleaning up, I got in the Corvette and drove myself to town. By this time my eye had swollen shut. The doctor examined me and said that I had been very lucky that the blow hadn't killed me. It struck the soft spot next to my eye and fractured the eye socket. He said there wasn't much he could do for me except give me some pain pills. I walked around with a black indentation on the side of my head for the next six months. The indentation looked exactly like the end of a tire iron.

• •

A year and a half after I bought the Corvette, I needed to refinance and obtain a bigger loan. My banker informed me that one of the terms of the new loan was that my level of fun was going to drastically be reduced, and therefore, I had to get rid of the Corvette.

I stopped at a dealership one day on a whim and told the salesman I needed a pickup. I must have also said something like, "I really want to get hosed," because that's exactly what happened. We walked outside and looked at their fleet of new pickups. I pointed to one a couple hundred feet away and said, "I'll take it."

I left for an hour so they could get it ready. Five minutes after I left the dealership, I called the salesman back and asked how much it was going to cost. A few minutes later, I realized that I wanted an automatic transmission. After another call he assured me it was. Good. I felt a little stupid. I should have asked about these points before I bought it. I chalked it up as something I should remember to do in the future.

A little later I wondered if it had air conditioning. I called. It did. Good. I should have asked about that too. After a few more minutes, I remembered there was a $1,000 rebate on their pickups. I called and asked if I got the rebate. "No, that wasn't part of the deal," he said. Not good. I paid list price for the rig and the dealer kept the rebate. "I really should have spent a little more time shopping," I told myself.

Two days later I remembered that I had left a loaded .357 magnum under the seat of the Corvette I had traded in. I went back to the dealership. No one knew anything about it.

This was similar to the time when I sawed off a double-barreled 12-gauge shotgun because I was having so many problems with theft at my tire store. I kept it behind the seat of my pickup so I could have quick access to a firearm in case I accosted a burglar. A few mornings later, I noticed it was gone. Someone had rifled, pardon the pun, through my pickup during the night and grabbed the gun.

• •

Speaking of guns, in the early 1990s I purchased a bunch of them.

During the early years at my tire store, I amassed a large amount of junk tires of all sizes and types. A conservative and fairly accurate estimate of the tires piled on three lots behind my tire store was 30,000 to 40,000 tires. It was a huge liability.

The county health department began giving me grief and ultimatums. I figured the tires were on my property, not the county's so it was none of their business. Another angle I took was that they weren't my tires. Other people (tire customers) had left them there. The guys at the health department didn't buy any of my arguments. Over a period of years, as time went on, the county got harder to work with.

As near as I could tell, it was going to cost me at least one hundred grand to clean up the mess. I didn't have the money, but the threats from the county were becoming ominous. One day, I had an epiphany. Why not turn the lemons into lemonade?

The next time I rendezvoused with the inspector, I asked if they would keep bothering me if I turned the tire-laden lots into a paintball course and used the tires as barriers and shields for the paintballers. He stammered and hem-hawed around and finally admitted he had no idea. He called me a few days later and said that after much research they had determined the junk tires in a paintball course would no longer be junk tires.

This was just as I suspected. By sticking a sign up advertising a paintball course, my junk tires were now an essential part of a paintball course maze. For once, the government helped me win a round and kept the code enforcers at bay.

I had to make my field of dreams take shape. For three months one summer, my kids and I moved tires. It was a job! Tens of thousands of tires were pulled off the pile and laced into walls and barricades. Tractor tires, truck tires, car tires, pickup tires, and implement tires—nothing was exempt.

We made a nice looking course. Toward the end of the transition, another tentacle of the county stopped by in the form of the fire marshal. He wanted me to get rid of the dry weeds and cheat grass so as to negate the fire hazard. I agreed.

That afternoon, I was out in the maze moving the last few hundred tires into position. I picked up one side of a truck tire and suddenly noticed that there was a fully grown skunk that had been under the tire that was now standing between my legs.

I was in shock and awe. The manifestation of my startled state required me to yell, jump, and throw my hands outward as fast as humanly possible. Unfortunately, the ring finger on my left hand came in contact with a tire situated three feet above the skunk's tail. The finger jammed back with such force that the bone in the back of my hand snapped.

I was in pain, but first things first; I had to get out of there! The skunk exited one way and I went the other. I'm sure we had about the same amount of adrenaline flowing. Soon after, I came up with a slogan for the paintball course: "Adrenaline by Appointment!" You could always count on the adrenaline kicking in when you were at this location, anything from paintballs flying at you to skunks appearing between your legs.

The next day I went to the hospital and was operated on. Walt Hales, who was just beginning his practice in the Tri-Cities and who later became close friends with my family, pinned the bone back in my hand. I no longer sport a knuckle at the base of my left ring finger.

The day after my operation, I was feeling a little weak and wasn't planning on working. However, I figured I should get somebody to clear the weeds out for the fire inspector.

I grabbed a helper at the tire store. We went out to the old junk tire pile/new paintball course and I gave him instructions for clearing and burning the weeds. I even lit up a couple of small fires to demonstrate. I was just getting ready to head home when I looked back and saw that a fire we had started earlier had crept over and lit up some tires. There was a substantial blaze going.

I yelled for someone to call the fire department and then hurried over and did my best to fight the flames. The fire trucks showed up and we fought a large tire fire for a couple of hours. It was a scary time, but not near as bad as the fire we had several years later.

The same thing happened again. The fire marshal came out and told me to clean up the weeds. We started the process, being very careful not to let the fire get away from us. Unfortunately, within ten minutes we had a blazing inferno going. The two times we had major infernos at the tire pile were because the fire inspector had bugged me to get rid of the weeds. We would never have had a problem if he had left us alone.

The second fire was very serious. Farmers in the vicinity brought dozers, backhoes, and tractors. At least 100 people showed up to help or gawk at the flames. I had a 12,000 gallon, full propane tank across the road in major jeopardy from the heat. The utility company showed up. Power lines were in danger and transformers were disconnected. Black smoke billowed up and filled the sky. Five or six fire engines were there. Several came from Connell, 18 miles away.

We did our best to separate the rows of tires from the flames. They were hot and fast moving. Water from the fire engines did little to douse the flames. It took over four hours before we finally had things under control.

The next day I was out among the ruins with my backhoe, trying to straighten up the mess. A county truck pulled up and an inspector from a different department got out, ticket book in hand. He wrote me up for the unauthorized fire, oblivious to the fact that the bogus county order to clean up the weeds was the instigator of the problem in the first place.

Years earlier I met up with this same inspector who was accompanying a deputy one day at a fertilizer business in Connell. They were very concerned because they had found an empty plastic 5-gallon bucket on the side of the freeway.

They had their hazmat manuals out and were quizzing the fertilizer employees as to what type of chemical had been in the bucket. The name of what they thought was the chemical was molded on the bottom of the bucket—Ropak. In looking through their materials, they were unable to find a chemical labeled Ropak. The fact that the spilled chemical seemed to be unlisted and top secret heightened their concern.

I chuckled at the cutting-edge intelligence of these "hazmat investigators." I told them that Ropak was the name of the plastic bucket manufacturer. They closed their hazmat book and left as quickly as they could without turning their lights and sirens on.

● ●

We finished the paintball course in the fall and immediately began hosting parties. I bought 50 paintball guns and the related equipment I needed to be functional.

We operated for 15 years or so. I built a large balcony with Plexiglas windows overlooking the field for spectators. I planted trees around the entire perimeter in an attempt to shield people on the outside from getting hit by the ammunition being shot on the inside. I put a shed in across the road to house the equipment and supplies.

After the repositioning of 40,000 tires, I installed ten tall power poles around the field. I borrowed a climbing belt and some climbing shanks to strap around my legs and began learning to climb the poles. It's harder than it looks! Not only did I have to climb up to dizzying heights with two, little pointy pegs sticking out of my insteps, but I needed to stand there for extended lengths of time working on the light installation.

The muscles would tighten up after a few minutes and it became extremely difficult to concentrate on the work. Now when I see a guy on the top end of a power pole, I have a greater appreciation for his service.

Liability was my biggest worry as I ran the paintball course. I'd heard many accounts of people losing an eye because of an errant paintball. I had masks for everyone, but I still worried. The rules of the game were that when a player got hit, the game was over for them and they should make their way out of the course until the next round.

The normal human tendency is to leave the mask on until the game is over. When a player gets hit, the game is over for him, but not for everyone else. Many times when the player got hit, the mask would come off while the bullets (balls) kept flying at him. He continued to get shot at until he got out of the field of play. When he pulled the mask off and yet was still in the field of play, those eyeballs were big targets just waiting to get hit. If that ever happened on my field, I would be one big target for those formerly functioning eyeballs' attorney. I never carried insurance for the enterprise. I knew I couldn't afford it.

My son Derek and I had to constantly monitor the field and scream on a regular basis at people to put their masks back on. One afternoon, a party was going on and a player was put out. He took his mask off just as another participant 50 feet away shot at him. The ball nailed him an inch below his eye. It was scary. This happened on the same afternoon that I got the first visit to my store from the president of Les Schwab, Phil Wick.

When he arrived, I showed him around the store. He asked what all the popping noises were emanating from the paintball field. I took him out with all the other Schwab brass. They climbed up onto the balcony and watched. When it was time to go they had a hard time pulling Phil away because he was enjoying watching so much.

I was relieved that he wasn't bugged that my store was so unorthodox.

Most of the paintball parties were in the evening. Big parties from the Tri-Cities, Yakima, Walla Walla, and other communities would show up. We even had one group from Portland make the 250-mile trip several times to enjoy the facilities.

The only problem was that most of these parties would stretch into the wee hours of the morning. I made good money, but as I got older I got tired of the hassle and the late nights.

Finally, I shut the field down. Not because of the hassle, but because all my equipment got ripped off. Some local scoundrels broke into the shed and took a good share of the equipment. When I discovered the theft, I slept by the shed, figuring they would come back for the rest. After a few nights of waking up with icicles in my hair, I gave up. A night or two later, they came back and got the rest.

A few months went by and a kid called me from Connell. He told me that some kids were selling paintball guns at the high school for $20 each. The guns had originally cost me $220 each. I contacted the cops and they apprehended the scofflaws. I ended up getting paid back for the loss, but I never opened the field again.

This brought back the county enforcement people, however, by this time I had started clearing out the tires. I eventually made them happy with the depletion of the former paintball accoutrements. Les Schwab had initiated a junk tire disposal program which allowed me to reduce the no-longer-a-paintball-course pile.

• •

When I opened the paintball course, I was on the lookout for opportunities to advertise the facility. On the 4th of July each year, the residents of the Basin City community have a parade down the main street. I enlisted the help of Eppich Grain and one of their 40-foot semi trailers. We set a few straw bales at opposing ends of the trailer and I grabbed some kids to participate in a free paintball demonstration.

As the truck and trailer made its way down the parade route, we blasted away. Paintballs flew back and forth like crazy. It was a lot of fun and gave the crowd a firsthand look at the sport of paintball.

I worried that a shot might go awry and nail someone in the crowd. Fortunately, everyone stayed safe. The only casualty was a little kid who saw all the brightly-colored paintballs landing on the road. He thought they were candy like all the other paraders were throwing to the spectators, so he picked one up and started chewing. It soon landed back on the street. Paintballs taste very nasty.

• •

For many years, I entered one type of display or another in the parade. One year I got in my Les Schwab pickup and drove it in the parade. It was just a Schwab pickup with no displays in the back, idling down the street. Nothing unusual except it didn't have a driver. I had a handheld radio and had given Kent another radio. He was in the Eppich Grain truck right behind my entry.

I lay on the floor of the pickup with one hand reaching up to the steering wheel and the other hand grasping the brake pedal and the other hand operating the radio. Kent gave me steering and braking instructions. I would have trusted no one else to guide me. I barely trusted him. It was very frightening to be motoring down the way with crowds on both sides and yet not having a clue as to where I was. Every few seconds I would engage the radio with my third hand and ask Kent if everything was okay. He constantly assured me it was but I still felt worried.

I could hear people saying stuff like, "How are they doing that?" and, "That is crazy!" I even heard one teenager say that he was going to look and see if anybody was in the truck. He ran up, looked through the open window on the passenger side and returned to his friends saying, "Nobody's in there. I have no idea how they're doing that!" I was surprised he didn't see me on the floor.

When I reached the end of the parade, Kent told me I could sit up and take back the controls. Just as I raised up, I saw the sheriff of Franklin County, Richard Lathim, standing 100 feet in front of me, in the middle of the road, directing traffic. When he saw me emerge, he simply shook his head side-to-side, as if to say, "Now I've seen everything."

Which reminds me of a story about Richard. One night at a Connell High School basketball game, I was sitting in the stands. I noticed Sheriff Lathim come into the gym and take a seat in the bleachers, far from where I was sitting. He never saw me or looked my way. We are friends but seldom cross paths. When we do, it's usually because one of his deputies and I have had a run-in.

At halftime, he stood up, took his nice leather jacket off and laid it on the bench where he had been sitting. He walked down and out of the gym. I saw my opportunity. I made my way to his leather jacket, quickly procured it and found my way back to my remote location.

After a good five minutes had passed, the sheriff came back in the gym and walked up to his former seat. He saw immediately that his jacket was gone and he started looking around. A maximum of five seconds elapsed before I read his lips. I have never really been able to read people's lips before but I was successful on this particular evening. They distinctly said "Where's Casper?"

I chuckled all the way over as I returned his coat. I'm glad I left his wallet in the pocket.

CHAPTER 22

LEST I DIGRESS—A FEW TANGENTS

Many years later I met an older gentleman who told me that he had heard of a way to burn tires with no smoke. This seemed impossible to me so I set out to see if it could be replicated. For weeks, I fabricated and re-fabricated a smokeless tire incinerator. Many test burns with lots of smoke ensued, but eventually I got it to work. I'll never forget the amazement I had as I watched lazy, blue, smokeless flames emanating from my custom smokestack. It clearly was a success, but lack of capital, a few remaining technical problems, and the need to generate a living stopped further tire burning, at least for the moment.

A decade or two after that in the winter of 2004, having been continually haunted by the memory of my past success, I decided I would take a few days and investigate a tire burner that was being assembled in Cedar City, Utah. It was 903 miles away and even though the weather was foreboding, I had a window of free time and became determined to make the trip.

Once I lock onto a plan or an idea, there's usually no turning back. The roads were icy and snowy from my home in Washington all the way to Cedar City. My wife advised me of the dangers of driving that far in the snow, but I'm not scared of a little frozen water. I love a challenge and felt that it was an ideal time to check out the machine.

I took off in the late afternoon, which meant I would be driving all night. At least 80% of my trip was over slick roads. Traffic crept along at 20 mph. Cars and trucks were scattered regularly along the roads, usually in a bent up or upside down condition. Cops were busy at all the accidents so there were no speed traps. I didn't have to worry about speed traps anyway since the speed limit was 75. I kept it between 60 and 70mph.

In retrospect, I went a little fast for the conditions. I made it to my destination even though several times during the trip I lost control and slid back and forth, front first and then rear first, multiple times progressing sideways down the icy trail that is usually called the interstate. I did slow down when I came upon other traffic.

I checked out the burner and headed home. Coming back, I got word that my very likeable and alcoholic brother-in-law had passed away by employing the use of a low budget pain killer, sometimes referred to as a bullet. I had to make a detour over to Prineville, Oregon to do some Les Schwab business before heading home. Soon I was heading north up the Columbia Gorge where the roads were clear. This allowed me to step up my speed a bit. Before I made it out of the Gorge, I got stopped by an Oregon cop for doing 82 in a 65. I told him my situation, but he had no mercy. At that point in my trip I felt justified because I was on a medical emergency to get home and comfort my wife.

Speaking of untimely deaths, I had a service man named Gary Ford who did a lot of our outside tractor tire repairs for many years. He was a little slow, but very dependable and a good guy. He worked for me for a good 12 years. One afternoon he was on a service call fixing a Harobed tire. He had a jack under the front axle of the machine, lifting it up. The axle slipped off the jack. He sensed it was slipping and pulled his head. The tire and wheel had been taken off when the axle dropped down to the ground. Gary got his head out just in time, but not his hat. It was crushed under the axle.

I sometimes got a little frustrated with Gary as far as him getting up to speed with some of the work he did. One day I was out in the side yard of the tire store and heard a semi truck grinding gears and making its way to the area I was in. The truck would grind gears, lurch ahead, and then grind a few more. I saw that Gary was driving the truck. After he finally got it parked, I walked over and told him that if he couldn't drive a vehicle without grinding gears he should get someone else to drive who could do it correctly.

I asked him what he had done to the truck. He replied that he had just put a new tire on the trailer. I looked back at the rear of the trailer and could see that the new tire he had just put on was not touching the ground. I walked back and saw that he had put a 9-00x20 tire on a trailer that had 10-00x20 tires on it. This took me over the edge. I knew if I let him continue working, someone was going to end up dead from one of his mistakes. I walked into the shop and told Don that Gary needed to go.

Before this incident, the last few times I called the shop and Gary answered the phone, it sounded like he was drunk. His speech was slurred and he didn't make sense some of the time. I had never known Gary to drink. I appreciated his service in the past, but I felt like I just couldn't keep him. I felt bad.

A few months later, I felt much worse. After he left my employment, he was diagnosed with ALS. I visited him at his home, but he was in the throes of Lou's disease by then and was unable to speak. He died soon after.

• •

During the early 1990s, a few of my friends and I bought snowmobiles. For some reason, the majority of us drove like maniacs. Full throttle was the desired setting. We went on a lot of night and Saturday rides and had loads of fun. It is against all odds that we didn't have a fatality. We would ride for a good six hours as hard and as fast as we could over trails, meadows, hills, mountains, and whatever else we came upon. Looking back, I feel a little foolish at how hard and fast we moved along.

Machines did get buggered up and close calls were the norm. There were probably 15 of us that actively rode over a span of several years. I don't think anyone even broke a bone.

A couple of experiences come to mind from those days.

Courtney Calaway and I had just started a Saturday ride in the mountains around Ellensburg. We were blazing across a meadow at 50 or 60 miles an hour. Courtney was off to my right a couple hundred yards. I happened to turn my head and look at him just as he encountered a tree bowl. A tree bowl is caused when the wind whips blowing snow around a tree and doesn't fill the void in downwind from the tree. The bowl can be five or ten feet deep and as large as 20 feet in diameter, depending on the size of the tree.

Tree bowls are invisible to riders coming upon them, especially when the speed is cranked up. Courtney and his machine were doing fine one moment and were flying in a downward angle the next. The machine nose-dived into the opposite bank and Courtney crumpled like a rag doll into his handlebars and then flew over the front of his machine. I was shocked by the sudden accident. I figured he was seriously hurt and headed toward him.

He lay in the snow for a long time. I assumed we were done for the day. His body was beat up and his hands were hurt and bleeding. We stayed there for a good hour while he recovered, but finally he got back on his machine and rode the rest of the day. Courtney is tough and loves to snowmobile.

• •

One afternoon a bunch of us from around Basin City went riding. At one point, we came upon a long, tall slope that culminated in a very steep ridge at the very top. It was probably a climb of at least a quarter of a mile. Everyone started trying to tackle the mountain.

Lynn Eppich made it almost to the top before he stalled out. Tim Taylor had a machine *that* had seen better days and by that time was duct-taped together. It stalled halfway up the hill. I couldn't see Lynn from the bottom, as the route curved around to the left as it reached the top.

I took off and was moving at a swift clip as I went around Tim and continued my ascent. I reached the top but was unable to go over the ridge because Lynn was stuck and parked in my path. I stopped and found myself in a precarious position, trying to inch back down the hill in a backwards position. Unfortunately, my sled started slipping and I quickly lost control of it and bailed off.

The snowmobile began rolling downhill and then started flipping end over end, picking up speed as it headed straight for Tim and his sled. Tim was intently working on his machine with his head down. I started yelling at him to watch out. Tim looked up, saw the flipping problem, and jumped out of the way. My sled continued to endo until it nosedived into Tim's.

It was a pretty awesome crash. I expected Tim would be a little bugged, but I was more than a little surprised at his reaction. He was mad, even though his machine hadn't been in all that great of shape before the crash. He hurriedly made his way through the snow to my snowmobile.

I am not kidding about this next part. My sled weighed at least 500 pounds. Tim was so ticked that he grabbed my machine, pulled it out of the side of his machine, picked it up, and threw it down the mountain. It slid down to the place where we had originally begun our climbs, crossed a trail, and continued on down to the bottom where a creek ran.

I was a little dumbfounded. My sled had been thrown to a location almost a half a mile from where I was standing. I trudged down and after some extended exercise finally got it started, intending to rejoin the group. Unfortunately, the crash had busted a tie rod end and I was done for the day. We cobbled it up so I could at least make my way back to the trailer. I sat there in the cold at the trailer for several more hours until the crew had had enough riding and returned to go home.

I'll never forget the way Tim threw my snowmobile through the air that day.

• •

When our oldest daughter Hauni was 16 she was invited to go water-skiing with some friends at Scootney Reservoir. We knew the family who extended the invitation and didn't worry. Michele and most of the other kids went to a family party while Michael and I stayed home. Michael proceeded to cut his foot on a tin can lid so I ran him in to the emergency room to get stitched up.

While in the hospital in the middle of the afternoon, I got a call that Hauni had gotten tangled up with a boat prop and was on her way to the hospital. I hung around the emergency room and soon Hauni arrived.

Our friend Debbie was backing her boat up and had forgotten about Hauni being in the water right behind the boat. The prop made four nasty gashes on both legs and cut ligaments in her knee. They prepared her for surgery and rolled her in. She recovered from the accident with no problem except some long scars on her legs. I still shudder when I think about how close she came to losing her legs or her life.

• •

Michele and I decided we wanted a hot tub. We built a deck behind the house and bought a tub. I enjoy sitting and relaxing in the cold winter air, surrounded with the hot water. Many are the nights I will retire to the tub when I can't sleep.

I generally use it in the middle of the night when no one else is up. I've gotten in the habit of wearing my birthday suit since no one else is around and I hate having wet clothes on in the cold air when I get out. This mode of hot tubbing has become a habit for me. Even if my family is still up, I unobtrusively do the tub in my natural condition. No one is the wiser as I wrap up in my towel when I exit the water.

One evening after a relaxing session, my towel and I made our way back into the house. Michele and the kids were in a bedroom off the hall watching TV. There was a chair in the middle of the hallway next to the bedroom they were in. I figured I would run down the hall, leap over the chair, and glide into our bedroom at the end of the hall. If I did it fast enough, they would just see a blur out of the corner of their eye as my towel and I flashed by.

Everything went as planned until I landed. About the same time my feet landed on the floor, my head landed on the top edge of a tall, wooden dresser that was just inside the bedroom door. It nearly knocked me out. I struggled to maintain consciousness while trying to keep my towel in place and find the correct words to express my displeasure. I decided, and verbalized instantly, that whoever put the chair in the hallway and the dresser in the bedroom were at fault. In retrospect, it was probably me.

Everyone came running in to see what had happened. I was not in the mood for a public viewing. I shooed them out and used my towel to mop up the blood, au natural.

CHAPTER 23

BACK ON THE RANCH

In 1992, I decided I wanted to farm again. My dad had MS and was easing out of the farming picture. Even though my tire stores were struggling, I wanted to be on the farm. I approached my dad with the idea. He was violently opposed. As we had done for 35 years, we argued. Neither side budged. This process went on for several weeks.

About this time in my life, I had kind of decided that maybe I wasn't as normal as I had always thought I was. Michele and I were visiting a psychiatrist in Spokane on a regular basis. I went through a very complex battery of tests. They determined I was bipolar. Through my conversations with the shrink, I also started realizing that a lot of my attitudes could be traced back to the relationship with my dad.

The stuff I went through with him as a little kid was still haunting me. Our back and forth hadn't matured much since my early years. The doctor told me I needed to just forget my anger and forgive my dad. One of the manifestations of my anger was our arguments. He told me that even if I was right, I should quit arguing with Dad. This advice was extremely hard for me to accept, but I finally realized he was right. I determined, at 35 years of age, to quit arguing with Pops.

I went home. The next day I knocked on his door. We sat down, as usual, to argue except I didn't sit down to argue. He started the conversation. "Ben, I am dead set against you farming. You don't have the time or the..."

"Dad, I've decided that you are right. I'm not going to farm."

He looked at me as if I had just spoken in a foreign tongue. I had never started out agreeing with him before, during, or after a conversation. He must have thought he hadn't heard me correctly. He recovered his thoughts and then started again. "The reason I don't think you should..."

"Dad, you're right. I'm not going to farm."

This time he looked like I had just stabbed him through the heart with a javelin. He started crying. I think this was the only time in my life I saw my dad cry. He didn't know how to handle this new set of conversational rules I had just handed him. He was dealing with the shock and depression brought on by just recently finding out he had MS.

And now his oldest son, who had always done battle with him, was acting totally out of character. "Everybody hates me. I'm worthless." Shocking statements started coming from him that had nothing to do with my offer not to farm. It took me a while to reassure him that I loved him and that I just wanted to get along.

As soon as Dad saw that I was going to go along with his way of thinking about not farming, he said, "I'm going to sell you the land and I think you should farm." It is amazing what a little reverse psychology and agreeing can do.

It was the beginning of a new way of life for us. We quit fighting. We got along so much better. It was one of the best things I've ever done. He died 17 years later. I am so glad we cleared the air. I have no regrets concerning him. Had I kept up the arguing, I would have many.

Many years later we were discussing a minor difference of opinion and it was starting to escalate. I dropped out of the argument and mentioned I wasn't going to argue. I also commented on how nice it had been that we had gotten along so well since we changed our debating style. He said, "Yes, and you know who started it, don't you?" I responded that I did know. Then I asked him who he thought initiated the change. He said, "It was me." I just laughed and said, "You're right, Dad." Saying that didn't bother me in the least.

So we battled for 35 years and abruptly stopped the pattern in just one morning. No more anger. No more frustration. We should have tried that tactic 32 years earlier and saved ourselves a lot of bad times. But I didn't have a shrink when I was three.

• •

So I farmed for the next five years. I worked my butt off. My tire business suffered because I was never there. I loved the hard work. I bought the 100 acres from him that I had learned to drive on when I was five, picking up hay on the old truck while he stacked it. It was the same farm that had the pond that I had almost drowned in as a young boy. It held many memories.

I farmed another 80 acres up by my folks' house. I had wheat in it the first year. Kim had just invented a wheel that ran on circle irrigation systems. It eventually became the Agri-Trac. It was on my circle of wheat that we tried to work the bugs out. The circle was always down. Kim's wheel was tearing up my gearboxes. The crop suffered from not getting enough water. But it helped Kim discover the Agri-Trac's weaknesses and develop a product that has sold millions of dollars worth since. I even made a little on it as I gave him money at the beginning for a slice of the action.

Several other years I had alfalfa. I did most of the work myself. I bought a little old tractor to pull a baler. I bought some beat-up rakes to turn the hay and a baler to bale it. I used my dad's tired and worn-out swather and Harobed. It was an enterprise doomed for disaster. Even though I worked hard, I didn't do it right. There are many things I should have done differently.

One night I was baling and having trouble with my tractor keeping the generator charged up. I shut the lights off and baled from the light of the full moon. After a few hours of baling in the dark, I noticed a pair of headlights coming up the road toward our shed and grain bins. The lights went out when they reached the buildings. I was sure it was some thieves moving in for the steal.

I was in the field a good half-mile away. I shut the baler and tractor down and ran toward the culprits in the moonlight. All I had was a flashlight in the off-position for protection.

I got in the vicinity of the shed and all of a sudden heard a woman scream and male voices yelling. I ran over to the grain bins and found the car hidden behind them. I turned on my flashlight. Two Mexican guys were in the back seat assaulting a girl. Some of her clothes were torn off. She was sobbing and telling them to get away.

I asked the girl if she wanted me to call the cops. She said, "No!" The guys jumped out the doors and got in the front seat and drove away. I think I interrupted a rape, but the girl was so afraid of her attackers that she didn't want the cops coming.

I'm lucky the guys didn't come after me.

• •

The first year I got back in the farming game and bought the acreage from my dad, it was a real struggle. There was a lot of underground, steel mainline pipe that had been buried decades before to service the irrigation needs of the farm. I spent a lot of that first summer digging 3-foot trenches and locating holes that had rusted through the old pipe. Then I tried to fix them.

The pipe was usually filled with water, and the leaks always ran a few inches of water into the trench that I was standing in. Since the only way to fix the rusty pipe was to weld it, I had a difficult job on my hands. Rusty pipe doesn't weld. Water seeping out of the holes complicated the repair. I soon learned that standing in water while welding is always a shocking experience. I was given regular, hefty, and jolting doses of electricity as I worked. It was a very unpleasant summer as I worked to keep the system operating and the crops watered.

One Saturday evening after I had spent the majority of the day in a trench welding pipe, my wife called and said I needed to get home in a quick hurry so we could go out to dinner with our friends, Vard and Verdene Jenks. Hauni, my oldest girl, was with me. She was ten at the time.

I had a problem. I had two pickup trucks in the field where I was working. I needed to get them both back up to the shed for the weekend. If I left one, it would be vandalized or ripped off by Monday. The shed was about a mile away.

I often assume that just because I know how to do something, I can give a 30-second spot of training and the trainee will know as much as I do about the subject. I thought this would be the case with Hauni.

She had never driven before, but I needed her to drive one of my pickups to the shed at that particular moment. She didn't want to. I insisted she obey her father because I was in a hurry to go to dinner.

I put her in the cab of one of the pickups and told her to stay behind the truck that I was going to drive. She kept protesting, but it did her no good.

I told her how the steering wheel operated. "You simply turn it the direction you want to go. If you need to go fast, you push on that pedal on the right by your foot. If you need to stop, push on the bigger pedal on the left. Okay, let's go." I put the transmission in gear for her and told her to push on the brake until she was ready to go.

I jumped in the other pickup and motioned for her to follow me. I drove down the main county road and turned left to go up the lane to the shed. A car was coming the other way. I didn't even think about her traveling behind me. Luckily, the car passed before she got to the intersection or she probably would have had a head-on collision when she made the turn. I had neglected to give her instructions about yielding the right of way to oncoming traffic.

I drove the remaining half-mile to the shed and got out to wait for her. Soon I saw her coming. She made a slight turn into the large parking lot where I was waiting with far too much momentum. I became instantly alarmed that her foot hadn't made the transition from the gas to the brake.

She sped past where I stood, clipping along at least 30 mph. She was starting to lightly press on the brakes, yet not paying much attention to where she was going. She went past the edge of my dad's big steel shop, missing the corner of it by no more than two and a half inches. She got a little more braking action going and finally came to a stop about the same time she ran into some farm equipment.

I went back and looked at her tracks. She literally missed the corner of the shop by inches. If she would have hit it, it would have been a bad situation, as there was a thick steel beam on the inside corner of the shop. I felt like an idiot for several weeks after giving Hauni, almost literally, a crash course in driving.

• •

Quality hay back then was selling for around $105 a ton. Farmers are always fighting the weather as they struggle to put up good hay. If it gets rained on, it drops substantially in value.

One night I baled a half circle (50 or 60 acres) of beautiful hay. I couldn't pick it up the next day because the Harobed broke down and I was waiting for a part to come in. The next night I baled up the rest of the field. I had a field of primo hay waiting to be picked up, stacked, and sold. Just as I finished baling on the second night, it started raining.

Farmers usually fear the rain before the hay is baled, when it's still in the windrow. A little rain on the hay after it is baled is usually not a big problem, however that was not the case this time.

It was in the middle of the summer in an arid climate. But it rained. And rained. And rained. For a straight Noah week. The bales were soaked. After it stopped raining, I had to wait almost two more weeks before the bales were dry enough that I dared pick them up. The re-growth of the alfalfa was taller than the wet bales and was almost ready to be swathed again. The bales were spongy and very heavy from the moisture they were packing. The value of the hay had gone in the toilet.

I set out one morning to pick up the hay; crappy, spongy bales of waterlogged hay hidden in a field of green re-growth. It was depressing. I wanted to quit.

Shortly after I began picking up my first load, the Harobed stopped. The motor ran, the transmission transferred the power, and the driveline turned like a top, but the machine just sat there; the rear-end had gone out. I spent the rest of the morning taking the thing apart and pulling it out from underneath the machine. It was the heaviest item I have ever lifted.

I was by myself. I lifted it up into the pickup, flirting with a hernia and a bad back. I hauled the gear cluster to town, got it fixed, hauled it back, unloaded it, and put it back in. Another entire day was shot.

Because the hay was so heavy and spongy, it took a full week to pick up and stack the hay when usually it was a two-day job at the most. And the spotted field of green continued to grow and laugh at me. That was the most depressing field of hay I have ever had to work in.

And the nightmare wasn't over.

I finally got the mess cleaned up. It was a real drag trying to stack the soggy bales and get them to remain standing in the stack. If they didn't fall or slough down as you stacked them, eventually they would do it after you left. My stack yard was on the corner of Road 170 and Casper Lane, available for the whole world to see. It was an eyesore.

Most hay stacks are uniform, square, neat, and pleasing to look at. These stacks were falling down, tipped over, twisted, and pathetic. I felt many negative emotions every time I drove by. The hay was next to worthless.

One morning I drove by the stacks and noticed a large, white sign with red and green letters leaning up against the hay.

It said "CUSTOM STACKING, BEN CASPER, 269-4974"

Custom hay stackers haul and stack hay for other farms. They are usually very professional and "put up" the haystacks in a neat and orderly manner. The sign was propped up against one of the worst looking haystacks ever put together. I was not in the custom stacking business! My hay had been rained on, depleted in value, and now someone was rubbing it in.

To put it mildly, I was mad. I ran over and threw the sign face down in the dirt. The whole world was laughing at me! I vowed to swath, rake, and bale up the sign painter if I ever found who he was.

I drove up and told my folks. They thought it was funny! My mom got her camera and went down and took a picture of the sign up against the hay. I have an enlarged version of her picture. I look at it for a reminder every time I think about farming again.

The next day I went down to the farm and . . . the sign was back up! The heartless culprit had come back that night and reinstalled it. I grabbed the sign and hauled it off and buried it.

Years later I found out who the sign maker was. Terrill Nielson, a sixteen-year-old from the Sunday school class I was teaching, had done the deed. I think he did it as a friendly prank. I have to admit, it would have been hilarious to me if it had been done to someone else.

He's just lucky I didn't catch him. He wouldn't have been healthy enough to attend church without a wheelchair. And I wouldn't have been allowed back in church, namely because I had maimed one of my Sunday school students.

• •

During this time I had a friend who owned a dairy and was struggling to pay his tire bill. He asked me if I wanted some Holstein calves in lieu of his bill. It had been long enough since I'd had the last Holsteins that I had forgotten how stupid they were. Besides, I wanted to get paid and if I didn't take the calves, I probably would get nothing. So I got back in the cow business.

I fenced the ditch bank at the bottom end of my farm and seeded it to pasture. Technically, what I was doing was a no-no. Even though it was my land and I was paying the taxes on it, the irrigation district had a right-of-way that extended ridiculously far out into my field for 100 feet or so. The easement was intended in case the district had to dredge soil or weeds out of the ditch and needed some place to put them.

The district hadn't driven on that section of road and ditch for years. It was overgrown with grass and weeds and was ideal for grazing cows so I fenced it in.

Soon Bruce, the district water master, somehow found out what I had done. He called me up and told me to move the fence even though it wasn't bothering him. He sent a surveying crew out and drove stakes with bright orange flags on them into my field, just to show me where his right of way was. He was a consummate bureaucrat. He believed that the farmers were subservient to the district. He didn't realize that without the farmers, he wouldn't have a job. We paid his grocery bill.

I requested that the Pasco office send someone out with more authority that I could talk to. Don Olson came out. He had previously been a water master and was now working in the central office. He was a great guy. He listened to my story and then told me not to worry about it. The problem was solved in about five minutes. We then spent several hours leaning on the back of my pickup talking about all the people and common experiences we'd had together. It was a good afternoon. I enjoyed it much more than I would have if I had been talking to Bruce.

Don was a great friend with my dad for many years. A few years later, after my dad had passed away, I heard that Don had ALS, Lou Gehrig's Disease. He continued to work, but was going downhill fast.

One day I passed a district pickup while traveling down to the farm. As I passed, I was surprised to see that Don was driving it. I realized that he was going to get out and work just as long as he possibly could. I stopped at the end of our lane and waited for him to come by. I flagged him down and walked up to talk to him.

I was surprised at how far down the ALS path he had progressed. He couldn't speak. So I talked. I told him what a great guy he was. I told him what a great family he had. I told him how much my dad thought of him. Tears ran down both of our cheeks. I told him that I loved him. I could tell through his eyes and his tears that he had the same feelings. He drove off. I am very grateful I had that opportunity to say goodbye to him.

A short time later he passed away. Without design, with the many cemeteries and hundreds of thousands of graves in the area, he is buried 20 or 30 feet away from my dad. They both would be, or I should say are, pleased.

• •

That wasn't my last run-in with Bruce. I owned a small water system in Basin City. The previous owners decided they were tired of dealing with the state water requirements and were going to shut it down. I had to have water at my tire store so I bought the system from them.

J Wood put in a big potato storage building across the street and asked me to provide water to him. I ran underground pipe toward his building. I asked the county road engineers if I could go under their paved street with a water pipe. They said, "Sure, no problem, as long as we don't know about it."

I had to tunnel under the road, which was no small feat, and then run the pipe across a district canal. I planned on running the pipe alongside a bridge that went across the canal. Normally, I would just do it and no one would be the wiser. It wasn't going to bother anyone.

However, since I had already had a run-in with Bruce, I decided I'd better go by the book and ask his permission. He said I had to fill out a permit application. After I did that, he would get back to me. When he came back and delivered it, the permit stated that I could put two inch pipe in. I had requested three inch pipe on the application. It was a small thing, but it bothered me. Some people with a little power always seem to throw a wrench in the works to show off their authority.

I complained to him and he said he had no control over it. The engineer in Pasco had made the decision. It was out of his hands.

So I drove to Pasco. I went in and talked to the engineer. He said he didn't care what size pipe I used. He told me Bruce was the one who had made the downsizing stipulation. I told the engineer I was going to put three inch pipe in. He said, "Fine."

I drove back out to Basin City. Bruce pulled into my parking lot shortly thereafter and tore into me for "making him look bad." I told him I was not trying to make him look bad. I informed him he had his program and I had mine. I was going to do what I could to make my program work. He drove off, a very unhappy water master. I continued installing the three inch pipe. (Many years later I was very glad I put the three inch pipe in. I sold the system to the Basin City Water and Sewer District. They hooked my line into their line at the very spot where Bruce tried to force me to downsize. The three inch pipe was an absolute necessity for their hookup to have sufficient flow to my old system and customers.)

I had one other experience with Bruce. Down below my farm is a bridge that spans the waste way canal going to the Columbia River. The bridge is part of the main road that goes to the Tri-Cities. The county decided they needed to replace it and began dismantling it. They closed the road. Somebody ordered the wrong parts and instead of taking a month to put up the new bridge, it took an additional five months before they got it finished.

This greatly inconvenienced the locals. We had to drive back north and around a long circuit every time we needed to go south to town, adding an extra fifteen miles to our round trip.

Within a mile of this bridge, just below my farm, another bridge provides access to an orchard. It was possible to take this alternate route through the orchard, bypassing the broken bridge and continuing on to town. The manager of the orchard is Rick Orozco. He's a great guy and understood the problem. He didn't have a problem with people taking the alternate route through his orchard until the bridge was fixed.

Bruce decided to do another maneuver. He talked to Rick and told him that he could put up some barriers for him and block the traffic so they couldn't go through the orchard or use the ditch road leading to the main road. Rick said no. He knew what an inconvenience it was if people couldn't use his road. He said, "I'm not going to do that to my neighbors."

The next afternoon, I came home from town using Rick's orchard road. In spite of Rick's demurring of the road blockage, Bruce had ordered his men to load up, haul, and smack down two large and heavy grates.

Where did these grates end up? You guessed it— road-block to our short-cut.

I was a little bugged. I jammed the pickup into four-wheel drive and went through some scary terrain on the steep side hill below the road before I was finally able to get around the grates. I drove down through the orchard and found Rick and another neighbor marveling at Bruce's handiwork and audacity. I got out and we discussed the situation. I told them that by morning the grates would be gone.

That night, I called Scot Haws and asked if he could help me around midnight. He showed up and we drove to the site. The grates weighed four to five hundred lbs. each. We hooked a chain to them and dragged them out to where we could access them easier.

We lifted and grunted. After a good hour's time, we had both of them loaded on the back of my pickup. They measured 20 feet by 20 feet. They were so long we had to chain them on or they wouldn't stay on the bed. We then gingerly drove down through the orchard in the moonlight. It was a covert operation.

Arriving at the functional bridge, we got out, unchained one grate and pushed it off the bridge. It was dark. When the end of the grate hit the water flowing under the bridge, a long and narrow white splash could be seen. A few seconds later, the entire cross section of the grate fell over and hit the surface, resulting in an awesome moonlight-enhanced splash. The same process occurred with the second piece. Mission accomplished.

The next morning Rick called me. He said that many people had complained to the Pasco office the previous day about Bruce blocking the road. Pasco had read him the riot act and told him to get those grates picked up! Two guys were there at Rick's home, asking where the grates were because they needed to put them somewhere else in a ditch. They couldn't fathom how someone could have moved the heavy suckers. He whispered in the phone that he wasn't going to tell them who did it.

I told Rick, "That's where they are—in the ditch."

He asked which ditch and I said, "The one under the bridge below your orchard." He laughed and said the workers couldn't understand how the grates were moved because there were no tracks. (This was because we had to drag them for a ways before loading them on the pickup. The grates erased all the tracks.) They thought maybe a helicopter had swooped down and carried them away.

They had to bring in a truck with a crane on it to retrieve the grates. I would imagine one of them had to take a swim in the ditch to get the chain around the grates.

I love it when common sense wins in the end. I haven't locked horns with Bruce for several years now. It's been nice.

CHAPTER 24

WORKING WITH THE STUBBORN

Over time I built up a nice little herd. I really enjoyed having the cows. I brought a bull in to breed them in the early summer. Getting a new batch of calves the next winter was very satisfying. I had originally started out with Holstein bull calves, but gradually acquired some Hereford and Charlais beef cows.

The only problem was that I didn't live on site. I lived eight miles away in Basin City and the dang things were constantly getting out. I burned a lot of gas driving back and forth, checking my little herd, and making sure they stayed inside the fence.

One Sunday morning I took Derek, who was about 12 at the time, down to check the cows. They were out. I told Derek to drive the pickup down the ditch rider's road and stop at the end. I told him to make sure the pickup blocked the road where I was going to herd them. He was to herd them through a gate near the road and not to let any cows get past him. With him blocking them, they would move off the road and into the pasture where they were supposed to be.

I sent him on his way and then walked a half a mile to retrieve the cows. Once I got them started Derek's way, they took off running. I looked down where Derek was supposed to be standing and saw nothing. He was sitting in the pickup reading the Sunday comics. It had taken quite a bit of time and energy to put this plan into motion and now it was disintegrating because of Blondie and Dagwood.

I started screaming at him with words that weren't appropriate for a Sunday morning, pre-church activity. About the time he heard me yelling, he also heard and saw a herd of cows stampeding past the pickup he was sitting in. It didn't take him long to realize he had really screwed up. He jumped out of the pickup.

It was too late. The cows went running into the neighbors hay field and we spent the next hour trying to herd them back.

The closest neighbors we have are a German Baptist family named Root. On a regular basis, our home phone would ring. It would be the Roots. "Your cows must be out. We just heard a car slam on its brakes and skid to a stop."

Many times these calls came at night. I am one lucky cowboy that I didn't have a lawsuit from a car vs. Ben's livestock accident in front of Root's home.

I would often check on the herd and find cows outside the fence, grazing in the neighbor's hay field. In the fall, the green, luscious hay would paralyze the cow's stomach valve and cause it to bloat and die. It always seemed the cows that bloated were the best and biggest of the herd.

It's a relief to be out of the cow business.

• •

One summer while I was farming Michele's brother, Doran, came up and stayed with us for a month. He was living in Utah on the tail end of his marriage that had produced four children. He was alcoholic. He was a very likeable, talented guy who couldn't leave the sauce alone. We knew he was about at the end of his rope so we offered him a place to stay and an opportunity to try to dry out.

He showed up one Sunday morning while we were at church. We got home with our little kids and Doran was sitting on our steps, drunker than a skunk.

He started crying and carrying on. We felt bad for him and promised we would do everything we could to help him. We gave him a bedroom upstairs and tried to set some ground rules for the future. I felt that not only should he quit drinking, but he should quit smoking at the same time. I felt the drinking and the smoking were connected. He wouldn't go for that. It was too much. He was probably right. So I started buying his cigarettes.

He had a lot of bills that were haunting him and his wife in Utah. Not only did we babysit him for a month, but we helped him catch up on his past-dues to the tune of five grand plus. It was a 24-hour a day sacrifice. My work took second place to watching him every minute. If he got out of my sight for a few minutes, he headed for the bar.

One time he made it into the bar before I realized he was gone. I found him there, just getting ready to order. I guided him back to our home.

At nights he would sit in the open window of his bedroom smoking. We didn't smell it and didn't realize what he was doing until I found a pile of cigarette butts on the ground below several weeks later.

He was an electrician and did some work for me. I put a new sprinkler package on my circle on the farm and had him do most of the work. We played basketball with the kids in front of the house in the evenings. He was a lot of fun, but the situation was unnatural and a drag on all of us.

He toyed with the idea of getting an electrician's job in our area. He surveyed the want ads and got an appointment at the Lamb Weston potato plant. I still remember that the boss who interviewed him was named Joe Dosh. When Joe asked him what he wanted to accomplish if he got the job, Doran said, "Joe, I want your job."

Joe offered him a job, but Doran must not have been serious. He didn't take it.

Finally, after a month had passed, he pronounced himself cured. He left one morning after I had gone to work. That evening when I talked to Michele about his departure, she mentioned she had given him a couple hundred dollars to get home on. This was in the days before high-priced gas.

I told her she should have given him $50 for gas money. With all the dough she gave him, I knew the first thing he would do was buy beer. I told her he wouldn't make it home.

We went out to eat that night. When we got home, one of the kids had written us a note: "Doran called. He's in the Jerome, Idaho jail."

Michele's grandma died a week later. We picked Doran up on the street in Jerome on our way down to the funeral. They had just released him from jail. It turned out that on his way home from our place, his pickup heated up and toasted the engine just before the cop pulled up and arrested him for DWI.

He had been sitting in the slammer for a couple of weeks. I've never seen anybody so glad to get a ride home.

He was always threatening suicide. What do you do?

One afternoon several years after his extended visit, he called. He was obviously drunk. "Ben, I've got a bomb duct taped to my body. I've got it wired up and I'm holding the switch. I'm going to blow myself up."

Doran was always a kidder and I thought he might just be drunk and goofing around. We talked for a while, but he seemed serious and intent on ending it. Finally he said, "Alright, on the count of three I'm going to kill myself. One..., two..., two and a half..."

I burst out laughing. He was starting to count in fractions. That made him mad. He started yelling at me and I tried to stifle my laughter. We spent a lot of time on the phone that afternoon. I told him to go take the bomb off, take a nice warm bath, crawl into bed, and sleep it off. Things would look much better once he rested and sobered up. He finally agreed to follow my counsel.

He called later that evening and thanked me for my advice. The booze had worn off and he was feeling much better. He went through several rehabs.

He never did get away from it. When he was 47, he put a bullet in his head.

● ●

I had a nasty experience the fall that Doran left. I had rented my ground out to J Wood for spuds. Like an idiot, I hadn't run the water and tested the system since we had changed the sprinkler package. The last weekend before the water was going to be shut off in the canals, J planned to fumigate. Fumigation is usually done by injecting nasty chemicals through the sprinklers. It is designed to kill all the bugs and vegetation (and probably people) it comes in contact with. When a field is fumigated, the government requires poison signs with skull and crossbones to be placed around it.

Saturday afternoon the chemical man came down and set up his equipment. I hung around just to make sure everything was okay. We started the circle and a few new hoses that Doran and I had installed blew loose. Torrents of water jetted from the disconnected lines. We shut the circle down and I went out and fixed the problems. We started it again and a couple more blew off. We shut the pump down, I fixed them, and we figured all was well. The fumigation process was expensive and it was critical that everything got covered. We simply could not have sprinklers blowing off.

It was starting to get dark. It was crucial that we get the water and fumigant going. It was getting late on Saturday evening and the field man was itching to leave. We started the circle and this time started the fumigation. The guy left for home. I stood around, hoping for no more trouble. Trouble soon began. First one sprinkler, then another blew off. I couldn't shut the circle down because the fumigation was going. The chemical was Vapam. I soon learned how nasty and potent it was.

I drove out to the offending water streams, located the sprinklers that had blown off and struggled to push them against the water pressure, back into place. It was a job. More heads blew off. I was standing on the top of my truck and sometimes on the truss rods, doing my best to secure the situation.

My clothes and body had been soaked in seconds. My skin started to burn. I couldn't quit. It was getting dark and I knew it was essential that all the sprinklers and hoses were intact. I would guess after the Vapam started I fixed seven or eight sprinklers under pressure, spending an hour getting constantly drenched in the potent poison.

Finally, in severe pain, I got the last nozzle secured. I drove lickety split to my parent's house. I ran into the bathroom while peeling off my clothes. I got under the shower and washed for a long time. My entire body was burning. The cavities under my arms and the soles of my feet were the worst. If I ever come down with a chemical-induced illness, it will be because of that night.

Unbelievably, when I checked the next morning, all the sprinklers were still in place. It ran for the next 24 hours with no more problems.

• •

The first few years my dad had MS, he continued to farm. One of the jobs that irrigated farms require each year is the winterization and servicing of the circle irrigation systems. Gear box oil being topped off, water being drained out of gearboxes, and valves or pipe that might freeze and break, are items requiring attention. Another job is pumping up all the tires that may be underinflated.

One fall day I walked into the shop where Dad and a couple of his helpers were working. I could hear his compressor running in the loft above the office and tool room. That was nothing unusual. I noticed that in the back of the shop he had a big air tank filling with air. For years he had used the large tank to pressure up in the shop and then haul out to the fields in the pickup to fill up tires on circles.

My brother-in-law, Bret, was in the front of the shop talking to me. We started to walk over to a piece of equipment when all of a sudden there was a huge explosion. I looked toward the back of the shop where I'd seen my dad a few minutes before. All I could see was a big cloud of dust and possibly smoke. The oxy-acetylene torch set was back there and I figured Dad had somehow blown up the back end of the shop with it. I headed toward the center of action not knowing what I would find.

I was pretty sure that Dad would be dead or have some serious injuries. As I got closer, I could see that a steel walk-in door that opened inward was gone. A heavy steel work table was down on its side with equipment and tools scattered around on the floor. The metal pipe legs had been blown off, dropping the table and its contents. I looked around, but couldn't see Dad.

He came hobbling up behind me, thinking I'd been hurt. When we ascertained that everyone was okay, we began trying to figure what had happened.

The tank that Dad was pressuring up was an 80-gallon hot water tank. It was designed to hold 60 or 80 psi of water, not 160 psi of air like it had just experienced. When it reached its maximum capability, it decided it had had enough and took off. It had been in a horizontal position on the shop floor. The bottom of the tank blew off and exited the shop through the steel door, taking the door and the frame with it. We found the tank bottom and the door out in the field behind the shop. Then we started looking for the tank.

The tank acted like the space shuttle on liftoff. It hit the two heavy pipes that were welded as legs to the shop table and broke them off. It then zoomed across the shop and under Dad's pickup that was parked on the shop floor. It struck the pickup fender just behind the left rear tire and tore the rear bumper of the pickup off. It then hit one of the front roll up shop doors and bent it out.

It was then that we realized that Bret and I had just had a very close call and narrowly avoided serious injury. We were walking across the front of the shop when the tank took off and shot underneath the pickup. Bret had been walking a few steps ahead of me and the tank made its way *between* us after taking off the bumper of the pickup. It had happened so fast, neither of us saw it. If it had hit one of us, somebody would have been hurting. I'm not sure there would have been a fatality, but at the least there would have been some broken bones. The tank was no longer used to fill circle tires.

CHAPTER 25

WHO NEEDS BRAKES?

A few years ago, we decided to take a trip back east in my folks' motor home. My dad had been diagnosed with MS a few years before and his last, major work project of his life had been this motor home. It had been a transit bus in San Francisco. He worked on it for several years, spending a lot of money and time in the conversion. My parents did a great job on it. It became a very nice, luxurious mode of transportation, although the mechanical components were still overworked and packed with high mileage.

The engine, transmission, and numerous other parts all had to be rebuilt or replaced at various times after they began traveling in it. Looking back, I took a big risk driving that monster around the country.

Before we left, I was told that my brother, Brent, had adjusted the brakes. However, after we hit the road, I could see that we had very little braking action. I found out later that when he did the adjustment he turned the adjusters the wrong way. This backed them off even further instead of tightening them up. I should have turned around and gone home until I could get them fixed. However, we were on a tight schedule and already on the freeway so I thought maybe we would be all right. This was the first of several unwise decisions.

We headed for Utah to pick up Hauni, our oldest daughter. We met her late on the first night in Salt Lake and then headed east. We had eight souls on board, one of them an idiot.

We drove night and day. I did most of the driving, but once in a while I would slither out of the seat and hold the wheel until Derek, our 18-year-old son, could crawl into the pilot's chair. My wife hates changing drivers while barreling down the road, but I consider it a very efficient use of time, fuel, and brake linings. However, because of Brent's brake adjustment, we didn't go through much in the way of brake linings on this particular trip.

After driving nonstop across most of the country, we turned off the freeway in West Virginia. I thought we could save a few bucks by not going on the toll road so I prepared to take the exit to a different route, a side road.

I approached the exit with a little more speed than I should have. There was a semi truck in front of me taking the same exit. I started downshifting the automatic transmission and stomping on the brakes as the back of the truck got bigger and bigger. By the time I got slowed down to the same speed as the truck, our windshield was less than six inches away from the back of the truck van.

The space stayed at six inches for a good minute or two, and then gradually, the distance increased until we were back to a safe distance behind the truck. Eventually, I passed him. As I went by, I could see the driver twisting around and looking at the front of our bus. He must have seen us come up on his tail during the exit. From the looks he was giving, he was positive that we had contacted his rear end and he was looking for his trailer paint on our vehicle.

Since we had opted to take the scenic route off the toll road in order to save a few bucks, we were relegated to a narrow and windy road through the hills of southwestern Pennsylvania. It was dark by this time.

We soon ran into thick fog and accumulated a substantial following of cars behind us. The bus struggled to maintain speed going up the hills. Downshifting and slamming on the brake pedal, I struggled to keep the acceleration within reason as we went down the hills. It was a little spooky in the heavy fog. The whole family was very apprehensive as we navigated our way along.

Late that night we arrived at an RV park in Gettysburg. It was quite a relief to be able to stop and relax once I got the diesel behemoth backed into a narrow space between sleeping neighbors.

We toured the Gettysburg Park and headed for Philly, my old missionary stomping grounds. We pulled into the city late that night. After getting lost for a bit, we located the house on West Queen Lane where my friend Art lived. We parked in front of his house and waited until the next morning to knock on his door. The next couple of days were enjoyable as Art loaned us his car to make a trip to Washington DC one day, and then took us for a tour of Philadelphia the next.

We next headed for Jersey where we stayed with friends before parking across the river from New York City. We took a ferry and began experiencing some marital difficulty as we tried to decide what to do during the few hours we had to tour. We ate lunch and traveled through the city, checking out some of the sights.

Eventually, it was time to head back to the ferry, which would take us to our bus on the opposite shore. We had a mile or so to go to get to the ferry. Michele wanted to get a taxi, but I felt we could save a few bucks and get some good exercise if we walked. She got a little upset, but she and the kids followed obediently behind as I set out. It was a lot like Chevy Chase conflicting with his family in the movie *Vacation*. Kind words and affectionate looks were not our companions through the rest of the evening.

It was not a wise decision. We walked through neighborhoods that most cops would avoid. If we had been a white mother duck with her seven albino ducklings in tow, we wouldn't have gotten more stares. This was not a good neighborhood for albinos. My biggest problem was that one of my ducklings named Michele was not waddling behind as obediently as she should have been. We exchanged more unkind communications as we traversed the Big Apple back to the ferry.

The kids were pretty upset. We ended up not having pleasant memories of New York City. I must admit, we were lucky we didn't get accosted, mugged, robbed, stabbed, or shot on our stroll back. Perhaps the natives didn't dare intercede while Michele and I were exchanging volleys.

When we finally got off the ferry on the Jersey side, things got even more heated. The kids sat in the bus while we debated in the parking lot. At one point, Michele threw up her hands and said she was going to walk to an airport and fly back to Washington. It was a serious situation, but we finally got on the bus and headed out.

• •

A day or so later we had an experience that I still shudder to think about. We were heading into Hazelton, Pennsylvania. Booking down a hill into town, I was intently watching the green light at the bottom of the hill. We were rolling along about 45 mph.

I knew we were going to be in trouble if the light changed. We had too much momentum and not enough brains or brakes. Several seconds after we had passed the point of no return, the light turned yellow. I froze. I could see that we were going to go through our red light, crossing a good five seconds after the intersecting traffic got their green signal to go. We had a nice, loud air horn available for pulling just above my head, but because I was frozen, I couldn't grab it.

A fellow in a pickup to our right began moving into the intersection. I was so horrified I couldn't move. We were headed straight toward the driver's side of his vehicle. At the last possible second, he happened to turn and see us hurtling toward him.

He jammed on the brakes. Luckily, his brakes worked better than ours and we flew past him, missing his truck by inches. He put his fist and at least one finger out his window, yelling vociferously. I couldn't hear him, but I would imagine he was saying, "Welcome to Pennsylvania. Enjoy your stay! As you can see, I think you're Number One!" We wouldn't see another hand signal like that until a few days later when I let Michele drive the bus.

I don't think I've ever been that close to killing another person, at least unintentionally. Oops. After reviewing a few other incidents I've experienced, I guess that statement may not hold water.

We toured some of the LDS Church sites in Pennsylvania and New York. As members of the Church, it was a great experience to see the buildings and places that hosted the events of the Restoration of the Gospel in the early 1800s.

One night we decided we would check out Niagara Falls. We drove to the Canadian checkpoint to drive in to the falls. A guard came out and started talking to me through my side window. He asked me the usual questions about where we were going, what kind of food we had on board, etcetera. All of a sudden, he asked a question that I wasn't prepared for. "Do you have any weapons on board?" I froze. Again.

Up until that point, I hadn't even thought about the heat I was packing underneath my seat. I thought, "You know, I could save myself a lot of trouble if I just told the Mountie that we were defenseless. On the other hand, if my kids hear me lying, their whole perception of me would be crushed. Furthermore, if the Man came aboard and did a search and found my Ruger, I might be in some major trouble." So I said, "Yes, I've got a 9mm."

He immediately sprang to attention. "Is it loaded?" What kind of question was that? If it wasn't loaded it might as well be a squirt gun. I responded that it was. He told me to freeze. Unbeknownst to him, I had been frozen since he asked if I had a gun with me.

He turned and yelled at several other inspectors and they raced to the door of the bus. They climbed on and asked where it was. I pointed under the seat. They grabbed it, took the clip out and ejected the live round. Then they proceeded to go back and go through all the cupboards and drawers in our mobile home. They took quite awhile rummaging through our belongings and interrogating me concerning the gun. I had simply brought it along to protect my family.

Isn't it something how few rights we have left when it comes to protecting ourselves and our families?

Finally, they informed me that they were going to keep the gun until we came back through later that night. However, they were also going to call the New York authorities and let them know I was packing.

They told me that if I hadn't fessed up that I had a gun and they had came on board and found it on their own, they would have taken knives to all the upholstery, mattresses, and anything else they could find. My folks' motor home would have been in shambles.

We enjoyed the falls and returned several hours later. They gave me the Ruger back and called New York. The New York authorities had a conniption fit, much bigger than the Canucks. I was there for several hours. They did a background check on me and conducted a thorough interview. I thought it was severe overkill. Finally, after much cajoling on my part, they let me have the gun back provided I kept it unloaded and in one of the compartments underneath the bus.

We moved on to our next adventure.

We finally headed home after touring the Church sites around Nauvoo and Carthage, Illinois. Some of my ancestors were part of the group of Mormons that inhabited Nauvoo in the 1840s. My great-great-great grandfather is buried there. His farm bordered the Prophet Joseph Smith's farm outside of Nauvoo. Joseph stopped and said goodbye to my grandpa's family as he rode to Carthage, only to be murdered by a mob a day or two later with his brother, Hyrum.

• •

Heading west on the interstate through South Dakota, I was getting pretty tired from all the traveling. Since we were going down a multi-lane highway, I figured there was very little chance that we could have trouble. I asked Michele if she would drive while I caught some shut-eye. She didn't want to, but I insisted. We switched seats on the fly and I lay down on the couch and zonked out. Not for long, however.

The next thing I was aware of was a tremendous BANG! I jumped up and started looking for the trouble.

"What happened?!" I yelled. Michele responded with a meek, "I don't know." We were cruising along at 60. Meg was sitting in the other front captain's chair. She said she thought we hit a sign. We continued motoring along while I moved up front and tried to see if there was visible damage. Soon I noticed that the big power rearview mirror on the right side was AWOL. That was the only thing I could see at that point that was unusual.

Michele asked what she should do and I said to keep driving. I could see that we were now on a two-way road mingled with a road construction operation.

I didn't want to stop for several reasons. We had no brakes so we would have had to coast to a stop. There was a lot of traffic behind us. The construction crews weren't agitated. I figured if we had done some damage, someone would have radioed ahead and gotten them to flag us down. I was pretty upset and asking a lot of questions at that point.

When the road turned back into a regular freeway, the semi behind us passed and the driver was yelling and giving us the finger. I pointed to Michele who was driving. It wasn't my fault!

I was starting to figure out what had happened. Michele had been driving along and didn't notice the construction signs that were telling the traffic to merge into the left lane. She stayed in the right lane, took out a few orange cones, and then ran head-on into a big obstacle before finally deciding to merge. That's when she cut off the semi that had been creeping up along her left side. But I was starting to wonder, "What was the big obstacle?"

We drove past several weigh stations and continued on with my train of loco-logic, I decided if we had done any damage, the construction guys would be on the interstate flagging us down. The roadway was bare, therefore, no harm, no foul.

We continued on our merry way. We switched seats and I took over the driving again. There was no way I was going to get back to sleep.

We drove through South Dakota and into Wyoming. We had probably gone 150 to 200 miles. I looked in the rearview mirror that was still intact on the left side of the bus and noticed some flashing lights way back, probably ten miles in the distance. Gradually the lights became brighter, redder, bluer, and more ominous. Eventually, a Wyoming State Patrol car pulled up behind us. I figured it was time to pull over, brakes or no brakes. We coasted to a long, drawn-out stop.

The officer came up to the door and I opened it. "I've got the South Dakota State Patrol on the phone in my car and they want to talk to you." My heart sank. Would we be returning to spend the night in the hoosekow in South Dakota? I hoped they had family accommodations.

We walked back to his car and he handed me the phone. A very irate trooper came on the line and asked me why I had performed a hit and run with a mobile electronic road sign in South Dakota and then fled into another state. I was able to truthfully say, "I'm sorry, sir, you have the wrong person."

After I had correctly affixed the blame, he asked to speak to the guilty party. I gladly walked back to the glorified but brakeless bus and retrieved her.

She was in a mood of mortification. I don't think she's ever got so much as a parking ticket and here she was a wanted fugitive throughout the Midwest. I felt bad for her, but a little relieved that I was not going to end up cuffed in the back of the squad car.

We walked back. By this time, I could see the Wyoming cop was starting to feel a little sorry for her. She tearfully told the South Dakota constable what had happened. By the end of her story, that guy was also feeling bad for her. This was a good development. It just might save me some money and her some time in the clink.

We gave him all of our information and were then released back into the wild. Luckily, I had taken a two-week insurance policy out on the bus before we left so we didn't end up in that bad of shape. The insurance paid $8,000 for a new South Dakota electronic road sign and I ended up spending a little time fixing up the damage on the bus. As with most experiences we have had, it could have been a lot worse.

I believe Michele is a legend throughout South Dakota and Wyoming, at least in State Police offices, road construction crews, and electronic road sign stores.

CHAPTER 26

FAMILY LIFE WITH BEN

My wife and I have been blessed with six wonderful children.

Derek is our oldest son. He fulfilled an LDS Church mission to Japan and graduated in electrical engineering at BYU. Toward the end of his schooling, he was trying to decide if he wanted to stay in that field or do something else. On a whim, thinking of my need for patent legal work and how a law school education might broaden his horizons, I suggested he become a patent attorney. He fasted and prayed about his decision for several months. One night he called and said he was going to go to law school.

As he applied for admission, he submitted the following story for the essay portion that was required for his entrance:

"One summer afternoon I was driving to a football game with two of my younger cousins. Upon cresting a hill, I found that a large truck carrying alfalfa hay was in my lane moving slower than molasses. Assuming that the truck had just pulled onto the road, I moved into the left lane and hit the gas. All of a sudden my cousin looked at me with wide eyes and yelled, "Derek!" The truck was not accelerating, it was turning left. I quickly hit my brakes and swerved out of the way. Unfortunately, a large wooden fence pole aided my stop. I got out of my vehicle and immediately noticed that my car's front end was ruined.

To teach me a lesson about cautious driving, my father fixed the car up in a comical fashion. The new bumper was constructed of muffler tubing, there was chicken wire in place of a grill, and I recognized that the new right headlight had been stolen from one of our old tractors. My dad was tickled with himself. I was mortified. Due to my conspicuous position on the high school math team, I felt that my stock with the ladies was already low. This would be the final blow. I had to come up with a solution. After racking my brain for a couple of hours, I approached my father with my fingers crossed. I was scheduled to take the ACT in a month. I asked my dad if he would fix the car up in a conventional manner if I earned a score of 35 out of 36. He agreed and I went to work.

I visited a bookstore and bought some preparation guides. After getting my hands on every practice test I could find, I spent my bus rides and weekends cramming through study materials. Test day came and I gave it everything I had. When the results arrived a few weeks later, I anxiously ripped open the envelope. Upon seeing a "35" in the box labeled "composite score," I filled the house with a triumphant shout. Mission accomplished!

A few years later I found myself facing another challenging situation. I had been a missionary in Japan for about ten months when I was assigned to work with a young man from northern Japan named Hiraku Oba. I soon realized that Hiraku suffered from depression and a lack of motivation. One morning, as we were planning for the upcoming week, Hiraku went into a funk. He slumped over in a chair with a disconsolate look on his face and would not reply to my questions. We had a lot to do and I was frustrated with his lack of responsiveness, but I held my tongue and told him to take some time off. I began thinking about what I could do to help him.

My father is bipolar and I had observed that he responds positively to honest compliments when in a depressed state. After careful contemplation, I wrote down Hiraku's strengths and talents. I knocked quietly, opened his door, and knelt by his side on our tatami floor. I handed him my findings and he looked at me in disbelief. Shortly thereafter Hiraku cheered up and we resumed planning.

In the ensuing weeks I offered support, allowed him to progress at his own pace, and did my best to be patient and understanding when he was down on himself. A few weeks later I transferred to a new city and did not hear from Hiraku for a while. Six months later I was surprised to learn that Hiraku had been called to a mission leadership position in which he was responsible for the periodic training of about twenty missionaries. I was later informed by the president of our mission that I was the first missionary to work with Hiraku who did not give up on him. I was thrilled to see that my faith in Hiraku had strengthened his confidence and bolstered his morale.

Another experience in Japan showed me that a positive attitude enables one to rise above any demoralizing situation. I spent the last six months of my time in Japan in the city of Hiroshima. While the city has been completely rebuilt, the devastation of the atomic bomb remains in the minds and hearts of those affected by its wave of destruction.

I remember two faces. The first is the hot red face of an older gentleman. I met him in the parking lot of an electronics store. The bomb had caused him a great deal of pain. He seemed intent on forcing me to feel that pain. I made an effort to calm him down, but he remained incensed. Each time I tried to interject or change the subject his voice grew louder. The graciousness that is normally embodied by the Japanese people was nowhere to be found in this man. I finally had to give up and walk away.

The second face I remember was kinder and softer. It was that of an elderly gentleman employed as a guide at the Hiroshima Peace Memorial Museum. I asked him what he thought about the bombing. His eyes were sad as he replied that it was very unfortunate. He expressed regret for the events that led to this horrible incident. He told me that he had been in Hiroshima when the bomb went off. After guiding me around the museum, he stopped and looked at me with hope in his eyes. He announced that we must learn from the past, forgive, and move on. I have never forgotten this powerful example of hope and attitude. I am convinced that it was this spirit that rebuilt Hiroshima.

These three experiences have taught me to move forward when adversity strikes and to make the best of every day. As there is a silver lining in every cloud, there is a creative solution hiding in every grim situation. My car wreck, Hiraku, and the gentleman at the museum taught me that patience, hard work, and a positive attitude facilitate the finding of those solutions. I want to solve problems and help others. I am convinced that law school is the best venue for me to learn how to do this. I am excited to learn how those who came before me approached the dilemmas of their time and to see how their solutions affected mankind. I look forward to the challenges, relationships, and experiences that lie ahead."

Derek graduated from the University of Virginia, School of Law and now practices patent law in Texas.

• •

These thoughts can be a great lesson to others. I remember sitting in the tub one night after work and all of a sudden hearing Derek scream with joy concerning his ACT results. Years later, Will, our next to the youngest, also achieved a 35 on his ACT, just a few months after he appeared on Jeopardy!.

Speaking of sitting in the tub, one night back in the 80s I was relaxing in a hot bath after work. No one else was home. I heard Will, who was about six at the time, come in the front door and walk down the hall. Just as he passed the bathroom door where I was located, I heard him utter a string of expletives that would make a seasoned sailor blush.

I flew out of the tub, grabbed a towel, and cornered him at the end of the hall. He didn't have a clue what was wrong. He had no idea what the words were that he had just pronounced.

"Where did you get that kind of language?" I demanded.

"Robert," he said.

I told him never to talk like that again and he was not to play or be with Robert until he was given permission from me.

A few days later I saw Robert walking down our street. I met up with him and asked him if he knew why Will couldn't play with him anymore. He sheepishly admitted that he knew. I asked him where he had picked up that kind of language. He said his mom and dad used those kinds of words all the time.

Years later, I told Will that he could hang with Robert again. Robert never used those words again, at least not when Will was around.

When Will turned 19 he went on a two-year mission to North Carolina and then majored in computer sciences at BYU. While at school he got jobs for a New York attorney writing programs to help the attorney scan patents. He made good money and also talked to Derek about working with him doing patent work.

One night our family was together and he announced proudly, "Derek says after I graduate I can go to work for him and make a three figure income!" He got lots of job offers that night and has been teased mercilessly ever since. He will probably never live down that faux pas.

During the time when Michele's mom was starting to lose touch with reality because of Alzheimer's, Michele and I were visiting her parents in Utah. One evening, Michele went out with her mom for some type of activity while her dad and I stayed home and watched a movie.

The movie was an edited version of *The Notebook* which is a poignant love story about a couple of kids who fall in love with each other. The story takes place over a long period of time and has some strong similarities with my decision-making conundrum over whom I would marry. I was really relating to the movie.

Wrapped throughout the length of the story are the two main characters that end up loving and marrying each other. The only problem is that later in life, the woman gets Alzheimer's, and except for a couple of special scenes, can't remember anything about her husband even though he stays right beside her. They end up dying in each other's arms. It was the perfect ending for that moving story. I began to realize that Karl, Michele's dad, was also relating to the story as his wife was in that downward spiral of losing touch with reality.

Just as the movie ended, Michele and her mom walked in the door. Karl jumped up and ran over and grabbed his wife Rayma and hugged her for a long time. He didn't want to let her go. Michele was surprised since Karl wasn't usually that affectionate. I knew just what was happening. It was a sweet moment. She died a few years later.

• •

Through the years, Will and Michael, my two youngest boys, helped me during the summers when I needed them. In 2005, I had thirteen-year-old Michael down at the shop doing various jobs. I had a bunch of steel tubing I needed cut into shorter pieces. I gave him a short primer on how to cut with the cold saw and then left him with the monotonous job.

A guy stopped by to visit with me. We were outside the shop for a half hour or so. Finally he left and I went back in the shop. Michael didn't have his shirt on and was crying. I asked him what was wrong and he led me over to the saw.

The cold saw is a very powerful saw that cuts through thick pieces of steel without slowing down. It shows no mercy. It has a strong motor that is geared down for even more power.

Michael was cutting away and when a tube got crooked in the cutting channel, he reached across the saw bed with his right arm to straighten it. The piranha-like teeth of the saw blade caught the short sleeve of his

287

tee shirt on his right arm. It immediately started reeling in his shirt and pulling him into its deadly path. He got so close to the teeth there were a few scratches on his arm.

He fought it. He twisted and pulled as hard as he could. The saw sucked the shirt relentlessly as he struggled to get away. His shirt began ripping and he was barely able to get the shirt to pull and rip off his trunk and head. The shirt was torn in two. His ears were hurting from the pressure that it created around his head as he struggled out of it.

It was too close of a call. I have cut metal with that saw for years without a problem. One critical mistake in my judgment: I neglected to remember that Mike was not operating with the same experience that I was.

I felt terrible. I was in shock. My dear little baby boy, by all rights, should have been sawn in half. The manner he got snagged and pulled in would have cut him in two from his right shoulder clear across his body had he not been able to pull himself free.

I honestly believe I could not have withstood the experience had he been killed. Walking into that shop and finding my boy sawn in half would have taken me over the edge.

I have used that saw hundreds of times since. I never fail to think of Mike. I generally get tears in my eyes as I think of the terrible possibility and the miracle of escape that Mike, and I, had that day. It's been years and I'm still rattled and emotional about the experience. Tonight, as I write this, I went down to Mike's room and hugged him. It is one of the closest calls and most traumatic experiences I've been through.

I still have the torn up shirt to remind me of the close call and great blessing.

• •

In the winter of 2007, we had the opportunity to attend a few live sessions of *Jeopardy!* in California. Our son Will is a fairly bright boy. He had gotten to the point where he could beat his folks while watching the show on TV. We tried for several years filling out applications for him as a contestant, but weren't able to make connections with the show.

In the fall of '06 we received notice that *Jeopardy!* was giving an online test for wannabe contestants. Because he was a senior, this was his last opportunity to appear on the Teen Tournament.

The night of the test found him waylaid in Connell after football practice. The kid is in his own little world much of the time, often missing deadlines and schedules and such. A very common happening, him missing his ride home, had just happened. He was going to miss the test!

Michele got on the phone and made arrangements for someone at school to start driving home with him. She picked him up halfway and he ended up in front of the keyboard with less than a minute to spare. We were told about 10,000 kids took the online test.

A few weeks later, Will checked his email. This was an exercise that he did very rarely. It contained a message that *Jeopardy!* had selected him to travel to Los Angeles, on my nickel, to audition for the show. They were auditioning 300 kids in several major cities across the country in order to pick 15 kids to appear in the tournament.

We were caught in a bit of a dilemma. His high school football team was heading for the playoffs. The audition was scheduled in L.A. at the same time as his first playoff game. We felt that football games were a dime a dozen, even if they were the state playoffs, and this *Jeopardy!* experience was once in a lifetime, however, it was his choice.

He chose *Jeopardy!*

The coaches were not happy with his choice even though the team they were playing in his absence was not a formidable opponent. While Will and I were waiting at the airport to fly to L.A., we checked the score. Connell won 44-7.

Will had started and played all year, but things were about to change. After we got back from Los Angeles, the coaches taught him a lesson. He sat on the bench for the next game. The next few weeks came and went. Connell won their games and Will was back in the starting lineup.

The audition in L.A. was interesting. I could tell that all of the kids there were sharp. Will was nervous. I could tell because he gets giddy when he's nervous. Most of the other kids looked like bookworms. He stood out because he was a big, strong football player who was missing a playoff game. He also did well at the mock *Jeopardy!* games they put on.

The deadline for notification was looming and we hadn't heard anything. We figured he hadn't been chosen. On the morning of the state finals, Michele and I headed for the game to be held the next day in Tacoma. Michael and Will had already left on the team bus.

We were traveling over the Vantage hill when my phone rang. It was Robert from *Jeopardy!* We talked for a while about the weather and what a fine boy Will was. He asked if he could talk to him. I told him he was on the team bus. I gave Robert Will's number, but told him that he probably shouldn't talk to him until after the game the next day.

I didn't want Will to get mentally sidetracked from the game. Robert agreed. We hung up.

I had kept my end of the conversation shielded so Michele didn't know who it was, however, as we spoke, she gradually became suspicious that it was "The Call."

After hanging up, Michele looked at me and asked if that was *Jeopardy!* I affirmed. Now let me tell you a little something about my wife. She is majorly low key. She doesn't get excited. She drives me crazy sometimes with her non-emotional approach and microscopic responses to life's ups and downs.

But her personality shifted on this day. She went into hysterics. She started screaming. She began jumping around inside the van. The girl was grabbing and hugging me as I drove. After that experience, I was determined to find out if I could somehow get *Jeopardy!* to call me every day or two. Michele was a lot more fun after a call from *Jeopardy!*

The only problem was, after everything had settled down and she asked me what he said, I was unable to say that Will would be on the show. Robert had just asked to talk to Will. I kind of assumed from the call that he was in, but maybe he was calling to tell Will that he had done poorly on the audition and they didn't want him.

A few minutes after the call, I happened to notice a tire off to the side of the freeway. I pulled over and backed up a half a mile with traffic whizzing by. It was a brand new backhoe tire, a 17.5x24 probably worth a good five hundred bucks. There wasn't a name on it so I figured it was mine. This was turning out to be a great day.

I called the State Patrol after we got to Tacoma and asked if anyone had reported a tire missing. They said no. I gave them my information in case anyone did call.

The boys got their butts kicked the next day. The refs blew the game. The coaches didn't make the best decisions.

However our family didn't care. While everyone around us was solemn, mad at the refs, and down-in-the mouth, we tried to echo their sentiments on the outside, but inside we were basking in the knowledge that Will was going to *Jeopardy!* It is harder than you think to cry crocodile tears on the surface while laughing your head off under the skin. I even muttered a few complaints about the refereeing when friends walked by.

We still didn't know for sure if Will was going. The question hung in the air until the next Monday when Robert called Will and gave him the formal invite.

That same day, I pulled out the backhoe tire and happened to notice some little letters inscribed on one of the bars of the tread. It said "ELS." Having been in the Les Schwab program for twenty years, I immediately knew it was a tire that belonged to the Ellensburg Les Schwab tire store. I knew I could no longer keep the tire.

It so happened that a couple of weeks before, as we traveled to Tacoma for a playoff game, I'd had a tire blow out. I limped into the Ellensburg Les Schwab store and the assistant manager put on a nearly new tire and didn't charge me anything. I called him up and asked if he was missing a tire. He was. I sent it back. What goes around comes around.

Jeopardy! paid for our plane tickets, gave us a thousand dollars for spending money, and put us up in the Hilton at Universal Studios.

Will did well. He was in last place going into Final Jeopardy on his first round. He bet his entire bundle and answered the question—correctly! He ended up with enough points to be a wildcard for the semi-finals.

He did well in the second game, but didn't win. He was pretty bummed for a bit, but soon recovered. It was a great experience for him and our whole family! He won ten thousand dollars.

• •

My blog entry in September, 2010 (Ben's Risky Business):

So Tyler, our red-headed stepchild, and I have been batching it the last couple of weeks. My good wife Michele has been living the life of luxury and no responsibility whilst in Utah with our daughters and grandbabies.

It is time she got back to the real world; you know, the world where the husband doesn't have to do the laundry and fix the meals while simultaneously fighting to keep the wolves away from the door. Two weeks is a dang long time without a maid!

I own a little community well. While my wife was in Utah, I'd been looking around for, and finally found a 120-gallon water tank for a little extra capacity. I got it from my brother, Brad, who is generally a cheapskate, but I must have caught him on a good day. He offered it to me at no charge. I understood why when I picked it up that morning.

After cleaning the mice nests, rocks, hard water deposits, and rust out, I soaked it in bleach to disinfect it from the various contaminants that had been shacking up for years in the galvanized, round steel mouse house. A company on my well system had just put in a big lawn with a sprinkling system that really taxes the well. I felt an auxiliary tank would keep the pump from cycling on and off so much.

I spent most of the morning getting it squoze through the well house doorway, plumbed in, and up to pressure. I have learned through a long, and sometimes violent, history of trial and error that the Basin City natives do not like their potable water AWOL. Several times this day as I worked, Michele called and asked when my flight was. I was under a little pressure from the downed well. Being fairly certain I could hear war drums in the distance from the water patrons, I told her I'd call her back when I got home and could check my ticket. I was quite positive it was far off in the late afternoon.

Toward the end of the job, Michele called me once more and asked if Tyler or I had mowed the lawn. Her tone was more like, "That lawn had better be freshly mowed when I roll back in the driveway or you may be sleeping on it for the next week."

Of course, we had mowed it twice since the Vacationer had been gone, but it needed it again. When I finally got home just before the noon hour, in order to maintain marital bliss, I went out and pushed the man killer, grass clipping Toro around the patch again.

I finally finished, went in, and stirred up some liquid refreshment. It was 1:00 and time for me to take it easy. I relaxed and turned on the TV. I had another hour and a half to kill before heading out— plenty of time to lunch, shower, pack, and head for the airport. I usually cut it too close when I have to catch a plane, but today was different. I had oodles of time.

I bought a ticket to Utah last week so I could check up on Michele and be in church for the blessing of Emma Crockett, my fifth grandbaby and actual niece of Davy Crockett. I really hadn't checked for a few days, but was under the vague assumption my plane left around 4:00 pm. I figured I was doing fine on time.

It was right about then that I began receiving a prompting that maybe I should recheck the flight. Much to my horror, I saw that the flight was leaving at 1:40 from Pasco. Forty little minutes till the plane overcame gravity! I was a good 30 miles from the airport and the passenger-halting blockade of Homeland Security.

I freaked. Quickly weighing my options in nanoseconds, at first I figured my goose was cooked. I might as well forget the trip. I was in dirty, sweaty, lawn-stained work clothes, not packed, and completely out of luck. People were without a doubt boarding the plane as I sat in my home in Basin City, reading my ticket with sweat dripping down my grass-smudged brow.

Most grown men would have thrown in the towel and called it a day. But I'm not quite a grown man so I grabbed my dress that was in a plastic bag (actually a dress my sister, Teresa, gave me to take to Utah for her soon-to-be-married daughter, Crystal). I frantically looked for my wallet and found it in less time than I normally do and yelled for 18-year-old Tyler to lock the house up when he left to be babysat by our friends, the Hawkins. I then flew out the door. There was no time to pack. No time to get ready. Brushing my teeth or even grabbing my toothbrush would eat up time I didn't have.

I jumped in the seen-better-days SHO, which has bad tires (the day before, I had noticed steel belts poking out of one of the black baldies), and gunned it toward Pasco, hoping there would be no blowouts for the afternoon. I hadn't grabbed my glasses so everything was a blur. The 100+ mph made things even blurrier.

Being a religious man, but still struggling a bit when it comes to obeying all the laws of the land, I began praying that the entire Franklin County Sheriff's Office would be at Dunkin' Donuts and nowhere near Glade Road for the next little bit. If a cop had appeared, I wouldn't have seen him until he turned his dreaded flashers on as he licked the doughnut jelly filling off his lips while reaching for a reckless driving ticket.

A couple of times I ended up behind people who had gotten their days mixed up and thought they were out on a Sunday drive when it was actually still Saturday. I tried to be a little more careful than I was when I drove to the hospital after I had cut my wrist with the paper cutter, but not much more. However as soon as it looked safe, I would pass the lines of cars and continue to accelerate to the necessary speed required to traverse the thirty miles to the Pasco Airport in respectable time. My Arrest-Red-SHO-Taurus and I completed the journey in 15 minutes.

Up to this point, I had tried to be fairly careful and make good decisions, however, after arriving I made a boneheaded decision. My brother Brad had told me how he parks in the Fed Ex parking lot so he doesn't have to pay a king's ransom for parking at the terminal. For some reason, I thought I could run to the airport, which was probably ¾ of a mile away from Fed Ex, as fast as I used to run the 100-yard dash on the high school track team.

The day was hot. I had already worked up a good sweat installing the water tank, mowing the lawn, and playing race car driver. Now I shifted into my marathon running mode, grabbed the dress, jumped out of the car, and began sprinting toward the faraway airport. I realized this cost-saving measure was ill advised after the first few steps. I should have gone back to my car and drove to the parking lot like a normal late-for-his-plane passenger would have done.

However I didn't. The 100-yard dash speed of 10.5 seconds I achieved decades earlier at BYU was surprisingly nonexistent. The extra 60 pounds I was packing underneath my sweaty work shirt, plus the plastic sack containing Crystal's dress, were slightly impeding the travel time.

Did I mention the day was hot? Off in the distance, through the chain link fence and across the heat waves emanating from the concrete tarmac, I could see a jet with its engines churning, anxious to get going. The portable stairs were still there and the cabin door open, but I would not have been surprised to see it close at any moment. I was starting to melt with exhaustion and had not even covered half the distance to the terminal.

I was sprinting full bore. Actually, at this point in my weight and life, what I would call sprinting is what others would call a limping, pathetic, hobbling crawl whilst in an upright position. Admittedly, I wasn't covering a lot of ground.

Right about then, as in other tumultuous times in my life, I began to feel a heat stroke/heart attack coming on. In the past, I've read where overweight, middle-aged guys often drop dead from heart attacks while they're out shoveling snow.

I would have loved to have been shoveling snow. The heat was a major factor in my premonition of the impending heart attack.

My gait slowed to a crawl. My lungs were burning, my osteoarthritis in my right knee was flaring up big time, and my visible world was spinning like the weather vane on the airport control tower in a hurricane. I thought I would probably go down with my face slapping the hot asphalt and the next time I would enjoy anything even remotely cool would be in the more comfortable confines of the local funeral home.

I finally slogged my way into the airport and made my way to the desk. The two female attendants looked at me with a bit of shock. There was not another person in line. It was completely deserted.

I knew I looked like a day laborer from Death Valley. I also knew they would bet their entire life savings I would not be riding any airplanes that day.

I told them I was very late for the Salt Lake flight. They told me Horizon Airlines didn't fly to Salt Lake, and maybe I should try the Delta counter down the way. I thanked them and sprinted for the Delta desk in my familiar running style.

The counter was deserted. I looked around, saw a buzzer, and began jamming with both thumbs on it with all the energy I had left in my totally dilapidated, but more than adequate, sweaty body mass.

After a bit, a guy appeared and ran me through the ticketing process. He said I might make it, but I might not. I sprinted toward the heart of Homeland Security.

The first thing they wanted me to do was take my shoes off. My heart sank, I had these work boots on that required a lot more work than most shoes do to take them off. I finally got them unlaced and pulled them free and lugged them into the basket along with my keys and phone. It was at that point that I noticed that I didn't have a belt that needed to come off. Maybe that's why I had had to keep tugging my pants up during the entire exhausting marathon run to the terminal.

After that it was a breeze. I didn't even bother to put my boots back on as I made my way to the Delta gate. The guy at the counter was surprised that a passenger would dare show up so tardy. For some reason, his computer wouldn't take me at this late date.

Finally, he said something about how I wasn't cleared, but he thankfully wrote a seat number on my ticket and pointed me toward the plane.

I was aware as I began moving down the aisle that my seat was in the back of the plane. I knew that my disheveled appearance was something akin to an illegal alien who had just crossed the southern border heading north. I was also painfully aware that my body odor was similar to a Middle Eastern camel rider who hadn't showered for a month and had been regularly spit on by his long-legged ride. I did not enjoy the experience of making my spectacular and heavily-scented way to my seat.

I huddled down in the seat, keeping my arms tightly locked to my sides, doing my best to emit as little locker room fragrance as possible all the way to Salt Lake.

After landing, I waited until everyone else cleared the plane before I exited. Michele picked me up in the parking lot. I was surprised and even a little disappointed that she was not more excited to see me. We drove straight to Deseret Industries where I acquired an entire Sunday wardrobe for less than $20.

Emma got blessed the next day with her very well-dressed grandfather standing in the circle.

• •

An entry from my journal:

About 7:30 this morning I was over at the tire shop talking intently to the manager when my phone rang. It was Mom, telling me she was locked out of her house and she was down at the trailer. Yesterday we had talked about me taking the key to her house and getting some duplicates made as it was the only one she had.

She said she had seen me take the key and needed me to come and help her get back in the house. I said I would, but then got lost in work at the tire store. About 45 minutes later, my phone rang again. It was her and I felt stupid because I had completely spaced her out. I immediately left and went over to my home to retrieve the key to her abode.

An hour and a half before, I had scoured my house for the key to the machine shop, as I was going to make duplicates for it, too. I went through everything I owned trying to find the shop key, with no success. Finally, Michele mentioned that she had thrown my pants away. I went dumpster diving and after the third, gross trash bag, found my pants. I finally fished out my shop key.

Back to the present: I went back to the house and went key hunting again, but this time for my mom's key. It was nowhere to be found. I dumped out boxes, rechecked vehicles, and ran over to Bret, my brother-in-law's, to see if it was in his van. Finally, I decided I was just going to have to go down, pick up Mom, and break one of her plate glass windows to gain entry.

I stopped at the trailer where the hired man who doesn't speak English lives. They had let Mom in. She was in her pajamas and her 76th year. No shoes. She had tied some scrap foam rubber around her feet that she found in the garage.

She had used string she found after getting locked out. I helped her down the steps and into my car.

At this point, I should mention that this morning was slicker than any day this year so far. It had rained during the night, while freezing, and there was a good 3/8 inch of ice on everything. She had walked down the hill from her house in bedclothes, in freezing weather, with no shoes, and on such a slick surface that Sir Edmund Hillary, even in his prime, wouldn't have tackled that descent without ropes, a pick axe, and spikes on his boots.

After getting a long run for momentum, we spun our wheels up to the house. I went into the garage and went straight to her car as I had been in it yesterday and we thought I might have left the key there. All this time, she kept insisting that she had seen me take the key and put it in my pocket. I've lost most of my memory so I didn't argue with her, as I knew it was probably true, even though I had no memory of doing so.

The key wasn't in the car. I figured I would look at the door in the garage and then go outside and break a window. Mom had already tried to break a window by striking it numerous times with a tool, but it stayed intact. This failed attempt happened before she had bee-bopped down the mountain.

The door was open.

I walked over to it, wondering what in the dell was going on. I felt on the ledge and there was a key, just like always. I went back out to the car and told her. She called me a liar. I told her if the door was open, I got twice my inheritance. If it was closed, I got nothing. She agreed. We shook on it.

I took her in the garage and she couldn't believe it. The crack of space between the edge of the door and the door stop was just a hair more than three feet, wide enough, I might add, for both of us to slide through at the same time. I showed her the key and she informed me it didn't work, it was for the bomb shelter. I stuck the key in the door and unlocked it.

I am left to ponder two things: One, will my eight siblings have a problem giving up their inheritance to pay off the bet? And two, why would mom want to leave her warm house at 7:00am to go outside in 25-degree weather without a coat to play like an elf at the North Pole? I'll be up all night wondering what she'll be calling me about in the morning.

• •

Another journal entry:

We went out to eat with the family down in Utah. Michele got back to Hauni's home a little before the rest of us. We got back and after a bit, Hauni started screaming and flapping her arms around and throwing a conniption fit. I couldn't understand what was going on. I ran in and asked Michele what was up since it was impossible to talk to Hauni.

Michele said that she had just whispered to her, "Hauni, you have a little visitor in the house."

We finally got her settled down. She was upset because the next morning she was going to have 50 visitors for dinner and didn't want the mouse showing up. She was also upset because she knew the mouse was probably going to have to die.

We set a trap. We went to bed. I was just settling down for a long winter's nap, when all of a sudden there arose such a clatter I sprang from my bed to see what in the heck was the matter. When out by the fridge, going crazy with surprise, a mouse was thrashing, 'twas music to mine eyes.

Hauni came tearing out with the same sour attitude she had previously exhibited. I escorted the mouse to his final lift-off pad and threw him over the deck, hopefully not to be retrieved on the lawn by the kiddies partying on the lawn the next day.

She said that as she was kneeling down praying that the mouse would just leave ... Presto! The trap sprung, the spirit left the body (and her house), and her prayers were answered.

And speaking of mice . . . one night Michele and I settled down to watch a movie. After a few minutes I left the dark room and went to the kitchen to do some foraging. I looked for graham crackers without success. I went downstairs and pulled a pack out of a new box. I returned to the theatre locale and started chowing down on the grahams.

As I ate, I noticed that Michele must have switched brands as these crackers had a unique taste and texture. I didn't care for them, but figured they needed to be eaten so I continued. After eating a good half of the cracker pack contents, I decided I was done with the strange brand of crackers.

They just did not taste good. I got up and turned the light on. Much to my surprise, I realized that the brand was not different.

What made these crackers different was that a mouse had decided it also liked Nabisco grahams. The crackers had been selectively nibbled on with little caverns chewed throughout the pack. The mouse had also used the bag and its contents as a multi-tiered restroom. I had been eating crackers that the mouse didn't want and also many little black lumps of excrement that the mouse also didn't want. Needless to say, I've been sick ever since.

This experience would not be complete without a picture of the actual package of Grahams and the eventual resting spot of the responsible party.

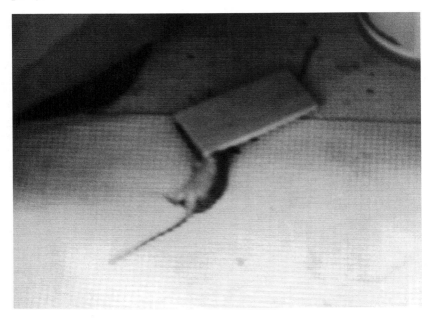

CHAPTER 27

VARIOUS TYPES OF STUPIDITY

Now to educate the reader with the author's vast wealth of personal knowledge concerning fiscal stupidity. For most of my life, I have lived with an exceptionally high debt load. I have always operated with the expectation that my rosy projections for the future would always occur and they haven't once.

At least 25 years of my life were out of control when it came to debt. It affected my very being. I didn't sleep because of the stress of trying to constantly figure out how to keep going financially. Usually, I found my answer into positive cash flow territory by incurring even more debt. Everything feels better for a day or two, but then the world turns dark again.

My familial relationships took a hit from the pressure. My relationship with my employees was often strained. They had no idea what situations I was dealing with in just trying to pay the bills, including their paychecks and bennies. I know they thought I was a tyrant and a jerk. It was a struggle for us all.

The 80s, 90s, and a good share of the early 2000s cycled by with me paying horrendous interest. I had over a million dollars of debt with over a hundred thousand in interest payments going out each year. In addition to the interest, quite a few of those years resulted in large operating losses.

After more than three decades I finally caught on to the fact that it is no fun being in debt. I liquidated assets and focused on reducing debt. Miraculously I've been able to keep my head above water. It was hard changing fiscal habits, but life is far less dark and much more fun.

Many of the times when I was in dire financial straits, I borrowed against equity I had to keep the cash flow going. I bought my house in 1983 for $65,000 which brings up one of the stupid things about me. I bought it from a very good friend, Bill York. He had built it a couple of years prior. When I asked Bill how much he wanted for it, he said he was asking $65,000, but he would take $60,000.

What did I do? I said, "I think it's worth $65,000 so I'll give you that." And I did.

Since then, I've refinanced the home a minimum of four times, taking the available equity each time and plowing into the cash-hungry tire store. After more than 25 years of making house payments and initially buying it for 65 grand, I had leveraged it for over $145,000.

I had big bank debt. I had big supplier debt. I had many charge cards that I used to jockey my problems back and forth between. Finally, I decided to do something about it. I began cutting expenses. I began downsizing. I began liquidating losers. I began trying to operate smarter. I am much happier since I've regained a bit of control over my financial destiny.

I believe this problem of fiscal stupidity permeates a great number of households across the country today. A friend of mine asked a car dealership credit manager how many people were upside down with the debt they had on their autos. He said something like 80%. If you owe more than the rig is worth, you'd better downsize. Maybe start walking.

People must quit the useless spending and fix their problem. If they don't, they'll die in debt. Their lives will get better as they regain some financial control. If they don't know how to solve their problems, they should get counseling or find an advisor or friend who can help. I have a perfect knowledge that this tenet is true.

And since I'm on my soapbox, permit me to wax a bit about our government, which is supposed to be an instrument of the people. Unfortunately, oftentimes the people are an instrument of the government. For many decades, the people of America have relied more and more on the government to take care of them. Each time the government has taken a step to provide more services, entitlements, stimulus packages, handouts, and many other keep 'em happy programs, a number of things have happened. My observations:

- We are hog-tied and hamstrung more closely than ever to the government teat. Once we are in that position, it's for the long term. The government rarely takes services away, they just keep adding to them. They advertise and promote their programs, especially the lottos, as the accepted norm. The public is trained to embrace instead of shun.

- Each time one gets wrapped up in a government deal, it comes with regulations, snares, and rules designed to further smother those who are under Big Brother's power.

- Each time a program is initiated numberless concourses of people are employed to promote that program. These people become administrators and slaves to those same programs. None of these tricks produce anything of value.

- The government, in order to keep the people happy, pays out big, incomprehensible dollars in entitlements. Keeping the people happy gets the rulers reelected.

- The government makes the money, but it never makes any money. If it were a business, it would be a colossal failure. It would be bankrupt immediately. And every day thereafter. There is little production and massive waste, no common sense, and lots of lies and behind the scenes manipulation.

- The country's problem now is that the majority of the voters are hooked on a government paycheck. How do we get out of this predicament?

- I believe the government should provide basic services and tax its citizens minimally. Instead, it now takes more than half our income. And it wants more.

I believe the founders of our country did not have our present socialistic state in mind when they wrote the Declaration of Independence and the Constitution. I don't believe God is pleased with the many aspects of the present governing mass.

• •

Sometime around the turn of the century, a neighbor friend approached me about working as a volunteer EMT on the local ambulance. Bob and his wife have worked for many years on it and I felt indebted to give some service because of theirs and many others' sacrifices. After taking a three or four month course, I became a certified EMT. I served for the next five years. Many interesting experiences came from that work.

My first run on the ambulance left a lasting impression. One morning I had just opened the tire shop. A fellow EMT named Chet drove up in his pickup and yelled at me to get in. I climbed aboard and we drove down to the ambulance barn. He told me a guy had just had a heart attack. We took off in the ambulance and drove eight miles to the victim's farm with flashing lights and siren. After traversing another mile of gravel road we finally arrived and ran into the poor guy's house.

His wife was frantically pumping on his heart as he lay unresponsive on a sofa recliner that was laid back. He had been watching the morning news on the TV that was still on in the background. He had suffered a massive heart attack. I knew from my training that it did no good to perform CPR while someone was lying on a soft chair or couch.

I told her to move away. I grabbed his feet and pulled him off the sofa. My partner, who was much more experienced, jumped over the man and started doing chest compressions. He instructed me to start giving air to the dude via mouth to mouth. I was a little hesitant, but did as I was told.

This fellow and I had had a slight disagreement years prior at my tire store. I don't remember what it was about, but it was enough that I didn't feel inclined to put my mouth on his. There might also have been another factor.

He was naked as a jaybird. I guess that's the way he watched the morning news. After suffering the attack, he didn't have gumption enough to get up and get dressed before we arrived.

I did as I was told and clamped my mouth on his. I'm sorry to say he never made it. It wasn't from a lack of trying on my part. I never got over the memory of my first ambulance call. Unfortunately, Chet was killed years later in an ATV rollover while fighting a fire.

• •

One Sunday afternoon I got a call to respond to a home fairly close to ours in Basin City. When we arrived in the ambulance, we were ushered into the house. A young Mexican lad of 17 or 18 years of age lay on the floor motionless. His eyes were glassy and reminded me of the eyes of dead cats I had seen on the road after they had been run over. He was gone.

However, after asking a few questions of the lady of the house, who was the guy's sister, the captain in charge decided we would start CPR. I was against it because I felt sure there was no way we were going to resuscitate him. I knew that by law, once we started we couldn't stop until we got him to the hospital. We began the process.

CPR becomes tiring after a few minutes. We loaded him up and drove him to the hospital. Because of the distance, we were performing resuscitation for over a half an hour.

The emergency room personnel took over and did their best, but to no avail. Because the kid had such a strong heart and was in good shape, his heart stayed active for quite awhile after we got him to the hospital. However, he had internal injuries that doomed his future. The hospital workers eventually pronounced him dead.

His problem? His seatbelt killed him. Earlier that morning, he and three of his friends were driving down a road and ran into a ditch. He was in the back seat and had his seat belt on. None of his friends were wearing their restraints. The other three exited the vehicle with no injuries.

He had no injuries except where his seat belt had been. He got out and walked home in great pain. Several hours later, he collapsed and died on his sister's floor. His injury stretched across his lower abdomen and was visible because of the hemorrhaging that had occurred. It was in the exact form of his seat belt. The only good thing about this experience was that it gave me ammunition later on to get a seatbelt exemption.

• •

Whenever we got a call, all the local volunteers were supposed to drop what we were doing and head for the ambulance barn or scene of the injury. I enjoyed the calls when we were able to help. I felt bad when we transported fatalities. And I especially didn't enjoy the calls that were bogus. There were times I received a call, dropped what I was doing, and missed out on the next two or three hours of work to run to town on the ambulance, all because somebody needed a ride to the big city. A faked illness was guaranteed to bring a taxpayer funded fancy taxi and a high speed ride to town.

The deadbeats would call and report a problem, feigning a condition just so we would haul them to town. Once arriving, they would miraculously improve. Most on the ambulance crew had jobs and it was usually a major inconvenience to respond. I soon developed a bad attitude from these situations.

One night my family and I came home from a basketball game that had been held in Connell. About three miles from home, we passed a car that had been stopped by a cop. After we got home, I got a call-out. We responded back to where the cop car was.

The deputy had stopped the car a few minutes prior. After calling in, he had discovered there was a warrant out for the girl who was driving the car. He told her to get out because he was going to cuff her and take her to jail.

Her mother was in the back seat and suddenly developed a major health issue. Actually, it was a convenient distraction intended to get the attention off her daughter. When we arrived, she was completely unresponsive. Her other children in the car were hysterical, as they didn't know what she was up to. We loaded her in the ambulance. The protocol was to take the patient's vitals before beginning the trip. I took them and they were perfectly normal. But what do you do? I didn't know because I wasn't that experienced.

But now I know. I'll tell you what you do! You get out the smelling salts and give the "patient" a good whiff. That would have brought her out of it! Or, you can do as the experienced hospital nurse did and as soon as you size up the situation, you take your knuckle and drive it into the "victim's" sternum and start twisting. Miraculously, the nurse's knuckle brought the faker back to a conscious state immediately.

Rather than retiring to bed and getting my beauty sleep, my fellow service providers and I rushed 30 miles to town in hopes of saving a life. Meanwhile, the lady on the gurney was putting on an act to keep her offspring out of the clink. Grrrr. By the way, her daughter still went to jail.

• •

Another memory that rubs me wrong is the call we received late one evening. It was at the trailer court for a woman in labor. When we arrived, a young illegal-alien teenager was inside the trailer having contractions. No one else was there. We had someone on the crew who spoke Spanish and soon learned that her family had all gone to Mexico for the winter, leaving her alone in the trailer for several months to wait for the delivery. This was all done so that the baby would be born in America and thus automatically be an American citizen, complete with free health care and all the other goodies.

• •

One afternoon I was in Mesa working in Kim's machine shop. I got a call to go to a wreck just outside town. A semi-truck had been barreling down a hill on the state highway and lost control going around a curve. When I got there, I was instructed to help extricate the passenger of the truck who was seriously hurt. The driver was okay and just standing around. The hitchhiking passenger kept saying, "I told him to slow down. I told him to slow down."

After the truck had lost control, it smacked head-on into a car that had two women and two children in it. There were a couple of ambulances there. One of them hauled the truck passenger off as soon as we got him out.

Many people were working on the car, trying to get the occupants out. They were finally able to free the two kids and one lady. They were seriously hurt and were placed in the back of the remaining ambulance. The lady that remained in the car was in bad shape, but still conscious. A half dozen EMTs and several deputies were trying to cut the car apart and get her out.

I was in the back of the ambulance with another guy named Jacob, attending to the three injured. I felt like too much attention was being focused on the lady in the car; I figured she was a goner. Several times in a span of 30 minutes, I went up to the crushed car and told the head honcho that we needed to get the people in the ambulance headed to the hospital.

No one would break loose to help us. There were more than enough of them working on the patient in the car and not near enough working on the other three. Finally, sick of hearing me complain, the EMT in charge said, "Just take them to the hospital."

I was itching to go because of all the pain in the back of the ambulance. I jumped in the cab and we were on our way. Poor Jacob was alone in the back, split three ways trying to care for the three. It was a ludicrous situation. I drove as fast as possible and we finally arrived at Kennewick General. For the next hour, we helped get the patients into the system and began filling out reports.

Eventually, we heard that a medivac helicopter was arriving with the final patient. She was dead on arrival. She had severe injuries and had been kept alive because of the compression against her body from being trapped in the car. As soon as they cut the car apart and got her out, the pressure was off and she began massively hemorrhaging, dying right away.

The person that had finally given me the command to head for the hospital arrived with the fatality in the helicopter. He/she began asking us a few questions. When this "leader" found out we had traveled with three patients and only two EMTs, one of whom was driving, it wasn't pretty. We were informed a report was going to be filed on us because we had broken the rules.

I could tell it was the intention of said "leader" to nail us as well as the person who made the decision to send us. We were questioned about who gave us permission to take off for the hospital. When I informed this "leader" that "he/she" was the culprit, there was a step back and a reevaluation of the situation. I then heard muttering of something like, "Well, we'll let this go, but don't let it happen again."

• •

One other situation that always bothered me was the expanding protocols the medical authorities required of us. It seemed that when we arrived at a serious situation, we had to jump through a bunch of hoops and relay all kinds of information to the hospital concerning the patient before we could go.

This often resulted in delays of 30 to 60 minutes. We were part-time amateurs and had no business doing stuff that was completely out of our realm. I felt the sooner we got the patient to the hospital, the quicker they would get the care they needed. It frustrated me to no end to stand around and twiddle our thumbs when we should be speeding toward a facility that could treat the problem.

One Saturday afternoon the radio announced that there was a bad wreck outside of our area and I should respond. I drove to the incident and jumped in to help. A car had barreled down a side road and blown through the stop sign, t-boning another car, spinning it off into a pond.

There were three expired Mexicans in the car. Several of us started working on the injured driver of the car that had caused the wreck. It was a good looking girl dressed in a very short skirt. As we got her on the stretcher, we checked her for broken bones and other unapparent injuries. To all of our dismay, one of us discovered this was not a girl; it was a guy! The ambulance took off while I stayed behind and helped drag the other car out of the drink and extricate the poor souls that got nailed by the cross-dresser.

After five years of ambulance chasing, I gave it up. I figured I had done my time and was a little uncomfortable with a few aspects of the job. We were rank amateurs in the medical field, and yet, personally liable for our actions. I always had a fear I might get involved in a malpractice situation.

• •

One evening, several years after my EMT period, my wife and I were driving home from a movie. The familiar blue and red lights came on behind us. I stopped and a state patrolman walked up. In a fairly excited tone, he asked me if I knew how fast I had been going. It was a 55mph zone and when I told him I didn't know my speed he said, "You were going 67 miles per hour!!"

I had the thought that I should start screaming "What? You are kidding me! I can't believe I was going that fast! Oh no, my world is ruined!" I then would get out of the car and start crying and banging my head on the asphalt. I also had the simultaneous thought that this cop was making a big scene over nothing. I talk big sometimes. Actually, all I said was, "I'm sorry, sir."

He then asked for my license. I rarely carry my billfold and this evening was no exception. I'm not a paperwork kind of guy, and therefore, couldn't produce my proof of insurance or registration either.

I could tell he was a little bugged and was going to write me up for several infractions. He said he would be back in a few minutes, turned, and started walking back to his car. I called out for him to come back. My wife doesn't like to stir things up and she started hitting me in the leg to shut me up, however, as usual, I was a man on a mission and therefore politely ignored her.

I told him I just wanted to explain something. I mentioned he had probably noticed that I wasn't wearing my seatbelt. Before he wrote me up for that, I wanted to explain why. He said that no, he hadn't noticed, but he had noticed now. My wife was thinking I was doing an excellent job of hanging myself.

"So why aren't you wearing your seatbelt?" he asked.

I launched into the story of being in a serious wreck when I was a youth on the cloverleaf, which was ironically just ahead of us. I told him that if I'd had my seat belt on, I would have been killed. I didn't tell him the cops were chasing us at the time.

I then rehearsed the story about working on the ambulance crew and hauling the kid in who was killed by his seat belt.

He responded with the reply that he had seen many people thrown out of vehicles because they didn't have their belt on.

I responded that I didn't think the state should dictate how I might die.

He responded that the state has to take care of paraplegics after they get hurt from not wearing their seatbelts.

I responded that I had insurance and that the state wouldn't have to pay for me.

It was a spirited discussion. After we finished, he said that he felt like I was a good guy and he wasn't even going to go back to check on my information. He also wasn't going to write me a ticket.

I was pleasantly surprised. I told him he seemed like a nice guy also and that if he ever had any kind of car trouble when he was in the Basin City area, to give me a call. I told him I owned the Les Schwab tire store there and I would make sure he got helped.

His response surprised me. "What? You own the Les Schwab in Basin City? I had a run-in with one of your employees a few years ago!"

"Oh, great," I thought. "Who?" I asked.

He answered that he didn't know.

"I was going to a wreck in Mesa and one of your guys was driving a Les Schwab pickup on the highway going a hundred and ten." All of a sudden, I knew just what he was talking about.

"That wasn't one of my guys!" I stated.

"Yes, it was!" he responded.

"No, it wasn't!"

"Yes, it was!"

"No, it wasn't!"

"Yes, it was!"

We traded opinions several more times before I more fully explained the situation. But first I need to fill in with a little background . . .

A few years before, while serving on the ambulance crew, I was in Eltopia with my propane employee Aaron doing a tank installation. My phone rang and our good ambulance captain Bob told me there was a wreck in Mesa and I needed to head that way.

I didn't want to go. I had work to do. I asked Bob if I could possibly skip the call. "No, you'd better come; it sounds like a bad one." he responded.

I threw my tools in the back of my Les Schwab pickup, told Aaron to hop in and we headed north. We got out on the freeway and I decided that if I had to go and it was such a serious wreck, then time was of the essence. I hammered down on the gas pedal. We soon were clipping along at 110 miles an hour, passing cars like I was trying to get somewhere quickly. I had my emergency blinkers on hoping people would think I was on official business and get out of my way.

After covering the next six miles at warp speed, I happened to look in my rear-view mirror and noticed a state patrol car was five feet behind my rear bumper with his red and blues blinking away. We were still doing 110.

All of a sudden, I was in a bind. I had to think fast. If I followed the natural human tendency that occurs when people see cops, especially with blinking lights, I would hit the binders and pull over. However, by hitting my brakes, it would mean I was pleading guilty to driving too fast and I would probably end up with a reckless driving ticket.

If I kept my speed up and acted like I knew what I was doing, I might be able to bluff my way through this little problem. I moved over to the right lane and kept the speed up. The cop pulled up a little closer alongside me and got on his loud speaker. "Where do you think you're going in such a hurry?" he yelled electronically over his loudspeaker.

I glanced out the side window and noticed that the lawman looked a little upset. He also looked as confused about what to do in this situation as I was. I pointed ahead and mouthed the words that I was on my way to a wreck. He couldn't hear me in the 110-mile an hour headwind, but since I looked halfway confident he must have figured out I was headed for the wreck. He then demonstrated that his Mustang cruiser could go faster than my Dodge Ram pickup, raced ahead, and took the lead.

I continued on. When I reached the scene, I jumped out and told Aaron to take the truck back and finish the job in Eltopia. I would ride the ambulance to Pasco and have him pick me up at the hospital there.

As soon as I ran to the wreck, the Stater ran up to me and said he wanted my name, rank, license, and serial number, as soon as I finished administering to the wreck victims. He also wanted to talk to my supervisor. I said, "Fine."

After we got the patients loaded and were ready to leave, the cop came over and I introduced him to Bob. He told Bob off and then started in on me. Eventually, I gave him my info and then hopped into the exiting ambulance.

During this time in my medical career, I was often puzzled by the way things worked. Whenever we responded to a wreck, we weren't supposed to go in excess of ten miles an hour over the speed limit. The cops can go as fast as they want.

Yet when we all get to the wreck, which are the essential workers? It's the EMTs who usually get their hands dirty, and bloody, and at times the county deputies dive in to help. In my experience, the state patrol guys stand around and watch. Therefore I'm thinking common sense dictates that the EMTs should drive as fast as they can to get to the wreck, along with the deputies who are actually willing to help. The other officials should be restricted to the no-more-than-ten-over-the-limit rule.

After Aaron picked me up at the hospital, we went about our business. That afternoon, Don called me from my tire store. He said that the Pasco Les Schwab store had called and said that the state patrol was looking for the driver that was speeding in a Les Schwab pickup from Basin City.

I was shocked. I had already given the officer all of my information. Now he was calling other stores to find me when he already had my number. I had the thought that he was never going to be promoted to detective.

I called the state patrol office and asked to talk to the head guy. A lieutenant came on the line. After I introduced myself he launched into a diatribe about how he had information that another person had driven me to the wreck going way past the speed limit and then I falsely represented to the officer that I was driving. I was shocked. The state patrol was really getting their facts messed up. I tried to set the lieutenant straight, but he kept getting more hard-nosed with me.

Finally I said, "Listen, I'm the one who is going to take the heat for this. I was the one driving." This last statement really set him off. He interpreted my statement that I was going to take the heat to mean that I was covering for someone else. He growled, "If you keep lying to me, I'm going to hang up and call the Franklin County Prosecutor and you're going to end up in jail!"

This last statement really set me off. I emphasized as firmly as I could the following, "I was the one driving the pickup! No one else was. If you call the prosecutor, I'll call my lawyer. I told you what happened, but you won't believe me. Arrest me and I'll sue you for false arrest!"

A few moments of silence passed. Then I heard a meeker, milder, and friendlier voice on the other end. He simply said, "Well, if that's the truth, that's what I need." We then spent the next ten or fifteen minutes talking about my mistake in driving so fast and how we should go out for lunch sometime.

Back to the traffic stop with my wife: after I convinced the officer that I really was the guy who was in the pickup, he rearranged his memory files and finally agreed that I was right. He was a nice guy. He didn't try to get his ticket book out to pay me back, but just told me to have a good night. I drove away from the cop, toward the cloverleaf overpass and location of where Brian and I had crashed so many years before.

CHAPTER 28

TEMPTING FATE

I struggle when it comes to doing things by the book. This is why I should have an occupation that has no dangerous elements involved— something like pushing a dry mop in a gymnasium with a football helmet and knee pads on.

I have been involved in farming, selling and working on tires, flying airplanes, doing brakes and front end work, and pumping and trucking propane. I've probably set a thousand propane tanks, trucked heavy loads, and spent a good share of the last four years working 40 or 50 feet in the air on top of grain bins.

These are all businesses that have a fair amount of risk involved and carry an extreme amount of risk when I'm in the picture. More than a few people have met their maker because of ineptitude in these areas. I am inept. I haven't had to practice it. It comes naturally. At times, wisdom whispers that I should not get involved, but since I've never been adverse to risk, I always dive in. I have to keep bread on the table.

Speaking of doing things by the book, I hate paperwork. I had neglected for years to get my medical card, CDL (Commercial driver's license), air brake certification, hazmat badge, and my tanker—you know, the standard stuff that keeps the driver's license office staffed.

• •

And then there's the propane business. With my record of near misses, how did I ever end up working in propane? Before going any further, I would like the reader to know that my safety record and procedures have continually improved, especially after I sold and got out of the business. It scares me to death to think that I could have been the cause of someone's demise.

One of my vocational setbacks is that I have never worked for anyone but my dad on the farm. Therefore, I've had no training in safety, paperwork, bureaucracy, or baloney. The major emphasis on my horizon has always been production, getting the job done, and making the buck. The second portion of this problem is that I have no fear and am willing to take on about any project that rears its "come hither" head.

I started my tire business in Basin City in 1982. It was nickel and dime, operating on a shoestring. I began with miniscule capital and as soon as I got a little ahead, I would take on another project and be back to a negative cash flow position. After 30+ years of this financial masochism, I hope I am wising up.

One of my first projects after I got the tire store built was to get a propane tank and sell propane. This was done with a rented 500-gallon tank that I used for ten or twelve years to sell gas. Finally I got tired of buying from another retailer at high prices so I acquired a 12,000-gallon tank. Now I could buy tanker loads cheap. The first load of gas cost me 25 cents a gallon.

I was now ready for the next step of buying a bobtail and delivering gas, however, with all the other projects I had going I had to put it off for a good fifteen years.

Finally the moment arrived when I was ready to dive in. At least I thought I was. I didn't have a clue what I was doing nor did I know all the government regs I should be following. I was referred to a guy who had an old, dilapidated delivery truck in Oregon. The truck had two, 900-gallon tanks on it and was a good . . . scratch that . . . a bad 30 years old. It had more value as scrap metal than as a propane truck.

After making arrangements, I hitched a 250-mile ride to Portland to pick the old girl up. I arrived, my ride left, and I set about making minor repairs to the truck before I left for home. The truck hadn't been run in years so I brought a battery with me. After installing it I started the truck up. It ran! But then I pushed the brake pedal to the floor with absolutely no resistance. It had no brakes. The old girl had just become an old lady.

I rounded up some brake fluid, borrowed a few tools, and bled the system. That didn't help at all. I pumped and stomped on the pedal to no avail. I decided it was time to go, brakes or no brakes. It would be dark soon. I was in the middle of downtown Portland with a propane truck that had no brakes or license. I was lacking a CDL, but didn't know anything about it at the time. The truck wasn't licensed and I wondered what else might rise up and bite me before we coasted into Basin City. I felt I had no choice but to dive in the cab and see if I could make it home.

This was going to be an interesting trip, I told myself—another challenge in the game of my life. I took off into traffic. Remember, this was downtown Portland, the largest city in Oregon. Every time I needed to slow down, I would downshift. Every time I needed to stop, I turned the key off, eased off the clutch, and the truck would rely on the dead engine to lug down and halt. Stoplights were especially exciting when they turned red just before I arrived at the intersection.

Each time a red light appeared, a wild panic would flare up in my innards, but would gradually scale down to a livable level as the truck bled off speed and lurched to a stop. This cycle occurred numerous times before I got out of the big city. After each close call, while waiting for the light to turn green again, I sat back in the seat and luxuriated in the adrenaline fade. I would look at the drivers around me and wonder what their state of mind would be if they knew what was really parked next to them.

Finally, I got on the interstate where my unique braking system wasn't needed. The rest of the trip was uneventful except for the fact that the two-speed was stuck in low and I could only go about 40 miles an hour. Everyone was buzzing by me at 70. The truck was a beater, and therefore, a beckoning red flag to all Constables on Patrol (Cops) within eyesight.

I was a little concerned as I drove through the DOT scales at Bridge of the Gods. The highly visible red flags all over the white beater were beckoning strenuously, but I idled through without the big red "STOP" light coming on. Someone was asleep at the wheel that day. I was at Bridge of the Gods and the gods were on my side! There's no way the government-commissioned road warriors were looking out their window that day as I drove through. They would have pulled out their machine guns and ticket books. I would have been thrown in jail.

• •

A year or so later I decided to upgrade and located an old, used Suburban Propane truck in Medford, Oregon, exactly 515 miles from home. I caught a flight down and picked up the truck. It was in a lot better shape than the first propane truck I bought and babied home from Portland. Still, it left a lot to be desired. Once again, it was a truck that a propane company had worn out and was trying to dump. However, for me it was a brand new truck. The windshield wipers worked. The brakes would actually make the thing stop. It even had an air horn! It was the kind of truck I could afford.

I still didn't have my CDL and this truck also wasn't licensed to do anything but stay parked, however, I was getting calloused when it came to these types of situations. I made it almost all the way home without incident and decided not to stop at the scales going into Washington.

That evening when I crossed the border the sun was just going down. I drove past the scale house without turning off at the exit. I could see the inspectors inside stretching their necks out, watching me pass by. Every commercial vehicle is supposed to turn off and slowly drive through their facility for the critical once-over. For some unknown reason they didn't jump in their squad car and come after me. I had no idea what would happen, but figured there would at least be a long layover and a heavy fine if I got stopped. Whew!

• •

A few years later, our eldest daughter, Hauni, got married in Portland. I went to Portland with my family and picked up, yet another, overused LPG (Liquid Propane Gas) truck. Why make another trip to Portland if I could incorporate it into the wedding trip? My wife wasn't in favor of this, but I always like to kill two birds with one stone. (There was almost a dead bird or two in our family by the time this particular experience ground to a halt.)

Since the last truck acquisition, I had acquired my CDL, but I hadn't gotten around to licensing the newly purchased truck. At least I was making progress conforming by getting the CDL. I headed home with my wife and kids following in the van.

The truck stalled on the freeway just outside of Portland. I jumped out and messed with the propane fuel system as traffic zoomed by. The sun was going down. In a minute or two we were up and going again. The stress was constant. We had lots of heated, family discussions as we traversed the Columbia Gorge in the middle of the night. I wanted my wife to follow on my tail so a patrolman would be less likely to get directly behind me and see the former owner's lapsed license plate.

I knew I had already tempted fate far beyond the breaking point and that I had better avoid the scale stations, if at all possible. Instead of traveling the interstate in Oregon, I took the Washington side to avoid the dreaded outposts. We reached the Horse Heaven Hills at about midnight and I knew I was running on fumes.

I wasn't sure where the correct back road to the Tri-Cities was so I put my trust in Lady Luck and hoped my guesstimated headings would turn out right. They didn't. I drove into the isolated, strange, and dark countryside with my family following behind, all occupants sporting a very nasty attitude towards their fearless provider.

I coasted to conserve fuel every chance I got. All of these trucks used propane for fuel which made it a lot harder to fuel if one needed a refill. I blindly turned off the main road a couple of times and ended up at dead ends several miles down the road I had turned on. I eventually conceded I was lost and had not a clue which direction I should be headed. My family was still following.

To say the least, they were not patient or happy with the blind leading the blind. I think one reason Michele was mad was that she had to prepare for the wedding reception the next day. Finally, we ended up in Prosser and then traversed a familiar highway back to the Tri-Cities. Just as I pulled into town, the truck started coughing. I coasted off the freeway and came to a stop in a residential area. I got in the car with my hostile family and we finally pulled into the home driveway at 2:00 am.

My wife was so mad she slept in our daughter's room. Christianne asked my dear Michele why she was sleeping with her and Michele said, " 'Cause your dad's a jerk." Christianne simply said, "Gotcha." She said it in a low key and completely understanding way. Even though Michele was mad, she had to laugh.

I had been told by more than one propane veteran that there was a $20,000 fine if I got stopped with my propane truck in the shape it was in and me without a license. Every time I saw a Department of Transportation van I would start sweating and shaking and putting new grip marks on the steering wheel. Being in the tire business for 20 years, I have heard many stories from truckers about how ticket happy the DOT guys can be. Still, I didn't get my propane operation completely organized and legal until the last year before I sold the company.

I had the propane delivery and tank business for eight years. It was a constant chore and challenge, to keep the tanks filled with propane, and yet efficiently time the deliveries so that you weren't driving around and filling tanks that were still almost full. There was a fine line between making prompt deliveries and emptying your truck by the end of the day and driving around town all day long and returning home at dusk with a still full tank.

And setting tanks was another demanding task. There were days when I would have eight tanks to deliver and set. I pulled a trailer behind my pickup and used my YankATank to maneuver the tanks at the customer location. Most propane service techs will set one or two tanks a day and call it good. I didn't feel like I was efficient unless I hit seven or eight.

I was in Richland setting a tank after a busy day for a nice guy named George Hanchette. I had sold him propane in the past and was there because he had decided he needed a bigger tank. I knew George had terminal cancer and wasn't doing well. I set his tank and said goodbye to him. I walked out and checked my schedule. I had one more tank to set before I headed home. I checked the trailer and made sure my load was secure. I stretched a rubber tie-down strap across my YankATank to keep it on the trailer.

As I pulled the strap tight, the hook slipped off the other end and shot at a very high rate of speed toward my eye. The metal hook hit me in the eyebrow and brought immediate pain, damage, and stars. I stumbled around trying to deal with my new and unpleasant point of view. Blood was spurting out of the gash and I knew I would have to get the bleeding stopped before I went anywhere.

I stumbled toward George's backdoor and knocked. With my good eye, I could see him in his kitchen. With my bad eye, I scared him to death. We had exchanged pleasantries less than two minutes before and now he was looking at a blood-soaked guy in some major pain.

He hurried to the door and was very concerned. I asked to use his sink which he readily agreed to. I then set about washing up and putting a compression bandage of toilet paper against the cut. George was kind to let me use his facilities.

He kept apologizing for causing my injury when he really had nothing to do with it. He told me that I needed to immediately go to the hospital or a clinic. I agreed. I was not feeling good when I left. This was the last time I would see George alive. I think his wife's name was Theresa. The next time I stopped by their home, she told me of his passing.

When I left George's place I headed directly for a clinic. My eye was swelling shut and I had a headache coming on. I walked into the clinic and signed into their system. I sat in the waiting room for 45 minutes without any visible signs to my one good eye that they were going to help me. I finally got up and left, still holding the toilet paper to my head.

I was feeling a little better. Some of the shock and pain had worn off. It was dark, but I decided I would drive to my last customer and set his tank.

I arrived and did the work. Just as I was finishing and walking toward my pickup, a car drove into the driveway and the owner got out. We walked toward each other and I informed him that his tank was set. We were next to his house and the outside lights illuminated our faces. He looked at me with great alarm. He told me that I needed to go and get treated as I might have some serious damage. I told him I had just left a clinic and it must not be that bad because they left me sitting out in the waiting room until I got mad and left.

He told me again that I needed to go get it checked. I told him I was okay and that I'd had injuries like this before. I appreciated his concern, but I wasn't going to go sit in another waiting room for an hour with toilet paper on my face. He insisted I go and get medical attention. I said, "Listen, I am more familiar with this kind of injury than you are. I've had many broken bones and traumatic injuries! I'll be fine."

He said, "Listen, I AM A DOCTOR! You aren't fine. You need to go get that looked at!"

I was surprised and started laughing. I told him that maybe he was right. I thanked him for his concern and his propane business. I strapped the YankATank on the trailer very carefully, keeping my face away from the killer strap hook direction of travel and left the good doctor's abode. And then I drove home.

• •

Another person I will never forget was on our propane route in Richland. His name was Gene Smith. He had formerly taught school in Connell and since retired. His wife had cancer and was in her last days. He took care of her in his home and whenever he wasn't doing that, he was out in the greenhouse he had constructed in his backyard.

He was raising orchids in his greenhouse. He needed propane to fire his heater to keep his plants from freezing in the winter. He had invested a lot of time and money in the project and was very hopeful that he would start making some money once the plants had matured. He showed me some of the flowers that were already coming out. They were beautiful!

His wife eventually died and every time I made a delivery, we had a nice talk. I thought a lot of the sweet guy.

The propane business got so busy in the winter; I hired a driver to keep up. His name was George. Delivering propane is not that hard. You just follow the route sheet, use basic safety principles, and keep track of the gallons you deliver. I think he even had his CDL.

Toward the beginning of spring, I was in Richland and I thought I'd stop by and see how my old friend Gene, the orchid man, was doing. It had been months since I had seen him. I figured by now he would have a full greenhouse of beautiful flowering orchids and I was looking forward to seeing the visual extravaganza.

I pulled into Gene's driveway and walked behind his house to get a sneak preview. I opened the door to the greenhouse and . . . there was nothing but bare shelves. I was shocked. I turned, walked to Gene's back door, and knocked. He answered the door and we exchanged greetings. Then I asked him what happened to all his orchids.

"They froze," he said.

I was now doubly shocked. "How in the world did they freeze?" I asked.

"Ran out of propane."

I was mortified. I had George doing the Richland route every couple of weeks that whole winter. Gene informed me that I had been the last guy to deliver to him back in November. He then said it was no big deal and that the Lord must have other plans for him.

Most people who salted that much money, time, expectation, and labor into a project like Gene had would have been royally ticked. Most people would have sued over the deal and I wouldn't have blamed them. Gene was a better man than most of us. He didn't complain once.

I apologized profusely to Gene. I felt so bad. He said everything was fine and not to worry about it.

George had quit just a week or two before.

I hunted George down at his new job and asked him why in the heck he had not delivered gas to Gene as he was supposed to. He gave me a lame excuse and walked off. I could see the guy never had any concern for his former employer or his former customer.

Gene Smith is a rare and wonderful man. I kept in touch with him until he remarried and moved to the Midwest.

• •

When I first started selling propane I needed tanks for my customers. I located some tanks in the Portland area that were 40 or 50 years old and were cheap. They actually turned out to be very expensive because it took a lot to upgrade them and many of them were problematic.

Basin City is in the middle of a farming area and farmers always need propane tanks they can pull behind their pickups to burn weeds. I adapted a few of these old tanks for this purpose and put them on trailers. This was a big liability and worry for many years. If one came loose from the back of a pickup and smacked into a car coming the other way, I would have been toast along with the occupants in the car.

In fact, one Thanksgiving Day, my good friend and great truck tire customer Lee Eppich needed propane to heat his swimming pool. He must have figured I was running a do-it-yourself propane company. He drove to my shop and hooked on to a tank and started pulling it home. He didn't have it hooked up right and as he went over a small bridge, the tank and trailer came loose, tried to pass his pickup on the left side, and then finally flipped end over end, crashed, and rolled on the other side of the road. Fortunately, there were no cars coming the other way and Lee retrieved and fixed the tank and trailer.

As I mounted these tanks on the trailers, there were several instances when I needed to weld attachments on the tanks. This was hairy!

Propane tanks are filled with very explosive gas. However, after using some basic physics and applying them to the situation, I deduced that since there was only fuel and no oxygen inside the pressurized tank, I could weld on the outside of the tank without incident. I just had to make sure I didn't get the weld too hot and compromise the integrity of the steel tank. The first few times of beginning a weld on the tanks made me close my eyes and hold my breath and brace for an explosion. I always got a good shot of adrenaline during this exercise.

One time I delivered one of these old 500-gallon tanks to a customer and filled it. The customer called me the next day and said he thought he could smell propane. I drove out and saw that the leak was on one of the old fittings. That particular tank wasn't set up to drain the liquid back out so my options were limited. I got my welder and welded the fitting. There was a little fire from the fuel leak but I finished the job without incident.

I would not recommend welding on propane tanks for any reason whatsoever!

• •

I had a few customers ask me about big field burners they had seen and needed. I located one down in Amityville, Oregon. It was a trip of about 300 miles. I made arrangements to buy it and drove down to pick it up one evening.

It was a monster, even without the thousand-gallon tank on it. It had two big wings that would fold down and cover a 45-foot swath with violent flaming under its metal flaps when burning. When it was running, it sounded like a jet getting ready to take off. The wings folded up for transport on roads but it was still very wide, tall, and heavy.

By the time I completed the transaction and headed out, it was getting dark. The thing rattled and clanked, especially when I went across rough spots in the road. Before I made it to Portland, it was completely dark. I was bouncing and clanking along the interstate, taking up every inch of my lane and then some. Flying around a curve, I saw two state troopers sitting on the side of the road. I crossed my fingers, held my breath, and my luck held. Neither cop pursued me. I guess my biggest infraction was I had no lights on the back, but I don't know how anyone could have missed it with the orange paint and gigantic profile it had.

I stayed in Troutdale that night and made it home without incident the next day.

A few months later I rented the big weed burner out to the Simplot farm down around Wallula. This was probably 45 miles away from Basin City. Every time someone rented the big burner, from a liability standpoint I felt like I was hanging out in a big way. It was a traffic accident waiting to happen. The guys using it usually towed it behind their pickups at regular highway speed, which was far too fast for the flotation farm tires that carried it. The full 1,000-gallon propane tank on board multiplied the danger. No flashing lights or pilot car, just a big monster cruising down the road behind a little farm pickup, looking for trouble.

After the machine arrived on site at the Simplot farm and ran for a day or two, it was out of gas. I had to deliver 900 gallons of propane to the tank attached to the burner so they could finish the job. I headed for Wallula with my first, impossible-to-license truck loaded with 1500 gallons of liquid propane. The trip was uneventful until I got to the general location where the burner was. I wasn't sure just where to go so as I was driving past the Iowa Beef plant, at the last second I got the bright idea that I should pull in and ask for directions. I was going a little too fast to make the turn into the parking area, but since I was committed mentally to arriving at that location, I did a little off-roading in order to reach my destination.

Unfortunately, my speed in the old overloaded jalopy was around 40 mph. We hit a large berm as we exited the road. The truck made a horrific bounce and skidded to a stop. The entire rear axle, including four dual truck tires, was completely ripped away from the driveline and springs. The back of the truck now lay on the ground, three feet lower than it had been a moment earlier, and the axle and tires relaxed in the barrow pit, freed from their former load.

I called my shop in Basin City and gave them a list of what I needed. One of my guys Tom drove out and by the end of the day we had the truck back up on the rear axle where it was supposed to be. I delivered the gas and headed home. Luckily, no piping damage or leaks occurred during the unplanned and instantaneous axle removal. A fire could very easily have occurred and that would have been disastrous.

The truck looked like a wreck for several hours before we got it fixed. I felt very fortunate that a cop or DOT guy didn't drive by and see the situation. Since the truck was loaded with propane and was sitting adjacent to the Iowa Beef lot, they could have declared the situation a major hazard and shut the plant down. This would have involved a minimum of several hundred Iowa Beef and Americold employees evacuating the area. It would have been very expensive and would have had severe negative financial and public relations ramifications for me.

I'm sure I would have been sued for loss of production at the two plants. The state would have nailed me for various and sundry violations and the newspaper and TV stations would have had a broadcasting hay day at my expense.

Speaking of hay . . . one day I sent my propane guy at the time, Ron Hay, out to deliver propane in the old beater delivery truck. For some reason, he stopped just past the intersection of Russell and Glade Roads heading south. The truck was loaded with gas. When he started to take off again, he had pulled so far off to the right that the soft shoulder of the road began giving way.

The further he tried to go, the deeper the right rear tires sunk and tipped the truck. Top heavy with the load of propane that was shifting to the right, the truck was on the verge of rolling over and crashing down the incline where he was located.

He called me and gave me the news. I drove out to the truck and surveyed the situation. It looked scary. Any further movement of the truck, or even sloshing of the fuel, would mean tipping over and certain disaster.

Just then, a friend of mine from Pasco drove by with a tow truck. He stopped and told me that for a couple hundred bucks, he could hook a cable on to the truck and winch it back up on the road and out of harm's way. I was ready to do the deal until he added that he would have to block traffic on the busy road, which required that he notify the sheriff's office, which would require that they notify the state patrol and close the road until the job was done. I asked him how long it would take and he thought somewhere around an hour.

This was way too much red tape and sure trouble for my liking. I told him no thanks. I called the tire store and had them send down my boom truck with several chains. In a few minutes the truck arrived. I had Tom pull up alongside the stuck truck, put his arm out the window, and motion traffic past us. I jumped up on the teetering ensemble and hooked some chains to the frame and over the top of the tank to my boom truck. Getting in the cab, I felt pretty nervous, as I was sitting at a sharp angle dropping off on my starboard side.

I instructed Tom to inch the boom truck slowly ahead as I began creeping forward with the propane truck. I told him to keep an angle toward the left which would keep the chains between the two trucks tight. We eased forward and gradually the truck leveled out and ended up back on the road. The tow truck driver had stuck around because he was sure his truck would eventually be needed. Sorry, Clemente! Another minor problem alleviated without the authorities getting involved!

• •

One evening at twilight I headed to Royal City, which was about 50 miles away, to deliver propane. As I arrived at the customer location, my truck quit. The lights on the truck were dim so I assumed the battery was bad. It wouldn't start so I hoofed it a half-mile down the road and enlisted a fellow's help to jump start the truck. We got it going and I delivered the gas. It was dark and as I got back in the truck I noticed my lights weren't working. A quick moment of decision-making and I had my course of action mapped out. I put it in gear and concentrated on the wild hope that I could drive back the 50 miles without meeting any traffic or running off the road.

I began driving 50 mph down the road with a partial load of propane in the 2,500-gallon tank on the back and no lights. Every time I met a car or truck I had to slow down and try to safely move to the shoulder of the road. I finally made it three quarters of the way home without an accident. The only way I had made it that far was to stick my head out the window and try to watch the white striped line in the middle of the road.

I turned onto Radar Hill Road and saw that there were no more white lines. The county had just paved the road and hadn't marked it yet. Now I could see nothing but blackness. I started idling up the hill, absolutely clueless as to where the road was. On the left of the road, there was a drop off that stretched down a half-mile or so. If I went off that shoulder, I'm sure the truck would have rolled fifty or sixty times before coming to rest. I finally made it to the top and pulled off in a parking area on the side of the road. I sat and thought for a few minutes.

I concocted a plan that I would wait until a car came up over the hill behind me and then I would pull out ahead of him. The illumination of his lights on my tail would show me my way home. Soon lights appeared and I accelerated as fast as the old truck would go. Soon we were clipping along at 60 mph and the lights behind illuminated the road ahead.

Unfortunately, and unexpectedly, the car passed me. In seconds, the road disappeared from view and I jammed on the brakes. I slowed to a crawl and ran off the road to collect my wits and get out of the way of traffic.

I sat there for a while trying to deal with reality. With no cars in sight, I took off again. The only way I could see was to look out the side window toward the sky. I could see the tops of the power poles against the night sky every once in a while on one side of the road. I inched along for a few more miles and decided I'd had enough when I got to the top of a hill that traversed down through a small ravine above Basin City.

I knew that since I had no way of telling where I was (there were no power poles in this area), and since I was a basket case, it was time to do something different. I sat for a few minutes and then did what I should have done an hour earlier. I called my wife to come help me.

Making this call was probably the hardest part of the whole night for me and my ego. She showed up shortly thereafter. I told her to get behind my truck and follow me home. I could see the road illuminated by her headlights and had no fear someone would rear end me because she was behind me. The rest of the trip wasn't bad at all. I told my shop guys to replace the alternator. They put it off which further complicated my life.

A short note: While I was doing the propane thing, I was also doing a trucking thing. One afternoon I had to make an ill-fated trip to Spokane with a load on my semi. It was a week or two after I made the initial propane trip with no lights. While on this trucking excursion, my customer in Royal City called and said he was out of propane. He was one of my biggest customers and I knew it was critical that I get the gas out there by first light the next morning.

I got home from the trucking trip to Spokane frazzled and exhausted from all the excitement the trip had generated. I tried to sleep. Because I knew the alternator in the propane truck was still not working, I knew I could not make the trip in the dark. I went to bed, but was wide-awake from the trip I had just gotten home from. I was also anticipating the trip I was about to embark on the next morning.

I tried counting sheep for a couple of hours, but the wooly effort found me still awake. I finally decided to borrow a line from Gary Gilmore and Nike and "Just Do It."

I drove over to the shop, I jump started the propane bobtail, let the battery charge on the truck for a few minutes, and then took off.

There was a little more moonlight than the last time. It was midnight, however, and I should have been home in bed. One nice thing about driving that time of night was that there was very little traffic. I got it up to 60 and cruised through the night with my head out the window. I worried a little about someone parking their car on the road without lights and me plowing into the back of them. That's how my Uncle Glade died. He slammed into the back of a disabled coal truck with no lights. I got my middle name from him.

Just past Othello, I got a big scare as I flew past that very car I feared. I didn't see it until it flashed by my right side as a dark shape. Luckily, it was parked far enough off the side of the highway that we didn't make contact.

I reached my destination and pumped the fuel. My return trip was fairly routine, if you call driving a bomb down the highway with your eyes closed routine, until it started raining. Luckily, my wipers ran on air pressure so I was able to keep the windshield wiped off, however, it was still very difficult to see outside the cab in the dark.

Five miles before my arrival in Othello I noticed headlights coming up quickly behind me. Soon the car was right behind me and then the familiar blue and red lights began their familiar dance. I knew the jig was up.

The officer pulled up to my door and asked me what in the heck was going on. It was an Othello cop. He had been out in the badlands chasing a car and was just returning to town when he came upon my un-illuminated propane dispenser and its cautious and careful driver.

He told me to park the truck immediately. He was mad. I think he was torqued off because he hadn't caught the runaway driver out in the badlands and decided to take it out on me.

He told me if he called WSP or DOT they would throw me in jail and confiscate the truck. I meekly answered that I agreed. He told me I was not to drive another inch or he would lock me up. I asked him if I could catch a ride with him into Othello and he said, "No way," and then directed me to pull the truck off into a field. I couldn't believe he was going to make me walk in the dark and the rain.

It turned out he actually was a very nice guy, although I had to beg him several times before he would give me a ride. He dropped me off on the outskirts of Othello and I stood in the pouring rain for an hour before someone finally picked me up. It was 4:00 in the morning by this time. I was able to hitch a ride to Basin City and went to bed for a few hours.

Around 7:00 am I caught a ride back to the truck with Kim Haws and drove it home by the dawn's early light. I kept realizing how dumb my actions were, and yet, I was still inclined to take big chances that nobody else would even think about. I truly needed to get out of the businesses I was in. They were too hazardous and risky for a personality like mine.

• •

I had many not-quite-up-to-code experiences as I developed my propane business. There are quite a few regulations in the books that are well and good and necessary. Over the years, I made great strides in my quest toward getting in compliance with most of these codes. I found along the way that there are quite a few that should never have been made, providing no benefit to anyone except the regulating agency. They displayed very little common sense and were last on my list of things to do.

I admit I took too many chances. Several times I had tanks dump their fuel through the liquid ports, sometimes semi-intentionally and sometimes accidentally. This is always a little disconcerting and very dangerous, especially if there is a source of ignition anywhere close to the incident.

I had a few near misses, especially when I first started working with gas. One night I had been trying to load a partially filled 500-gallon propane tank onto my truck in pitch black darkness. The chains on my crane slipped and broke the liquid valve off. I ran and shut the engine off.

A migrant family whose house was in the same proximity came out and marveled at the beautiful liquid plume shooting up 100 or so feet in the air. The helpful and nervous fellow asked me in broken English if I wanted him to call 911. I said, "No thanks, they are the last people I need right now." I told him he probably ought to go in and shut his stove off. He did that and then we stood and watched the Old Faithful replica for the next 30 minutes until it ran out of juice.

Since I had acquired a bunch of old and outdated tanks, there were times I had to remove a gauge or a valve out of a loaded tank of propane and replace it with a new one. The escaping vapor rushing out of the ¼" bung hole sounds like a jet engine. This particular situation has been attacked and conquered by the author several times.

However, vapor line blowouts are child's play when compared to dealing with an Old Faithful style gusher from a liquid line. The liquid gas blowing out at 44 degrees below zero and the blast of product shooting skyward makes it nigh impossible to screw the new valve back in. However, following my usual path, I have tried to do the impossible—and even succeeded once.

The most memorable LPG experience I've ever had happened many years ago. It was a cold winter day and I was out in the middle of an orchard servicing tanks. I took a faulty liquid valve off of a 500-gallon tank as I needed to replace it with a new one. The internal safety valve was supposed to snap shut and stop the flow of liquid if the valve broke or came off. Unfortunately, it did not.

I stood there watching expensive gas shooting up in the air under tremendous pressure, 80-100 psi. It was venting liquid propane to the tune of 50 bucks a minute. I knew I was going to be the one who would have to replace and pay for the fuel. I stood next to the tank, watching the 100-foot plume shooting skyward and the percentage gauge rapidly dropping.

After about a hundred gallons had escaped, I began to feel myself falling into a deep financial depression. I was going to have to replace the lost fuel. With this background pressure, I succumbed to a wild idea and decided to sacrifice my body. Taking a deep breath, I climbed on top the tank with the new valve in my hand. The tank was covered with ice and I had a hard time balancing on top of it. I stuck the valve down where I thought the hole was located. Liquid propane was spewing all over me at 44 degrees below zero. Several times I took deep breaths, jamming the valve down into the screaming liquid and making attempts to screw the valve in a clockwise direction. After the fourth time of trying to get it started in the threads, I made it! As I turned the valve, I sensed I had engaged the threads.

I was amazed and thankful since I figured there was about one chance in a million that I would be successful. I gently turned the valve while pushing it down against the tank as hard as I could. The gas slowly stopped escaping as I screwed it in. I was coated with frost, but hadn't gotten frozen or burned, both of which you usually get when coming in contact with liquid propane, especially in the cold temperatures of winter.

I'm sure you could count the number of people in this world on less than ten fingers who have tried to stop a liquid propane geyser like that. The number of people who have actually stopped it is likely to be counted on less than five fingers because the other fingers would be frozen off. In reality, you could probably count them on one finger.

I felt like I had just won an Olympic gold medal. In fact, maybe they should make this activity an Olympic event. I guarantee it would be fun to watch from the safety of the stands. If they do make this an event, they should do it in a "No Smoking" stadium.

• •

As I developed the propane business, most of our calls for service came from the Tri-Cities, a 30 to 40 mile trek from Basin City. It was very inefficient to drive the truck back out to Basin City every time we needed to fill it with gas. I looked for a place to park my semi-tanker around

Pasco to fill the bobtail up. A couple of guys let me use their lots, but their welcomes didn't last very long.

I started thinking I needed to buy a place when I remembered that a friend, Wayne Woodward, had a fertilizer business in the vicinity. He was very hospitable and I was able to keep tanks, trucks, and an old shed there to house my parts and equipment for the next several years. Years before, I had hauled the shed up around the tire store and used it for an equipment shack for the paintball enterprise.

After Wayne said I could squat in his yard, I transported the old shed down to Pasco on the back of a Harobed bale wagon. The shed had been used out at Hanford for a multi-user outhouse on the reservation when government employees were working on mixings for the A-bomb they built to help end World War II. Dad bought it from the government in the late 50s and used it for many years to milk a cow in every night and morning. It was very handy to use Wayne's property for a staging area. Thanks, Wayne!

One day in October while working there, I noticed a guy with a big backpack and sleeping bag hung on his back trudging up the road. He looked like he had seen better days and I felt a little sorry for him, but was busy and didn't stop my work to go out and say howdy.

About a week later, I left Basin City on my way down to my farm and machine shop. It was a rainy and cold day. As I drove along the bottom of the bluffs, I happened to see a tent out of the corner of my eye, barely visible up in a ravine. I braked and walked up the hill to see who would be camping up there on a day as miserable as this day was. Just as I got to the tent, this same guy I had seen a week before down by Pasco, came struggling out.

He was in rough shape; cold and dirty and without a plan. His name was Dan.

I asked him if he needed anything. He was shivering and asked me if I could take him to a store as he didn't have anything to eat. I quizzed him further and realized this guy was in trouble. If I hadn't happened along, I think he would have died from hunger, thirst, or hypothermia. It was just by chance I had seen him. Most people wouldn't have stopped.

I took him to the store in Basin City and then offered him a place to sleep down at the shop. He accepted. I hauled him around and then fixed him a bed in the office at the shop. He stayed there all winter.

Every week, my wife or I would buy him groceries. A couple of times I took him to my home so he could bathe and get cleaned up. The only thing I didn't like was buying him cigarettes.

He hung around the shop all winter. One day I was working on moving stuff around with my forklift. Dan was watching and was giving me advice every once in a while. I drove over to pick up a pallet and Dan was standing a little too close. The front wheel of the solid-tired forklift ran over his foot. He started yelling and hopping around. I was instantly bummed out about the bum.

My forklift was a solid-tired machine. There was no give to it like there is on pneumatic tired forklifts. Both of us were very lucky. He got a large blood blister on his big toe and he limped around for several weeks after. I don't know if he broke any bones, but his big toe was smashed. I do know I was very fortunate that the tire didn't roll over more of his foot. He definitely would have had a multitude of broken bones. I'd have been on the hook for a big judgment if his foot had gotten smashed.

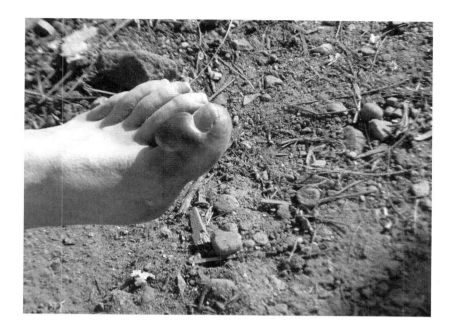

One day he was out of cigs and begged me to get some for him. I stopped by Villa's Department Store in Basin City and asked for a couple packs of whatever brand he wanted. Just as I was paying for the cancer sticks that were lying in front of me on the counter, in walked my church bishop at the time, J Wood. He looked at the cigarettes and then at me. I started laughing and didn't even try to explain what I was up to.

I think he remembered that I was taking care of Dan and knew I probably didn't have a nicotine problem.

Dad died in December of 2004. After the funeral, the hearse and funeral procession made a final trip with Dad up Casper Lane, around his home and beautiful surrounding farms and view, and then back down the lane. We did this just to give Dad one last figurative peek of his place. As usual, Dan was standing out in front of the shop, smoking and watching all the cars pass. It was very contrary to the atmosphere of Dad's farm and, in spite of the somber day, everyone got a kick out of it.

Sometime in February, I decided I would keep buying Dan food, but no more cigarettes. I had taken him into town several times so he could pick up his government offerings, so he knew which direction town was.

The next time I got groceries for Dan, I walked in the shop and he was gone. He had left during the night. I figured he had walked back to Pasco since it was pretty lonely and boring around the shop. He should have asked me for a ride, but I think he was too embarrassed after all the help I had given him.

A few days later I talked to Bob Andrews, the ambulance man. He said someone had found my new friend, Dan, five or ten miles up the Columbia River from where the shop was located. I was shocked. Why would he take off in the opposite direction from town and head into an area that was isolated and without any services?

I guess he was found in his tent by a game warden. He was near death from starving and hypothermia, in a little worse shape than when I found him on the side of the hill. They hauled him into town in the ambulance and got him revived. All of his earthly belongings, including his coat and his camping gear, were left behind by the ambulance.

Bob stopped by to tell me where his stuff was. I drove up the river, but never found it. Someone must have needed Dan's belongings more than he did. I never heard from him again.

By the time I finished using my dad's old milk barn for a propane equipment shed at Wayne Woodward's, it was in such dilapidated shape that it couldn't be moved again. One foggy winter day, I decided to take my chances and eliminate it without a burn permit. I'm sure there would have been a lot of red tape and bureaucrats conjuring up senseless and expensive barricades if I had done it the "right" way. So I threw a match in it and hoped the fiery demolition would be complete before a fire truck or cop car appeared.

It went up like a tinder box. When it was fully engulfed, I began watching up and down Glade Road, wishing and hoping for no traffic for just another half hour or so until the burn was completed.

A couple minutes later, I saw a sheriff's car hightailing it toward my location with his red and blues flashing. I prepared myself to assume the position. He was moving along about 80 or 90 when all of a sudden he noticed my inferno. He slammed on his brakes and screeched to a stop just a little ways past the fenced entry gate. We stared at each other and I could see that he was a little confused as to what he should do.

After ten or fifteen seconds of the stare down, he jammed his car into gear and took off on his original route. I realized that he must have been on another call. When he saw the fire, it was so impressive that he had to stop. After weighing his options, he must have figured his other call was more important and off he went. I breathed a sigh of relief and went back to watching the historic outhouse go up in smoke.

CHAPTER 29

JUST ONE LAST TRIP

Around the time I got the propane business started, I decided I might as well get into the trucking business too. I bought an old Western Star semi truck and a couple of older, homemade flatbed trailers. I didn't have a clue what I was getting into. I already had more than my share of problems—massive debt, several poorly managed businesses, unfinished projects, lots of uncollectible receivables, etcetera.

When I take on a project, I always think I can beat the odds and surprise everyone with my excellent management skills. This never happens, mainly because I have no management skills, especially not excellent ones. I surprise people with my brazen, instantaneous, and monumentally stupid decisions that I always do on the cheap. Baling wire, chewing gum, and clothes pins are my tools of the trade, any trade. My trucking enterprise was a classic example of this trait.

Kim needed trucking done from time to time and complained about the hard time he had getting trucks when he needed them. I offered my services and then went out and bought the oldest and least expensive equipment I could find. I had to get a friend to show me how to shift the old, brown Western Star that a gypo trucker happily brought by (he got his check and left in a big hurry). Another buddy showed me how to hook the trailers up to it.

Okay, I was ready to be a trucker. No CDL, no weight permits, no insurance, old equipment, bald tires; still, I figured I was ready to haul.

A day later Kim needed a load hauled to Spokane so I saddled up and ground gears over to pick up the load. It was a hot summer day. That is not the best time to make a maiden voyage with a beater truck and a loaded trailer, running on old recap tires. Tires love to blow out on hot days. I took my 16-year-old son, Derek, and we headed north on the freeway. The only thing I was worried about was the weigh station halfway to my destination. If it was closed, all was well. If it was open, I would be in jail. I wasn't sure what they would do with Derek. The weigh station was closed. Derek could relax.

We were having fun—windows down, elbows hanging out in the breeze, and not a care in the world. The rumble of the big diesel and the availability of 13 speeds made us feel like real truckers. Every once in a while, if I felt like it, I would reach up and honk the air horn. I was on top of . . . OH, NO!

Two state patrol cars were parked in the median with their occupants shooting the bull, just waiting for somebody like me. We passed them and I stared in the rearview mirrors for the next couple of miles. They faded out of sight.

"Today must be my lucky day!" I thought. Just then, KA-BOOM!! The explosion was right below and behind where my outstretched elbow was hanging. I glanced in my rearview mirror and saw rubber flying everywhere. Several cars were dodging every which way trying to evade the shredded tires. Two of my drive tires had blown out at once. I was hauling a full load of Kim's steel and had my hands full trying to ease the truck off the highway and get it slowed down.

We finally got stopped a half-mile down the road from the blowout location. I looked back and could see remnants of the tires scattered back down the freeway with cars and trucks dodging them.

I sent Derek to run back and pull the big shards of tire tread off the road. I grabbed my cell phone and called the Les Schwab in Ritzville, thirty miles away, for help. I then settled back to wait for one of the state patrol cars that was sure to arrive at any minute. It never happened. Years later, I still can't believe it. I was as illegal as I could get and I was stuck on the interstate—ripe for a ticket, but the ticket book didn't show up.

A half hour later, the tire truck pulled up and we both grabbed a tire and started mounting. We had that truck back on the road ten minutes after we started. For once I was glad I was a tire man.

We traveled up the road another ten miles and since I hadn't been to the destination before, I took the wrong exit. We finally figured out that we were on the wrong road. We needed to turn the truck and trailer around but were out in a forest on a small road with no culs-de-sac. I finally found a small drive leading off the road and pulled in.

The road had just been asphalted and, after a break in traffic, I backed out onto the main road and the traffic started piling up. I had to crank the trailer real tight to make the corner. With the new pavement and the 100 degree day, this maneuver rearranged the new pavement in a fairly significant manner. I finally got inched around to where I could take off and cease being the cause of a traffic jam. Eventually we got back on the freeway.

The rest of the trip was fairly uneventful except for the DOT guy coming the opposite way who did a major rubbernecking job when I drove by him with my piece of junk. Unbelievably, he didn't come after me. The gods of trucker heaven were smiling down upon me that day. I really didn't deserve it.

It seemed that every time I climbed in the truck I would have problems. I took a load up on a dark winter's night. All was well until I hooked onto the load coming back. It was cold. Everything was frozen including the 5th wheel mechanism on the truck that hooks onto the trailer. I thought I was hooked up and started off. As soon as I pulled onto the street, a big crash told me I wasn't hooked up. The loaded trailer had dropped off the 5th wheel, but luckily was still held up, resting on the truck's rear tires.

I grabbed the landing gear handle and started trying to crank the load back up. I didn't have gloves. The digits got cold fast. The landing gear mechanism was old and worn out. It's hard enough jacking up a load with a good system. It was nigh impossible raising a trailer up in the snow and cold with a piece of junk that slipped cogs in the jacks 90% of the time. After an hour and a half, I finally got the load high enough that I could back the truck back underneath it. I was drenched with sweat, but my fingers were frozen.

With no flashlight, I couldn't tell if the lock had engaged on the 5th wheel. I suspected it hadn't. I had a towrope in the cab so I wrapped it back and forth between the trailer and the truck. Anyone familiar with trucks will know that I was dreaming if I thought it would hold my load on.

I jumped in and started driving. Slow was the speed I selected. I just knew I was going to dump the entire cargo right in the middle of the road. I idled along for about five miles. I had to make four 90-degree turns and those were especially nerve racking. I arrived at a mini-mart just before the freeway entrance and decided I couldn't go any farther. If I dumped the load on the freeway, the best that would happen is the law would nail me in a major way. The worst that would happen is I would kill somebody.

I parked the truck and weighed my options. I could see a motel in the distance so I waited around the mini-mart until a girl came out and started to get in her car. I was greasy, dirty, and cold by this time. I really had to beg to get her to give me a ride to the motel. My sales experience proved very helpful as she finally relented. Once at the inn, I drew a hot bath, thawed out, and finally was able to relax.

I called my brother Brad and told him the story. He is much more capable in these types of situations. He said he would skip church the next morning and drive the 120 miles up to help me.

The next morning he showed up and we went over to the truck. Sure enough, the 5th wheel wasn't locked. I still can't believe I drove five miles and didn't lose the load. We spent an hour or more working on it before it was ready to go. He found several other serious problems with the truck and I promised myself if I could get the mess home, I would never attempt another trip in this truck. We made it and I kept my promise.

Several months later I took another load up to Spokane. This was in a truck that I didn't own. A guy owed me $22,000 for a tire bill and then went banko. He said I could take a truck of his. I assumed he was giving me the truck for part of his bill. I took the truck, but before the thing hauled a complete load, it broke down over by Seattle and I had to put in another $10,000 in repairs to get it home.

A few months later the "owner" informed me he was going to charge me rent on the thing. Next thing I knew, repo guys began chasing down all his equipment and came after the truck. I told them they couldn't have it unless they paid me for the work I had done on it. This made them cool their heels because the truck wasn't worth half the money I had put in it. I must admit I was totally stupid as I did this deal—starting with the guy who owed me the 22 grand to the ill-fated trips I took the truck on.

My next load couldn't be hauled until I replaced the landing gear on the trailer. I hired a guy to do the installation who claimed to be an expert at that sort of thing. After he finished, I turned the handle. One leg jacked up and one jacked down. He redid it, but still didn't get it right.

I hauled the load. I unhooked it from the truck and pulled away. The landing gear shifted until it had assumed a precarious angle. I started feeling uncomfortable about the looks of it as I stood there and watched it. The more I looked at it, the worse it looked and the worse I felt. It was dark and though I couldn't see clearly, I sensed it was sinking.

I ran over and asked a forklift driver to hurry over and take some of the heavy racks off the front of the load. He drove over and as he lifted the first rack off, the landing gear failed to a point of no return. I could see that a big mess was imminent. I ran around screaming for another forklift and directed both of them to get under the trailer. This they did just in time.

The landing gear became useless. The load was so heavy that the forklifts were tipping forward, their rear wheels off the ground. We rounded up some blocks and stabilized the trailer. They unloaded the racks and I asked myself why in the world anyone would want to be a trucker. The guys in the yard said they would fix the landing gear, which they did. I loved those guys! They were always so patient with me. I headed home and arrived without further incident.

I kept one trailer at the yard in Spokane and the other in Basin City. Whenever needed, I would trade the trailers. One day the Spokane outfit called me and said one of their guys was walking by my trailer and a tire exploded. It scared the daylights out of the guy. How often does that happen? That trailer had been sitting there for several weeks.

On my next load, I took an extra tire with me. Things went fine until I got about 30 miles from Spokane. I heard an unusual noise and looked in the mirror. I could see that I had just had another double blowout, this time on the trailer. I pulled over and made a call to the Les Schwab in Spokane. I told them I owned a Les Schwab store and needed a couple of tires. Just then someone knocked on the passenger door. I looked over and saw a state trooper peering in. I motioned for him to open the door. He asked if I knew I had tires on the road a mile or so back.

I said no, all I knew is that I'd had a blowout. He said there was rubber scattered all over the freeway. He was not a happy camper. He then gave me the news that a car had hit a big piece of tire tread and the guy's grill and headlight had been knocked out.

I could see this day was going to get worse before it got better. I told him I would pay for the damage, but I needed to know where the car was so I could make arrangements with the driver. He looked around and scanned the roadway in both directions. Finally, dejectedly, he said he didn't know what happened to him. The driver must have left.

The officer then started looking around at my tires and trailer. He asked to see my paperwork. I had my CDL by this time so I handed it over. However, I didn't have my medical card. I didn't have proof of insurance or the registration for the trailer. The truck was registered to a different owner, a friend of mine who owed me money and had loaned me the truck. He looked for the license on the trailer, but it was gone. The tonnage was expired on the truck. The tires were bald.

He crawled under the trailer and looked for a serial number, but was unsuccessful. It was a homemade trailer that was built in 1955, the same year that I was built. He started wondering aloud if the trailer was stolen. I asked him who in the world would want to steal a trailer like this particular model. He responded by asking me who in the world would want to drive a trailer like this on the open road. I decided we both had valid points.

The trooper was getting upset. I could see that this was going to be a major ticket. In fact, there would probably be several tickets as all the charges would not fit on one sheet.

I decided now was the time to bring out the big guns. I asked him if he knew Randy Hullinger, a brother-in-law of Brian Cook and also a state trooper. I told him that Randy used to be my neighbor and we were good friends. He said, "Yeah, I know Randy. He and I went through the academy together."

He looked at me and said, "You know what? I don't care if you ARE best buds with Randy Hullinger. In fact, I don't care if you are friends with the head of the Department of Transportation. Come to think of it, I don't care if you know the governor. You know, I don't even care if you know the President of the United States. YOU CAN'T DRIVE JUNK LIKE THIS ON THE HIGHWAY!!" His tone grew sterner and the volume grew louder with each passing word.

Thus chastened, I decided maybe it hadn't been such a good idea to bring up Randy's name after all. Randy might end up in jail with me just from guilt by association. With that final statement, he retreated to his patrol car and sharpened his pencil.

A few minutes later I saw the Les Schwab tire truck coming from Spokane. He drove across the median and headed toward us. I was afraid the cop might get out and talk to him. If the tire guy happened to say something about how he couldn't believe I was running bald tires on a beater truck, especially since I owned a Les Schwab Tire Store, I was dead. If that happened, I knew the cop would write me up for every illegal thing he could, including each bad tire on the old 18-wheeler.

I decided a little diversion was in order. I ran up to the cop and told him he should probably back his car up so the tire truck could pull in behind me. I then ran over to the tire guy and told him, "Don't tell the cop I own a Les Schwab store!" He said that would be no problem. He had just gotten a ticket that morning on his way to work and he wasn't in the mood to help any cop with information that would help him write more tickets.

We jumped on the job and changed the tires in a jiffy. I loved the feeling of being a bona fide truck driver, and yet, being able to immediately switch vocations and change a truck tire faster than the tire man who has been called out to do the work.

Just as we were finishing up, the cop beckoned me to come over and get in his car. Once I was seated, he proceeded to list all the laws I had just broken. He told me to get them fixed and handed me a warning ticket. Another lucky break! I love troopers named Randy! I got the tire guy to follow me into the Spokane yard where we switched out the tire on the other trailer that had blown out and scared the worker to death a week earlier.

My trucking days were coming to an end. I had flirted with the fickle over-the-road Lady Luck and could see that sooner or later, I was going to end up in a hellacious wreck, the penitentiary, or locked up at the DOT scale house. But before I quit, I just had to haul one more load. I wonder how many truckers keep making that same promise

• •

Another load was ready to go. I enlisted my good pal Scot Haws to tag along with me on a cold winter afternoon. I thought it would be nice to have some company. He turned out to be more than just good company.

We headed out. Everything was fine until I noticed my temperature gauge climbing. I was watching it intently when steam started blowing out from under the hood. I pulled over and we climbed out to see what the problem was. We popped the hood and found a split water hose.

About then, a truck from Walmart pulled over. The Walmart driver walked back to see if he could help. When he saw the problem, he went back to his truck and got several gallons of water and some electrical tape. We temporarily taped the hose back together and dumped the water in. I gratefully thanked the Walmart angel. We climbed in and took off for more adventure just over the horizon.

We pulled off at the next exit and stopped at a truck stop. Surely they would have the little hose we needed to replace our broken one. It was leaking more each passing minute. They didn't carry hoses. The clerk told me to slip out the back and cut a piece off the garden hose laying there. He even loaned me his knife. We installed the hose, filled up with water, and took off. This was turning out to be just the usual trip for me.

We arrived in Spokane, switched trailers, and headed out. That is to say we got about six feet in the yard and, Boom! Another crash! Again, I hadn't gotten the 5th wheel locked! We jumped out and saw the trailer was twisted at a dangerous angle and the load precariously hanging.

One side was resting on the truck tires while the other side was resting on some very thin air. Two big metal boxes that had been sitting on the front middle section of the trailer had fallen off and spilled their contents. We had strapped the racks filled with heavy metal plates to the trailer. If we hadn't, the entire front half of the load would have been on the ground. The racks on the front were tipped at least 45 degrees.

Once again, I had a wreck occurring in slow motion right before my eyes. I ran and got a forklift driver to get under the low side of the trailer and lift it as much as possible. We then slowly raised the landing gear. Once we got the trailer stabilized, I backed the truck back underneath it and made sure the 5th wheel was locked. By this time, Scot was trying to remember why he had come on this trip. He helped me tremendously throughout the ordeal.

Now that the trailer was back on, we set about picking up all the pieces that had spilled out of the boxes. This job took over an hour and it was dark by the time we finished. I noticed the temperature gauge was climbing again so we looked under the hood and discovered a small leak in another hose. We got the forklift driver to put the boxes back on the trailer and took off in search of our next fiasco as we headed home.

The temperature gauge continued to climb. By the time we neared Ritzville, it was approaching the red. There were no more towns for 60 miles, and yet, I started talking myself into the idea that I might be able to make it home without stopping. I mentioned this idea to Scot and he hit the roof. "Pull off and get some water," he demanded. I resisted. I always look at each emergency situation that comes along every half hour or so and view it as a challenge to see if I can get through it. You know, "Beat the odds!"

He again commanded me to stop in a screaming sort of tone. The exit was approaching and at the last second, I reluctantly pulled off just to make him happy. After all, he is bigger and probably tougher than I am.

It's lucky that I kept Scot happy. We pulled into a gas station and steam blew everywhere. It took a good 15 minutes of watching the engine get steam cleaned before we could get close enough to get the cap off. We then spent 20 minutes pouring water down the spout. I could see then that if we hadn't stopped, the truck would have blown up in just a few more miles. We drove home. Thank you, Scot.

CHAPTER 30

DANGEROUS LOVE

I love flying. I soloed while in Utah and then ran out of money and was unable to continue the lessons. In 1986, I bought a Beechcraft Musketeer 4-seater with my brother, Brent. I don't have the personality to be a real cautious pilot, therefore I've had a few too many close calls while flying. Essentially all of these occurred because of pilot error.

My first hairy experience occurred while I was still a student pilot. Brent and I had just acquired the Musketeer. I took off one Saturday morning in the fall and flew around the area. Down by my farm I noticed a few friends were standing around so I decided to show off, land, and shoot the bull with them. One of them, Karl, had hit me up for a ride the day before, but then he had decided he wasn't brave enough. I couldn't take him anyway since I didn't have my license yet.

I circled around and lined up with the highway that bordered my farm. I slowed the plane up and came in on the final approach. All of a sudden, directly in front of mine and Brent's Beechcraft, were three power lines with a ground cable underneath them, hanging 20 feet above the ground. I had lived in these parts all my life and knew that there were power lines there. However, in the process of looking for cars or other potential crash participants on the road, I had forgotten about the high voltage lines.

In a nano-second, I shoved the stick down and dove under the lines. Then, just as quickly, I jerked it back up so I wouldn't plow into the ground. All would have turned out non-momentous and I would have been able to flair out and land except for one problem; Karl's Ranchero was parked off the side of the road, under the power lines, with its hood up.

My front landing gear hit the hood and folded the gear back under the fuselage. The plane slammed down on its nose and slid for a quarter of a mile down the road. I was powerless to change anything after the initial impact. I just sat there and enjoyed the ride as the crash unfolded. It was loud and quick and felt a little like I was at Disneyland. When we finally stopped, I jumped out and surveyed the damage. The prop was badly damaged and the nose sat on the ground. The main gear was intact and the tail was sticking eight feet up in the air. My buddies arrived and Karl ran up out of breath. He was shook up, much more than I. He was saying something about how that could have been him in the propeller bender. I got a kick out of how upset he was. You would have thought he was the guy who had been in the wreck.

We hooked the tail of the plane on to the back of a pickup and started pulling it up toward my dad's shed. My parents came driving down the lane just as we were pulling my broken plane up the road. They stopped at the stop sign, looked at the wreck, turned, and went the other way without even stopping to ask what had happened. I couldn't believe they didn't even care if I was dead or alive. I arrived at the conclusion that they were a little jaded when it came to worrying about my wrecks.

We pulled the plane up behind Dad's shed and parked it. I decided I probably wouldn't report it to the powers that be. I wanted to collect the insurance, but didn't want to answer all the questions the government was sure to throw at me. Why stir up a hornet's nest?

The next morning at 4:00 am my phone rang. I answered and the guy on the other end identified himself as some kind of brass from the Civil Air Patrol in Yakima. He asked if I owned a Beechcraft airplane. I answered that I did. He then asked if I was the pilot when it wrecked. After another yes, he told me that the ELT (Emergency Locator Transmitter) had gone off when I wrecked and a satellite had picked up the signal. They had been flying around the area all night trying to locate it. He also told me that since they had gotten involved, they would have to report it to the NTSB and the FAA.

During the night, my folks heard a plane circling and buzzing their house. They had no idea why. They were a little bothered that it disturbed their sleep.

The FAA called me later and said they wanted me to come over to Seattle and take a flight proficiency exam. I didn't feel like driving 500 miles just to show them I could fly. I asked the gentleman if they ever came to Pasco. He answered, "Yes." I said I would be glad to take their exam if I could take it in Pasco. He said that was okay. I never heard from them again. I eventually obtained my pilot's license.

After I wrecked the Beechcraft, collected the insurance, and paid my brother for his half, I took a short hiatus and then bought an old Mooney. My 1963 M20-B Mooney was a relatively fast 4-seater airplane. It had a variable pitch prop and retractable landing gear so it was faster than most other small airplanes in its class. The landing gear was extended and retracted by grasping a big handle in the middle of the console and manually pulling it back or pushing it up to raise and lower the wheels. It was kind of like a big emergency brake handle located between the seats. It was dependable and fun to operate. The big challenge for me was remembering to put the wheels down before landing. Just one time forgetting would require the purchase of a new prop, overhauling the engine, and dealing with the ridicule that would come from my local detractors and customers. I managed to get through the ensuing Mooney years without an incident. Well, at least one involving my landing gear.

• •

I used to fly to La Grande, Oregon regularly while I was wrapped up with the Valve Alarm. I had several misadventures on this route. One of the first times I flew down, I ran into cloud cover just past the Tri-Cities. I climbed on top of the clouds to about 12,000 feet and flew in the general direction of La Grande. At the time, I had no GPS or Loran. I had no clue exactly where I was or how far I had gone. The further I went, the more concerned I became. The clouds were completely covering my view of the ground and stretched as far as the eye could see. There were no breaks or holes. I was starting to feel desperate that I would end up running out of fuel and dropping through the clouds into a mountain. Finally, I saw a hole and dove down through it. Unbelievably, I came down right over La Grande. I kissed the ground after landing.

Another time I flew to Prineville, Oregon, the headquarters of Les Schwab, and ended up with the same problem. When I finally found a hole, I was a little hesitant going down through it because I could see that the ground was somewhat close to the bottom of the clouds. It was hard to judge if I should make the vertical trip down as there were mountains around. I didn't want to get down, get stuck in the clouds, and slam into a hillside that was hidden in the clouds. Once again, I lucked out.

Connell High School had a good football team one year and I decided that I would fly up to their game in Ephrata. The air strip in Basin City that I always flew out of had no runway lights of any kind. I decided that I would solve this problem by putting out some little, low voltage plastic lawn lights on each side of the runway. I put a car battery at the end of the runway and hooked it up before I took off for Ephrata. The trip up was uneventful. The game was good although I remember Connell got beat.

Back at the Ephrata airport (the movie *Always* was filmed there), I cranked the Mooney up a little after 10:00 pm and took off into the darkness.

The first few minutes were uneventful, but soon I was disoriented. I had a Loran which told me exactly where I should be headed to go home. However, I also had a brain that told me the Loran was all wet. Something must have gone wrong with it as it was pointing me in the opposite direction of where I was convinced I was supposed to be headed. I looked at the compass and it was off, too, about 180 degrees. Many pilots die from this phenomenon of wanting to believe their head instead of their instruments.

I tried to guess the different towns from their lights and where I was in relation to the towns I thought I recognized. I flew and flew and finally concluded I was completely lost and better get some help before I ran out of fuel. I called Seattle Center, told them I needed some help to get to the Tri-Cities since I didn't think they knew where Basin City was. They gave me a transponder number so they could find my location. Immediately, they gave me the correct coordinates which I once again found hard to believe, but I followed their instructions and soon was flying over the Tri-Cities. From there it wasn't hard heading north to home to land by the dim flicker of my lawn lights. Beat the odds again.

I flew at every opportunity that materialized. Whenever I needed to go somewhere, if there was a landing strip, I flew. Even that restricting factor didn't stop me at times.

Speaking of landing at night, I never learn. Once I get set on landing at a certain place, I get a one-track mind. Several times I came close to crashes with this mentality. Growing up on a farm, we always took chances most folks wouldn't. That is because we had to get the job done and we were used to going against the odds. This usually works on the farm, but is not a good trait if you are sitting in the left front seat of an airplane.

It is a paradigm that often makes for a wild ride.

One evening I had just finished work and arrived home. Dave, the manager of my store in Connell, called and said his sister-in-law was having big marital problems in Hood River, Oregon. He wanted me to fly down and pick her up. I didn't want to and told him so. He told me if I didn't, he would have to drive down and it would take him away from work for a day. I knew it would be close to dark before we got back, even if everything went like clockwork, which it never seemed to do. I finally reluctantly agreed.

I had to wait for Dave to drive over to Basin City and we took off. We arrived in Hood River in about an hour and picked the girl and her two kids up. We were soon back in the air with a payload of five souls in a four-seater. It was getting dark.

By the time we reached Basin City, there was just a hint of light available. The sun had been down for a long time. I could barely make out the town and was just guessing where the runway was. I came down in a final approach landing configuration three times and had to abort each time at the last minute because I was not lined up with the runway. It got darker during each go-around.

This was particularly distressing and stressful because of the other people I had in the plane. I had been cajoled into doing this good turn and now I was completely responsible if something went wrong. The fourth approach was close enough and after some yawing and crabbing, I forced the plane onto the ground. As happened on a regular basis, I kissed the ground after arrival. I felt like kicking Dave in the hind end.

Another eve, I don't remember where I had been, but I arrived in Basin City well after dark. There was absolutely no way to tell where the airport was. After flying around scanning the lights, I got the general idea of where the landing strip just might possibly be. There was a mercury vapor light at the front of the hangar at one end of the runway. I kept focused on this particular light as I came in on final approach in line with where I thought the runway could be.

I knew there were some power lines and a tree on the left side of the runway. Just to be safe, I stayed higher than usual as I approached since I had no idea where they were. I didn't want to hit them. I couldn't tell how high I was off the ground and I couldn't tell where the runway was located as everything was dark . . . no . . . more like black. When I flew past the light at the hangar, I could see I was far too high.

I should have gone around, but I was scared and tired of being in the air. I dove for the ground, picked up some unwanted speed, and finally touched down about 2/3 of the way down the 1600 foot strip. I was going way too fast and the runway transitioned from pavement to dirt right where I touched down. I stomped on the brakes for all I was worth and skidded with the wheels locked for the next 600 feet. When I finally came to a stop, I looked out the side window and the plane landing lights revealed an irrigation ditch full of water two feet away from my front wheel and left main landing gear. I again beat the odds and, miraculously, my plane was still in one piece. This would be the last time I landed in the dark without runway lights.

• •

And yet another night found me heading home from La Grande after dark, running on empty. I figured I had just enough fuel to make it to Basin City. I called my wife before takeoff and told her when I arrived in Basin City I was going to call her on the radio and have her drive out to the airport. I told her to drive to the far end of the runway and shine the lights down the runway so I would have a rough idea of just where the runway was.

I made it to Basin City and radioed her. I was nervous and out of fuel. I watched the Suburban headlights as she slowly and carefully drove from our home out to the landing strip. I whispered under my breath that she should speed it up as I periodically glanced at my empty fuel gauge.

It was then that things went dreadfully wrong. She parked down at the far end of the strip as instructed, but instead of facing the runway and shining her lights down its length, she was perpendicular to it!

It was about 11:00 at night and as dark as it could be. Her headlights were pointed toward the trailer park and gave me no clue as to what direction I should come in at. I circled a few times hoping she would figure out my hesitation and satisfy my needs. However, she just sat there. I guess she wanted me to land in the trailer park. Unfortunately, the radio at home was not a remote handheld so I couldn't communicate with her.

I shook myself out of my landing mode and wondered if I had enough fuel to make it back to Pasco, the closest field with lights. The gauge was on empty. I swear that was the longest trip I've ever made from Basin City to Pasco, even when I've hitchhiked.

I arrived at Pasco and began getting ready to make my final approach. I was expecting my engine to conk out at any second. To make matters worse, I noticed the landing lights from a Delta jet from Seattle. He was making his approach from the opposite direction, but was still about 20 miles out. Even though I could see his lights, I figured if I hustled I could land and get off the runway before he arrived at the point of impact. The control tower shut down at night so I was on my own.

As I announced and began my final approach, the Delta pilot came on the radio and told me he was coming in and I had better go around. I didn't want to get in an argument with him, nor did I want the FAA to get involved. I crossed my fingers, jerked the stick back to gain as much altitude as I could in case I ran out of fuel, and went around. The jet landed and I came down directly after. I borrowed a buddy's car at the airport and drove home to find out what trailer space my wife had in mind for me to park the plane in.

• •

On a late afternoon, the day before Thanksgiving, I was looking for an excuse to fly. I jumped in the Mooney and headed for Pasco to pick up some automotive shocks that were needed at the tire store. Who flies 25 miles to pick up a pair of shocks that they'll make $20 on when it costs them 30 or 40 bucks to make the trip? A guy who loves flying, that's who!

About halfway to my destination, I started smelling gasoline. It got stronger and stronger. I looked around and discovered a significant stream of gas flowing from underneath the instrument panel. It was puddling up on the floor.

I immediately had visions of an electrical spark from the radio or other instruments inside the plane igniting the napalm-like fumes. My ride and I would go down in a fireball. I would be dead from burns and smoke inhalation before the plane hit the ground. Panic set in. I didn't dare use my radio because I had just acquired a sudden phobia toward anything electronic, therefore, I couldn't call the tower for clearance to land. I began circling and waiting for them to shine their green light at me as is standard procedure if a plane appears with no radio traffic.

I flew around for a few minutes with nary a green signal. The gasoline was making a big pool on the floor. I was scared to death and choking on fumes. Finally, I decided to abandon the reason for the trip and head for home. The Basin City airfield could not arrive fast enough. Fifteen minutes later I landed and parked.

The next day I checked for the leak and found that the fuel line going to the fuel pressure gauge had cracked. I had beaten the odds again.

• •

One winter Michele and I went to Hawaii for a Les Schwab Manager's week. We were to catch a flight out of Spokane. I wanted to get a Loran GPS installed in my plane. I decided we would take the plane to Spokane and leave it for the installation while we went to Maui. We would fly it home after getting back to Spokane.

Michele had never flown with me before. We had to leave well before daylight on a frosty morning. We took off in the dark on the strip that had no lights. It wasn't that bad. Landing on one is a billion times worse. At least you can kind of see which direction the runway is headed with the plane's landing lights while you're taking off.

I assured her that things would be fine. She was scared. Perhaps I was a little overconfident. I was excited to show her how good I was at piloting. This was the first and last time she flew on an airplane with me in the driver's seat. We traveled a good 75 miles in the dark with no problem.

All of a sudden, without warning, we were in the clouds. In the dark, you don't know where the clouds are until you're in them. Vertigo can hit a pilot in seconds. Immediately, I became under confident. I thought back on my training under the hood and focused solely on my instruments until we finally broke back out of the clouds. It was exactly this type of flying situation that brought John Kennedy, Jr. down along with thousands of other pilots through the years.

Michele could tell that I was a little uncomfortable in that situation which scared her to death. She never flew with me as chief pilot again. Instrument rated pilots do fine in clouds, but wing nut aviators like myself need to see where the ground is at all times.

• •

Years later a friend of mine named Russ had a little plane that he had just soloed in. We had him and his family over for dinner one evening. He and I talked about planes and I warned him concerning how fast you could get into irreversible trouble with the contraptions. I told him to be aware of all power lines since not seeing them led to my crash. He assured me that he was smarter than that, he flew safe, and knew all about power lines.

A few days later I was at home and the electricity went off. I called the tire store to see if they still had power. They informed me not only that they were powerless but that Russ and his plane had crashed into the power lines in front of the tire store.

It turns out that Russ had a low tire on his plane and decided to land on the street adjacent to my store and fill his tire with air. They hauled him away in the ambulance. His back got a little messed up and his ego was in critical condition for several days after.

359

CHAPTER 31

HOW I FEEL ABOUT RESTRAINTS, FINANCIAL AND OTHERWISE

Throughout my career, I have been a haphazard manager of money. I've taken great chances and lost large amounts through my risk-taking and loose management style. In order to accomplish my lofty goals, I've constantly needed to borrow more and more money to keep a positive cash flow. I often neglected my "old" and boring sources of cash such as receivables and moving out excess inventory. It was much more exciting and challenging to apply for loans and get a larger credit line.

During the many years of borrowing, I often ended up at the desk of a banker friend of my father's named Mick. He worked at four different banks over the twenty-four years that I was in my aggressive borrowing mode. It was always a convoluted relationship between us. For the first few years, whenever I applied for money, this particular banker would talk to my dad and ask him what position he should take with the loan, even though my dad usually had nothing to do it. It was very frustrating.

A few years after I started my tire store, I went in and applied for a loan. Mick told me to come back in a week, which I did. When I sat down with him, he told me I was bankrupt and that I had two choices. I could liquidate everything I owned or get a loan from him with my father acting as co-signer. I told him neither was acceptable. I went to another bank and got a loan without my dad's involvement. I've never declared bankruptcy so Mick had it wrong. I know . . . never say never.

Ten years later, I was in dire circumstances and looking for dough. Making my rounds, I stopped in at a new bank that my old banker Mick had just gotten a job with. I laid out my financial situation to him and he told me he would get back to me in a day or two. My folks were down in Reno, Nevada at that time. My dad was doing everything he could to fight the

Multiple Sclerosis that was attacking his body. He was in Reno for several months at a place called Century Clinic, hoping for a cure to the disease that left him in a wheelchair. That experience ended up costing him lots of money and great pain while providing no benefits.

It just so happened that I was playing the lead in a play at our church called "Capricious Pearls." My mom also had been in rehearsals prior to accompanying Dad south and had just returned home for a couple of days to be in the play. The day she arrived home, Mick called her and said, "Joan, I just called to tell you that Ben is in a lot of trouble financially." He then proceeded to give her the stress-inducing details of my money situation.

It shook her up. She called me to see what was going on. I told her that nothing was out of the ordinary. I was always in that kind of shape. I calmed her down and as soon as we hung up started considering the possibility of suing the bank and banker for divulging my personal business.

He had disclosed confidential information without my permission. If my dad had been home at that time and gotten Mick's phone call, it would have greatly upset him. It was not something he needed on his plate at the time. I couldn't believe this guy would do that. It seemed to be a constant theme with him, always trying to do some backdoor move on me with my dad on the hook instead of a straightforward financial relationship with me.

I had always paid my bills and never left him in the lurch. I swore I would never do business with him again. The only reason I didn't go after him legally was because it would have greatly upset my folks.

●　●

Years later, I needed another big loan. I went to a new bank where it just so happened that my old friend Mick had just, once again, gotten a job. I knew better, but like I always do, I thought, "THIS TIME THINGS WILL BE DIFFERENT!" We both apologized for our past mistakes. He told me this deal would be different.

Predictably, by the time it was completed, he had gone back to his old ways. The loan was for $690,000. I got it, but only after working through a lot of extra-curricular garbage propagated by this same guy.

My personal banker was a gal named Jan, but Mick was doing all of the coaching. I had done some new construction and bought several semi-truck loads of propane tanks. I needed new money. I applied for the loan in August. Mick told me I would have the loan proceeds in September. Month after month rolled past and I was still jumping through his hoops via Jan. I was in deep trouble with Les Schwab and other payables. Finally, in the last few days of December, the bank board met with Mick and came up with a list of new hoops for me to jump through. Words cannot express the agitation I experienced.

One of the eight new items they wanted was for me to send out forms to all of my customers who owed me over a thousand dollars. My customers were to verify and sign off, acknowledging to the bank that they owed me the amount. I probably had 300 customers in that category. I assume this was because the bank (Mick) didn't believe me when I listed my receivables.

I was livid. In the roughly 20 years that I had been in business, I had never heard of such a thing. In my mind, it had Mick's fingerprints all over it. After much debate I got them to loosen up on some of their stipulations. They agreed to randomly pick a few customers out of my pile and send them the questionnaires.

The day after I sent out the forms, Jimmy Parnell walked into my office. Jim was a great guy. He was short in stature, but didn't mince words when he had an opinion. On this day he had an opinion. He slammed the form down on the counter and said something like this: "Ben, I've been doing business with you for many years! I don't know why you don't trust me to pay my bill! I don't know why your bank is coming after me for money! I'm going to pay my bill right now and you are never going to have to worry about me buying from you again 'cause I won't."

Jim didn't understand the purpose of the letter he had just received. Of course, I really didn't either. I then explained what was going on with the bank. I informed him that I had been dead set against sending him the letter. I told him I would like him to tell my banker what he had just told me. He said, "Fine."

I dialed Jan and gave Jim the phone. She got an earful. Afterwards, I told Jim I valued his business and he said he would keep doing business with me. Several other customers followed with similar complaints. I had them all call Jan. The bank withdrew their outrageous demand. I got the $690,000 soon after.

Five months of misleading promises, last-minute stipulations, and unreasonable hoops to jump through, all while my financial life hung in the balance. Mick liked the power he held over his customers. I talked to other people that also had the same kinds of experiences with him.

Several years after obtaining the loan, I paid the bank in full. One day, Mick simply dropped out of sight at the bank. No one knew what had happened to him. I think some of his tricks must have caught up with him.

• •

Seatbelts have always been my pet peeve. I agree that they have saved a lot of lives. However, I propose that they have also cost a lot of people their lives. I feel strongly that this is one of those areas that the government ought to keep their nose out of. I don't believe they are all that concerned about our safety. If they were, they would outlaw tobacco, sugar, alcohol, high-speed police pursuits, wars overseas, and women drivers. Just kidding on that last one!

I don't know that the surveys they tout to promote seatbelts are all that accurate. I've read that death rates have increased in some states after seatbelt laws were instituted and enforced. I've obtained this information off the internet so I know it must be correct.

The only reason I can think of that the government is so set on requiring seatbelt use is revenue. They refuse to release any info as to how much dough they generate from seatbelt violations, but it is substantial. One good estimate is a billion dollars a year. These dollars are flowing out of our pockets, many who can ill afford it, and going into public coffers for something that we should not even be stopped for.

One winter, on a Sunday afternoon, I pulled out of my driveway and headed down the road to visit a couple of families on a monthly church visit that we call Home Teaching. This involves visiting assigned households and making sure their needs are being met, sharing a short spiritual message, and having a prayer. It is a great program and has helped many people who needed, but otherwise would not have received, help and support.

Anyway, back to my seatbelt story. I noticed a sheriff's car stopped at the intersection in front of a stop sign about a quarter of a mile from my house. By the time I backed out of my driveway and traveled the distance to the official vehicle, it had probably taken 30 or 40 seconds. He was still there. There was no traffic on the intersecting street for him to wait on. It bugged me a little that he was blocking the road for no good reason. If he wanted to park and look for violators, he should have found a parking lot.

I, on the other hand, should have pulled up behind him and laid on the horn. Instead I politely scooted around the right side of him going partially off the road, turned right, and went about my business. In a heartbeat he was on my tail with his lights flashing. He was a young kid, still wet behind the ears.

He asked why I wasn't wearing my seatbelt and I told him. He asked for my paperwork, which I gave him. The only problem was that I didn't have the current insurance card. I had one that was outdated by several months previous. I told him I still had the same insurance as was on the card. If he wanted we could drive back to my house and I could show him proof. He walked back to his car.

In a few minutes, he came back with a $650 ticket for having no insurance card and no seatbelt. My experience has been that for the first couple of years after he gets his official certificate from the police academy, a new cop can't think for himself. He has lost all social skills, thinks he's one step above deity, and makes everybody mad that he comes in contact with.

After spending some time dealing with everyday life experiences, the majority of these constables (in my estimation about 20%), wake up and realize that they are serving the public and that they need to use some good judgment and common sense in their application and enforcement of the law.

After one of Franklin County's finest handed me the large fine, I simply asked him how long he had been out of the academy. He responded that he didn't have to answer that question, but that he knew all about me and he didn't care who I called.

This made me mad. Although I had started my trip on a spiritual mission, I was now dealing with a guy who essentially was telling me that he was gunning for me. I wondered if the reason he was stopped at the stop sign for so long was because he saw me pull out of my driveway. I suspected he had waited around to see if he could nail me for something. If he "knew all about me" it was obvious that he was going to nail me to the wall as hard as he could.

This incident occurred during the Christmas holidays. Derek was home from law school. He was accompanying me on my home teaching route. Every time I exchanged pleasantries with the cop, Derek would say softly, "Dad, shut up!"

The official walked back to his cruiser, I told my rearview mirror that he was a little jerk, and proceeded on my spiritual visits. It took me a while to get a Christlike spirit back. I'm afraid the families we visited that day could sense the lack of Christmas cheer in me. I was upset for the next few nights and finally penned the following letter to my doctor after my brother Bryan gave me the suggestion.

Dear Dr. *****,

I am writing you to find out what I should do. If you want to charge me for an office visit for taking the time to read this, I'm okay with that.

In 1970, I was involved in a serious auto accident. My side of the car was smashed in. I did not have a seatbelt on and I ended up being pushed over on top of the driver. I had serious injuries to the right side of my head, my right ribs, my right arm, and hand. I know without a doubt if I had been belted in, I would have died. I would have been restrained in place by the seatbelt and taken the full impact of the car caving in on my side. The cops thought I was going to die as it was.

In 1979, a buddy of mine, Scot Haws, got T-boned by a truck that lost its brakes and ran a stop sign. The truck tore the car in half, taking everything behind his seat including his seat belt one way while Scot and the front end of the car went another. The two halves ended up several hundred feet apart. If Scot had had his belt on, the belt certainly would have cut Scot in half, maybe even killed him.

It's interesting that a few years later when the seat belt law first came out in WA State, a state patrol revenue generator stopped Scot and I one night and gave us both tickets for no belts on. Because we didn't have belts on in our prior accidents, we were both still alive for the cop to tax us.

In approximately 2002, I was serving on the Basin City volunteer ambulance crew. We were called to respond to an accident victim. He and 3 of his friends ran head on into a ditch. He was belted in and died from one injury, caused solely by his seatbelt. He had no other injuries. He was a healthy young man and suffered severe lower abdominal hemorrhaging, visible by the mark of his belt. His companions were fine. They each walked away without a scratch. None of his friends were wearing a seatbelt.

I have had several other similar experiences. I am not writing concerning the pros and cons of wearing a seatbelt. I am fully aware of them. I believe it would be best to be wearing a seatbelt in a rollover. However, I would not want to be wearing a belt in a side impact, some head-on collisions, a broadside t-bone, fire, or submersion. Belts trap and keep people from moving away from oncoming impacts or escaping imminent danger. Contrary to the commonly publicized law enforcement generated statistics, there are also studies that show fewer fatalities in states before passage of seatbelt laws than after. Of course, the public is not made aware of this argument because of the adverse effect on government budgets and increased revenue from seatbelt infractions (somewhere between 600 million and 1 billion dollars).

I have been stopped several times by WA State troopers and after having explained my situation, they have let me go without issuing a ticket. However, last Sunday I was cited for not wearing a seat belt by a rookie sheriff. Since then, I have been very worked up about the situation. I've slept very little at night even though I've been taking 25 mg of Amitriptylin each evening. I am now sick with a bad cold, congestion, and exhaustion brought on solely by my dilemma.

Because of my experiences and concerns, I feel that wearing a seatbelt is injurious to my daily well-being and health. It could possibly be life threatening if I am involved in an accident. I am experiencing sleepless nights and anxiety daily by this conundrum. My blood pressure jumps every time I get in a car and have to make a decision whether to buckle up or not. My anxiety is high if I wear my belt because of my previous experiences. My anxiety is high if I don't wear my belt because of the threat of a ticket. Therefore, understanding all the risks involved and assuming all liability for this request, I am requesting (actually pleading for) a medical release or exemption from wearing a seatbelt.

My brother Bryan has Crohn's Disease and has been given a medical card that allows him to avoid wearing a seatbelt. When it comes to seatbelts over the long term, I believe my health is just as threatened as his, or even more so, if I am required to wear one.

Please respond via email as to whether this is a viable option from you. If it is, I will make an appointment to come in and discuss/obtain this desirable document. Thank you.

Sincerely,

Ben Casper

My wife said I didn't have a chance of swinging this deal. I thought I did. The doctor called and said he was willing to talk to me. I went in and he asked me what I wanted him to do. I told him a letter would suffice. He asked what he should write as far as detailing the reason. I told him the reason was nobody's business except his and mine. He agreed.

He then asked what kind of expiration date he should put on it. I said I thought it should be permanent. "They'll never go for that," he said. I pulled out the copy of my brother's card and we looked at it. It said, "Permanent." "Sounds good," he said.

I got my exemption. Free at last!

• •

The only time I have ever really needed a seatbelt was when I flew my airplane. One day, I jumped in the plane and hurriedly ran through the checklist and took off. It was a windy day and as soon as I lifted off, I knew I was in trouble. The plane was bouncing around in the turbulent air like crazy and I was bouncing around in the captain's seat even worse. I had forgotten to put my seatbelt on.

I was the only one in the plane and therefore couldn't ask someone to hold the wheel while I buckled up. Hanging on to the wheel for dear life, I was doing everything I could just to keep the thing under control. Every time I would bounce up, my hands would pull the stick back and the plane would start climbing.

After I hit my head on the roof and began a rapid descent to my seat, the stick would move forward and the plane would dive, searching for another upward wave of air to ride. This went on for some time. I didn't dare let go of the wheel to fasten my belt and yet the crazy flight pattern I had established was a little disconcerting. Finally, I let go of the wheel, got hooked up, and then was able to regain control of the airplane.

Okay, seatbelts are a good thing once in a while. In fact, once in a while when I'm inspired, I hook it up. It's my decision, not the legislatures and code enforcers. I let the Spirit guide me. It's a beautiful feeling.

One last thing . . . the news always reports when people are killed if they didn't have their belt on, suggesting that is why they died. They never report when a belt kills someone. Vehicle fires, submersions, and impacts from the side are just some of the times you would rather not have your belt on. Being restrained and trapped without being able to get out of vehicles has killed many people.

CHAPTER 32

A FEW MEDICAL NOTES

Speaking of doctors, permit me to share a couple of stories concerning experiences with them. A fellow in our community died at the ripe old age of 102. A friend of mine asked him a few years ago what the greatest invention was that he had seen in the past 100 years. It wasn't the airplane, automobile, cell phone, computer, space shuttle, iPhone, YankATank, or TV. He testified with all sincerity it was toilet paper. So what does toilet paper have to do with doctors? Hang on.

Decades ago I developed a pain in my side that became unbearable. I spent the entire night on the floor, unable to lie down, let alone sleep. It was exhausting and excruciating. I was on my knees the entire night, ready for my nighttime prayers.

The next day, Michele ambulatoried me to the hospital. They probed, x-rayed, and did all the tests they thought I could afford, but even after all my money was gone, they still hadn't determined the culprit that had incapacitated me. The emergency room doctor did a little research in his medical book, discovered I had insurance, and suddenly prognosticated that I had a kidney stone and was still a source of income. I was immediately checked into the hospital.

I spent the next several days on medication and undergoing more tests. They fed me nothing but liquids and a watery broth throughout the entire stay. I guess they were thinking that if they scrimped on my food budget, they would have more of a net profit to show for the period that I was under their care.

I was starving. I started spending less time dealing with the kidney stone pains and more time doubled over dealing with acute hunger. In retrospect, the kidney ailment never subsided. The hunger pangs just overrode them. The nurse came in on the third day and asked me how I was feeling. Under the covers I pressed one hand hard against my stomach so it didn't feel so empty and the other hand tightly gripped my side so as to stifle the stone pain. I was then able to smile.

"I feel so much better!" I happily fibbed through gritted teeth. Whatever it took to get out of this sterile gulag and chow down on some vittles, I was up for. The nurse stated that she had just witnessed a modern-day miracle and on her clipboard wrote a glowing report for the doc.

The doctor/miracle worker confidently strode in a few minutes later and said they were going to release me. He appeared to be very happy with himself and his medical acumen after reading his nurse's accolades. He then produced a paper outlining the things that I should avoid at all costs, namely greasy and fatty foods. He also had a master menu of things that I could drink and eat. This master menu consisted of two food groups, water and ice. I assured him I would avoid the multitude of forbidden foods found on the first list so he signed my release papers.

My wife arrived to pick me up. They carted me out in a wheelchair and I gingerly eased myself into the car. In addition to the pain of my tender kidney-stoned side panel, I was in the throes of starvation. I instructed my wife, in no uncertain terms and over her vehement objections, to drive me Code 3 (screeching tires, flashing red blinkers, and an occasional horn honk) to Roy's Chuck Wagon.

We spent the next hour feasting on fried chicken, ham, potatoes and gravy, and all other possible options available in a respectable western smorgasbord buffet. The pains left. I'm now of the opinion that the grease dissolved the stones, or at least provided a little lubrication so they could pass on their merry way south just a little bit easier. The pains never returned. I'm thinking greasy and fatty foods were the cure, not the culprit.

The doctor turned out not to be the miracle worker. Roy of Roy's Chuck Wagon was the real hero.

• •

Several years after the kidney stone experience, I bought tickets to go to Spokane with my wife and relatives to see Styx and REO Speedwagon, two bands that were popular in the 70s and 80s. On the days leading up to the concert, I had stayed very focused on delivering propane and setting tanks. However, I noticed a slight pain in my abdomen that increased over time until it was very painful to work. It was a little like the kidney stone pain I'd had years before, but was in a slightly different spot.

By the time the day of the concert rolled around, I was in agony. I couldn't stand to wear anything that put pressure on my abdomen. Even underwear was unbearable. I could hardly walk. I was torn as to whether to try to make the concert or not. However, I have always hated to be a party pooper so I committed to make the 120-mile trip to Spokane.

The only apparel I could stand to wear was some very loose fitting sweat pants. I had to hike them up so there was no pressure whatsoever on my lower tummy. Instead of heading out for a music fest, I felt like I should be heading for an operating room. Even though I was dressed like a jock with the sweat pants and tennis shoes, I think at least some of the visual athletic effect was lost on the onlookers. This was due to the fact that I had to wear the sweats hiked up to just below my nipple line in order to keep the tie cord from putting any undue pressure on my painful abdomen.

I remember my wife commenting several times that I should pull my pants down a bit as it looked like I was preparing for a flood or being raised in an invisible helicopter sling that was hooked on to my belt loops. I was wearing ultra high-water, dark sweat pants with the bottoms of the legs a good three inches above the top of my white tube socks. I must say that through that entire evening, I had no concerns whatsoever regarding my outward appearance.

We arrived in Spokane early. Everyone wanted to grab a bite to eat except me. But like the sport I am, I dealt with the pain and hobbled into the restaurant with my kin. I remember my brother-in-law Todd had a huge, horrific looking boil on his lip. I felt sorry for him, but was absolutely certain he was in less pain. He was ugly outside. I was ugly inside.

The concert was probably good, but all I remember was trying to get comfortable in my seat for three hours. I was never successful. The strongest memory I have of the evening was trying to walk back to the car in the parking lot afterwards. I was bent over and hanging on to the coattails of my brother Brent since it was too painful to look up. I limped with both legs every step of the way. I thought we'd never get to the car. We should have parked in the handicapped zone that night. I would have gladly paid the ticket.

Something was definitely haywire in my innards.

It so happened that the next morning we had been planning to head for Utah to visit Michele's parents. I had a terrible night and told her the next morning that there was no way I could make the trip. We decided that she and the kids would drive down without me. However, just before they left, I came up with a solution.

I would ride into town with them. We would visit a clinic, find a solution, get healed, and then make the long trip to Utah. We pulled out the back seat in the Suburban and I lay down in the most comfortable position I could find with my head resting on the spare tire. All the kids were crammed up front with Michele.

Arriving at the clinic in Kennewick, we found they were booked up and couldn't see me for three hours. We called several other clinics and got the same story. It was late in the morning and there was still over 600 miles to cover before the Promised Land of Utah appeared. A very long drive was shaping up for one in the shape I was in. I decided to take one for the team and told Michele to drive on.

Several times on this most memorable trip, Michele would call out, "Who needs to use the restroom?" I wanted to join in with the kids chanting, "I do! I do!" I felt kinda like I really did need to, but also knew the pain of my, as yet, unknown malady would prevent success. So I stayed in the least painful fetal position I could find while screaming in agony every time Michele ran over a piece of gravel or center-line stripe.

I bounced around in the back of the Sub all the way to Utah, wondering if I could continue taking the abuse. As we passed through Salt Lake, we called Mitch's folks in Orem and got the number of a clinic (I call Michele "Mitch" when I'm feeling particularly needy). The clinic told me they closed at 10:00 pm. I told Mitch to hit the gas and stay off the brakes.

We pulled into the clinic parking lot at 9:58 pm. I clenched my teeth and found my way inside. I was dying. The nurse handed me a clipboard with an introductory multiple choice quiz with several hundred questions concerning exotic diseases I wouldn't have been caught dead with. I'm not a fan of these questionnaires and I sure wasn't in the mood to take a written test on this particular evening.

I handed the quiz to Michele to take and then bent back over the counter. The doctor came out and after glancing at my pale face, took me in and immediately ordered a series of x-rays to try to find out what insidious monster had attacked my system. A few minutes after the x-rays, he walked back in the room while hiding a smirk and asked me when I had last had a BM?

I was a little taken aback. At that particular time in my life, I hadn't been keeping a written record of such incidents and didn't think I had a problem in that neck of the lower woods. In my mind, I thought I had been fairly regular. I was therefore inclined to think it was a waste to talk about my waste when my waist was so pained. I was sure I had appendicitis or stones or cancer . . . something a little more glamorous than a non-BM.

He got this know-it-all look on his face. Pulling out an x-ray, he clipped it on the lighted panel. My pain lessened as I gazed at the board. I gravitated from insolence to embarrassment and finally, at last knowing what the problem was, I became, you might say, basically relieved. Well, not *really* relieved.

My intestines looked like they were packed to the max. I could tell I had missed an important opportunity about a week earlier. He handed me a bottle of laxatives and bid me goodbye. He said something like, "Adios, Senor mucho packo."

My wife was incredulous, mad, and laughing at me for the next few days: incredulous that I hadn't known what my body was up to, mad that I had been such a baby making her drive all the way to Utah and spending a few hundred hard-earned dollars just so a doctor could tell me to hit the head, and laughing because . . . well, I don't know for sure why she was laughing.

Anyway, she shifted back and forth between these emotions for a good week. That's about how long it took me to get the pipes back in shape.

I have since found that if I start approaching the threshold of irregularity, it pays to cinch the belt up a couple of notches past the comfort zone. This, coupled with two or three hundred sit-ups, usually breaks up and gets rid of the problem.

The longer you live, the more you learn about yourself.

• •

Speaking of attacks, I had my own little heart attack one evening. I'll quote from my wife's entry on our family website:

> *"You'll like this one. Yesterday, Ben's chest was hurting him all day. It got worse and worse until he was in quite a bit of pain by early evening. His mom thought it might be a heart attack so I took him into the hospital. Fortunately, it wasn't a heart attack. The diagnosis was pleurisy, which is an inflammation of the lining of the lung and is very painful. Here's the funny part of the story.*
>
> *The night before, Ben shaved half his chest. He did it for shock value and to see how long it would be before I noticed it. It got the desired result, too. It did shock me when I finally noticed it. Well, the first thing they have you do when you get to the hospital and you think you're having a heart attack is—you guessed it—take your shirt off. As he was taking his shirt off, Ben recalled that there was something odd about his chest, but he couldn't remember what it was."*

I'll take over at this point.

I knew I didn't want to take my shirt off, but I couldn't remember why. I pulled the top of it out and peeked down and saw the baby's behind on the one side and the gorilla chest on the other.

I asked them several times, "Do I really have to take my shirt off?" They were in a frenzy because they thought I was in the middle of a heart attack. They couldn't believe I wouldn't take the shirt off. Finally, I reluctantly said, "Okay," and pulled it off.

The doctor and several nurses stood there and stared at my chest. They must have thought I was a nut case. One of the nurses said, "I don't even want to know. I don't even want to know."

Michele had been parking the car. She walked in about this time and I pointed at her and exclaimed, "She made me do it!" Through the rest of our hospital visit that night, the medical staff looked at Michele with a bit of apprehension and none of them wanted to get too close to her.

After a bunch of tests, they determined I was okay and gave me a few pills. This quickly took the pain away. We left, leaving behind a few medical personnel shaking their heads.

• •

One summer I remodeled my tire store. I built a canopy over the driveway areas without a building permit. Soon I was getting letters from the building department and then the prosecuting attorney's office, threatening me with jail time if I didn't get their all-important building permit. I was then privileged to go spend a bunch of money to have an engineer draw up plans on a structure I had already built, just to make the inspector happy.

A few years later, I decided to enclose the area next to the office and make it into a showroom. After enclosing the area for the showroom, I took a torch to remove part of the frame and siding of the office. After tearing out the front wall, I went back to work at the tire store. A couple hours later, I smelled smoke. It registered immediately what was going down. I ran upstairs in the loft and sure enough, I had a fire on my hands. It had started in the insulation when I torched the steel framing.

The guys who sold me the insulation years before told me it was non-combustible so I hadn't worried about it. By the time I discovered it, the fire had spread to the wood frame in the loft. Another 10 minutes and I would probably have lost the shop. I had tires stored in the loft and they were just itching to create an inferno. Luckily, I hadn't done the cutting in the afternoon or the fire would have gotten going after we left for the day.

After the inside framing was done on the showroom I started hanging sheet rock. I spent several days on the walls and then embarked on the ceiling. It was about 12 feet high. I was using scaffolding that wasn't the best. I held each heavy panel of sheet rock above my head while balancing on some planks suspended about six or seven feet above the floor, while at the same time trying to get a few nails started to hold the sheet up.

A couple of days later, I had the job almost done. As I was hanging the last full sheet above my head, the scaffolding slipped out from underneath me and I went straight down. Everyone had left for the day except Tom. He heard the big crash and ran in to see me lying on the floor, writhing in pain. I thought my ankle was broken and my elbow and arm were numb so there was no telling what damage had been inflicted on that extremity.

I called it a day and limped out to my pickup to head home while Tom locked up. As I drove away, I stuck my numb arm out the window and heard cracking and popping noises, kind of like you hear when you pour milk on a big bowl of Rice Krispies.

That night it started hurting—badly. I'd broken at least 23 bones up to this point. This one hurt the worst. I was in terrible pain and spent the night crawling around the house with one traumatized wing and one badly sprained ankle. The next day I headed for the doctor. He said the elbow was shattered and they would have to operate. I went to the hospital that afternoon.

They wouldn't let me eat anything that evening, as I was scheduled for surgery the next morning at nine o'clock. The next morning, I was ready to go. Nine o'clock came and went. I started getting restless; my elbow was killing me, I was hungry, and anxious to get into surgery. The hours ticked by. Every couple of hours a nurse would come in and assure me that they were running a little behind, but would soon be around to get me.

Finally, at eight o'clock that night, they came in and gave me a shot to prepare me for surgery. I guess they'd had some emergencies that day and that was why I'd been pushed back 12 hours. At 9:00 pm, they wheeled me into surgery.

We rolled into the operating room and they transferred me from the gurney to the op table. I was a little rummy, but still intent on getting the show on the road. There were a couple of doctors and four female nurses. One of them tugged on my gown and said it had to come off. I figured I would save her some trouble. I jumped off the table (I'm sure doped-up patients jumping off of surgery tables is a major no-no in the hospital rule book) and pulled the gown off. This action left me standing there naked while five or six medical professionals looked at me with their jaws dropping. I climbed back on the table buck-naked and wondered what the big hesitation was all about. Hadn't these medical experts ever seen a naked dude before?

They all started chuckling and the nurse said she didn't mean the gown had to come *completely* off. It just needed to come off my arm. They helped me get the gown back on and then we pulled it down over my arm. I can remember I didn't feel embarrassed. I was just bugged that I'd had to wait so long. Soon they turned me over to the anesthesiologist and he put me out of my misery, at least for a couple of hours.

CHAPTER 33

THE PRACTICAL, THE IMPRACTICAL, AND THE SENTIMENTAL

When I was hooked up with them, every five years Les Schwab had a manager's meeting in Hawaii. In 1994 Michele and I went to Maui for the shindig. The day after we arrived, my sisters Jill and Lisa and their husbands surprised us. They had decided to come to Maui on the spur of the moment, and knowing we were there, hooked up with us. The first night, we hit the tourist traps and had a great time.

We returned to the Marriot and as we walked past the karaoke bar, all my relatives started urging me to go in and sing a song. The place was filled with inebriated Les Schwab managers and I had no desire to make a fool out of myself. I declined. They continued to press me as we went up to our room. Finally, I said I would do it if they chipped in a hundred bucks. After a few more minutes, they came up with $100. I was still unwilling, but decided it was easy money.

We went down and I surveyed the song list. I had sung "Magic Carpet Ride" in our old high school band and since it was kind of a catchy tune, I decided that it would be my number.

I did it. I quickly retreated out of the bar and collected my money. Over the next couple of days, I felt kind of bad taking my kinfolks' money so I bought everybody a couple of lunches and paid for a few other things; in my mind, this kind of evened things out.

The next year I turned forty. My wife arranged a dinner out with Bill and Joanna Easterday. Joanna's birthday is on the same day as mine so we used to celebrate together. After dinner, my wife surprised me with the information that she had rented a motel room for the night so we would be staying in town.

We got to the motel and when we entered our room, SURPRISE! There was a big crowd of friends and relatives there, throwing me a surprise party. After a few minutes of banter, I looked around the room and noticed that it was decorated in a Hawaiian theme. I commented on it and remarked how we had just been in Hawaii the year before. One of my sisters piped up and said that since it was like Hawaii, I should sing "Magic Carpet Ride." I declined. I said I needed music to sing karaoke. They produced a recorder with a tape that had that very song on it.

"Oh, no!" I didn't want to do that thing again. I racked my brain and came up with another excuse. I wouldn't do it without a microphone.

They shoved a microphone at me. Can you smell a rat? I should have, but didn't.

"Okay, I'll fix them," I thought. "Sorry, I need a hundred bucks, just like it was in Hawaii."

They started scrounging around and people started throwing money in. They came up with eighty dollars and looked to Karl Eppich, a guy locally known for the iron grip he keeps on his wallet, for the remaining twenty.

He pulled out a twenty, but then thought better of it. He didn't want to give it up. Finally, they pried the bill out of his hand.

I didn't like it, but I did the song. I pocketed the hundred dollars.

The conversation bounced around for a while and then someone said something about how I had just sung for my own money. Everyone roared. It took me a minute to start understanding what had just happened. Michele had given out a hundred dollars of my money to my supposed friends earlier who had then just returned it so that I would make a fool out of myself. I had been had. I remarked how hard it had been to get Karl to cough up the twenty bucks he had of mine.

Then it got worse. I mentioned that at least I had made a hundred dollars over in Hawaii, even though I had given it back by buying everybody lunch. The room filled with laughter. Michele had given my sisters and their husbands a hundred dollars of my money there, too. It was a good joke, but I would have preferred it would have happened to somebody else.

In 2004 Michele and I took our last Les Schwab manager's trip to Hawaii. They put on a good party, but it cost a lot of money that I didn't have, as did most every other program Les Schwab has. I think I kind of sensed it would be the last time, as my situation with them was getting more tenuous by the year.

A night or two before we left to come home, I got a call from Kent Mackay that his brother-in-law Lee Eppich had died. Brothers Lee and Lynn Eppich, along with brother-in-law Kent owned Eppich Grain. They had always been good friends and big tire customers of mine.

Lee was a short, gung ho, and happy guy who always had a laugh and a joke for you. He ran the trucking side of Eppich Grain and had a lot of dealings with me through the years. We were great friends. He often stopped at my tire store, rolled the window down, and yelled that he would buy me lunch if I went to town with him. I seldom turned him down even though it would take three hours out of my day. Our trips were always entertaining.

I remember a couple of times when he was feeling blue I would bring my daughter Meg by his shop. She would play him a few tunes on her fiddle. One morning she had been working on a song and really had it nailed. I called Lee and told him to stop by our house on his way to work. He came by and she played the number. It made his day. As he was leaving he handed her a hundred dollar bill.

Lee had polio when he was a kid. He walked with a pronounced limp, having a steel brace on his shrunken leg. I watched him for years, walking with a pronounced limp in the truck yard, fixing trucks, and staying abreast of their transport business. His walk made me hurt. It had to have been very painful on his body to have to work and walk like that.

I knew Lee had been sick, but it was quite a shock to hear he had died. I was glad that I was going to make it home in time for his funeral. Someone called me the next day and told me I was going to be a pallbearer.

We flew home from Hawaii and got to bed fairly late. Around 2:00 am, I got a call from my burglar alarm informing me there was a problem at the store. I threw on some pants, grabbed my gun and phone, and drove over as fast as I could.

At first, my eyes were unable to comprehend the sight that greeted me. There was a gigantic hole through the front of my showroom and office. Inside, I could see the back end of a backhoe. I pulled up and jumped out. It was a cold February morning and I was barefoot. As soon as I got out of my pickup, I could hear the backhoe roaring at full throttle, still in gear. I knew that it had to be shut down immediately so I ran into the building and climbed up on the machine. I shut it down and then jumped off and ran back outside, not sure if someone was still in the building.

I grabbed my phone and called 911. Since the backhoe had gone through several plate glass windows, I had stepped on a bunch of broken glass on my way in and out to shut the backhoe down. I waited for 15 or 20 minutes without anyone showing up.

Finally, a couple of sheriff's cars arrived and I told them what the situation was. I mentioned to them that my feet were cut and I was going home to get some clothes and shoes on and would be right back. I pealed out of the parking lot in frustration which probably didn't endear me to the doughnut patrons standing there gazing at what had been my tire store.

I was pretty upset. It was a constant battle for my property, waged between me and all the low-lifes that lived within 100 miles. I often felt that law enforcement did not help me protect my property and sometimes knowingly hindered. My service room was trashed. Displays, tires, wheels, computer screens, and other items were destroyed.

I arrived back in less than five minutes. The cops were still standing there. One of the first questions they asked me was if I had a safe and if it had been taken. The safe had been in my back office, but at that point I had no idea if anything was missing. I said, "I don't know, I'll go in and see."

The cop jumped in front of me and said, "No, you won't! It's not safe in there and you are not going in!" At this particular moment in my life, I was not in the mood to be told by a Johnny-come-lately bystander that I could not go into my own building. I told him I had already been inside to shut the backhoe off and I would go back in if I so desired. This was my property.

He raised his voice and told me that I could not enter. I raised my voice and told him I could. This conversation repeated itself several more times until I grew tired of arguing and started walking in. He again jumped in front of me and pushed me.

"You just assaulted me!" I yelled.

"You are disobeying the direct order of a police officer and if you take another step, you're going to jail," he retorted. I was ready. I immediately decided that this was a great time to assert my Constitutional Rights. "Fine, let's go." I said.

I took another step and he once again said he would take me to jail. All of a sudden, I thought of Lee Eppich. Of all the times for him to die! I couldn't go to jail or I would miss his funeral. The service would be starting in a few hours and if I went to jail, I would probably be there for a day or two. I backed off solely out of respect for Lee.

I am still bugged that it didn't happen on a different day and that Lee picked such a poor time to die. I just don't believe that an outsider should be able to come onto my property at my invitation and then start telling me where I can walk. If I had possessed his chicken attitude, I never would have gone in the "hazardous environment" to kill the machine. My entire store would have burned to the ground after the backhoe heated up. The full throttled hoe was in high gear and straining mightily against the obstacles in its path. If I hadn't come along and shut it down, in a few more minutes it would have cooked the hydraulic transmission and caught fire. The tire-filled store would have burnt down and possibly blown up the 12,000 gallon propane tank that was behind the shop.

The perpetrators (not the cops, but the guys who operated the hoe) had stolen the machine from J Wood's potato storage across the road. I believe they stuck it in high gear, gave it full throttle, pointed it toward my store, and jumped off. The major destruction and noise probably scared them off. Nothing was taken. Most likely they did it as a drunken lark.

The showroom was severely damaged. After crashing through the front, it pushed racks of tires, wheel displays, and other items toward the back of the office. The tall boom of the rear bucket sliced through the rafters at the top and created a very precarious situation. I called J and he came down. We shored up the roof and backed the hoe out.

I went to Lee's funeral later that morning.

• •

I am a devoted fan, focused instigator, and undeserving recipient of practical jokes. They add spice to life. I probably enjoy them a little too much. Permit me to share a few of the more memorable ones I've been involved in.

After I sold the rights to the YankATank, I was under obligation with American Standard Manufacturing to do the Western Propane trade show in Reno with them. One year, I took Michele with me to the show. She spent most of her time shopping, but agreed to come down on the last show day and hang around our booth.

David Day is the manger of American Standard and was in the booth. Dave and I get along well. He is soft-spoken, "saved", owns a Harley, and has no guile within—except when he makes fun of my religion. Michele is the opposite of me, quiet and very low-key. Michele and Dave are of the same type personality.

Michele arrived and shortly thereafter I walked up to the booth where she and Dave were talking. Dave had a picture of his Harley out and as I approached he said, "Hey, Ben, I'm just showing your wife the picture of the Harley you just bought."

Knowing Dave, I think this was probably the first time he had played a practical joke on anyone. He was a novice.

I played along with him. Michele didn't know what to believe. After living with me for seemingly countless decades, she knew there was a real chance that I had bought the bike. I told her I was going to fly back to New York and ride the hog home. On the one hand, she thought we were kidding her, but on the other she knew there was a good chance we were serious and I would be flying to the east coast.

I was instantly up to speed with Dave. In fact, I flew right by him. In two shakes of a Harley Softail, I had latched on to a brilliant idea. I would turn

Dave's own joke around and bite him with some much bigger teeth than he had used on Michele.

I kept my cool and told Dave we were going for a stroll. I was going to show Michele the rest of the booths. We walked away. Dave smugly and happily watched us move down the aisle of the show.

As soon as we got out of sight, I grabbed Michele and emphatically informed her of what she had to do. She was to walk back down the aisle storming mad. She was to buzz by Dave and if he tried to talk to her, tell him to get lost. I wanted him to think that I had convinced her that he really had sold the bike to me and she was mad and ready for a divorce. It was a great reverse to the prank he had just pulled.

She wouldn't do it. She was willing to let a once in a lifetime opportunity go by just because it would put her a tad bit out of her comfort zone. This was one time in our marriage that I decided I had to act decisively. I pulled out all the stops.

I told her that if she didn't do it, I would be mad at her for the rest of the trip and it was going to be a long drive home. I had to repeat myself several times before she finally understood the import of my stance. I gave her directions again and told her to wait until I could position myself in a spot where Dave couldn't see me, but I could watch the action. Then I motioned her to proceed.

She did a great job, probably because she was mad at me for giving her the ultimatum. She stomped down the aisle in a big huff, blowing right by Dave, who tried to talk to her as she whizzed by. Dave stood there in a perplexed position with his forefinger in the air, suddenly realizing that he may have just broken up a marriage. She did an admirable job, more than I expected, but just as I directed. She stormed by his booth and then stood behind the curtain at Dave's own booth and waited.

Now it was my turn to act. I ran over to the main aisle and began frantically looking down the side aisles, presumably for my dear wife. Dave saw me and started walking over. He could see my entire focus was on finding my wife. He was very, very concerned.

As he got to me, I hurriedly asked, "Dave, have you seen my wife?" He said that she had just stormed out of the building. I immediately put my hands on my head.

Then he asked, "Did I do that?! Did I do that?!"

I could tell he was heartsick and was internally making a solemn commitment to never ever pull another practical joke, especially on a married couple. Inside, I was laughing my head off. Outside, I was one very worried husband whose wife had just left him.

I ran toward the exit and turned just past the curtain and met my wife. We both stood there laughing. Thirty seconds later Dave rounded the corner, hoping in some way to salvage the situation.

When he saw us laughing, he knew he had been had. "YOU DAWG! YOU DAWG!" He couldn't stop calling me a dog for the rest of the day.

It is truly a wonderful moment when my wife and I can pull something like this off as a team. I personally think this type of moment is the pinnacle of marriage. Okay, maybe not the pinnacle, but pretty darn high on the list.

• •

When I first started up my tire store, I sold a lot of motor and farm lubrication products. I also put in a fuel cardlock system and tanks. I developed a relationship with a guy named Bill Luber. He was my source for the oil products and I rented my cardlock station to him. We did a lot of business together and became good friends. We also spent some time on the golf course although he was a much better golfer than I.

He sold his business and we drifted apart. I didn't see him for 10 years or more. One day I was driving in Kennewick and saw him parked, fueling up his pickup. I pulled in and we did some catching up.

At that time, he had just put in a nice mini mart and fuel station in Kennewick. He told me that he was just finishing the construction and was way behind with his vendors and contractors. He had done the project before he got the financing. He said that he had been in the loan application process for months and that that very day was the day he was going to be closing the loan. He was just waiting for a call from his banker at ACME Bank in Spokane. He was ready to go to Spokane and get the money as soon as his banker called. It was for a substantial amount, around a million dollars.

He told me that he was on pins and needles. He had a lot of people he needed to pay. We talked for a little longer and then I said I had to go. I asked him for his phone number so we could get together again and play golf. He gave it to me.

He drove off and I followed. I was right behind him at a red light when an idea hit. I picked up my phone and called him. I heard and watched him answer his phone. I said, "Hi, is this Bill Luber?" He said it was. I said, "Yeah, Bill, this is Jim Smith from ACME Bank." (I couldn't think of a better name on the spur of the moment.)

Bill was thrown off balance. He knew Acme Bank, but he didn't know Jim Smith. He said, "Who? Oh, oh, yes Jim, how are you doing?" He was so hungry for loan money that he didn't want to rock the boat by not remembering everyone at ACME.

I had him hooked. I said, "Bill, I just called to tell you that your loan has been turned down at our bank." I could see Bill's posture slumping and sinking lower in his pickup seat. He was devastated. A few terrible seconds passed by in Bill's pickup while a few wonderful seconds passed by in mine.

"What's that Jim? I think we've got a bad connection. What did you say?"

"Your loan didn't go through. We can't help you."

Bill's world had just crumbled. "Why?" he asked and demanded simultaneously.

My mind raced. What answer would sound like it was coming from a banker? What would Bill buy into? "Insufficient collateral, Bill, we just can't make it work." (Believe me, I am very familiar with banker's jargon when it comes to telling customers no)

Bill was devastated and started sputtering unintelligibly, something about his world turning completely black. I was watching it in living color from the front seat of my pickup. After a few seconds had elapsed, I decided it was time to let Bill off the hook and time for me to get about my business. The light had turned green and he wasn't moving. "Bill, this is Ben. Just kidding."

"Who?!!! Ben, you . . . you . . . (Insert whatever words you deem applicable. They were probably enunciated at this juncture.) I'm never going to speak to you again." He hung up.

I have spoken to Bill since. He has either forgotten the incident or decided it was a pretty good practical joke after all.

• •

Brian Cook has a sister named Sherri who is a couple years older than we are. She is blonde and attractive and doesn't look like she's had the 12 or 14 kids that she has. She is a sweetheart and believes everything you tell her.

One April Fools morning I dialed her number. She answered. I said, "Hi, this is Bill Jackson from KFOOL Radio and we are calling you because you have the chance to win a great prize."

She was excited and nervous. I said, "You are on the air. We are going to give you 30 seconds to sing me a few strains of a pop tune from the '60s." I asked if she was agreeable and she said she was. I told her I was starting the clock. She stumbled and muttered and stumbled some more. I kept telling her that time was running out. I needed a song.

She couldn't think of anything. I kept prolonging the contest, waiting for her to sing. She just couldn't think of anything. I begged for just a few melodic words to a song, any song. Nothing.

After a good five minutes had passed I said, "Time is up. Did I tell you that the prize if you had correctly sang a song from the sixties was one thousand dollars?"

In less than a heartbeat, Sherri immediately launched into Bobby Vinton's "Blue on Blue." I cracked up. She wasn't happy when she finally recognized my cheerful voice.

Sherri lives five miles away from us. Three, maybe four minutes passed by and she came tearing through our front door. No knock. Wild-eyed. Not singing. Fists clenched.

I am a very lucky man that I can run around my kitchen table faster than she can. Even while I'm laughing.

• •

When I banked at Key Bank, I became good friends with a lady named Rita. My folks banked there also and she always gave my dad credit for helping her quit smoking. She was a nice lady and always helpful.

One day I was caught in a bit of a usual quandary and was going to be overdrawn about $50,000 in my bank account for a few days. I figured I better call Rita and warn her of my situation.

I said, "Hi, Rita," when she answered the phone. She said "Well, hi, Joe."

I had no idea who Joe was, but I decided to play along. We chitchatted for a bit and then she told me she had my papers ready to sign. From the way she was talking, it sounded like the bank was ready to loan Joe some money.

"So how much did I end up getting?" I asked.

She shuffled through some papers and then said, "Fifty thousand dollars."

I couldn't believe it. This was exactly what I needed to cover my overdraft. I asked her if I could change the name of the person the check was to go to. She hesitatingly answered that I could.

I said, "Okay, I want you to make the check out to Ben Casper."

She slowly said, "Okay."

I gave her my address and asked her if she could get it in the mail that day. She said she could. Even though I knew I could use the money, I decided it was time to straighten Rita out.

"Rita, this is Ben." It took her a few moments to gather her wits. We had a good laugh. I never got the check, Joe did.

At one point, I got a relatively large loan from Key Bank. Part of the agreement was that I sign my life insurance over to the bank as collateral in case something happened to me. Rita called me several times to come in and sign it off, but I never got around to it.

One day I was driving back from Hermiston after a Schwab meeting. I happened to remember that I was supposed to stop at the bank and sign my life insurance away. I called Rita to make sure she was there. When I said, "Hello, Rita," she said, "Well, hello, Brad."

That woman really needed to quit guessing who people were before they identified themselves. I decided I needed to teach her another lesson. I figured she probably thought I was my brother Brad.

"Brad, when is your brother Ben going to come in and sign these papers?"

My conscience was a little pricked, but I couldn't help myself. "Oh, you didn't hear? He died in a car wreck a couple of weeks ago." (I agree; it was mean.)

Rita felt terrible. I don't know if it was because I was dead or because she hadn't gotten me to sign my life insurance over to the bank before I croaked. She expressed her condolences and we talked a bit more about poor Ben and then hung up.

I headed straight for the bank. After climbing the stairs, I walked into the offices and made a grand circus entrance, complete with outstretched arms, in front of Rita's desk. "Hi, Rita!" I exclaimed.

She looked at me like I was Casper the Ghost, back from the dead. Once again, we had a good laugh and I really do think she was glad I was back, even if it was only so I could sign her papers.

A few days later, I stopped at a flower shop and bought a bouquet of flowers and delivered them to her. It was the least I could do.

CHAPTER 34

EVERYBODY NEEDS A MARBLE

One of the people I remember since I was a small boy was Leonard Marble. He was a bit older than my dad and was one of the first settlers of this area. He and his wife LaWana raised four beautiful daughters, two of whom were good friends with my sisters. Leonard was a veteran of WWII and Korea. He was a dedicated and outstanding farmer here in the Basin, growing mostly sugar beets. He farmed around 300 acres.

Most farmers ran a tractor and cultivator through their beets two or three times a season to get rid of weeds. Leonard was famous for running through his beets ten or twelve times a season. He babied his crops. He was often seen walking through the fields, monitoring the progress and health of millions of his beet plants. The story got around that Leonard was so familiar with his sugar beets that he had names for each one of them.

In 1973, my family and Leonard's family loaded up our gear and headed to northern Idaho to Priest Lake. This was the first of a long string of vacations to that beautiful area I've been lucky enough to enjoy. We camped at Indian Creek campground for a week.

One morning, Leonard, my brother Brad, and I arose early and went out fishing. I don't remember if we caught anything, but later on in the morning, a strong storm came up and we decided we had better head in. As we got close to the campground, we watched as the high waves and strong winds combined to blow a sailboat over. We motored over and helped them right the boat and get to shore.

• •

A year earlier, I had wanted to learn how to slalom ski. We didn't have a boat at the time so Brian Cook and I found a homemade, flat-bottomed ski and headed for an irrigation canal on our farm. Flat-bottomed skis are not made for slalom skiing. To use a single ski, it should have a concave bottom in order to allow the skier to stay in control. Learning to slalom was hard enough, but I was trying to learn how to master the one-ski program on a wooden ski that made me feel like I was slip-sliding on ice.

To top it off, the canal was six feet wide and three feet deep. A spill meant you connected with a bank of earth or the shallow bottom. We hooked a rope to the back of Brian's dad's pickup and I jumped in the water. Brian spent the afternoon taking off in the pickup and trying to pull me up. After many spills I mastered the balance point of slaloming. I went out and bought a nice slalom ski soon after.

• •

Back to our vacation at Priest Lake . . . one evening my dad and Leonard decided to take our boat and travel down to Coolin which was on the south end of Priest Lake. I asked if I could water ski down. It was about a 12-mile trip. I was in good shape and made the entire trip without stopping. We fueled up and I decided to attempt a return leg. Even though I ended up pretty tired, I did it. Leonard always talked about how he couldn't believe I skied that far without falling.

Leonard had a heart attack when he was 46. Health problems continued to haunt him. Several times through the later decades he came close to death. I remember visiting him in 1980 when he was on his deathbed and not expected to recover. He eventually had to sell his farm to get rid of the stress. However, the farmer in him yearned to return to his former livelihood and he soon was working for another farmer. It took a lot of the stress away and still allowed him to do the work he loved.

Fast forward to 1988 after I purchased the new Corvette . . . for some reason Michele didn't enjoy driving it. However, she needed a ride to a seminary graduation one Sunday evening in Pasco so she took it. Seven-year-old Derek went along with her.

After they parked, the burglar alarm started honking. Michele was embarrassed because she didn't know how to shut it off. Derek felt bad for his mom. They hurried inside hoping no one would notice they were the responsible party. The meeting started and the stake president, Lowell Barber, got up and made an announcement. He said, "There is a red Corvette in the parking lot with its burglar alarm going off."

Michele was embarrassed, however, it reached a whole new level when Derek immediately sprang to his feet and looking right at President Barber yelled, "You shut up!" He was just trying to protect his mom. He accomplished just the opposite. When they got home that night, Derek wrote a nice long letter of apology to Lowell.

One night Michele pulled the Vette into our garage. Derek hit the button to lower the door before she got the car inside. It came down and broke the power antenna off the car. I took the car back down to the dealer in La Grande to fix it and remedy a defect with the paint.

After the car was fixed, I had to travel down to pick it up. On a whim one afternoon, I stopped by and asked LaWana, Leonard's wife, if she would do me a favor. She was probably 60 at the time and I don't think she was accustomed to doing things on the spur of the moment.

However, she took a deep breath and agreed so we drove over to the local landing strip and jumped in my plane. We flew to La Grande and she drove the Corvette 155 miles home while I flew back. She didn't even tell Leonard she was going. Leonard later told me that she told him that it was one of the most fun trips she had ever taken.

• •

LaWana got cancer and died in 1994. Leonard lived two doors away from us and I made the decision to visit him at least an hour every day. He was 70 and alone. This was one of the best opportunities for service I've ever had. Usually, I do a lousy job when I make a commitment. I often don't follow through like I should. I performed this commitment far differently.

I'm happy and grateful for the time I spent with Leonard. We talked for thousands of hours. At least seven hours a week were spent in his house shooting the bull for that decade and a half. Our time together was a treasure even though it was sometimes hard to visit him every day.

He had grandkids, several of whom served two-year missions for the LDS Church. His daughters sent him via snail mail the emails they got from their kids on missions. One day I dropped in and he was upset. He had seen some of the email addresses of girls on the page that were also receiving the missionary letters. He said something like this: "I am mad! This isn't right! Girls should not be sending a missionary Hotmail! Hot mail is the last thing a missionary should be getting from a girl."

Leonard was a very modest guy. One day he was complaining about his leg hurting. He pulled up his pant leg and showed me where it hurt. As an afterthought, he pointed out a scar on his leg. He said shrapnel in Korea had caused the scar. He was in charge of a group that operated a big mobile gun that lobbed large shells 15 or 20 miles at the North Koreans.

His group was traveling down a road and all of a sudden started getting heavy artillery fire from the North Koreans. They raced away from the barrage seeking safety. Leonard said he was sure he was going to have some casualties by the time they got away. The group found sanctuary in a gravel pit where they took stock of the situation. He went to work checking out his men. Some were wounded, but he was surprised to find there were no deaths.

Soon a Jeep came down the road and spotted them. It drove over to them. There was a general or bigwig of some sort being driven by a driver. He yelled at them and asked why they were parked there. Leonard told him that they had just come from some heavy shelling and were taking stock of their situation. The cocky officer told them that they were full of baloney and were a bunch of chickens, something to that effect except in cruder language. He then told his driver to proceed down the road Leonard and his company had just traveled from. He was still ridiculing and cussing out Leonard's group as they drove off.

This was when Leonard checked out his wound. His leg had been hit by an exploding shell. The shrapnel was hot and painful. He had a medic dress it and bandage it and then he went back to work.

About fifteen minutes had gone by since they had seen the officer and Jeep. Then they heard shells exploding from that same direction. Soon they heard a Jeep engine racing toward them and saw it go by without slowing down. He said the driver and the officer looked like they were scared to death. They never saw them again.

I couldn't believe that Leonard hadn't made a big deal out of his injury. Not only had he not applied for a Purple Heart or grabbed at least a few days of R&R from the war, but he threw a bandage on it and carried on. I asked him who knew about it. He said no one. He had never told his wife about the experience or anyone else in the years since.

In some ways, we were very different from each other. Me? I would have taken pictures of it and sent them to the *New York Times*. We never got tired of each other. We always found something to talk about. We sometimes disagreed. We even had a few heated arguments, but always managed to patch things up.

One winter he got worried about a giant sycamore tree outside his house. The roots were coming up through the ground and he was concerned that a large branch or the tree itself might topple onto his house which was just a few feet away. I told him I would take care of it.

I grabbed my chain saw and a rope and started climbing. The tree was so large and close to the house, I knew it had to come down piece by piece. I crawled up the tree 25 feet or so and cozied up to a large branch that was probably a foot in diameter. I tied the rope securely to the branch past where I was going to cut and then again below the imagined cut location. The rope was intended to keep the limb from dropping to the ground and possibly falling on the house.

The first amputation was the scariest. It was on a section of the tree that was leaning toward the house. I knew that if my plan malfunctioned, Leonard's house might immediately and substantially depreciate in value. I was also a little concerned about my ability to maintain my present altitude when the large limb dropped. The rope would stop the timber's fall and I had no idea what my perch would do as a result. I was concerned that something might go wrong and I might lose my grip on my post.

I started up the chain saw and hung on for dear life with two legs and one arm wrapped around the limb's lower portion. I held the chain saw over my head with my right hand and began cutting. As I cut the limb, it began cracking and the large section of tree began dropping. Still holding on with one hand, I let the chain saw fall back over my shoulder. I gripped the saw handle as tight as I could with my right elbow applying additional traction against the tree. The motor was now idling and the chain had stopped moving.

As it fell, the limb snatched up the slack in the rope and hung like an executed felon at the end of a hangman's noose. I was greatly relieved because I was still hanging on to my perch in the gallows. However, something was different. A funny smell wafted into my nostrils, especially my right one. It was because the chain saw muffler that was slung against my arm on my right side was sizzling away on the bare skin it was in contact with.

I had been so preoccupied with hanging onto the tree that I hadn't noticed the burning sensation. Once the limb dropped and I could see that I was still standing on wood, my other senses began kicking in. I quickly jerked the saw away from my arm and began climbing down. I had a good-sized burn and still sport a visible scar from it today. It was similar to Leonard's injury on his leg, but my injury was incurred under much more hazardous conditions than his was.

I worked for several days on the tree and finally the entire sycamore was dissected. I planned on doing it for no charge, but after I finished he insisted I take $400 for my trouble. We were both relieved that his house survived.

In March of 2002, I got a call to head out one morning at 3:00 am to fill some orchard tanks with propane. In the spring, orchard farmers run wind machines during the night to keep their orchards from freezing. These machines run on 500-gallon tanks of propane and it is critical that they don't run out. I got back to Basin City around 5:30 am and noticed that Leonard's lights were on. I stopped to chat and after walking in the door, yelled for Leonard. He weakly called out and said he was in bad shape.

For years, Leonard had been constantly complaining of angina and chest pains. He had had quadruple bypass surgery years before. Recently his doctor told him that he had some obstructions and that only about 30% of his heart was working. The doctor had essentially told him to go home and die. However, Leonard was a tough old bugger. Even though he constantly complained that he wanted to move on, he kept going to the doctor.

Every time he went to this doc, he got mad because the physician would place his stethoscope on Leonard's chest for one second, move it to another spot for another second, and then call the checkup good. Leonard said there was no way the guy could hear what was going on because of the limited time he listened to each spot. I told him to change doctors, but he wouldn't because he said the doctor had saved his wife's life at some point in the past.

Leonard looked rough on this particular morning. We realized later that he'd had another major heart attack. He had been sitting in his chair, enduring the pain for the last 17 hours. He hadn't called anyone for help. He just sat there.

He told me that the day before, he started having severe pains so he popped a couple of nitroglycerine tablets from a new bottle he had just gotten. Doctors tell heart patients that they should get to the hospital ASAP if three pills don't alleviate the pain.

Well, Leonard just sat in his easy chair and popped 90 nitro pills for the next 17 hours.

I should have called the ambulance right then, but since I had served on the crew in the past, I had developed a bad attitude about all the time that was taken to "measure" a patient before transport. There were times when a guy would have to wait for an hour getting checked out in the ambulance by amateurs before the wheels would even start rolling to head for the hospital. I preferred the scoop and run method and to let the professionals work on the patient so I initiated the scoop procedure.

With my pea brain kicking in at about 15% efficiency, which was far less than the function of Leonard's heart, I told Leonard I was hauling him to the hospital. He resisted. He said he wasn't going because he hadn't shaved for a couple of days and he was dressed improperly. I told him I needed to run home and get dressed myself and he should do the same. If he hurried he could get a shave in too. I told him I would pick him up in ten minutes. He reluctantly agreed. Reflecting back, I'm lucky he didn't croak while under my care.

I drove him to the hospital. The staff jumped on him and soon painkillers were doing their thing. His doctor arrived in a bit and after looking at his chart, started laughing. He told the nurses what his medical situation was and they joined in laughing. They couldn't believe he was still alive. Leonard kept us all laughing because the sedation he was under was bringing out some hilarious commentary from him.

The doctor was incredulous when he heard that Leonard had downed a whole bottle of nitros before I found him. He laughed some more.

Leonard stayed in ICU for the next week. I thought he was going to die. I was pretty upset. I realized that a guy I had known for most of my life and had spent thousands of hours with over the past seven years wasn't going to be around anymore.

His daughters arrived over the next few hours and expressed their gratitude to me for finding him. They appreciated the fact that I had been so close to him since their mom had passed. They told me that I was the son that Leonard never had.

The next day, I drove into town to visit Leonard. I cried most of the 30-mile trip because I was really going to miss the old codger. When I got to ICU, the nurse asked me if I was family. I said no, but I was like an adopted son. She then blew me away with the statement that his daughters had left strict instructions that only the four of them could see Leonard.

I drove home that day with different emotions than I had come to town with. It took me a while to mentally reconcile with my adopted sisters.

He didn't have surgery. The doctors said he wouldn't be able to handle it. Gradually he improved and came home a week or so later.

Since then, even though he had no invasive procedures, he had a lot less pain and rarely complained of angina. Go figure. Seven years later, at 89, he died a day or two after he left his home and went into a retirement facility. I miss the guy.

CHAPTER 35

A PAUSE FOR POETRY

I used to write quite a few poems. Here are a couple of little ditties I've scratched out over the years.

Turkey Bowl

Across the lawn, past the cold road and wandering in circles on the deserted church ball field. . . my little boys wait.

I watch them with affection from a distance in my warm, dry car. My neck is stiff-that was the best excuse I could come up with when I left them there alone.

Through the bare branches of shrubs whose leaves left with the first chill, they walk and I watch until a green bushy evergreen slides in and blocks my loving view.

Waiting with them, skeletons of summer trees in front of gray skies keep watch around the field-expectantly scanning for more brave boys and excuseless dads.

It's time for the annual Turkey Bowl. But this Thanksgiving morning, the wet drops and slick grass are keeping all other hardy heroes home.

My boys stand, looking. Their hope is dimming, their excitement waning. Heads down, they begin walking again. Heads down, they finally walk for home and a different Turkey Bowl.

I drive from my vantage place. "Hop in, I'll take you home." Both heads shake and they say in unison, "We're going to walk and wait a little longer."

Impressions of Clouds
(written while I was in Pennsylvania)

That far-off blue and gray colored cloud,

With the orange sun shining through loud.

Takes me away, at least in my breast,

To younger days, yes, way out west.

Standing for hours looking across,

To the dunes and clouds and waves that tossed.

Standing there with work to be done,

Immoveable, watching shadows of cloud and sun.

Now is today, but my heart yearns for yesteryear.

I'm happy but lonesome, I feel a tear.

Vapor trails place man's mark on nature's mural.

A speck of dust upon a perfect pearl.

Cottony white and impressions of blue,

Lonesome gray, forbidding black is there too.

The sun, though hidden, flings his rays,

Yellow, orange, and red, hundreds of shades.

Willow trees and veins of blue,

Marching armies and faces too.

The summer breeze constantly changes the scenes,

Rearranges the clouds and brings rain that cleans.

With evening drawing the day to his close,

She pulls the blinds and away the light goes.

But the clouds are still there, watching and seeing.

Day and night take turns. Coming, then fleeing.

Sparrows speckle the sky, while night draws nigh.

Back I lie and breathe a deep sigh.

I still remember standing on those hills,

And as I remember, thrills and chills.

CHAPTER 36

THE THRILLING LIFE OF AN INVENTOR

After chasing my inventing dreams vicariously for 20 years by investing a substantial amount of spectating, money, and time in Kim Haws' projects, in 1999 I struck out on my own. I had never been able to invent anything up to that point. I was convinced I didn't have the ability. However, necessity is the mother of invention.

One day I was in Benton City, about 50 miles from home, retrieving a propane tank. The majority of a sweltering hot summer day was spent trying to move the tank out of a yard, through a gate, and onto my truck. It was a very exhausting experience. The half-full tank passively laid there and watched while I spent several hours grunting, dragging, tipping, and scraping the tank. I was lucky I didn't drop from heat stroke. After the ordeal, I decided there must be an easier way of moving tanks than the method I was presently using.

After much contemplation, I came up with an idea that eventually evolved into the YankATank. This was the beginning of my venture into inventing that would become my life's work in the middle-age period of my life.

I developed two carts that performed separate jobs in moving tanks. I sent out some primitive brochures in the winter of 1999 and was surprised that I got a couple calls of interest. So I set about building 40 or 50 units to satisfy the two callers plus anyone else who might want one. I borrowed a trailer, loaded my pickup and trailer up with product, and headed for Portland.

Arriving in Portland, I called my friend John Bailor, who had initially convinced me to get into the propane business, and we arranged to meet for lunch. I was packing a large and heavy load of tank movers. I stopped for a red light at a busy intersection going in to Portland.

When the light went green, I went nowhere. My quite new, Dodge pickup just sat there. The first transmission of the next three to go had just gone out. I was blocking traffic in the center lane as I hurriedly called John for some help. I never had good luck with pickup transmissions until I bought my Tundra a few years later.

In a few minutes, John pulled up and towed me to the eatery. After lunch, he pulled me and my junk to the Suburban Propane yard in downtown Portland. I unloaded the fairly primitive equipment I had cobbled together. He proceeded to pull me to a transmission shop where I was informed it would be several thousand dollars and several days before it was done.

I had previously committed to the manager of an Amerigas outlet in Springfield that I would deliver a unit the next day. I had no idea what I would do. And then inspiration struck.

Years before, a Washington State trooper lived close to us in Basin City and we had become good friends. He later was transferred to Vancouver, Washington, just across the Columbia from Portland. He was my only hope. His name was Randy Hullinger. You might remember that his name alone saved me from an ultra large ticket and possible jail time a few years earlier.

After I called and explained my situation, Randy immediately volunteered to let me use his little pickup as long as I needed it. I drove around Oregon for the next few days peddling tank carts in a Stater's ride.

The trip was a success. I was about to head home when John suggested we go to the Suburban yard in Vancouver. He had set up a presentation with several store managers to check out my tools.

We arrived and I confidently wheeled my cart over to a couple of tanks that I lifted and moved with ease. "But will it lift that 330?" they asked.

"Sure," I replied. I actually had no idea. I hooked on to it and gave a jerk. It didn't budge. I had numerous pairs of eyes watching so I decided I better give it all I had. I leaned ahead and then jerked back with all my might.

SNAP! I dropped to the ground in pain. My problematic left hamstring had just decided it wanted no part of this 330-gallon tank, especially seeing that it was half-full of propane. All initiative and salesmanship immediately left my spirit and body. I literally crawled over to the side of John's pickup and used his front tire for a pillow. I knew several dogs had probably marked their territory on the tire previously, but I really didn't care at that moment.

John was taller and stockier than I. He was a good friend and hated to see me lose a sale. He walked over, gave the cart several tugs, and lifted the tank. He then helped me into the pickup. I never tried to lift a tank again without checking the liquid level gauge first.

Kim stopped by my tire shop in Basin City and looked at my new inventions. He liked them, but advised me to combine both of my products into one unit, which would make a much better cart. I figured that would be an easy job. I set about making arrangements to market my new invention before I even sketched out the initial prototype.

This is a trap I fall into every time I come up with a new idea. I often order a semi-truck load of materials in order to get a volume discount for my dream machine. I start making sales calls and highlight the imaginary vision of my dream. I even get offended if I don't make the sale. If I do make the sale, the pressure is on and I set about making the initial prototype.

And so the manic side of me kicked in. I immediately decided I would market my new product in Atlanta at the propane tradeshow that was in a couple of months. I assumed the new "imagined" product would be simple to come up with. It wasn't.

After a month and a half of intense R&D tribulation, I was ready to give up. The show was in a few days and I had nothing. I decided I was a failure at inventing. However, I knew Kim could do it. I went to his shop and asked him if he could drop everything and make my product for me. He said he was busy, but that for a price he would drop everything and do it, if . . . I would give him my half ownership of the press.

Several years earlier when he had first started working on the Agri-Trac, he needed a big press to manufacture it. He located a 1100-ton press in Portland. However, he didn't have enough money to swing the purchase and asked me if I wanted to be a part of the action. I was always ready to risk borrowed money so I gave him something like $13,000. It was a great deal and worth far more than we paid for it. It was a monster. It stood about 28 feet tall. Unfortunately, in the 25 years since, I've never made a dime on it.

I was torn. I was afraid I might miss out on a big opportunity or money to be made with the press. But I needed a product to show in Atlanta.

I remember vividly walking around outside his shop for several hours trying to decide what to do. It was excruciating. I thought. I prayed. I listened. I made the right choice.

I decided I would keep my share of the press and keep on trying. It was a pivotal moment. I know if I had turned it over to him at that time, I would never have invented another thing. I am so grateful I kept plugging away at it.

I must interject here that Kim has helped me tremendously over the years in many different ways. Every time I've been in a spot and needed a tool or advice or work done, he immediately takes care of me. He has shared so much with me and I consider him a good friend. Many years later we worked the press deal out. It remains to be seen who got the better end of the deal.

• •

The *BPN (Butane-Propane News)*, a national monthly trade magazine for the propane industry, published a six-page story that I wrote about my initial experience with the YankATank. I had given American Standard Manufacturing in Central Bridge, New York, the rights to manufacture and market the YankATank in 2002. They submitted my story to the *BPN*. This is it:

> *This account of the YankATank's wild debut in Atlanta in 1999 was written by Ben Casper, the inventor. It is the unedited and grammatically incorrect, yet factually accurate, account of the article that appeared in the April 2002 Butane-Propane News magazine starting on page 50. Enjoy.*
>
> *After watching a TV show about a guy who sold propane and propane accessories, I decided to get in the business. I bought a few tanks but ran out of money before I could buy a boom truck to move the tanks around. Without a boom truck, I could see I would need some form of mobility to set my tanks where they needed to go. I needed a YankATank.*
>
> *Penniless, but imaginative, I invented it. At least my confidence level was high enough that I was sure I could concoct a workable prototype. I was absolutely positive it would work, since I had it all drawn out inside my head.*

I furthermore decided to take a giant step toward the edge of the entrepreneurial cliff and market it, even before I had my first prototype. I figured I could sell it to fellow propane dealers and started looking for a venue to take some pre-orders.

Why not take another step and go all the way? I made a call and signed up for the world's largest propane show. It only cost me $5,000 (all on charge cards) to gear up with the entry fee, airfare, hotel, all the trimmings. Naturally, I would pay them off after the show with my expected large YankATank income. The show was in six weeks so I decided I probably ought to get moving and start inventing an as yet imaginary YankATank. It would be a piece of cake.

Unfortunately, I was majoring in Confidence and minoring in Comedy. I had just flunked out of Realism 101.

Nightmare City became my new address. Inventing was not as easy as I had envisioned. I built cart after cart. No worky. Cut, weld, hammer, swear, chuck in the junk. Out with the old, in with the new. Cut, weld, hammer, swear, chuck.....you get the idea. Work all day, worry all night. The show date was looming like a 1,000 gallon loaded propane tank rolling straight at me. My self esteem had gone from 60 to 0 in 5 weeks flat when ... Eureka! I got it! One night at 2:00 in the morning, I got the vision.

The single most welcome cart of my life emerged the next day, just a few days before D-Day. I slapped a coat of paint on it and packed my bags for Atlanta. I knew it still had some bugs, but I was not going to get the Raid out at this late date. Since I still had a few hours before the plane left, I decided I needed a video of the thing in action. I did some more brainstorming and decided to buy and haul a 20" TV/VCR on the plane.

I figured I could save some bucks by being a TV transporter-upon-the-airlines innovator instead of shelling out big bucks for a TV rental unit at the show. I also thought I could save a few more pennies in freight and slip the YankATank (complete with 6 tires) on the plane. To keep my packages within size and weight limits I made many modifications to the cart. After disassembling into many small clocklike parts, it would fit in the box. Big unit crammed in little box.

On the spur of the moment and in one more poorly-thought out whim, I decided to invent a small base/roller assembly to carry my boxes and duffel bags around the airports I soon would be cruising through. 3 pieces of muffler pipe with matching caster wheels were the ticket to my saving 3 bucks for an airport cart.

When I went to check my bags, I could dismantle the roller thingy and place it in a duffle bag along with the concrete blocks I had stored there. I erroneously thought I might need the blocks for demonstration purposes at some later time. I did not realize at the time that this was going to impact the entire weight and balance calculations of the flight crew, not to mention the way it kept dislocating my shoulder as I drug it through the airport.

Three days before I was to leave I finally started on my promotional material. I hired a high school kid to help me with the technical stuff. I got some harebrained ideas about what we were going to film and we were off to the races.We started early and worked late videoing tanks getting YankATank'd on trailers, pickups and yards. I built and wrecked two sets of ramps. I now understand that beginning an advertising campaign on an untested prototype that keeps falling off a trailer with a propane tank hooked on it creates major stress. One day was wasted building rickety plywood ramps with no usable video footage. My mom and dad (who are in their 70's) came around that night and Mom started trying to give me advice on how to get the tank on the trailer. I was so stressed out by that time I think I told my dear mother to get lost. The YankATank had taken me over the edge!

The next day went better. We spent the day videoing, picture taking, inventing, picking up, hauling, moving, losing a camera, demonstrating the Yank and setting tanks. We were finally rolling! In fact, we did in one day what a Hollywood production company would spend months on. We didn't have quite the same quality only because we didn't have a Hollywood timeline, starlet or budget to work with.

We got the brochure done and that evening (the night before my flight) we started trying to get the video transferred over to a VCR tape. Things were not working. It wasn't happening. I didn't have a clue what was going on or how to help. My contribution was stewing, sweating and fretting.

About 1:00 that night (or morning) with no success in sight, I started wondering just what the proper procedure was for a propane man to commit Hari Kari. My carefully made, albeit rushed plans were quickly vaporizing. I started calling people who I thought were friends asking if they knew anything about how to transfer a YankATank from a hard drive format to video. Lots of hang ups. No help. Finally, late into the night, the transfer occurred. Whew!

A couple hours later I left in my pickup for Seattle. The YankATank paint had still been wet when I stuffed it in the cardboard box before I left home. I stopped in Ellensburg to buy some paint to touch it up after I got to Atlanta (a wasted effort as later I forgot the paint in my pickup at the airport.)

At the paint store, my pickup started spewing brown, steamy water. I decided my water pump had crashed but I couldn't stop now. I burned my hand and got dark brown radiator water spots on my nice white bellbottom pants. Every exit thereafter was used to search for water, as the engine kept heating up. I pulled into the airport garage a little later than planned and my transportation monster was belching steam like Mt. St. Helens.

I was 45 minutes late according to airline recommendations. I hurried and loaded the two 80 lb. boxes on my 3-wheeled cart and topped the combo with two duffel bags. I had just started pushing the top-heavy load when before you could say timber, over they went. Three little crazy wheels mounted on a triangle ain't exactly the best base. This was right in front of the elevator at SeaTac International Airport.

People were coming and going, looking at this idiot goofing with cardboard boxes, duffel bags full of concrete and a funky looking 3 wheeled cart made out of muffler tubing. Not exactly designer luggage. Oh, and don't forget the pickup still spewing steam about 20 feet away from the center of trauma. I finally got the load in the elevator and up to the counter. Already sweating and trying to be inconspicuous, I did my best to hide the rusty brown radiator coolant on the white pants. I don't think it worked.

There was hardly anyone at the TWA counter while the other lines were packed. I understood why as the trip progressed. The guy threw my boxes on the scale and said I was overweight. This was not news to me, as my wife and our family doctor have told me that same thing for years. In fact, a good friend of mine always asks me if I'm in my second or third trimester.

"That will be seventy five additional bucks, payable now". I didn't have cash like that! I pulled out my newly issued credit card from Circuit City. They had provided me with the card because I didn't have any cash when I bought the TV for the trade show.

His machine wouldn't take it. It hadn't been authorized. I borrowed his phone and spent the next 20 minutes in the front of the line getting that done. People were grumbling behind me. I next went through the beeping x-ray machine and they stopped me to ask what the concrete block and all the pipe was for in my duffel bag. I wrestled with a big temptation to talk about bombs. Instead I told them it was a newly invented and highly popular luggage carrier and ballast system and they better get used to it. I assured them that soon everybody would have one.

I finally made it on the plane. We sat and sat and finally took off an hour late. The pilot announced that the baggage handlers were a little slow in getting the luggage loaded. I worried my overweight cardboard boxes had slowed the loading. Or maybe it was because they were worried about getting their next paycheck from bankrupt TWA. Or perhaps they needed a new muffler pipe luggage tool like my unpatented as yet cart.

I wasn't too worried about the extra hour, as I figured I would still make my connecting flight and if not, I could take the next one. We arrived in St. Louis and I ran to my flight lugging this very heavy duffel bag filled with pipe and concrete, YankATank tires, order sheets and brochures. I didn't know St. Louis was this hot in March. Sweating was becoming a permanent problem on this trip.

I ran up to the counter and they informed me my plane had just left. I was exactly two minutes late, THEIR plane from Seattle was the culprit and MY connecting bird had left without waiting 2 extra minutes! I couldn't believe it. I asked when the next plane to Atlanta was and she said 9:00 the next morning, arriving at 10:20. The show started at 12 and I knew that was cutting it close. They sent me to a hotel for the night. The last plane out for the night and they couldn't wait 2 minutes after they had held us up for an hour in Seattle. Bad night. Bad dreams. I couldn't shake the feeling things were going to get worse.

Next morning I started thinking about how much I had invested in this trip. Since the airline had goofed me up so bad, I figured the least they could do was help me out when I got to Atlanta. They should quickly escort me and my boxes in an airline van right to the Georgia World Congress Center. Seconds were rubies. Minutes were diamonds. I approached two people at the TWA counter with the idea and they started laughing hysterically. I stifled the temptation to smack them with my muffler pipe and coup d' grace them with the cinder block. However, if I did that, I might not make the 9:00 flight.

I arrived in Atlanta on time (Wow!) and since they graciously put me in first class for my troubles, I ran out of the plane and through the airport lugging my overweight duffel bags. I was at the baggage claim tapping my toes a good 10 minutes before anyone else. I rounded up a baggage guy and got him all lined out about my situation. I enlisted his help and paid him in advance for *his cart services. I didn't want to fool around with my tri-cycled invention at this late hour. After the longest half hour up to that point in my life, the bags started plopping out. The last to appear was one of my boxes. What??? Just one?*

12 o'clock was the magical hour of the show opening and I was pretty much YankATankless, without my new show stopping TV and still stuck in Airport Hell. It was now after 11. My helper could see how wild I was becoming and suggested we go to the baggage room on the off chance...At the baggage room, staring me right in the face was my other box and duffel bag. There was only one problem. A plate glass window and a locked door stood between us. Adding to my frustration was a sign on the locked door stating the room would be open from 8-5. It was 8-5 and the room was locked!

My baggage buddy said he would go to the TWA counter and get somebody. I watched him walk away until he was out of sight and wondered just where this TWA counter was located. The way things were going, it was probably on the other side of Atlanta. I sat there fuming and waiting and dying. After a good 20 minutes he came back and said they were sending somebody right down. We waited. And waited. After another 10 or 15, I blew a gasket and headed the half mile down the hall for TWA.

I didn't wait in line and I didn't apologize. I've always dreamed of crashing a line. However, I was under so much stress right then I didn't have time to enjoy my courageous audacity. I muscled past everybody and told the guy I needed the door unlocked. NOW! He said the lady with the key had already left.

I ran back and guess what? Nobody. No lady. No key. Nothing. We waited another 5 minutes and then my main baggage man said, "Here she comes!" I looked and way down the hall was this large female moving toward us about as fast as a snail in reverse. I freaked. I went her direction and after intersecting with her route, I let her know I was not happy about the gear she had it in. She stopped and refused to go any further toward the hallowed room I was trying to penetrate. She kept repeating, "Don't attack me, sir!"

I didn't feel like a sir right then. Finally, I could see this heifer was going to have to have a feed bag put in front of her if she was ever going to move again and so I apologized, not because I was sorry but because I wanted to get my boxes and bags and get the heck out of Dodge. After a good 5 minutes of her analyzing whether she was going to accept my apology and another 5 minutes of her examining all her keys, the vault was finally accessed. We grabbed the bags. I intentionally forgot to leave her a tip, sprinted to the taxi and took off for the Center.

I called the Center security and a helpful lady told me how to get to the loading dock for the show. Twenty minutes later we arrived and started looking for the dock. No luck, back and forth in the bowels of the Center. Nobody we asked knew what we were looking for or they gave us wrong directions. The taxi driver was getting nervous because he had been driving around a long time and was not making any money since he'd already quoted a fixed price.

Finally, I told him to take me back to the front entrance and I would get out and try to find the loading dock on foot. As we started back up the street, a mile-long train had materialized and was blocking our path, booking along at a strong 5 mph. Atlanta was hotter than St. Louis. I was perspiring buckets by now and feeling like a stroke was coming on. I had spent 5 grand to be at this show and it was blissfully going on while I was locked outside. Here I was, sitting in a stopped taxi, watching box cars meander by and my financial future heading for a train wreck. We waited 16 minutes and 2 seconds before crossing back across the tracks.

The people in charge of the show don't want you to set up while its going on. In fact, most people set up 2 days in advance. I thought I had given myself plenty of time, but as usual, I was a day late and a dollar short. In fact, by the time this adventure was over, I was much more than a dollar short. I knew it would take me at least an hour to set up and I would end up doing the setup while all these potential customers cruised by, never to return.

My boxes, bags and I got dropped off in front of the hour-old show. I started trying to assemble my baggage-handling machine. Someone told me I had to go down the steep street between the front of the Georgia World Congress Center and the CNN building to get to the dock. The taxi could have dropped me there in 15 seconds more if we had known that. As it was, I ended up strapping my 220 pound load on my little tricycle carrier and wondering how I was going to negotiate going down this 45 degree street with lots of traffic and no sidewalk. Running on raw nerves, I drug my load over the curb and plunged into traffic. I stayed in front of my cargo and hung on for dear life while walking downhill backwards, pushing uphill and trying to direct traffic around me.

Finally, my circus and I got to the unloading area. Curiously, the doors were locked. I pounded and yelled with no luck. I dialed security (who had given me the wrong directions) and asked them to please let me in. 10 minutes later someone materialized and after I explained my situation, they relented. I then had to run all over the building (twice the size of Rhode Island) to locate where my booth was. I finally found it and pulled my paraphernalia over to the spot. I felt that I had finally made it and the rest was going to be easy.

I started unpacking. First the TV. Before the trip I had congratulated my wife for saving a big bag of peanut Styrofoam. I figured the fluffy stuff would be just the ticket for packing my TV safely. I had loaded the box with the TV, my clothes, and then dumped the peanuts in to protect it during shipping. As I opened the box and pulled my clothes off the top, Styrofoam flooded the booth. Mommy and daddy Styrofoam peanuts were propagating little peanuts much faster than I could corral them. Unloading the TV, I realized I had a mess. Hundreds of bits of foam covered my clothes and the TV and immediately flew to every square inch of my booth and then some. Major mess. Major stress.

I finally got the TV out as all my potential customers were walking by admiring my Styrofoam. I set it up and tried to turn the VCR on to divert their attention away from the Winter Wonderland in Georgia that was partially covering my clothes strewn on the floor and fully engulfing everything else in my booth. I didn't want to pick the clothes up because they were doing a somewhat satisfactory job covering the popcorn mess. Next, the VCR wouldn't go on. I tried to eject the tape but no go. Pushing the door up, I looked inside at the tape but I couldn't see it. Styropopcorn was blocking my view. Stuffed full. Packed in. White on white.

Death would deal no sting at this point. I unpacked and assembled my YankATank, which was a whole new ball game. Tools and nuts and bolts and pieces and tires and popcorn. A half-hour to forty-five minutes later my cart was together, floating on a sea of foam. Every time I tried to shoo the stuff away, it returned with a vengeance. Static electricity was having a heyday with the white foam! People walked by shaking their heads and giving their condolences at the casket. The folks in the booths on each side of me were thanking their Maker that they weren't me. I was wishing I was with my Maker.

The next step, I decided, was to go on a scouting trip for some little tools and a hanger to try to unpack my VCR from the wedged tape and white packing. I started the operation and worked on the patient for a good hour. The crowds were still cruising and shaking their heads. I had my flyers out but I don't think anyone saw them, as they were so amazed at me sitting in my fluffy peanuts with my brand new 20" Panasonic torn completely apart. It looked like one of those TV's you might have seen thrown out at a junkyard.. The picture tube, electronics and wiring were strung all over as I forced a hanger down in the back of the VCR trying to eject the foam. A century later, I finally got it clean but by then I had busted a component or two and realized the thing was never going to work for this show. Gave up and sat there waiting for the show and the misery to end.

The next morning was full of promise. I called rental places and finally found one that was open. They would have a TV and VCR there in 15 minutes. An hour and 15 minutes passed. At least 20 minutes after the show started, they arrived. Things were going much better today. Stress was there but under control. Hustled it in and started the tape. Worked great. The next day and a half, showed lots of people the product and didn't sell a one. I was firmly convinced my marketing strategy was going to take a little work before I showed up in Atlanta again.

On the third and final day, out of cash, I took my new credit card and tried a cash machine. It wouldn't work because I didn't have my pin # yet. I called and they said they would put in a new number but it wouldn't work until the next day. OK, no dinner for Ben that night. I was so confused I forgot I could use the card to charge a meal.

Next day, I paid my hotel bill with the credit card and found a cash machine that finally put $100 in my pocket. It was a good feeling. After the show closed, I packed my stuff up (with just a few stragglers of foam hanging on) and caught a taxi. I hit the airport dejected and broke, but felt kind of superior knowing that I was now an expert at moving heavy boxes through airports. Got a lot of funny looks even though I didn't tip the load over once.

Nothing noteworthy occurred till I hit St. Louis. Switched planes and as we waited for takeoff, the pilot announced that since there were some other planes coming in late, we were going to wait for them. It would be just 5 minutes. I started heating up and wondered why they didn't do that for me a few nights before. The pilot assured us we would get to Seattle on schedule. This went on and on. We were there for a good 45 minutes listening to pure baloney from the pilot about how we HAD to wait for these people and we WOULD get to Seattle on time. I was ready to choke the nearest TWA employee.

It was then I noticed that the strobe lights outside were getting stronger and more frequent. Looking closer, I determined the strobe lights were quite dim. Lightning was providing the flashing visual effects. A big thunderstorm was racing toward us in the night sky (where we were supposed to be but weren't) from the west. I figured the next logical step was that our flight was going to be cancelled. There were lightning strikes every 3 or 4 seconds. We started hearing loud thunder just as our plane started taxiing. We finally took off and the pilot announced that they had closed the airport right after we took off. He mumbled something about a near miss or near death experience.

TWA is bankrupt and so we got nothing to eat from Atlanta to Seattle. The captain kept saying we were right on schedule. Lying through his teeth to make TWA and all their late flights look good to the unthinking masses. How do you take off 45 minutes late, fly against the jet stream and be on schedule?

We were somewhere over Wyoming when the good captain informed us we were over Seattle. "Unfortunately, the controllers are putting us in a holding pattern which is going to make us late." What a great trick to make everybody think that the pilot had made Seattle on time and now it was the tower's fault we weren't on the ground. I know we weren't in a holding pattern because we never turned. We were still hoofing it across the Idaho Panhandle. After landing my suspicions were reaffirmed as the airport was dead. It was after midnight for heaven sakes! Not a plane in the sky.

I waited another 45 minutes for luggage and then pulled my oversized bundle to the parking garage. What a relief! I went up the elevator to the fourth floor. I saw a machine out of the corner of my eye that said you had to pay right there to get out of the garage. I left my stuff on the 4th floor hoping somebody would steal the stinking YankATank. Ran to the 5th floor, got my parking ticket and hustled back. I stuck the ticket in and it said I owed $80. I had only been gone 3 days!

Didn't they know that I hadn't parked in the gold plated space? I think I got whacked an extra 20 bucks because our late plane made me stay past the midnight hour. We were supposed to have arrived at 10. Well, I pulled out my trusty new Circuit City credit card and stuck it in to satisfy the 80 dollar bill. Declined. I was maxed, to my surprise. Ok, I wasn't that surprised.

I pulled out the last 60 bucks I had from the Atlanta cash machine and stuck it in. It sucked it up and wanted more. I tried the card again and it made the last 20. Elevated my load to the 5th floor and crazy wheeled my load to my truck. I noticed a lot of brown water under my pickup as I got in. I drove through the dark garage maze, out the gate and onto the freeway at about 1:00 am. Tired. Broke. The pickup started missing and then completely quit. Oh, boy.

I let the pickup coast backwards down the hill to the last exit and stopped. I popped the hood and saw my propane vaporizer was completely frozen because there was no water circulating in the engine to keep it thawed. *Do not ever run a propane pickup if the water pump is out!* Grabbed a plastic bag and pretended that was my water bucket. Headed off into the night not knowing where I would find water.

A couple hundred feet down the grassy knoll I looked up and saw a cop had pulled behind my truck with his lights flashing. I ran back and explained the situation. He said, "Fine, but where's your back license plate?" I said I didn't know. That was the truth, because I haven't had it on for the last 5 years. It just hadn't been that high on my priority list.

He said, "OK, let's look at the front one." I didn't have to look but I figured I would go with him just to keep him company. Sure enough, it was gone too. He asked me where I had come from and I said the airport garage. He said, "Well, that explains it. Somebody has stolen your license plates." I didn't argue, even when he insisted that we fill out a stolen license plate report. Why make it worse?

After the paperwork, he took me back to the airport where we located another cop with a water jug and some doughnuts. Returning to my pickup, I gave it a drink, drove down the exit and up the street to find a service station with some more water. Filled it up and the cop left. I pulled on the street and the truck died. I coasted into a motel parking lot and noticed a fan belt had shredded.

Dead tired, I entered the motel to see if I could get a room. The clerk tried my credit card and it was declined. I tried to call the sleeping wife several times but no answer. My cell phone battery then went dead. I was cold and depressed by this time.

Finally I left, deciding to sleep with all my junk in my cold pickup. 15 minutes later, wide awake and shivering, I decided to see how far I could drive down Pacific Highway looking for an auto parts store that would open the next morning. I figured eventually the truck would quit but I could go the rest of the way after it recuperated and thawed out. Unbelievably, the truck and I drove about 20 blocks and found a NAPA. Parked in an empty lot across the street and tried to sleep. I was freezing.

Couldn't sleep. Thirty minutes later a security rig pulled up and I had to tell the female cadet what I was doing in her lot. I asked if I please just could get in her rig and warm up a little bit. She looked at me, snickered "no way" and drove off as fast as her warm little security vehicle would go.

Crawled back in the pickup and after freezing 10 more minutes, decided to try a little more driving and see if I could find a Denny's. I was sure the truck was going to quit at any time, most likely at a stoplight. Made it to Denny's. Asked the waitress to put me away from everyone else as I was feeling like a vagrant. I gave her my credit card and asked her if she could check and see if I had enough left on it for a hot meal. She did and it did. I ate and tried to doze for the next couple of hours. She left me alone as I think she sensed I was down on my luck. Poor lady didn't even get a tip.

I was freezing the whole time. About 5:00 a.m. people started coming in and I decided I better leave. Walking outside, I looked down on the sidewalk and saw two lost and beautiful credit cards that I'm sure would have worked at any motel in the city. Declined the temptation and stuck them in my pocket just in case. Went back to the NAPA store and waited. About 6, as it was turning light, I thought I would look and see just what was happening under my hood. I saw that the serpentine belt was still ok and just the compressor belt had broken. This meant that I should be able to run.

Motored home and got there about noon. Heated the engine up several times along the way and had to stop for water often. As soon as I arrived, I got my good friend Lee to fix the water pump while I took a nap under his space heater. After I told him my story he said: "Ben, you need to take a friend with you the next time you go on a trip. Just make sure it ain't me."

I had learned many lessons. Much to fix. Lists to compile. Things to remember such as...

- *Water pumps die when you need them most.*

- *A 55-gallon barrel of water hauled in the back of the pickup for the radiator should be standard equipment.*

- *Always carry a boatload of cash.*

- *A hammer is good to hang on your belt in case you need to get into any locked TWA luggage rooms.*

- *Pack a cot and a pillow so you can grab some zzz's as you wait for the lovely lady to open the sacred baggage room.*

- *A sack lunch is good if you're flying TWA.*

- *Throw away any and all muffler carts you have invented.*

- *Get license plates whether you need them or not.*

- *Carry a portable heater as female security guards will not warm you up.*

- *Ship direct, don't try to roll YankATanks around the airport.*

- *Get all the inventing done at least a week before the show starts.*

- *Leave for the trade show earlier, a month should be adequate, especially if you're flying TWA.*

I now have much more empathy for people who are down on their luck, hungry, and spending the night outside in cold Seattle. Next time I see a guy like that with his hand out asking for a tip, I'm going to take him to Denny's for a hot turkey sandwich and then see if he needs some help working on his water pump.

2 weeks after arriving home, I got a call from a big player in the industry who saw my YankATank at the show. Made me an offer that will heal my wounds. As soon as I get his check I'm going to put in a bid to buy TWA. I'm thinking they should go cheap. I'm also in the process of hiring an assistant to make sure I have license plates on all my vehicles.

• •

To be absolutely candid, I wrapped my first two years of Atlanta experiences into one. The first day of my experience selling YankATanks, I met a guy named Jim Reynaldo from New York. He had a large manufacturing company that produced quite a few fine tank handling products. When he saw the YankATank on the showroom floor, he said he could knock my patent claims off in just a day or two.

I was a newbie. I didn't know much about patents back then so I agreed with him and started to worry. I now think Jim would have had a hard time knocking it off. Anyway, the next morning as I was going down to the trade show, who do you think got in the elevator with me? It was Jim. As we traveled down, he said he was sorry about what he said about ripping me off. I got the impression he had felt bad all night about it. He never has tried to knock me off.

CHAPTER 37

IT COMES TOGETHER IN BITS AND PIECES

In the summer of 1999, after my YankATank experience in Atlanta, I decided to do another propane trade show in Reno. Derek had just been called to serve in the Hiroshima, Japan mission. Michele and I were going to take him to Provo, Utah, and since the dates coincided, we planned to proceed on to Reno after Derek's drop-off.

I loaded up the pickup with several boxes filled with YankATank components. And at the age of 44, I began my sojourn as an inventor. The beginning YankATank model that I produced was a great idea, but because of my lack of manufacturing experience, it was poorly put together. I had each unit cobbled together so when the customer received it, it looked like a jigsaw puzzle. Most of the orders I filled that first year worked, but a few of them had problems. There must have been at least 100 parts to each individual unit.

We all got in the pickup and headed out. I had to stop at our bank in Pasco. As I got out of the pickup at the moneychangers, I happened to notice that there weren't as many boxes in the back as we had started out with.

Instantly, our planned, pleasant drive south took on ominous overtones. I was short on product. I had no idea where the box was, but there was no use going to Reno if I didn't have it. It contained crucial components to the show units. I hurriedly completed my bank business and we began retracing our route. About 12 miles north of Pasco, we happened upon a stray YankATank.

The bright yellow frames were scattered on the side of the road, scraped and scarred, but nothing a can of spray paint wouldn't fix. The bigger problem was the nuts and bolts and thingamajigs that were scattered over the road and landscape after hitting the pavement at 60 mph.

The three of us got out of the pickup and scurried around, picking up parts for a good 15 minutes . . . make that a bad 15 minutes. It was a mess. I didn't have a clue if we had retrieved everything. We taped the box back together, threw the stuff in as best we could, and continued our travel while keeping a wary eye on the rearward, and potentially wayward, load.

Derek's drop-off was a memorable event. Our beloved son was leaving our presence and heading for a distant land of strangers in the country of Japan. In the Missionary Training Center, a large group of parents and siblings gathered to see their young family members off. A movie and a short program of details and testimony were followed with several missionary songs being sung. It was heart-wrenching for me.

Most of the mothers in the group were crying. I looked over at Michele and she was dry-eyed. I decided I would have to carry out that duty for our particular family. I did an admirable job. It was hard for me. I wondered if I would ever see him again.

We bid him goodbye and then drove over to the Boyd Simmons home in Provo. He was one of the original "hunters" from the old days and was in the last stages of Alzheimer's. Before we left, I bent down and faced him as he sat in his chair. I told him how our family loved him and his family. There was no response which is what I expected, but after a few moments a tear ran down his cheek. His wife, MaRue, was surprised. She said they hadn't had a noticeable response from him for quite a while. I think since I resemble my dad, something in him clicked and reminded him of Dad, hence the tear. It was a special moment. He died a week or two later.

An interesting aside: their son, Bob, worked for my dad and lived with our family back in the 70s. He served his mission in Thailand. He worked for the government and raised his family in Pakistan, Bangkok, and Indonesia. Since they weren't in the states, current U.S. events weren't on their menu. He traveled to Washington DC quite often. One day he was reading a magazine in a U.S. airport. He saw a picture of a guy and knew he looked familiar, but couldn't quite place him. Then he realized it was a guy he had gone to high school with many years before in Seattle. It was Bill Gates.

We got back on the road and headed toward Reno. We had no further incidents until we drove across the Bonneville Salt Flats an hour later. As usual, I looked in my rearview mirror and got a shock. I think I'm going to tear all the rearview mirrors out of my vehicles. They bring nothing but bad news. Among the multitude of boxes that we had in the back was a box filled with YankATank informational brochures I had procured.

Because of a strong northerly crosswind, the top of the brochure box had blown off a few miles prior to my revelatory observation. Full-color, 11x17 brochures at a buck and a half a copy were streaming out of the box and heading south. I looked out my side window and saw many pages loping across the median past the oncoming highway and picking up speed as they hit the Salt Flats.

I slammed on the brakes and was able to save a few brochures that were still lying in the bottom of the box. Coyotes that reside in the wilds of western Utah and eastern Nevada are now well-informed concerning the benefits of the YankATank.

• •

I was able to work through the sub-par manufacturing experience. After we made a deal, Cole Vickary of American Standard Manufacturing tweaked the design and began producing them. We had a good product. It was a great education for me concerning manufacturing processes. In later years, I offered substantial discounts on the new and improved YankATank to my original customers who bought the first YankATanks. Most of them took me up on it.

For some reason, I have always been far too trusting. I have lost large amounts of money because I trusted that people would pay me back as they agreed. I have lost large amounts of cargo because I have trusted that the items would be obedient and remain where I put them. My trust has been betrayed many times.

I have a fairly formidable list of items that have scooted, slid, and toppled out the back end of various trucks I've driven. It has gotten to the point that I almost don't trust anyone or anything anymore. It's so bad now that I have had to start strapping things down when I haul them. And I've tightened my credit policies up enough now that I'm to the point where I require the borrower to at least tell me what country he's from in case I need to chase my money down.

In other parts of this history, I have listed a few of the experiences I've endured from flighty cargo. Following is a sampling of a few of the other times when I have been betrayed by my freight.

During one of my high school summers, Nolan and I determined that we were going to transport our musical equipment from one home to another. I got my dad's two-ton flatbed truck and we loaded it up with amplifiers, guitars, and the rest of our stuff. Nolan stayed on the back and I drove. The amplifiers all had rolling casters under them.

Traversing a gravel road, I rounded a bend. I was probably humming the Credence song "Up Around the Bend" when I should have been worrying about another Credence line "Rolling, Rolling, Rolling on the…"

I heard Nolan scream and glanced in my rearview mirror, just in time to see my large, prized Carvin amplifier and speaker box roll across and fly off the back of the truck. It then dove into the dirt and weeds on the side of the road.

I stopped and we recovered the unit. It turned out to be okay. Nolan and I had a good laugh as we dusted it off and lifted it back up on the bed of the truck.

This was one of my first experiences with the downside aspects of hauling products.

• •

A few days after I had surgery on my shattered elbow, which occurred when some scaffolding dropped out from underneath me, I decided I was going to remodel my Connell store. My left wing was unusable, but since I was right-handed, I figured I could still drive with no problem.

I loaded up my pickup with a good amount of 2x6 12-footers and proceeded from Basin City toward Connell. After arriving at the stop sign that leads onto Highway 17, I looked both ways and turned left onto the highway. The mild acceleration and 90-degree turn, the upwardly inclining road, the extended length of the boards beyond the back of the pickup, the slick plastic bed liner and the sloped angle of the loaded pickup combined to slide my complete pickup load of lumber off the vehicle.

I had owned a nice stack of lumber that was now lying on the highway and was no longer a nice stack. A lot of traffic, including many trucks, constantly traverses this blacktop. Normally, it wouldn't have been that big of a problem, but at that time I only had one arm.

I pulled to the side of the road and backed up to the general location of the scattered wood. After jumping out, I began trying to pick up one stick at a time and reload it. Several vehicles went by. It was apparent that many other rigs were going to have to dodge my lumber before I got it gathered up. My work speed was greatly hindered. Then, an angel appeared. A high school ag teacher from Benton City pulled over and started throwing the wood back on the bed.

A few minutes later, my rearward-tilted Chevy and I were on the road again.

• •

Not too long after I started my tire business in 1983, I decided I needed to acquire a large plastic tank to pump calcium chloride in and out while working on tractor tires. I located a 300-gallon fertilizer tank in the Tri-Cities and drove down to buy it.

After loading it and giving it strict instructions that it was not to move, I headed home. There was a strong crosswind from the west that eventually grabbed my new tank and threw it off the back of the pickup. The hardtop blacktop did its job. The tank was now perforated and cracked instead of water tight. I turned around, drove back into town, and bought another tank. The second tank got strapped down.

• •

One winter night, after a hard day of setting propane tanks in the Tri-Cities, I headed toward my last installation. I had a small trailer and a 120-gallon partially filled propane tank on behind my pickup. I was on the phone talking to Kim as I went around the corner of a normally busy intersection in Kennewick. I heard an ominous noise and then a scraping sound.

I told Kim I would call him back later since a small problem had just arisen. The tank was lying on the street still attached to the strap I had secured it with. Luckily, no valves or fittings had been broken off and, after a session of heavy lifting, I was back in business.

• •

When I first began setting up my propane business, I went to an auction and bought a used 1,000-gallon tank that had several hundred gallons of propane in it. This was an older tank and had no lifting lugs or points available to tie it down securely. After securing it as best I could, I headed back to the shop. I knew it was questionable as to whether the thing was going to stay put so I drove as gingerly as possible.

As I turned the last corner, in my rearview mirror I noticed it beginning to roll off the back of the flatbed truck. Feeling helpless and holding my breath, I watched it drop four feet off the bed, roll a couple of revs, and stop in the dirt at the side of the road. Again, no valves got knocked off.

• •

One fall day, I received a call from Jed Pauley to place a couple of 1,000-gallon tanks at his corn drying facility a quarter of a mile down the road from my shop. I figured I would save a little time by filling them with propane and then transporting them down the street on my forklift.

The long and full tanks were quite heavy, somewhere in the neighborhood of 5,000 pounds. It was a stretch for my old forklift to make the lift and trip. The backward tilt of the forks was somewhat negated by the weight of the load, which gave a flat sort of look to my front tires and a forward tilt to the entire machine. I strapped it down with the best mediocre strap I could find and headed out with the first tank toward the jobsite.

As I turned off the street, I slowed down and carefully motored down the slope to the grain bins. Then, in slow motion, I watched in horror as the big cylinder broke loose from its mooring and obeyed the laws of physics and gravity.

When it hit terra firma, it began rolling. It was a brand-new tank and unlike some of the other tanks I have lost control of, it had a fitting partially break off before it rolled to a stop. Liquid propane began spewing out. I immediately shut off the forklift as it was a source of ignition to the volatile fumes that were quickly accumulating. Many men, greater than I, have died under similar circumstances.

I jumped to the ground and began trying to roll the heavy tank to its upright position. Somehow I got the job done. Since the broken valve was now facing up, the liquid stream went away and the vapor exhaust replaced the liquid. I was greatly relieved that the liquid was gone. Vapor is far less dangerous than liquid propane. Liquid propane expands to a thousand times the area it took as a liquid when it vaporizes. However a vapor leak, especially one of that magnitude, is still formidable, and I knew I needed to get it stopped pronto. All of this was going on adjacent to the main street in Basin City.

I ran back to the shop and grabbed a couple of wrenches and a new valve. For the fourth or fifth time in my propane career, I was able to replace the valve in spite of working in the extreme blast of escaping gas.

I then hauled the second tank over, strapping it to the forklift more securely.

• •

Speaking of Jed Pauley, I have a funny little story about him. He grew up in the LDS church but quit coming at some point. I've always invited him to come back to church, but he's always politely refused.

A few years ago I watched an old movie. It was a western filmed in black and white. Part of the plot involved a bunch of townspeople trying to harass a local rancher. A group of them rode their horses out to his place to do damage to him and his property. They all wore hoods over their faces.

The victim took the opportunity to confront them before they took action. He walked around the mounted men and quietly talked to them. The riders were hoping to hide behind their masks, but it didn't work. He called them each by name and commented on personal experiences he had had with each hooded cowboy.

When the rancher walked up to one mounted harasser, he brought up something about the rider and then said, "By the way, Jed, when are you coming back to church?"

I told Jed about the movie scene. Now, whenever I see him I say, "By the way, Jed, when are you coming back to church?" We enjoy a good laugh every time.

• •

A few years ago, my wife's family decided to have a family reunion at my family's cabin at Priest Lake in northern Idaho. Her brother is a FedEx driver in Wasilla, Alaska. Recently we found out that he lives a mile away from Sarah Palin, the former governor and vice presidential candidate. He said he periodically delivers packages to their home; once to Sarah in her pajamas.

Because Scott drove a FedEx van, he regularly needed to buy tires and at times purchased them from me. Since he and his family were meeting up with us at the cabin, he asked if I would bring some tires along so he could drop them off at FedEx to be shipped to Alaska.

We loaded up my pickup with a week's supply of clothes, food, and other incidentals, lashing Scott's tires on top of the big load. My wife followed me in the van and we proceeded toward the freeway.

After a few miles on the 70 mph freeway, I did my usual exercise and glanced in the rearview mirror, only to see the tires escape from their captive ropes and take flight. My wife, as we learned only too well in South Dakota, doesn't do well when it comes to avoiding things on the road. She ran over at least one of the 235/75R16 10-ply radials before she knew what had hit her. The others went rolling off into the brush on the side of the road.

We stopped and gathered up the vagabonds. The tires were undamaged. The van was okay. My wife was shook up. I tied the load on again and we proceeded without further incident.

Many other items have been lost out of my vehicles over the years. Fortunately, I have never caused an accident with my wayward cargo. As

I have matured, I believe I am using a little more caution as I secure my loads. By the time I hit 95, I would bet I'll never lose another load.

CHAPTER 38

BAITED BY SUCCESS

As I began inventing, I found that I also had to sell the contraptions after I invent and manufacture them. Several times I have gone out on the road as a marketer. It's a tough way of life. It usually takes me several weeks and many excuses to my wife before I arrive at the point of departure. I don't like going and put it off as long as I can. I finally go because Michele is tired of me hanging around and claiming that I'll go in just another day or two.

I feel like I'm climbing a 100-foot high dive and my wife eventually forces me to jump. I just don't want to do it. Whenever I have gone on the road selling my wares, I have had a terrible time forcing myself to make the leap. I don't like leaving the security and comforts of home. However, nothing sells when I stay home. After I get on the road, I'm usually glad I went.

I drive out of Basin City, generally with a huge load of product on the back of my pickup and a trailer, if I happen to be pulling one. My biggest fear is that I'll return home in a week or two with the same large load strapped on the back, unsold. Up to the present, I have always been pleasantly surprised that I have returned with an empty truck.

In the course of my marketing, I have put together my own brochures and printed material. I fought with several types of printers over the years until I finally broke down and spent big money on a nice Xerox machine. I ordered the machine from Bruce, a friend of mine, and was told it would be delivered in a couple of weeks. It was around $7,000.

I woke up around 3:00 the next morning. As I lay there, I happened to notice a bump under my arm. I felt around and found several more. I had heard that lymph nodes are located in the armpit and I started freaking out. I soon had myself convinced that I had cancer of the lymph nodes and that at that very moment the cancer was invading all of my internal organs. I didn't sleep the rest of the night.

The next morning, I called my friend Bruce and told him to cancel my order for the printer. I seriously did not think I would be around much longer and, therefore, wouldn't need it. He canceled it.

That afternoon I saw a doctor. He asked me what kind of deodorant I used and then gave me his prognosis. It was plugging up my sweat glands. What a relief! I dialed Bruce and reordered the printer.

• •

In the year 2005, I was coming to the realization that I wanted to develop my ideas into products instead of dealing with tire store problems. For the previous five years, American Standard Manufacturing had been building and selling the YankATank. It was good since they were doing all the work, but gradually I watched my check grow smaller and smaller.

I also saw some areas where they could make improvement on the unit. They didn't want to. Whenever I would complain about the diminishing returns and increasing cost to build, David Day would tell me that they were just following the contract. After a few rounds of this verbal sparring, Dave told me to go read the contract. I am so glad he did.

As I read, I realized we had put a performance clause in the contract that wasn't being met. They owed me $7,000 to meet a minimum sales guarantee. I called Dave and informed him of my review. He said he would check with the owner, Cole. I got a call that Cole wasn't going to pony up the seven grand. I told Dave I was going to take it back. We parted friends and remain so.

I am glad that this happened. I made the improvements and have been shipping out YankATanks ever since.

• •

In 2002, I came up with a rolling tire rack. I began "envisioning" it a year earlier. I'm famous among my friends and family for getting too excited prematurely and gearing up before I have a viable product, let alone any experience with it. When I envisioned the RubRRak, the first thing I did to prepare to build it was buy a semi-truck load of tubing. I hadn't even settled on the final design. Luckily, I was on the right track as far as the size of tubing. If it hadn't worked out, I would have had a shed full of useless metal. As it was, I sat on the load of tubing for a couple of years before I was ready to start building and selling.

My dad would drive on his electric wheelchair down to his shed where I had the metal. He would look at it and ask me what in the heck I was going to do with it. I know he thought I was nuts. It wasn't the first time or the last time that I over-ordered. I worked on developing and eventually decided to call it the RubRRak (Rubber Rack). I took it to a few tire stores in the area and told them to try it. After a few weeks, even though they didn't want to support me because I was their competitor, they had to buy it. They had become dependent on my Rak! It turned out to be a handy, simple, and unique tool.

Since I was a Les Schwab dealer, I decided I would try to market to all the Schwab stores. Since the Schwab Company was supposed to be one big, happy family, I wondered if I could get the top brass to agree not to compete with me. I called up their attorney, Dick Borgman, and asked if the company would agree not to steal my idea.

Essentially, he told me that if I didn't have it protected, they would steal it. Nice guy. It made me mad as I thought we were better friends than that. I thought Schwab would be more loyal to its dealers. I applied for a patent.

I was under a severe cash crunch at the time. I hired a young Mexican named Jose to build Raks while I went on the road and sold them to Les Schwab stores. It was a venture into the unknown. I put together a book with pictures showing how it worked so the managers caught the vision in a few seconds.

The first trip took me to Ontario, Oregon, and back. Starting out, my truck was loaded to the gills with Raks. I sold them all. I could see that I was going to be doing a lot of traveling and selling over the next few months. I stopped in Hermiston and bought a flat-bed trailer from a friend so I could haul more Raks on future forays.

I didn't want to spend a lot of money on motels so I came up with a plan. I bought a little propane water heater/shower made for mountain climbers and hikers. The water pressure was provided by a small pump powered by four, D-cell batteries.

I would work all day selling Raks and assembling them at the store locations. I went strictly to Les Schwab stores because they were by far the biggest and busiest tire stores. Their managers were autonomous and I didn't have to work my way up the food chain to get approval. It didn't hurt that I was also a Les Schwab dealer.

I went from Schwab store to Schwab store. By the time evening rolled around and I finally arrived at a store that was closed for the day, I would pull into the parking lot at the rear of the store. This was my home for the night. I was sweaty, greasy, and dirty by this time from assembling and setting up RubRRaks.

As soon as it was marginally dark, I took a bucket over to the store's water hydrant and filled it up. I then stripped down to an arrestable condition and cranked up my little shower. Once I got it primed, it fed from the bucket and heated up with the little propane burner. I stood between the two open doors of my pickup, naked as a jaybird, and washed up.

After jumping into clean clothes I would hop back in the Tundra, lay the passenger seat back, crawl into my sleeping bag, and try to sleep. It was nice getting clean, but I spent a lot of energy worrying about a cop coming around the corner and arresting me for lewd conduct.

I went through this process in Seattle, Portland, Spokane, and many other small towns along the way. I always got clean and never got caught. It was usually the most exciting part of my day.

I loaded my Tundra and trailer with Raks and headed out on Monday mornings. On one of my first trips, I left my sales book on the back of the pickup and got to Ellensburg, 90 miles away, before realizing it. I pulled over in deep despair. I then experienced a minor miracle. The essential sales tool was still perched on the back of the trailer.

One hot summer day, I had a full load of Raks. I was just getting started. I went around a corner a little too tightly on Division Avenue, one of the main thoroughfares in Spokane. The trailer tires went up the curb and sidewalk. The entire load of 40 Raks broke loose and tumbled onto the street. There was steel tubing and parts scattered across three lanes of traffic. I was dumbfounded. I grabbed my camera, jumped out, and snapped a couple of pictures. I knew no one would appreciate the experience unless I had proof.

The next two hours were spent dragging Rak bases and tubing off the street, reloading them on the trailer, and worrying about cops showing up to write me a littering ticket. Luckily, the law was a no-show. I traveled for a week on that trip and got home on a Saturday. The next Monday, I went to the Tri-Cities after posting pictures of my Division Avenue spill on our family website. My brother-in-law Tracy had just read about me dumping my load in Spokane and then left his office, driving down Columbia Center Boulevard.

About that same time, I was losing another load on the very street Tracy was traveling. Here's Tracy's post to the family website later that day:

Date Posted: Oct 6, 2003

Late this afternoon, I was driving down Columbia Center Boulevard when I saw this bald guy off to my left on a side street next to the Midas store. He was standing next to a wooden crate looking somewhat frantic. He was motioning to some guy with a dolly and they all looked to be in a hurry. I couldn't turn around immediately, but I thought to myself "that can't really be Ben again with a load in the middle of the street." By the time I got back to the scene this is what I found. (He posted a picture of me trying to get the crate out of the middle of Columbia Center Boulevard.) Ben, we love you.

• •

I traveled throughout Washington, Oregon, Idaho, Montana, Utah, Nevada, and northern California, selling my wares. Sales calls were made on over 350 Les Schwab tire stores. Many managers immediately saw and recognized the benefits of the Rak. A few did not. A handful were rude to me.

Most would not have even talked to me if I hadn't been a Les Schwab man. I found a few of the guys had large egos. Some Schwab people look at themselves as some kind of gods in the tire world. At a few of the Schwab stores I visited, humility was a job for the assistant managers and crew, not the manager. But most of them were great guys.

It was an interesting time. One manager in Seattle threw me out. He told me all the reasons he didn't need them. I sold Raks to most of his neighboring stores and after a few weeks had passed and the word got around, he had his assistant manager call me up and order three Raks.

In Santa Rosa, California, I met with a cocky zone manager who wanted nothing to do with me and my product. In the course of our conversation, I found out they were having a zone meeting the next morning at his store. I asked if I could make a presentation and he reluctantly agreed.

The next morning was a disaster. A negative aura hung over the meeting and I didn't sell a single Rak to the ten managers that were there. I slunk out in disgrace after my presentation. A few months later, this same zone manager was fired for stealing almost a million dollars from the company. When everything came to light, the reality was that his store and zone were in shambles.

I drove to Sacramento the same day and met with another zone manager there. He was much more open-minded and positive. There happened to be a zone meeting at his store the next morning and he invited me to make a presentation. I presented my wares and received a much different reception. I sold over twenty thousand dollars worth of Raks in a half hour and took 20 managers to lunch.

On my way home from this California trip, I decided to stop in Prineville. The manager of Midway, the equipment division of Les Schwab, Mike Crakes, had called me a year earlier asking if they could handle my product. I put him off because I wanted to get more units out in the stores and I knew I would have to do the selling for that to happen. Also, going through him would have significantly cut my margins.

Now, after hitting most of the stores, I figured this would be a good time for Schwab to take over. I was ready for a rest. I met with Mike and he was glad to handle my product. A week later, he called me and said that Phil Wick, the president of Les Schwab, had torpedoed the plan. They were not going to handle it after all. I was a little bugged and disappointed.

A year later, I stopped in Prineville and enjoyed the distinct advantage of meeting with a few of the key people as I had always done since becoming a Les Schwab dealer. I spent a little time talking to Les himself and then met with Phil Wick.

I brought up the subject of the RubRRak and asked him why he had nixed Mike Crake's plan of handling it the year prior. He expressed great surprise and said that he never said they wouldn't handle the RubRRak. At first I didn't believe him, but as he kept insisting, I realized that maybe Mike had been wrong. Emphatically, he stated that Mike was mistaken. Of course, Phil said, Midway and Les Schwab would sell RubRRaks to their dealers.

I left the room excited. It would help to have them on board. I went across the street and informed Mike that Phil said that he was mistaken. Phil had no problem nor ever had a problem with Midway selling Raks. Mike got a very perplexed look on his face. He told me in no uncertain terms that Phil had turned down the deal the year before.

I restated what Phil had just told me. Mike was still puzzled, but said that it looked like they were going to be buying RubRRaks from me in the future. We were both excited.

After a week, I hadn't heard from Mike so I called him. His exact words echoed the previous year's message: "Phil said we are not to sell your RubRRak."

Why didn't Phil have the guts to tell me what was really going to happen instead of lying to me? I just don't get it. Most of the people who work at Schwab are great. A few are not.

• •

So after I delivered and sold RubRRaks for a few months, I decided to get some boxes and ship them to save time and trouble. August of 2003 included one of the worst nights of my life and believe you me, I've had a lot of them. I decided that I needed two large boxes to ship each Rak out to the store that purchased it. As usual, I had high hopes for my newest venture and in order to get a quantity discount on these cardboard behemoths, I ordered eight or nine thousand pounds of these custom boxes from a company in Portland.

A week after placing the order, I got a call that it was ready. I borrowed J's trailer, hooked it up to my little Toyota pickup, and headed out. At the time, I was in the middle of trying to write a patent for this new invention. Since I had no clue what I was doing in the legal world, I looked up a patent attorney in the phone book, called him, and made arrangements to stop by and visit with him on my way to Portland. He said he would be home all morning so I agreed I would drop in around ten o'clock. He sounded like things were pretty low key and I got the impression it really didn't matter when I showed up. I had a couple of hours after making the appointment to make the forty-minute trip to his place.

I hooked up the trailer and realized I was putting a two and five-sixteenths inch trailer hitch on a two-inch ball that was attached to my pickup. I hunted around my disorganized holdings, but couldn't find a bigger ball.

I knew this wasn't good, but I felt that since gravity was fairly dependable and there was a little weight pressing down on the tongue, I should be able to drive thirty or forty miles to town and purchase the right size ball before the trailer bounced off the ball and made its own way to town.

I headed for the big city, figuring I would make it to the high-priced lawyer right on time, even if I stopped and bought a ball first. Halfway to town, disaster struck. No, the trailer didn't fall off. I happened upon a county construction crew that were busy resting on their shovels, alternately watching the traffic back up, and taking union-mandated naps. I immediately sensed that these people did not care in the least that I had an appointment, albeit a vague appointment, with a high-priced patent attorney.

Disgruntled motorists in front of and behind me made U-turns after waiting twenty or thirty minutes and left in search of an unobstructed road to town. I was stuck with a twenty-foot trailer balancing on my bumper. I knew I probably couldn't get turned around without big problems so I stayed put and waited. It was a pleasant summer morning and even though I felt a little pressure to get moving, I felt all was right with the world.

Forty-five minutes later, I was starting to steam. I dialed the county engineer's office and asked to speak to a guy, possibly the assistant engineer. Actually, Guy was the guy's name and he was the assistant engineer. I related my plight and he feigned great concern. I knew he couldn't help but get complaints from the citizenry every couple of minutes with a road crew moving like these guys were. Another ten minutes found the great caravan of cars starting to make forward progress.

I was late. There was no time to stop for a ball. I raced to my new legal advisor's home and found him sitting outside on his porch swing in Bermuda shorts, sipping on a cool one while he was checking his stocks on his laptop. I was greatly relieved. He hadn't missed any work waiting for me. I told him I was running late (it was eleven by now) because of the road crew. He said it was no problem.

I spent fifty minutes gleaning information from him and then finished. I didn't want to go over an hour as he was charging two hundred and fifty dollars an hour. I pulled out my checkbook and was more than a little dismayed when he presented a bill for five hundred bucks. I gave the robber my goods and then hurried to my truck before he added any more seconds to my bill.

It was getting late, almost noon. I had two hundred and fifty miles ahead of me before Portland would materialize and I needed the right ball. I hurried into Walmart and ran to their automotive section. Locating a guy with a blue coat on, I breathlessly jogged over to him and innocently asked, "Where are your balls?"

He glared at me with an alarmed look on his face. "Are you looking for trailer accessories, sir?" he asked.

"Yes, I'm in a hurry," I said. All of a sudden, I realized that I had not phrased my last question correctly. He directed me toward another gentleman behind a counter.

I ran to him and blurted, "Do you have two and five-sixteenths inch balls?" I got another alarmed look. What is it with these Walmart guys? After he regained his composure, he showed me where the trailer accessories were located. Naturally, they were out of that size.

I jumped back in my truck and headed down the road. Once into Oregon, I drove through a small town and bought the right size ball and screwed it on. Safe at last!

The temperature grew hotter as the day continued. A wreck on the freeway delayed me further and by the time I rolled into Portland and my destination, it was close to closing time. I signed the paperwork and started directing the forklift driver on how to load the huge bundles of cardboard. We stacked one large pallet on the back of the pickup and put five more pallets on the trailer. I intentionally broke one bundle and stacked portions of the bundle across the top of the load, attempting to level the top of the load for optimum aerodynamics. This turned out to be a major mistake.

I was, as my kids would put it, "like, way overloaded." All of my tires were essentially flat with the massive weight they had just received. I borrowed an air hose and pumped them up, far past the recommended dosage. They were still looking a little saggy.

The day was hot, over a hundred degrees. I had mixed up a perfect recipe for a blowout or two on the hot asphalt leading home.

I neglected to mention that one of the reasons I was trying to get loaded and out of town were my taillights. I didn't have any. The borrowed trailer had an electrical pigtail that had been ground off by being drug along the road at some point. Naturally, I knew I wouldn't get home before dark, but I at least wanted to get to the shores of Washington as I'm not fond of the artificially high-priced tickets that are issued in Oregon.

I hadn't had lunch or dinner because of the time element. I grabbed a drink of water at the cardboard plant and then headed out with great trepidation. I crossed my fingers and managed to navigate out of the streets of Portland. Fifty miles later, arriving at Troutdale, I figured I had better stop and see how the load was holding together. I pulled off and saw that the load had done some major shifting and loosening up. I hurriedly pulled the straps tight and headed back for the interstate.

At Hood River I stopped and tightened things up again. I began to see that I would have been much wiser to have left the last bundle bound together instead of breaking it apart and spreading it out across the top of the other bundles. The two hundred loose pieces, each larger than a sheet of plywood, were the culprits working loose and making me stop every fifty miles to re-secure. I was not making great time because of the stops and my limited speed. The heavy load was causing the trailer and my little rice burner pickup to sway from side to side.

Even though I'm locally famous for my brisk, autobahn style driving, forty-five mph was as fast as I dared push it. At least I hadn't had a blowout.

Another nagging problem that had cropped up was the inability to see traffic behind my first stack of cardboard. The bundle we had stacked on the back of the pickup was too wide. Vision was limited to brown cardboard in both of my rearview mirrors. Looking back, I can see that many factors surrounding my pickup and J's trailer were starting to howl for a major calamity. They didn't have to wait much longer.

A few miles past The Dalles, I sensed it was time to stop and tighten straps. Traffic was hot, heavy, and passing me like I was standing still. I was still swaying along like a drunken sailor with a shipload of cardboard at forty-five mph. The desire to stop was starting to pound in my head, but there was no place to exit. A guardrail located right next to the lane I was in stretched before me for another mile. I crossed my fingers and hoped my growing premonition of disaster was false. It wasn't.

Finally, I reached the end of the guardrail and pulled off onto the shoulder. I stepped out of the pickup and my senses were assaulted. A blast of hot, Columbia Gorge wind hit me from the direction I had just come from. A train was flying by on tracks located between my highway and the highway going the opposite direction. Cars and trucks were screaming by as I glanced back at my load. Since I had been traveling the same direction as the wind, my loosened up load had stayed on as there was no noticeable airspeed factor. However, as soon as I stopped, I had a forty-five mile an hour tailwind.

My last strap must have slipped off just as I looked back and VOILA!! My loose sheets of compressed and flat boxes began peeling off the top of the trailer and flying everywhere. Even though it was over one hundred degrees, I was frozen in place. I had not yet accepted the fact that the Gorge wind was a permanent thing. I thought perhaps the train was creating the horrendous wind and as soon as it went by, all would be calm. I was wrong.

Semi-trucks and passenger cars were slamming into large slabs of cardboard. Great tornados were suddenly visible behind each truck as the sheets twisted and flew in every conceivable direction. Some opened up into a form of the boxes they were meant to become and flew down the highway like gigantic box kites in a forty-five mph windstorm. Trucks and cars were dodging cardboard and other vehicles. The screeching of tires replaced the sounds of the train.

As I scrambled back and crawled up on top of the load, I waited for the massive pileup that was sure to occur. Cardboard was still peeling off the top like giant playing cards involved in a game of Fifty-two Card Pickup. Fifty-two cards wouldn't have been bad. As it was, more than one hundred and fifty five by eight foot, double-walled pieces had exited before I got on top of the load. I was grabbing straps and sheets like a mad dog and finally got the revolt stopped. I temporarily secured what was left and then surveyed the damage.

I was shocked. No vehicles had wrecked, at least that I could see. Vehicles were still sporadically hitting the boxes as they motored up the interstate, but at least the sheets had spread out and metallic carnage had not yet occurred. The wind was still whipping.

I looked down the highway and could see some of the brown wind surfers had traveled over a half a mile from my location. Some were lodged up against highway signs. Most had jumped the guardrail on the other side of the road and had landed in a rocky ravine between the highway and the railroad tracks. Some were most likely still plastered against the grills of northbound cars and trucks, never to fulfill their customized purpose as RubRRak containers.

I counted six sheets suspended in the power lines overhead. They were flailing around like crazy. Gradually, they slid downwind, riding the wires like a big troupe of trapeze artists. A few more lay in a suicidal-type prone position on the railroad tracks, waiting for the next train to put them out of their misery.

I wanted to cry. I wanted to die. I wanted to drive away and pretend like I had no connection to the massive mess of corrugated papyrus sheets.

However they were mine. I had written a check for them a couple of hours earlier. The first cop to happen upon the widespread clutter would see the brand of cardboard and call the manufacturer in Portland. Since it was a custom size, my name would immediately become associated. Besides that, I had a lot of dough invested in the units flapping around that particular neighborhood. For those reasons, I stayed.

It was hot. Already I was sweating. I grabbed my phone and called my wife. It was 8:00 pm and I had hoped to be home by 10:00. Our family was primed to go to a Mariners game in Seattle the next morning, but I told her all bets were off. She asked when I would be home and I said if I was lucky, maybe around 6:00 the next morning. At that point, I had no idea what was in store concerning my future.

I walked across the road, climbed over the guardrail, and marveled at the way the landscape had turned brown. Layers of corrugated materials stretched as far as the eye could see. Craggy, sharp boulders had covered the ravine minutes before. Now, paper products covered the rocks. Cardboard sheets hung like scarecrows from the barbwire fence next to the tracks.

I knew it was time to go to work. I ran down the road and peeled sheets off the guardrail and road markers for three-quarters of a mile. Nobody stopped; they were all preoccupied with dodging my boxes. The initial shock was wearing off and reality was setting in. I was winded and worn out by the time I finished clearing the highway. I started walking back to my truck, in disbelief and awe of the job ahead of me. This was a job that I had very little faith I could complete.

I got to my pickup and opened the door, intending to drive it a little farther off the road. The winds flung the door open and whipped open the file containing my patent papers. Papers flew in a whirlwind around the interior and then headed for the exterior. I slammed the door and managed to catch most of the papers that had blown out of the cab. Things had been pretty rough for me during the last half hour. I sensed they were going to get even rougher.

The wind was relentless and ruthless. The heat seemed to me to be a vivid preview of eternal hell and damnation. For the first time in my life, I started considering the fact that maybe global warming is for real. The climatic conditions were, for the most part, shall we say, unfavorable.

I started my gathering process. Oblivious to the traffic screaming by, I began a process that lasted through the night. I walked across the highway, crawled over the guardrail and down into the ravine, gathered two sheets and attempted to navigate my way back up and across the road. The wind whipped the boxes and it was all I could do to hold on to them. Many times the boxes flew up and hit me in the head, giving me a bloody nose at one point. I lay them on the side of the road where my pickup was parked and secured them to the ground with large rocks.

After fifteen minutes of this ritual, I felt like I was going to have a heart attack. This was extremely hard work! I was sweating like crazy and panting for air. Every step climbing that rocky slope and guardrail was way past the limit for this chubby and getting-older-by-the-minute bald guy. Each time I drug the boxes over the guardrail, the slats and edges would catch on the guardrail bolts. The only way to disengage this connection was to position the cardboard in the wind and make it aerodynamically fly off the bolt. When that would happen, I would say, "Houston, we have liftoff." More than once I thought the sheets were going to take me for a magic carpet ride.

Jay-walking the highway between speeding cars and trucks was nuts, but necessary! If I wanted to keep from becoming road kill, timing was all-important. I was becoming dehydrated and exhausted. I found myself praying one minute and swearing the next. If I looked at the multitude of heavy sheets scattered downstream, I became severely depressed. I soon found that the only way I could continue was to concentrate on two boxes at a time. Absolutely no more! I could barely handle two. Following this ritual, I slowly worked my way north.

Days before, I had finished reading a book about deaths in the Grand Canyon. One of the main causes of death in the Canyon is dehydration, hallucination, and then expiration, even though the victims are often within spitting distance of the Colorado River. I was a hop, skip, and jump away from the Columbia River. And here I was, dehydrated, hallucinating, and mentally desiring expiration.

I was gathering where no man had gathered before. After an hour of this process, I found myself teetering on the edge between reality and hallucinations. I still had many trips ahead of me. I had only just begun. I realized I had appropriately been absentmindedly singing the song "We've Only Just Begun" by Karen Carpenter. Remembering that she was dead, I knew there was a good chance I would be singing a duet with her, at her location, before the night was over.

At one point, I thought I would try to hoist three boxes up the valley and across the road. It was not to be. Several hours into the adventure and well after dark, it was as hot as ever. The jagged rocks stretching hundreds of feet into the air must have retained the day's heat. I continued clawing my way up and down, back and forth. Eventually, to retrieve some of the wayward boxes, I had to navigate my way through a five-strand barbwire fence and climb up to the railroad tracks.

At last, I rounded up the last two boxes that had escaped. I carried them over and piled them up in the last of many stacks I had accumulated on the far side of the highway. I could hardly believe the job was done! It was after midnight and I was done with the hard part, or so I thought.

I walked a half-mile back to the pickup, started it up and idled up to my first stash. I got out and began trying to lift a box up and secure it to the top of the load. This was a job for Superman! The wind was still screaming and my box and I were its primary targets. I would lift a box up and it would immediately begin madly gyrating and trying to take off. Things were just not working.

Just then, I noticed red and blue lights reflecting off of my pickup in the dark. I looked up and sure enough, there was an Oregon State Police car, just behind my pickup and up on the shoulder of the highway. "Why would he stop in this desolate place?" I wondered. Then I noticed a car had pulled over by the side of my pickup. The cop had stopped someone speeding! What were the chances that they would end up directly at the central point of my misery?

I watched as the cop got out of his car. He hadn't even seen me or my pickup. He was giving the car he had stopped his full attention.

"Hey!" I yelled. He jumped with surprise and concern. He recovered his composure after shining his flashlight down on me and seeing I was no threat. "Are you here for them (I pointed at the car he'd stopped) or me?"

He gave a nervous laugh. I thought I saw him put his pistol back in the holster. He responded, "I'm here for them."

I yelled back and said, "As soon as you get done with them, sir, would you come down here with your gun and shoot me in the head, please?"

He laughed again with a little more enthusiasm and said he would. Little did he know that I was serious.

I should pause here and inform the reader that every single incident I have recounted in this experience is the honest to goodness truth. I could not make this stuff up!

An Oregon ticket and a few minutes later the trooper came down and asked what was going on. I gave him a brief synopsis of the evening and told him he should probably call the power company to come and get the boxes off the power lines across the road.

He said he would and then congratulated me for being a good citizen and cleaning up my mess. I lied and said, "No problem." He asked me if I wanted a light. The cardboard panels seemed to glow in the moonlight so I declined his offer. I asked him if the wind ever stopped in these here parts. He said not usually.

Again he thanked me for cleaning up and left me alone to fight the wind.

I soon could see that a different plan was needed if I was to get the boxes back on the trailer. I decided that I needed to drive to the far end of my piles, flip a U-turn on the freeway, and load the truck heading back against traffic and the wind. This would make my pickup and the front end of the trailer a windbreak. It provided the only possibility of my loading up with the wind howling.

I motored up the highway and after passing the last pile, I turned to the right so I would have enough room to make the U-turn on the highway. I went slowly as I still had a very heavy load on the truck and trailer.

All of a sudden, I heard an ominous, "PSSSSSS." I sat and pondered. It was either a rattlesnake or a flat tire. I would have much preferred sitting on a rattlesnake than to have a flat tire at this point in my life. No such luck. A serrated rock about a foot in diameter had sliced the sidewall on my right rear tire.

I began to organize and assemble my emotions so I could have a good cry. With the over-maxed load on my pickup and trailer, the right rear portion of my pickup was drooping substantially. Since I hadn't had a flat on this rig before, I had no idea where the jack and wrenches were. The spare was underneath the rear of the truck which, because of the load, was a couple inches from the ground. I had no light. I had no hope. So I did what anyone in my situation would do. I called 911.

I explained my predicament and asked the dispatcher to tell the cop I could use his light now. Could she send him back so he could shed some light on my dilemma? She put me on hold for a minute and then returned to tell me that he was on a call down in Hood River. I said I could use his help if he got back up where I was. It was then that I noticed the wind had died down.

I began fumbling around in the dark, trying to find components to assist me. I found the Toyota owner's manual and used the dome light to read up on where all the tools were supposed to be. It turned out to be a pretty interesting book. I had a hard time putting it down.

I lay on the rocky ground between the pickup and trailer and dug basalt rock with my fingernails, trying to provide enough clearance to get the spare out. I could sense that this was not a five-minute job like your usual tire change. An hour later found me still working on it. However, I must say, I did an admirable job considering the situation.

A combination of finding tools and operating them by Braille, knowing all the tricks of the trade by having been a tire man for twenty years, and hallucinating that I was victorious in climbing Mt. Everest, helped me finally get the tire changed. I was tightening the last lug and feeling like I had just conquered the big hill when the cop showed up. I had managed to get the tire changed in just over an hour.

"I understand you need a light," he said. It crossed my mind to say, "Yeah, and do you have a cigarette to go along with it?"

Instead, keeping with my Mormon persona I replied, "I'm past that point. I need a drink." He looked at me with surprise and said he had no beer in his cruiser.

"I didn't mean that kind of drink. Have you got any water with you?" I asked.

He motioned to his car. "I've got a water bottle that I've been drinking out of. If you don't care about that, you can have the water."

I replied, "I don't care if you've got AIDS and cancer; I've got to have a drink." We made our way to his car and I quickly guzzled down his offering. A new lease on life!

I thanked the cop, he left, and I made my way back to the truck. I found the rock that had caused the damage and threw it in the back of the truck as a keepsake and proof, just in case my wife didn't buy my story of where I had been all night. I figured the rock was good, hard evidence and could possibly even hold up in court.

Now I had to finish making my U-turn. I leaned down and felt around for other sharp rocks in the vicinity. I then backed up and pulled the trailer up on the highway. I could vaguely see that the boxes on the trailer had shifted with all the wacko maneuvering that had been going on. I made a big U-turn across both lanes of traffic on the freeway and then stopped on the shoulder. I was now going the wrong way.

I did not want to get down in Paul Bunyan's arrowhead garden again. I didn't have another spare tire and I was pretty sure the cop wouldn't come back again. I left my headlights off so the oncoming traffic wouldn't freak out. I did leave the parking lamps on. At this time of night and in my state of mind, the last thing I needed was a head-on collision.

With my lights off, I gingerly pulled ahead on the shoulder to finish my U-turn and get the trailer straight behind the truck. The truck gave a sickening lurch upward and I realized I had just run over a big pile of boxes.

Walking over to the pile of cardboard, I picked the top sheet up, grateful that the wind had died down. Just then, the wind came back in full force and tore the cardboard out of my hands. I wasn't surprised in the least. In fact, I would have been surprised if the wind hadn't come up. Even though the hurricane-force breeze continued to make it difficult to load the boxes, having the truck in front as a windbreak was very helpful. It took another hour and I had all the boxes, torn up but back in my possession, loaded.

I made another loop across the road and started down the highway for home. It was three in the morning. I had just completed seven hours in hell. I soon had the rig back up to forty-five mph.

Gratitude for finally being back on the road was rudely interrupted by the sound of a pallet falling off the top of the trailer and skipping down the road. I had traveled less than a mile. I saw a few cartons taking off in the wind. I began the prayer/swear routine all over again. I didn't know how much more I could take.

I eased to a stop, jumped out, and climbed onto the trailer. I was beat. As before, there was no one around to hold the boxes while I tied them down. However, at least this time I hadn't lost a zillion of the buggers. I located, carried back, and prepared to reload the eight or ten boxes that had taken flight. I finally got them up and secured, maneuvering them into place once again by using standard aerodynamic principles of wind versus cardboard that I was thoroughly familiar with by now.

All of a sudden, I remembered the wooden pallet that I had heard fall on the road. Traffic was flying by. If somebody hit that wooden pallet, another bad experience might materialize, like a motorist involved in a rollover or an inventor involved in a suicide. I sprinted back a quarter of a mile and located the pallet in the road. Dragging it back used up the last reserve of energy I had. I threw it in the back of the truck, crawled in the cab, and headed for home.

Twenty miles down the road I found a mini-mart open. Running in, I bought three large bottles of Gatorade and a forty-four-ounce cup of ice. The attendant charged me for the ice. I didn't mind. I would have gladly paid him a hundred dollars for the ice if he had required it. I walked out, tightened my load up once again, and headed for home. The gallon and a half of Gatorade and the forty-four ounces of ice were gone within five minutes. I arrived home at 6:00 am sharp, just like I had told my wife I would while I was watching one hundred fifty giant cardboard sheets taking flight in the Columbia Gorge.

We made it to the Mariners game that day. She drove; I slept.

CHAPTER 39

NOT IN MY TOWN

In 2002, on a beautiful fall Saturday afternoon, I came home for lunch. Just as I got out of my pickup, I noticed a small red pickup driving down the street in a big hurry. Soon it returned, going backwards. It raced down a side street in the same fashion. I could see it was a young Mexican kid who had no concern for other traffic on the road. He was racing through stop signs without looking for oncoming traffic or bothering to slow down.

Several neighbors were standing outside their houses, yelling at the kid to stop. He paid no heed. I decided if something wasn't done right away, somebody was going to get hurt. I walked out and stood in the middle of the road as he sped toward me. He slowed to a stop and I walked over to his open window.

I asked him if he had a driver's license. I didn't think he did because he looked like he was barely in his teens. He had a punk sneer on his face and said yeah, he had a license. I asked if I could see it. He dumped the clutch and sped off.

I was a little uncomfortable with his attitude and the fact that he would leave in such a hurry before I finished talking to him. So I dove through his open window into the cab. He was kind of a pudgy kid and there wasn't room for both of us. I was half in and half out, dragging alongside the speeding vehicle, hanging on for dear life.

I was sure that the rear tire was going to be running over me at any second. The truck veered off the street as it continued picking up speed. We flew past a tree, barely avoiding a scrape-against-the-bark catastrophe that would have smashed me into oblivion.

Soon we were cruising through rough terrain and sagebrush and I was still hanging on for dear life. We were fighting each other for control of the vehicle and he was trying to push me out. Finally, I was able to shut the key off and we rolled to a stop.

I was a little upset.

I told him to get out of the pickup and he kept saying, "Okay, mister, okay!" The only problem was he was fighting to stay in the pickup. I kept trying to open the door, but in retrospect, I know that the door was locked because I had been lying on the lock during our prior travels.

He started the engine again and tried to take off. I shut off the ignition and pulled the keys out. He was still refusing to get out so I grabbed his head and we began playing tug of war. He was heavy enough that I wasn't winning, but I was mad enough that he wasn't winning either.

After several minutes of tugging and yelling, my brother-in-law, Bret, showed up. I told him to go around to the other side of the pickup and open the passenger door. As soon as he had the door open, I sprinted around and grabbed the polite young man who had called me "Mister" and pulled him out. I held him down and told Bret to call the cops. He said someone already had.

Finally, I let the kid up. He asked if he could call his dad, who I happened to know. I said, "Sure." I figured his dad needed to know what junior was up to so he could straighten him out. He called and said some stuff in Spanish and then handed the phone to me. His dad was mad at me for beating up on his kid!

After another twenty minutes, the cops showed up. I gave them my statement and then walked home for lunch, figuring that justice had prevailed. After lunch, I walked back up the street to see what was happening.

By this time, a large congregation of the lad's relatives had gathered. There must have been 20 people there and they were all mad at me. They were yelling and screaming in a strange Latin dialect. In the middle of this confusion, a pickup drove up and the kid's uncle got out. He began yelling in the cop's face that I should be arrested. The guy was drunk. You could smell it. You could see it in his manner.

The cop looked at him and asked him if he had been drinking. When the uncle said, "Si," the cop told him several times that he should leave. Finally the guy walked back to his vehicle and drove away. I couldn't believe it. The cop let an obvious drunk drive away. In fact, he told him to!

After this little incident, I became less sure that justice was going to prevail. The cop told me I'd better leave, as the mob was getting pretty nasty. I walked home. A little while later, the cop knocked on my door and informed me that he was recommending that I be charged with assault. I never hit the kid; I just evacuated him out of the potential death machine he was driving.

I couldn't believe that the cop had taken the route he had. I believed then, and still believe, I did the right thing. After a few days, I went down and tried to make peace with the kid's dad. He was mad and continued haranguing on me.

Within a few months of this incident, I heard his dad was arrested for a serious offense. He has been in jail for the last fifteen years. I think he has another fifteen to go. I guess I'm lucky he didn't come after me.

The cops never charged the kid. Six or seven months went by and I never heard anything more about the incident. I figured that cooler and smarter heads must have prevailed in the sheriff's and prosecutor's office and they had dropped the charges against me. I had forgotten that the wheels of justice grind ever so slowly.

One day I got a letter from the prosecutor. They were charging me with assault. I had to go to court and make a deal to be a good boy for a year. I paid them 400 bucks so I could be on parole.

I went downstairs in the Franklin County jail so they could get my fingerprints and mug shot. The girl who got ink on my fingers and who was taking my picture started laughing. I asked her what was so funny and she said that I was the first person she had ever taken a mug shot of who was smiling.

I was supposed to check in monthly with my probation officer.

After the first month, I called the probation office and after telling them who I was and a little about the situation, they told me I didn't need to call again.

I guess they just needed the 400 bucks.

• •

Some entries from my journal...

Last summer I was sitting at the kitchen table looking out the window when two cars raced by my house, side by side, doing at least 90 mph. Cathy Vowels, a neighbor, also saw them tear past. I ran out and jumped in the SHO and found them over by the library. I started to pull in to find out who they were. Just as I was getting out of my car, one of them headed toward me in his car at full speed. I was barely able to jump out of the way. It was a sneering, young Mexican. I got his license and watched him tear off back down Canal Boulevard.

The other car headed west down Road 170 so I followed him. Caught up to him after a four mile chase (he was driving as fast as he could in a Firebird), got his license plate number, and then went home. Called the cops and they came out, but said they couldn't do anything about it because they hadn't seen it. I gave them the license numbers, but it was a useless gesture.

I drove around the trailer park a couple of days later and found the car. I went in and found the kid. His folks didn't speak English, but his sister translated. The kid was 14 and his dad said that he couldn't do anything about the kid taking the car. I lectured him, but it probably didn't do any good.

• •

After eating lunch at home one day, I started driving my pickup back to work. I had some obstructions plugging the nostril region. I began picking and examining the specimens as my pickup picked up speed. I moved my eyes from checking out the nostril gleanings to the street just in time to see mailboxes and posts materialize and loom larger right before my eyes. There was no time to stop. I crashed into the postal receptacles. Mailboxes exploded off their moorings and numerous posts were mowed down. I pulled over, finished my nose job, and spent the rest of the day buying and installing six new mailboxes.

• •

One morning in the spring of 2005, I walked out of the tire store and met a friend and customer of mine. Kent McMullin was getting the tires on his brand new John Deere four-wheeler filled with flat-proof compound. He had just bought it and told me how great the machine was and what a good deal he had gotten. A wild thought struck me that I should get one for my boys since they were already twice as old as I was when I started off-roading. They had not yet had the experience.

Later that morning, Scot Haws and I went down to the John Deere dealership. The salesman was treating us like we were just tire-kickers which solidified my determination. We were standing around several of the four-wheelers as we talked. They cost $6,000 each.

Finally, I felt like I had to decide. I took out a coin and called it. I said, "Okay, if it lands on heads, I'll take one." The coin landed on tails. To be funny I said, "Darn it, I guess I'll take two." The salesman and Scot looked at me like I was nuts.

I filled out the paperwork and they delivered them to my machine shop the next day. I brought my boys down a few days later to ride them. We put a couple miles on each bike.

The next day, I walked in the shed where I had left them and there was only one bike. Make that one uninsured bike. The other uninsured, $6,000 bike with two miles on it was gone. I found some tracks and traced back to where someone had loaded it in a pickup and hauled it away during the night.

I reported it to the cops. Nothing ever came of their investigation.

I slept in the shed for the next two weeks, sure that the culprits would return for the other one. They never did. I endured many sleepless, disquieting, and wide-awake nights. Every noise caused me to spring out of my sleeping bag, grab my AR-15, and stand at the ready for ten or fifteen minutes until I decided it was a false alarm.

Finally, I could take it no more. I set up an alarm in the shed which called my home whenever it was activated.

Nine months went by. I never got a call. My lonely four-wheeler sat in the shed.

One early morning at 1:00 am, as I was sleeping at home, my phone rang with a message from the alarm at the shed. I didn't think it was a false alarm since I'd never gotten a call before. I was sure that somebody was ripping me off again.

The shop is about eight miles from where I live. I jumped into some trousers, grabbed my 9mm and cell phone, and ran to my pickup. I tore down the street as fast as the V8 would accelerate, through the stop signed intersection, and floored it through Basin City. Little did I know, a cop was parked at the fire hall a couple hundred yards away, licking his lips, and waiting for some action.

I drove through Basin City as fast as I could go. I was doing over a hundred miles an hour by the time I hit the west end of town. I was watching the road when I should have been watching the rearview mirror.

After traveling a couple of miles in this high-speed fashion, I decided maybe I'd better call the cops and get them headed to the shed so I would have some backup. I dialed 911 and told the dispatcher what was going on.

Just then I noticed my cab started glowing with blue and red flashes. I looked in the mirror and saw a cop behind me. I asked the dispatcher to tell the cop what was going on and she said I'd better stop. I didn't want to stop. I was sure that in another minute or two, my four-wheeler would be exiting its home and traveling to a far-off country, never to be ridden by my boys again, just like the last one.

Again, the dispatcher told me to pull over. I complied. I jumped out of my truck and yelled to the cop that my burglar alarm had gone off. He asked me where and I replied, "Casper Lane."

"Go ahead, I'll follow you" he said.

I proceeded as before, 100+ miles an hour. He stayed right with me minus his flashing lights.

We pulled up to the shed several minutes later. I jumped out with my gun and bare feet, gingerly tiptoeing through the gravel. He backed me up. I went in and checked the place out.

It was a false alarm.

The deputy was upset. He started yelling at me for my driving techniques and speed. I tried to defend myself, but to no avail. He went on for several minutes, got back in his car, and left. I figured he had gotten it out of his system.

Several days later, I was opening my mail and happened upon a letter from the sheriff's office. I opened it and was very displeased to find a ticket from the aforementioned officer. He had written me up for negligent driving and, in a chicken doo-doo sort of style, sent it to me in a letter so he didn't have to look me in the eye.

I sort of lost my cool. I called out a few names that my wife didn't approve of. Our stake president had asked all the LDS members to spiritually prepare for and dedicate their homes for spiritual protection and righteous living. Our family had just had a special meeting a few days before and I had dedicated our home toward those ends.

My response to that ticket had negated the dedication, according to my wife. I was a little embarrassed and had to agree with her. I tried to pacify her by assuring her that I would rededicate it as soon as I got this ticket thing straightened out.

Soon after, I headed to town to talk to the powers that be. The undersheriff was available so I went into his office. He was already well aware of the situation and even gave me the impression that he had encouraged the deputy to write me up.

Our discussion escalated to the point that we were yelling at each other. When I went in his office, no one else was around. When I exited after our differing points of view had been expressed, there were two deputies standing just outside his door, trying to eavesdrop and ready to rush in if needed. I bid them a courteous adieu and left the premises.

I felt bad about the screaming, even though he had done as much as I had. I went in a few days later to apologize. It was a Friday morning to be exact.

I promised the receptionist that I would not scream this time around and she buzzed me through the electronic door.

We talked. I told Kevin that I wanted to apologize for the audio level of our previous meeting, but I wasn't apologizing for the general theme and principles I had expressed. They were as follows:

- I was not out "joyriding" at one o'clock in the morning. My burglar alarm had alerted me to a potential problem. I had been sleeping, for heavens sake!

- I felt I had to take care of the problem ASAP. Many times when I have called the cops concerning an urgent matter, they haven't shown up until 20 or 30 minutes later. And then they can do nothing about it because they didn't see it.

- I was not driving recklessly or negligently. The definition of those driving infractions includes the fact that the charged driver is endangering the lives of others. There were no cars on the road that night during my travels. I didn't endanger anyone else.

- I was operating under the assumption that if I didn't hustle down to the shop, my four-wheeler would be gone and the cops had already demonstrated with the last one that they couldn't get it back for me.

- The cop drove just as fast as I did. His emergency lights were off the entire time he followed me down to the shed. Why didn't he write himself out a ticket and mail it right after he wrote me up?

I reminded Kevin about the 25 years worth of problems I'd had in the past. I rehearsed the time I had been charged with assault by his department for trying to protect my home and family and neighbors while the perpetrator walked.

I talked about all the thefts and vandalism I had endured through the years without getting much help from law enforcement. I talked about the drag racers that went past our house on our 25 mph street at over 90 mph, side by side. I spoke of how I chased them down and one of them tried to run over me. I reminded him of how I had furnished both of their license plate numbers and yet they told me they couldn't do anything about it because they weren't there when it happened.

I probably covered a few other things while keeping my voice down the entire time. He said he understood my position, but wasn't going to change his mind. I deserved the ticket. The prosecuting attorney already had the charges anyway.

I got up to leave, still mumbling about the unfairness of it all. I noticed the Herald was opened to a story about a small mom and pop gas station that was selling gas cheaper than anyone else in the Tri-Cities. Cars were stacking up on the streets because everyone was trying to get in to buy cheap gas.

The sheriff's department had started writing tickets to the vehicle owners. The *Herald* was echoing the sentiments of the community about the unfairness of it all. Kevin started grousing about how he was getting all these calls and complaints and it was making his job really tough.

I seized the opportunity. I told him that that was a great idea . . . I was going to call the *Herald* and tell them about my problem! I was sure they would be glad to write a big, juicy article about all the past injustices I had endured and the present ticket I had been presented. It would make for an interesting story and might make somebody think twice the next time before writing a bogus ticket, at least to me.

He didn't say anything. We shook hands and I left.

That was a Friday. The next Monday around noon I was working down at the shop. A red, unmarked patrol car pulled up outside. It was Kevin. He informed me that my visit with him the previous Friday had caused him three sleepless nights and restless days.

Bingo! The press is what those guys worry about. They don't worry about extenuating circumstances or common sense or what's right and wrong as much as they worry about the press. He then told me that he had talked to the prosecutor and my ticket was gone.

I thanked him and we parted ways.

A few days later, I got a slip in the mail informing me that I was to appear in court and answer to a negligent driving charge. I called the sheriff and he said he would check into it. He called me back and said that since I didn't have an attorney representing me, the prosecutor wasn't going to dismiss the charge.

I was back to square one. Kevin contacted me later and said that he was going to write a letter to the judge.

On the appointed day, I showed up in court. My friend J and his daughter Corianne were the only other defendants in the courtroom. She had been charged with speeding and J was there to do battle for her. Ironically, a reserve deputy had charged her with speeding on Road 170 just past Casper Lane. Without getting into the details, the cop had been misinformed or had lied about the posted speed limit on that very road. I know because I drove that road every day and I had even had conversations with the county engineer about the posted speed limit.

The judge wouldn't listen to J's argument. He said he believed the cop more than J and his daughter. They left in a huff. After J, Corianne, and the huff left, I was the only one left to try.

The judge called me up and read the charge. He glanced through some papers and pulled out the letter from the undersheriff. He took several minutes to read it. He then thought for a bit.

Pulling the ticket up, he read something like this: "The ticket number is 76291." He then looked over at another paper and said, "The docket number is 76292. The ticket and the docket number don't match. The state has no case. Case dismissed."

I don't remember the exact terminology he used, but I do know that he claimed that two numbers didn't match and therefore my ticket magically evaporated. Without the letter from the sheriff's office, I would have walked out of the courtroom more than six hundred dollars lighter in my right rear pocket cavity.

As I walked out, I turned and said to the judge, "Your honor, I've lived on Casper Lane since the 60s. Mr. Wood was right in his statements. The deputy was wrong." The judge simply shrugged. He didn't care. I left the courtroom a happier man than J had a few minutes earlier.

CHAPTER 40

LEGACY

Journal, family website posting, and eulogy I gave at Dad's funeral:

Dec. 18, 2004

It is finished. This evening, as everyone is probably now aware, Dad bid adios and headed for greener pastures. I remember as a child listening to him singing (as we worked, naturally):

"Oh, give me land, lots of land under starry skies above, Don't fence me in, Let me ride through the wide open country that I love, Don't fence me in, Let me be by myself in the evenin' breeze, And listen to the murmur of the cottonwood trees, Send me off forever but I ask you please, Don't fence me in"

He didn't sing all the words, but he sang enough of them to let me know how he felt. What a wonderful time we have had! I count myself extremely lucky to have Dad as my father, Mom as my mother, and the rest of you as my kin. I think 99.9% of the deaths that have occurred on this planet have not come close to approaching the peacefulness of this day and his passing.

We are encouraging our kids and ourselves to write down the events and their feelings of this last week while it is still fresh and unforgotten. This week, to some of us, has been the most memorable week of our lives. We are very lucky to have been so close to Bill Casper. He is a legend. Boyd's (Matheson, a brother-in-law) advice was so good— let the funeral of Dad be a starting point of changes in each of our lives. For you who asked, here is a copy of the eulogy I gave at the funeral:

William Vere Casper was born near Roosevelt, Utah to Joseph and Rena May Casper on November 28, 1927. He grew up on a farm in Heber Valley, Utah. He graduated from high school in three years instead of the usual four.

After World War II, he served in the Army as a paratrooper during the occupation of Japan and worked in the underground mines with his father in Park City, Utah.

Bill served a two-year mission for the Latter-Day Saint church in Bagdad, Arizona, part of the time serving as the branch president for the Bagdad branch. He then attended Utah State University and graduated with a Bachelor of Science degree in Vocational Agriculture. He went to India for six months as an International Farm Youth Exchange Ambassador.

On March 4, 1954, he married his sweetheart, Joan Riggs, in the Salt Lake LDS Temple. He taught high school in Manti, Utah and then moved to the Columbia Basin in 1957 and worked as a county agent while developing their farm in the Ringold area.

Together they raised four sons and five daughters and have been blessed with 48 grandchildren and three great grandchildren. Bill loved the gospel of Jesus Christ, was active in the LDS Church his entire life, and faithfully served in ward and stake callings. He cherished his family and friends, was extremely generous, and loved farming.

He was diagnosed with MS in 1985 and retired from farming in 1992. Bill and Joan celebrated their 50th wedding anniversary this year. He passed from this mortal existence on December 18th from complications of pneumonia, surrounded by his loving family.

Dad was tough as nails. It always seemed that nothing could take him down. Even when his sugar beets blew out three times in one spring, he bounced back. However, in order to proceed with his eternal progression, he finally accomplished his earthly assignments and has moved on.

Dad and Mom have each written autobiographies. I would like to quote a few lines from the Preface of his book.

"My parents and grandparents were farmers. I was born and raised on a farm, lived and worked most of my life on a farm, and hope to die here on my farm near Ringold, overlooking the Columbia River. I've had varied experiences from the deserts of eastern Utah, eastern Washington, and Arizona, to the mountains of Japan, Nepal, and Tibet, and have met and become acquainted with so many fine people.

I worked many long days, especially in the early development years, but they were the happier times of my life. If I have been a successful farmer, I give much credit to the people who worked along with me through the years—to my hired men and women, my wife, and my children—and to the migrant laborers, too. I couldn't have helped the Columbia Basin irrigation pioneers tame this desert without them.

The opportunities and blessings that have come to me were, and are, greater than I had hoped for. It's been said, "In every life some rain must fall." I used to take pride in being able to walk far and run fast; now I can do neither. I can frown and be sad or I can smile as I watch each of my grandchildren run and play, study and work, and prepare for their future. Life does go on, with or without us, but hopefully I have left an example of faith and work to each of my children and grandchildren. I'm thankful for the privilege of living in this day and age, for the modern conveniences, modern machinery, and all the things we have had that our pioneer ancestors did not have. It's been a wonderful journey and I now look forward to reaching my destination."

Around Dad's home and shop, every place we look, every step we take, and every improvement we enjoy, is filled with memories of life with Dad. He was a class act. He was a guy who taught correct principles by his example. He was driven to succeed. He was strong. He was fast. Many times he jumped wide irrigation canals in a single bound. Sometimes hired men half his age would attempt to follow him and end up in the middle of the ditch, soaking wet. In foot races at Church picnics in the 60s, Dad usually always beat the other men and high school boys.

I've watched him carry six sprinkler pipes at a time, time after time, down through the middle of the beet field. This went on year after year. In his 35 years of hard farming, he probably changed more hand lines than any other man who moved sprinklers. For many years he would often change five or six hundred head of pipe a day and sometimes, if he thought it was needed, even in the middle of the night, all at a full run.

Early mornings bring memories of Dad already on the run, breaking a sweat before dawn. The daylight hours, except on Sunday, were always filled with laying out new hand lines, shoveling corrugations, leveling land and constructing ponds, moving mainlines back and forth, working ground, planting, cultivating, swathing alfalfa, and stacking 110 pound bales of hay by hand in massive stacks that would reach 20 or 25 bales high. This was in the days before Harobeds, boom loaders, or any other type of mechanical stackers. He could always be found fixing machinery, setting up planting and cultivating equipment, and running from farm to farm to perform many other tasks.

Sometimes, if his kids and hired men were lucky, a half-hour nap was enjoyed after lunch. Then he would say, "Okay, back to the salt mines." After supper, he'd go back out and work until dark.

Spring always brings memories to our family of tilling and planting. Summer was filled with irrigating the sand and clay with siphon tubes, hand lines, wheel lines, and later circles. Fall brings the smell of past sugar beet, potato, and corn harvests. Winter reminds us of feeding hundreds of head of cattle in the snow, helping fix equipment for the next year to the sound of a loud diesel heater, pruning trees, building ponds, and putting in underground irrigation systems.

It wasn't all work. Boating, camping, and fishing trips were sandwiched in to the family schedule.

He built many structures including two homes, a machine shop, a spud shed, and a top-notch grain handling facility. I don't know if he ever heard the saying, "Wear out, don't rust out," but he was the epitome of that philosophy.

One fall, a truck spring dropped and broke his ankle. He had hundreds of acres of beets left to harvest. He worked from early each morning until late every night driving the tractor and beet digger, hobbling around with a plastic bag wrapped around his cast. As usual, he pushed himself and everyone else to get the beets out before the ground froze. At one point, with several truck drivers standing around watching and waiting, he crawled under the digger to make a repair. While tightening bolts and being totally exhausted, he dropped off to sleep on the cold ground. They shook him awake; he finished tightening the bolts and crawled back on the tractor.

Dad farmed every square inch of his land. One summer our balers weren't working so we had Nielsons bale our hay. Some of the windrows dropped off on a steep slope. You couldn't keep a Harobed on that sidehill and could barely keep a tractor and baler on it. We would just give the bales a little push and they would roll by themselves down the hill where we would Harobed them at the bottom. After the hay was baled, Rick Nielson came over to me and said, "Somebody really has to love farming to be farming a sidehill like that." He was right. My dad really loved farming.

He strongly encouraged and supported his children and grandchildren to obtain all the education they could. Six of his children served missions. He loved the Gospel of Jesus Christ. He never missed church on Sunday due to work. Farm work was not his top priority on the Sabbath. He served many years on the Stake High Council and in other positions. He was dedicated to his church callings. He set an example in calling on the Lord daily in kneeling down and having family prayer. Mom says he prayed silently many times each day.

Mom was, and is, just as diligent. Dad loved Mom. He did not put up with sassing or disrespect to her. In return, she was always his reliable companion. They were as one. For many years Mom could be found driving tractor, hoeing weeds with her kids, driving the beet truck, and doing many other farm jobs. She also found the time to raise nine kids and run a home. Both Mom and Dad are outstanding individuals in all the tasks they have undertaken.

The last 19 years of his life was battered with Multiple Sclerosis. He fought it valiantly every day. He had spells for years before this when he was overcome with fatigue, but he had work to do so he set his exhaustion on the back burner and continued to work his body daily in Olympic style efforts. He was very concerned about getting out of debt during this time and was greatly relieved when he finally accomplished that.

As the MS began its relentless damage, he told me that in the mornings he just wanted to stay in bed. However he didn't. He was always up and struggling to be constructive. The first years of MS found him fighting great depression, chasing cures, spending lots of money on promised remedies, working on his cabin at Priest Lake, building a nice machine shed, converting a San Francisco transit bus into a luxurious motor home, and gradually becoming confined to a wheel chair.

The later years found him still trying to drive, but because of his dead legs, he often crashed into other vehicles, his new shed, his house and garage, and various other items. It frustrated him greatly. Finally, he quit trying to drive. However, just in the last few months, on several occasions, I saw him drive his car down to get the paper. He would stop and talk to me on his way back up to the house. At these times, he had snuck out of the house without Mom knowing and somehow managed to get into the car. He would operate the gas and brake by moving his legs with his hands. When I would tell him he was being a bad boy, he would give me a "cat ate the canary" kind of smile and tell me not to tell Mom.

One of my saddest memories are the many days he would be found sitting outside the open garage door in his wheel chair, waiting and wanting to do something constructive, but unable to do anything.

One job he was still able to do, even up through this last summer, was to mow the lawn. Sometimes he got stuck, one time even sliding downhill on the wet grass and becoming stretched and wedged under a large branch in the orchard until my mom found him. He wore out five or six wheel chairs. He fell innumerable times. At Priest Lake, one time my mom had to leave and he promised her he would go nowhere near the water. As soon as she was gone, he was out on the dock. Soon he had rolled backward off the dock and landed in the water. Luckily, he was able to keep his head above water and after yelling for a time, two neighbors heard him and pulled him and his electric scooter out.

My brother-in-law Bret was having trouble with the hydraulics on a tractor one day. Dad drove up and saw the problem. He crawled out of the car, pulled himself up on the back of the tractor, reached in, and tried to feel what the problem was in the linkage. He pushed the wrong link and the 3-point hitch raised. It crushed his arm, including the veins and arteries, and peeled the skin off clear around it. Bret moved the lever back down, but his arm was wedged so tightly the tractor arm wouldn't drop. In control as usual, he told them to get a long bar and pry the 3-point arms down to release his arm. The doctor worked a miracle on him after five hours of surgery. I thought he would never be able to use that arm again which would have been disastrous considering he was wheel chair bound. Instead, he made his arm fully recover.

We finally got Dad a remote dialer with all the kids' phone numbers on it. If he fell, he would push the button, which would call us. One day my sister Lisa got a call that Dad was down. She told Todd to drive down and help him. She got a little frustrated because Todd sat down and had breakfast. He knew Dad wasn't going anywhere. Sure enough, when he finally got there, Dad was lying on his side next to the overturned wheelchair in the strawberry patch, happily eating strawberries.

He never gave up. He probably holds a world record for falling out of wheelchairs. He always had scrapes and bruises. We are still amazed that he never broke a bone from falling.

My mother is a saint for the way she has taken care of Dad. My dad is a saint for his life-long accomplishments and for enduring to the end. He suffered great frustration and indignities, and yet, still stayed true to his core beliefs. Even until the end, he made sure he had nice clothes on and was clean and shaved. This may not sound like much, but with the large difficulties each task entailed, it was quite an accomplishment.

He did his best to live the commandments. He always paid more than a full tithe and he gave the Lord credit daily for all his blessings. He had a strong testimony of the Restored Gospel and prayed daily for his family's happiness and well being. He followed the steps the Lord has outlined we each must follow to receive a testimony of the divinity and truth of The Bible and The Book of Mormon.

He had that testimony. He attended the temple regularly.

Of all his interests, he was most interested and concerned with his family. His main concern was that his family had faith in the Lord, Jesus Christ, kept the commandments, repented as necessary, received the ordinances of the Gospel, and endured to the end. Just as the Savior has done for all mankind, my father set the example for our family on how we should live.

Dad wasn't perfect. He was well aware of his shortcomings. He always tried to do better. It is my prayer that we will do the same.

Jun 20, 2005

This was the first Father's Day we've had without Dad. I am so grateful that the last words and conscious moments I had with him were grand. Mom and I took him to the hospital. Brent and I helped him get shaved, cleaned up after he got sick, and then said goodbye. He was very gracious and thankful as we left. We lingered in the doorway for awhile, waiting for Mom and talking to him. This was the last time we spoke—a great memory for me.

• •

After the passing of my mother-in-law we met up with Michele's side of the family in Utah to divide up the spoils.

We packed my pickup with all the stuff Michele was bringing home. It was a major load. It took over three hours just to get everything tied down in accordance with Michele's specs. It would have taken three seconds according to my specs. There were chairs and boxes and anything else you might find in a garage. The load was hanging out all over. I grabbed some cardboard and wrote a big sign on the back "The Beverly Hillbillies: Y'all come back now!"

We kept track on the way home even though it was dark by the time we got to Boise. From Orem to Boise we got the following numbers from the people who passed us:

Waves	13
Thumbs Up	8
Stares	Numberless
Smiles & Laughs	47
Bird	Possibly 1

• •

Since I've gone on and on about my dad, maybe I should talk about my mom for a bit. I loved her every bit as much as I did Dad.

Mom was born in Kansas during the Depression. Her dad was named after me. Or maybe it was the other way around. Regardless, his name was Ben. He struggled at farming and worked in the oil fields in Texas. After years of trying to support his family in the Midwest, the Riggs clan moved to Eugene, Oregon.

Mom spent her teenage years in Eugene with her folks, her brother John, and three sisters. Probably the most important occurrence of her teens was the night she was invited to a party by Nan Powell, a friend of hers.

• •

Fast forward to the day of Mom's funeral last September— this very same Nan came from Seattle with her husband to the funeral. She was close to

Mom. As our large family of 150 souls sat in the church's Primary room savoring our last physical moments with Mom before the service, Nan had still not shown up. We knew she was on her way and we didn't want to have the family prayer until Nan got there.

We told the church ushers to be on the lookout for Nan as we wanted her to be with us. We told them she would be in a wheelchair and wearing a pink outfit. We sat and waited. Finally, Nan showed up. Her husband wheeled her and her hot pink outfit into the room. She said, "Sorry, we're late. We couldn't find Basin City. The directions you gave us were very good, but they were wrong." In spite of the somber occasion, we all had a good laugh.

After the family prayer, the family made their way into the chapel for the service. After we were all seated, I noticed that Nan was seated with her husband. Next to her sat Julie Mathews. I wondered why, even though Julie was a good friend, would she be sitting with the family?

After the funeral, I found out why. Julie had arrived late also. She also arrived in a wheelchair and a hot pink outfit. The ushers figured she was the guest we had been waiting on. They wheeled her up and sat her right next to Nan in the pew that was reserved for wheelchair-bound ladies in hot pink suits.

• •

Back to the party Nan invited teenage Mom to in Eugene—it was a Mormon party that Mom was just a little apprehensive about. Even though Nan wasn't a Mormon either, she invited Mom. This was the beginnings of Mom's sojourn through life as a Mormon. Over the next few weeks she was taught by the missionaries and joined the Church shortly after. Nan did the same.

Mom died on September 20, 2014. My eight brothers and sisters and I were with her at my sister Teresa's home. It was as peaceful and loving an eve as Dad's passing ten years earlier.

About an hour after her death, Michele and I walked out of Teresa's house towards our home. Michele got a text that our daughter Meg had just had a baby at 9:45 pm. We looked at each other and had the same thought. That was about the same time that Mom had died. I walked back in the house and into the room with Mom and the other siblings. "What time did Mom die?" I asked. Several answered in unison, "9:45."

Meg's daughter Josie was born into this life at the exact same minute that her great grandma Joanne left this life. Josie is Mom's 50th great grandchild. Both of them are called "Jo" by those who love them most.

We believe we each existed as spirit children of God before we were born. We also believe that when we die, as the *Bible* says, our spirits return to God. (Ecclesiastes 12:7)

I don't think it is much of a stretch to think that two kindred spirits passed, and maybe even greeted each other with a high five, on that special night.

Mom had taken care of Dad through his 18 years of MS. As a caregiver, it was hard on her. She raised nine kids with her oldest being the most problematic. She served in many capacities in our church. As a farmer's wife, especially in the early years, she worked as a hired hand driving truck and tractor. I remember as a young kid hoeing weeds in the beet and bean fields with her.

She worked as hard as Dad. She loved and served her kids and husband. Several times, I believe, she was instrumental in saving my life. More than once she wanted to take my life.

Which reminds me of a story . . .

One afternoon when I was about 16, my brother, Brad, and I decided to go for a round of a fairly regular, ongoing shoe fight we often had. With nine kids around, there were always plenty of shoes available. We would assemble our ammunition and then start chucking shoes just as hard as we could at each other.

Most kids use a ball when they play dodge ball. We used shoes when we played dodge ball. I think we preferred the shoes because they were plentiful and inflicted more pain on the opponent when a direct hit was scored. The only rule we had was no high heels.

A variation of the shoe throwing contest that usually occurred outside on the lawn was done with sprinkler boots. They were a little softer but you could throw them harder since the high tops gave you more leverage when you threw.

So we were downstairs chucking shoes at each other. When we missed, the shoes would bang against the wall. Our house was fairly new and I'm sure that Mom was not pleased when she heard the walls being impacted. She yelled several times at us to knock it off without much success. Finally, she let us know that if she heard one more shoe hit a wall, we were going to be sorry.

Brad has always been smarter than I but this day was different. I took Mom at her word and quit. Brad picked up a shoe and threw. Being smarter than Brad, I dodged and the north basement wall took a hit. A loud hit! I knew Brad was in big trouble; so did he. He took off to hide in a bedroom closet.

Since I was innocent of the last transgression I felt no need to hide. I would hang around and let Mom know Brad was the culprit and the direction he had headed.

It just so happened that Mom had been getting ready to go to a church meeting in town. It didn't take her long to navigate down the stairs. She came around the corner and was loaded for bear, at least mentally. Physically, she was in a little more vulnerable position. All the gear she had on was underwear, a slip, and high heels. But there was blood in her eye. And I was all she could see.

I quickly explained that she should go looking for Brad and he went that-a-way. She was not interested in my suggestion. Someone was going to pay and I was the only one available. I shifted into "Drive" and ran around the downstairs fireplace with her in hot pursuit. The heels kept her speed reduced and I was able to shift into reverse. I started backpedalling down the hallway, protesting as I retreated. I lost her as I ran up the back stairway and into the garage.

I figured she had given up or picked up on Brad's scent. I was wrong. As I walked outside to get away from the very dangerous situation, the front door opened and Mom emerged. The only thing different about her appearance was the broom she now held in her hand.

I tried explaining again, but she was fixated and focused. I knew I could outrun her any day of the week. However, to make it a little more fair and easier to explain that she was after the wrong guy, I turned and jogged backwards once again as she chased me. I continued sharing my feelings about how I was not at fault.

I led the small caravan on a westerly course toward the cheat grass-covered hill between our house and the Columbia River. I was sure the rough terrain would soon force her to go back to her dressing room.

But no such luck. Mom, her high heels, and her broom were dedicated to the task at hand.

All I can remember her saying was, "I'm going to get you!" This promise was repeated multiple times. I pleaded and cajoled and explained, all to no avail. The situation was escalating and getting serious. This wonderful, little five foot two, eyes of brown mother would not stop, even if she was in heels, whites, and holding a sweeper attachment. I wondered if we would be swimming the Columbia before it was over.

I backpedaled through the field and up the hill as she continued the chase. We were not far away from each other, probably just a little further apart than the length of a broomstick.

We traveled a good quarter of a mile uphill in this fashion. Finally, I heard a pickup coming up the driveway. I've never been so relieved to see my dad in his work truck. My only problem was he was a long ways away, almost out of earshot. When he finally parked and got out, I started yelling for help. He looked out at us and, if I remember correctly, started rubbing his eyes to get rid of the image they had presented to him. He then proceeded at a fast pace toward us.

The chase was still on. I began circling back toward the unusual safety of my father. When we met up, I quickly explained the situation and surprisingly, he accepted my claim that Brad was at fault. He walked up to Mom and said, "Jo, get back to the house and get some clothes on; right now!" I was finally able to relax.

• •

This was probably the only time in my life that my mom was not my best friend. Well, in retrospect, there may have been a few other times. I loved her. As I may have stated earlier, Mom loved me like no one ever has. I truly feel that in spite of all the stress I laid on her and Dad, she was always in my corner. She wasn't very big, but she was a giant when it came to love, compassion, and service to her husband and kids.

When I was 12, Mom was called to be a stake Young Women's leader. She felt inadequate for the position so my dad recommended she attend a leadership meeting in Salt Lake City. She took a plane to Utah and didn't arrive at the Salt Lake airport until after midnight. She caught a taxi and asked the driver to take her to the Grand Hotel where she had reservations.

After they had driven a few miles, my mom was familiar enough with Salt Lake that she could tell the driver was not going toward her hotel near Temple Square. She asked where he was going and in response he turned down a dark street that had no other cars or street lights on it. She began frantically praying for help, certain that he was up to no good.

About then, the taxi stalled. Mom jumped out of the vehicle and ran a block or so until she finally saw another car. She flagged the driver down and told him what had happened. They looked back toward the location of the taxi and saw it was on fire. The young man who stopped invited her to get in and they drove back to where the taxi was burning. He retrieved Mom's bags and took her to the hotel.

I remember her telling us the story when she returned home. It was another lesson I filed away, teaching me of the power of earnest prayer.

After Dad died, she went on a service mission and worked in the Church Office Building in Salt Lake. She came down with Parkinson's Disease which made things tough for her in her later years.

She broke her hip several times. The first time, she was walking in the orchard by our house and tripped over a branch. She was able to crawl and painfully make her way back to the house.

• •

The second time, she and Dad were headed to Priest Lake, pulling a trailer behind their Jeep. They stopped at a grocery store in Spokane. It was a hot day in July. As she got out to walk to the store she tripped over the trailer tongue that was hooked to the Jeep. She went down on the hot asphalt, breaking her hip in the process. Dad was wheelchair bound and couldn't get out to help. She lay on the hot asphalt for several minutes before help arrived. She told me the burning hot asphalt hurt more than her busted hip until the ambulance crew got her on the gurney.

Not a day goes by that I don't think of Mom and Dad. Their love, example, teachings, generosity, and sacrifice have greatly blessed my life. I am privileged to work on the same road that I grew up on—Casper Lane. I am surrounded by memories I love. I am blessed.

CHAPTER 41

$40,000 CUSTOMER SERVICE LESSON

My journal entry...

September 13, 2005

I got a new paper cutter. I tried opening the box in my office and I could see a lot of Styrofoam was going to spread and make a mess. I've had a phobia about the mess Styrofoam can make since that trip I took to Atlanta. I took the box outside on the porch and pulled the cutter out. As I was taking it out of the box, the heavy, industrial-version paper cutter slipped and . . . (the following is Michele's description on the family website).

This morning some ladies were at my house for a meeting. Ben went on the front porch to open a package that had been sitting out there. He started yelling and came running in holding his arm up against his chest. He said that he had cut himself and had to get to the hospital right away. While I was still trying to figure out if he was joking (I didn't see any blood) or really hurt, he rushed out the door, jumped into the Taurus, and sped away. We looked out on the porch and saw a big-bladed paper cutter with blood spattered on it. I knew it was useless to try to chase him down. One of the ladies said, "I think he's in shock."

The only thing I could think of to do was call and see if a deputy could intercept him. About 15 minutes later (one can only imagine the ride) he called from Lourdes hospital. He said they were "working" on him. He also said he never saw a deputy. He was too fast for them. After a couple of other phone calls, I found out he had cut the artery and tendon in his wrist. He had to wait around all day for a surgeon to look at it. He's in surgery right now and should be released in the morning.

I freaked out when the blade got me. I was shocked at how sharp it was and instantly had visions of bleeding to death. Because I had previously worked on the ambulance crew, I was familiar with the time it would take to get a

response and all the paperwork and protocol that the medical higher-ups
required before the meat wagon even started the wheels turning. Therefore,
with the blood spurting, I was convinced that my only chance was to get to the
hospital as fast as I could. (End of journal entry.)

Admittedly, I was not thinking correctly. I jumped in the SHO and took
off for the hospital. I was trying to keep the wound compressed to my
stomach while shifting the 5-speed with my left hand and driving. Most
of the miles between home and Pasco were covered doing 130 mph. I took
some slightly inordinate chances passing cars on hills, etcetera—VERY
stupid. I started realizing the folly of my rush and regretted it after I got
to the hospital and realized I wasn't going to die. I could see that I should
have waited for the leisurely ambulance ride. It's even possible I might
have survived.

It wouldn't stop bleeding so they operated that night and fixed the artery
and a tendon.

This accident put a damper on my inventing work. After a day of recovery,
I headed back down to the shed with a big bandage wrapped around my
wrist, hand, and arm. The doctor really didn't tell me not to do anything.
I guess he just assumed I would stay in bed.

I got to work doing what I could. I remember lifting several heavy pipes
with the tips of my fingers that were protruding from the hospital wrap.
The wrist throbbed, but I worked through the pain. I worked for a week in
this manner and then headed back for an appointment with the doctor.

When he examined me, he noticed the dirt and grease that had been
attracted to his clean wrap and seemed immediately concerned. "You
haven't been lifting anything with that, have you?" he asked.

"Not too much," I answered as I swerved around the intent of his question.

He then enunciated in scary language what would happen if I lifted and
the stitches broke that were holding my tendon together. I realized I had
been flirting with losing the use of my right hand. Inwardly I breathed a
sigh of relief that my hand was still working and outwardly I promised
that I wouldn't lift anything. I took it easy for the next few weeks.

When I got home from the hospital, I examined the paper cutter. The
manufacturer had included a large Plexiglas shield for installation and
protection after the cutter had been set up for use. Unfortunately for me,
they hadn't made any provision for protection from the 26-inch long,

sharper-than-a-razor guillotine before the shield went on. If they would have installed a two-cent piece of wire to lock the blade down until it got out of the box, I would have been saved a lot of trouble.

The more I thought about it, the more it bothered me. I decided I would at least make them aware of my situation so I called the manufacturer, Martin Yale, and asked for the manager.

I told him of my trouble and the fact that they needed to secure the blade in transit. He said he would look into it and get back to me.

477

I didn't hear from him, which got my gears grinding. Initially, I had no thought of asking them to help me with my medical costs. But as the days went by and he didn't respond, I started thinking that maybe they should chip in and help me with my hospital stay.

I finally called him and he admitted that yes, he also was surprised that the blades weren't tied down. He had gone to their warehouse and checked out some units to verify my experience.

His next words kind of set me back. He said something about the fact that I was pretty stupid for allowing myself to get cut. I asked him if he was willing to help me offset my medical costs. He offered to give me a discount on the paper cutter I had just bought. I could see that he was thinking of giving me something along the line of fifty bucks for my trouble. I said I would get back to him. After my talk with this guy, my wrist was starting to hurt a lot worse.

I called Nate Henry, who had just passed his bar exam. We settled with Martin Yale for a little more than 40 grand. Calling me stupid turned out to be a customer service boo-boo for Martin Yale.

My wrist still gives me problems.

CHAPTER 42

SOMETIMES IT'S REALLY HARD TO QUIT

In 2005, after inventing and marketing products for six years and neglecting my tire store, I decided I'd had enough. I was tired of constantly having to find new places to borrow money so the store could keep going. I was tired of the constantly increasing costs required to satiate Schwab. I was sick of employee problems. I was weary of being the low man on the totem pole in the Schwab "family." I was tired of the mountains of bad debt I constantly had to write off. I was fed up when I drove through Othello on propane business and the Othello Les Schwab store manager called our zone manager and complained that I was in "his" town.

I figured that refinancing my home four times, and then having to dump the money into the store, was above and beyond the call of duty. I was tired of the risk. I didn't want to return and manage it. I wanted to invent products. I called Les Schwab and told them I was done.

Schwab charges and the related expenses of being affiliated with them were too much. It cost me almost $2,000 a month for their computer system and another $2,000 a month for their advertising charges, which I always maintained didn't do me a lick of good in Basin City. The tire business I had didn't come from their advertising; it came because I was the only tire service willing to be located in that remote location.

My "Schwab-inspired" employee benefits rang up another seven thousand plus dollars a month. The high wages Schwab set were an additional drain. As a Schwab store, I was paying over $150,000 more each year to be a Schwab store and *only then* was I able to start paying my normal operating expenses. When I first joined up with them in 1986, the Schwab costs were about $200 a month. It had grown into a blood-sucking parasite.

I had been losing over $50,000 a year for years because of my own inattention, risky charging, poor store management, and Schwab's high-priced program. It was a millstone around my neck. I hated to get rid of

Schwab's program because I had been with them so long and my customers were used to their services, but it had to be done.

I placed the terminating call to Prineville in November of 2005 and told them my last day with them was Dec. 31. The word spread quickly through the Schwab organization and soon after, Dick, an assistant manager at another Schwab store contacted me. He stated he wanted to buy my store and had a friend who would put the money up.

A big red flag should have started waving in my head right then. Several incidents in dealing with Dick in the Pasco store let me know that he could not be trusted.

I approached my Les Schwab zone manager and district manager and they were all for Dick buying my store. They knew the store needed a different manager/owner, new blood, and fresh capital. Dick and his buddy looked like a good thing to them. They told us to mail Dick's partner's financial statement to Prineville and if his paperwork proved to be adequate, it was a done deal.

The big cheeses in Prineville didn't even look at the financials. They didn't want to deal with anyone but me. I was surprised and disappointed that there was such a disconnect between Prineville (the headquarters) and their zone and district managers. It was a major conflict of policy between the people who were my bosses. Even though I owned the store, as long as I had their pole sign up in my parking lot, Prineville could dictate what happened. It had always been this way.

To make a really long story really short, to preserve family relations, to keep me out of a lawsuit and to cathartically get rid of some longstanding feelings that have just a hint of negativity to them, it didn't work out. I had stayed solvent in the tire business for 24 years and in just nine short little months, lost $550,000. The shenanigans that took place in those nine months would make your wallet curl. At least it did mine.

I slammed the store doors shut on December 31, 2006. Exactly one year too late. The community was shocked. Ben's Basin City Tire had been there 24 years. A few days later, as I was starting the huge job of cleaning out and buttoning up the place, a former customer, Brad Curtis, pulled in the lot. He got out and asked me the standard questions about why I was closing up. Then he hit me with some bad news.

He had given Dick a big check the previous spring for a pre-payment and still had a credit of $13,749.24. My heart sank. I was broke. Legally, it was Dick's problem.

However, I felt the right thing should be done, not the legal thing. It took a few months, but I finally was able to scrap together the funds and pay him.

Another old guy I've known for many years and who really struggles financially approached me with proof he had bought some tires and left them at the store to be mounted later. The tires weren't there. Once again, I could have just told him to go after Dick. Instead, I wrote him a check for four hundred bucks, the same amount he had given Dick for the tires. It was the right thing to do. Through the course of that year, I took care of numerous other credit and tire problems that occurred on Dick's short watch.

Several times after I booted Dick out, he would knock on my door, pleading for another chance. I knew by this time that the only chance he was looking for was to skim some more cash from my very skinny and curly wallet. I showed him the door and locked it behind him.

One morning about six months after I kicked Dick out, I pulled into my bank's parking lot. A red, jacked-up Ford pickup was parked in the lot. I was sure it was Dick's so I took a deep breath and walked inside. I scanned the lobby, but didn't see him.

I walked over to a teller and began my business. As she worked on my stuff, I turned around and began scanning the lobby again. I couldn't see him. He must be in the bathroom, I thought.

Then I saw him. He was scrunched up in a chair about three feet in front of me with his back facing me. Dick is a big guy, six foot plus. His gregarious, albeit double personality makes him even bigger. He usually stands out in a crowd. He didn't on this day. He was curled up like a drowned earthworm, looking like he wanted to crawl in a hole. After a few minutes, he got up and slunk toward the door.

I called out, "Hey, Dick! How are you doing?" He cringed and looked sideways back at me, gave an embarrassed, little nod and disappeared.

I spoke to the girl at whose desk he was sitting. She knew there was big trouble between us and when she saw me walk in the bank, she was afraid there might be some fisticuffs. She said when Dick saw me walk through the door, his mood completely changed. There was no doubt from his changed demeanor that she could tell he knew he had done me wrong.

After I hired a lawyer, depositions were taken. I wanted to be there to listen to Dick's side. He was there for three hours. I sat across the table from him, slightly to his right. Never once in the three hours of being interviewed did he glance my way, let alone look me in the eye. Once again, he knew he had done me wrong.

Dick left as soon as he finished his deposition. I guess he didn't want to hear my side.

I spent several hours telling my side of the story. I had submitted a lot of paperwork previously and felt I had a watertight case. Before we started, my attorney took me aside and told me to make my answers as brief as possible, yes or no would be preferable. He wanted to save the juicy stuff for court.

Unfortunately, like Dick, I am gregarious also. I told my lawyer, Shea, that I was going to have a hard time not telling it like it was. He told me several more times before we went in to keep my answers brief.

Dick's attorney started the questioning. I kept my answers brief; at least for the first 30 seconds. Then, unable to help myself, I would launch into how I really felt and what exactly had happened. Shea sat to the side of me, legally restrained from breaking in and stopping me from telling my story. I have to give him credit, however. He kept coughing and clearing his throat, fidgeting in his chair, and using every body language tool that lawyers can legally use to shut me up.

Periodically, I would hear his noises and realize he was trying to get me to shut up. I would then apologize to him, which I don't think he appreciated either. He was not supposed to be intimidating or coaching the witness. The timing of my apologies let everyone in the room know that he was trying to coach me with his unspoken sounds that essentially were screaming, "Shut the heck up!"

It went on like this for the next couple of hours. Finally, toward the end of my deposition, I was asked a question that I didn't like. It was most likely something from a point of view that Dick had operated honestly. I let her have it with both barrels. Shea shook his head and gave up at that point.

That night, I woke up in a cold sweat. I realized that by expounding on my answers, I had given the opposition much more ammunition and knowledge than I should have. Once again, my big mouth had gotten me in trouble.

I called Shea the next morning and apologized. He said it was alright. After I left the night before, he had taken Dick's attorney into the room where I left all the paperwork concerning him. Shea said she was shocked. There were several large boxes weighing a minimum of 300 pounds. He chuckled and said it was going to cost Dick a fortune just to have her wade through the paperwork.

I'm actually glad I expounded in the deposition like I did. Soon after, Dick offered to pay a partial settlement and I accepted. This stopped the legal fee hemorrhaging we both were incurring. I'm sure my deposition showed his attorney that I was not going to be a Caspar Milquetoast in court.

I got a settlement on paper, a small fraction of the losses. That lasted temporarily. He soon went banko and I got nothing except a big lawyer bill (billed to me) that has UNHAPPILY PAID stamped on the front of it.

• •

This experience has been the hardest buffeting in my life for me to get past and forgive. After almost ten years, I've finally clenched my teeth and forced myself to get over the grudge. I forgive. I've been very kind in the presentation of this saga.

I can't forget, however. I want to make sure it doesn't happen again. I wish them well. I'm glad to close this chapter of my life. It was a tough one.

On a related topic, I am perplexed concerning a phenomenon I have noticed with some people. It seems to me that the more moolah people make, the stingier they get. In contrast, poor folk are usually the most charitable and giving.

• •

Case in point . . . there's a well-heeled farmer in the area that used to rent my dad's spud shed for many harvests, always paying Dad twelve grand a year for rent. Dad died December 18, 2004. When my mom got the rent check for that year, it was for eight thousand dollars. My brother Brad and I noticed it and we wondered why the check got shortened immediately after Dad checked out. It must have been an oversight. Surely he wouldn't take advantage of a poor widow.

I ran into him shortly after and asked why the lesser number. He denied there was a shortage. He said they paid the same amount that they always had. I dug up the paperwork and sent it to him.

His hired man knocked on my door a week later and said, "My boss says you were right about the payment amount. However, he said to tell you they had a bad year last year and that's all they're paying."

All I can say is, "Wow!" And then there are people like me who shift into a completely contrary mode when it comes to finances. I hand out cash like it was going out of style and heaven knows I can ill afford it.

A few years ago I met a guy who had just gotten out of prison. He claimed injustices had occurred and that he was going to get a big settlement when he sued the county and state. He claimed the county prosecutor had already offered a big payment. The guy was fresh out of prison, destitute, and without wheels.

I felt bad for him. I believed the guy. Empathy made me give him our Taurus and before he was through with me, he had extracted 16 thousand dollars in cash from my back pocket. He kept promising that he would pay it back when he got his settlement. I got more concerned as each dollar exited. Eventually, I stopped the bleeding, checked out his story, and found it was a scam. I am gullible.

And then there's the dude who married into a good family in the area. He played me into believing he had a windfall coming and that his marriage was toast if he couldn't get some cash to tide him over till his ship came in. It was bologna. He got me for 16 also.

Sixteen, as in sixteen thousand, has not been a lucky number for me.

Every time I buy into one of these cons, I have to listen to my wife gripe afterwards. I know she's right so what can I say except, "I'm an idiot. And I guess I'm not recovering."

There's an old saying that there's a sucker born every minute. I've done my best to keep that adage alive. One of my big problem generators in life is trusting people. It happened all the time with my tire shop. There were so many tires back in the day rolling down the blacktop, owned by me and worn out by those with big promises. If any of you are reading this book and happen to need some extra cash, just call me. I'll even give you my phone number—it's 1-800-IAM-ASUCKER. But I'm slowly learning. Your story had better be good or I'll send you to my wife.

CHAPTER 43

NEEDS NO EMBELLISHMENT

At the end of 2006, when I was in the midst of kicking Dick out and trying to figure out what to do with my business, for just a day or two I decided I was going back to run it myself. I got a wild hair and fixated on the fact that I needed another service vehicle and it needed to be a 4-wheel drive Toyota Tundra. I'd had good luck with my 2-wheel drive Tundra so I figured a 4wd would be twice as good. I immediately went to eBay and bid on one.

Unfortunately, I was in too much of a hurry and dealing with too many problems so I got scammed in the process. Numerous emergencies and events prevented me from taking delivery of the truck until a year and a half later. And it was parked in Philadelphia. Here's the story with absolutely no embellishment.

I bought a pickup on eBay and finally got around to flying back to Philly to pick it up a year and a half after I bought it. Bad deal, no title, and no bill of sale. All I had was a note from eBay saying I had won the bid.

I arrived at the Philadelphia airport after midnight and Benny Walker, a young friend who was going to dental school in the big city, picked me up. I slept at his place for a few hours and then got up and experienced a very nasty shock when I saw the pickup. My lightning fast purchasing reflexes, eBay, PayPal, and Ceyon Ruddock had combined to scam me.

The rig was totally totaled—no taillights, no blinkers, one headlight, no insurance, no license plate, no bill of sale, no heater or A/C, a twisted frame, dead battery, multi-colored junkyard doors that wouldn't close, and an air bag that had long since deployed. The tires did a lot of rubbing against the frame if you tried to turn the vehicle while in motion.

Michele told me before I left that I had three days to return to Washington. We would be heading to Utah for Meg's graduation from BYU. I was in a bit of a tight spot. I had no choice but to buy a battery, hit the road immediately, and dodge the cops on a nationwide basis.

I drove away from Benny's apartment on Ridge Avenue, recognizing doors and streets that I had tracted out as a missionary in 1974, some 34 years earlier. I had serious doubts as I began my journey in the "100 dents, screaming-for-an-arrest, no paperwork, cop-magnet Tundra." Once I was on the turnpike and got my speed up, the passenger side door that was restrained by a strap, but still open a good foot, started emitting a noise in the cab similar to a jet engine. The noise continued unabated from the east coast to the west coast. I was initially surprised that I was able to uneventfully drive past 14 cops. I drove 255 miles to the west side of Pennsylvania before I met up with the 15th one, a state trooper.

He was just finishing up a traffic stop. As I drove by him, he pulled out behind me. I knew I was had so I had to think fast. It so happened that I was going around a curve and up a hill at the time. As soon as the trooper drifted out of sight in my rearview mirror, I slammed on my brakes and skidded to the side of the highway. I knew he would pull me over as soon as he passed me. I figured it would be better to be stopped before he saw that my brake and signal lights were inoperable.

He materialized from around the curve and slammed on his brakes when he saw me and my totaled Tundra. He backed up to find out what I was up to. I got out of the junker, put my hands in the air, and told him I was a dead man. There was nothing about the vehicle that came close to being legal. I explained my situation to him and he went back to his car to call the VIN in. I was in need of a restroom so I jumped down in the brush at the side of the highway while the cop called in for information. After a couple minutes of fertilizing something that looked a lot like poison ivy, I climbed back up on the blacktop to wait for news of my destiny.

When he finally walked back to me, he told me to put my hands on the vehicle and spread my legs. He pulled out his handcuffs. I did as instructed, at the same time thinking about how Michele was going to be driving to Utah on her own. I knew there was a good chance she would refuse to send me bail money.

To my relief, he then laughed and said he was just joking. He even holstered his handcuffs. He told me he was going to give me a break and let me go since the truck wasn't shown as stolen. He also told me that I was going to meet many more just like him before I got home, but that some of them might not be as nice. I got the distinct impression he saw no way I could possibly make it on my tour across the U.S. without spending a little time in jail.

My trusty, but twisted Tundra and I continued down the pike. I still can't fathom why we didn't get stopped again, even when I had an "accident" on the interstate in Wisconsin the next day. That first night I drove through downtown Chicago with the gas gauge on empty in rush hour traffic. I don't know why. I guess just to see if I could. Finally, I coasted into a filling station on the west side.

The next morning was Sunday. Just past Madison, Wisconsin, I had my accident. I was doing a little housekeeping, cleaning up the Big Mac wrappers in the cab. I was buzzing down the interstate at 70 mph when I accidently pushed my wallet off the passenger seat. Something in the back of my head whispered that things were just not quite right. I suddenly remembered that there was a 12-inch gap between the door and the cab where the wallet had dropped out of sight. I glanced in the rearview mirror and saw my wallet bouncing on the interstate, spewing cash.

Twenties, fifties, and hundreds, credit cards, my LDS temple recommend, driver's license, and other goodies were flying everywhere except back in the wallet. It was like a TV game show with a fan blowing cash all over the inside of a glass bubble. However, there was no bubble in my world. It had just burst.

Unfortunately, the cash did not consist of ones or fives. When I left home, I packed my wallet with lots of cash, mostly fifties and hundreds. I knew with my talent of attracting trouble, I just might have an emergency and need some greenbacks. This was not even close to the type of emergency I had envisioned. Vehicles were churning through my dough, some driving in a westerly direction with Ben Franklins and Ulysses Grants pressed against their grills and headlights. It reminded me of the cardboard fiasco from years earlier.

I decided I had no choice other than to have some fun and try to recoup some of my losses. I backed up the side of the highway to the point of the cash debarkation. Seventy-mph trucks and cars provided for exciting games of Dodge-all, Scoop the Cash, and the very fast-paced 3-lane Dash or get Smashed—all played at the same time. I finally recouped around $400 of the eight hundred that had taken wing. My gas credit card was among the hide and seekers that were never recovered.

Sometime in the next year or two, a guy in a pin-striped prison uniform working on a litter crew is going to strike it rich when he cleans that section of interstate.

I'm telling you, the people out for a Sunday morning drive that day on the interstate were royally entertained by a fat, bald guy scooping various denominations off the blacktop in the neighboring lane as they whizzed by.

With the price of gas, no credit card, and the miles left to cover, I could see that I was going to end up a few hundred short.

Since it was Sunday, I stopped in Eau Clare, Wisconsin, to see if I could find the local church and borrow a credit card or some dough from a fellow saint. The church was empty with a sign in the window stating they were all gone to stake conference in a town I'd never heard of. I drove on.

After 91.7 more miles, I stopped in Minneapolis to buy gas and stumbled onto a meetinghouse next to the LDS temple. This was the stake conference I had read about in Eau Clare! I was dressed like a hobo and was feeling pretty desperate. I walked in and mingled with all of the finely-attired saints who were just getting out of the meeting. I asked where I could find the stake president and made a beeline for his office.

There was a long line of people waiting for interviews at the door of the stake president's office. I barged my way to the front of the line and asked for the President. He had just arrived from the conference to begin his interviews. I told him I really needed to talk to him and it would just take a minute. He ushered me in and closed the door, probably more than a little concerned with the vagrant who was not familiar with waiting in line. I told him that, believe it or not, I was a member of his church. I needed $500 in gas money to make it home to Washington State since all my money had flown out the open door of my pickup while I was cleaning up Big Mac wrappers.

As I finished my story, I thought I detected looks of disbelief and surprise in his countenance. It was kind of like, "Wow! I thought I'd heard everything, but this guy comes in with a whole new twist on how to dip into the church coffers."

He quickly switched his look to one of compassion and told me not to worry. He would put me in touch with the bishop who took care of indigent transients. I had never been called a bum before, but decided this was not the right time to take offense and agitate my potential caregiver. I didn't argue. I was just glad I had found a positive cash flow source. I asked him where I should send the check to pay it back. He looked at me with a gaze of sorrow and brotherly kindness. He put his hand on my shoulder as he ushered me out the door and said, "Don't worry, you don't have to pay us back," in a soft tone that screamed, "Everybody always says they'll pay us back and they never do!"

I couldn't get in touch with the transient bishop. He wasn't answering his phone. I had to get back on the road! The clock was ticking. I knew Michele was waiting at home with a big, black skillet clutched in her throwing hand.

Just when I was ready to give up, I remembered I had a cousin who lived in Minneapolis. I called her number, but she was gone to visit her folks in Washington State, of all places! I asked her husband if he remembered me. He thought he did so I asked if I could borrow five hundred bucks. He said sure, he would be right down. A few minutes later, he pulled up to my new wreck that was parked in front of the Minneapolis temple and extended the loan without any paperwork. What a guy!

I was back on the road.

The weather had been in the 70 and 80-degree neighborhood as I traversed the nation's heartland. I even enjoyed a nice tailwind. That is, until I hit Bismarck, North Dakota. It was about sundown. It had been a long, but fairly pleasant drive until then, except for the cash dispersal in Madison.

In total, I traveled some 2,674 miles across the country listening to the constant roar of a jetliner-like wind stream flying through my digs. It was loud, but bearable until the post-Bismarck era. As I drove past the city limits, the wind did a 180, started double-time screaming into the cab, and dropped 50 degrees. I am not kidding.

We froze for the next 375 miles as we marathoned across the arctic tundra—me and my eBay scam-job Tundra. The temperature was hovering around 15 degrees Fahrenheit according to the weather reports I obtained later off the internet. No heater, no winter clothes, no coat, a gaping open door, and air rushing into the cab. I drove as long as I could stand the cold without losing consciousness. Finally, I pulled into a motel at 10:00 that night in Beach, North Dakota.

The inn had a room for me. I paid the bill in freshly borrowed cash. It was late and I was tired, but I sat in a tub of steaming hot water for over an hour. I finally quit shivering and went to bed.

The next morning I walked outside and it was still freezing. I wanted to get back in the hot bath, but then I thought of Michele and her skillet. I had to keep going. I fueled up and wondered if they had gloves in the mini mart. The only ones they had in stock were rubberized, uninsulated, bulky, bright orange sprinkler gloves. They didn't keep my hands warm, but did remind me of all the times of moving ice-covered sprinkler pipes as a kid. Driving gloves they were not.

The last 45 miles before Billings were very difficult. I spent those miles looking through a windshield that had a quarter inch of ice permanently plastered on it from the back tires of semi trucks I encountered. I had no way of defrosting or thawing the windshield and other glass. I couldn't have gotten out of the pickup anyway, as I was frozen in place. It was like looking through a frozen opaque shower door for the last hour of my drive. It was the exact same scene I had witnessed many years before just before I plowed into the back of a school bus. The only difference was that I had been driving less than a minute when I hit the school bus.

I was desperate for a Billings arrival by this time, having lost all my body heat about five miles outside of Beach. I kept my 70 mph speed up even though I lost control on the icy road numerous times. I was freezing. I was desperate. The Tundra was often in a sideways configuration, out of control, whipping back and forth as it headed down the slick road. It didn't scare me much since I couldn't see through any of the windows. All I knew was that I was hell bent for warmer climes.

What a miserable trip! And no, there should not be a question mark after that last sentence.

I sat in a Billings truck stop for two and a half hours, just thawing out. No one can imagine how badly I wished I did not have to get back in that 4-wheel drive nightmare. But remembering the black skillet, I had no choice.

I finally crawled into the cold cab and drove another 660 miles to the friendlier confines of home by the end of the evening. Three days were now thankfully history.

The next morning, my wife drove me to Utah. I slept in a nice, reclining, electrically warmed, toasty leather seat. It was so nice not to have to drive. The little cash I had left from my kin's loan in Minnesota was safely stored in my wallet, on the seat with no twisted and open doors to fall through.

I slept whenever I wanted. It was the most enjoyable trip I've ever been on.

CHAPTER 44

THE STAFF OF LIFE

As soon as I got out of the tire business in 2006, I had to clean the store so I could rent it out. There were loads and loads of oddball tires and equipment that needed to be hauled down to my dad's shop that I was renting. It was a major job. I couldn't do it myself. I called my old friend, Don Mitchell, who I had ran track with in high school and played in the band with.

He had worked for me in my tire store in Utah and then, for many years, at the tire shop in Basin City. He was the guy who drove the combine through the corn field to call the ambulance when I was run over by the tractor. He is a premium guy. Maybe that's why we clash so much. Anyway, he had left my employment a couple of years earlier and I heard he was between jobs.

I called him and asked if he could come out and help me for a day or two. He's still with me. We've worked together over 26 years at the time of this writing. He's exactly like my wife—no guile, dependable, honest, hard-working, calm, spiritual, and focused. All the things I'm not. He drives me nuts. I guess we make a good team.

We spent a month moving the stuff—many unorthodox and slightly illegal loads. We lost a few items off the trailer, but there were no fatalities.

Then we set to work inventing. YankABigTanks, YankAnUprights, Tank Dunkers, Tank Rollers, Tire burner, Arm and Leg Powered Bike, Teeter Skeeter, Tire Squire, PartyTimeChimes, Truck Tire Squire, Tire Buddy, Forklift 24 TankLot Carrier, SDS Grain System . . . the list could go on. Each of these products, a few winners and a lot of losers, took us several months to individually construct and 30 or 40 thousand dollars a pop to develop. R&D is consuming, expensive, exciting, and depressing. It's never boring which, ironically, is also the way my wife describes our marriage.

• •

A few years ago, I started receiving correspondence from Amerigas, the country's largest propane company. A safety director had caught the vision of the YankATank and wanted to do some testing on it. They found that it was a great product, their dealers liked it, and it could help reduce many injuries that often occur while handling tanks. It was not just another tank cart. I mentioned to her that with the YankATank's special configuration, a guy could easily lift a 500 pound tank with one arm. They ran some tests with a few units. The next time we spoke, she told me that they were surprised that my lifting claim turned out to be true.

After they finished their testing, the person who initiated the interest, Dr. Bouril, pulled the strings necessary to make the unit a standard piece of equipment for Amerigas plants. They gave us large orders for the next four years until their quotas were filled.

When she placed the first big order, she quizzed me about the lead time. I told her we could get it filled in a month. She was happy with that, but then quizzed me. "Just how big is your company?" she asked. There was no way I was going to tell it was just Don and I, so I responded that it was confidential information and I hated to give her the exact number. "Oh, Mr. Casper, please don't tell me you are just a five-man operation," she said. I shaped my reply to sound incredulous. "Oh, Dr. Bouril, you are not even close if you think we have five employees." She was happy with that answer. I got the feeling she had mentally just moved our company up into the Fortune 500.

• •

The SDS Grain System has consumed my life for the last half decade. Several life threatening experiences have occurred, but we're still in one piece. At this writing, I am on my fifth year of R&D at the grain bins. This has been the longest sojourn I've experienced in developing a product. I'll start from the beginning. So how did I get into inventing a new way to dry corn? An innocent little tiff between siblings got things rolling.

Dad built a nice shop back in the 80s. By the year 2000, everyone in the family and anyone else who happened by was using the shop. The roll-up doors were always open and it was in total disarray. Birds flew in and out. Tools were constantly walking out the door.

I decided if I was going to be an inventor, I needed a place to work. I made a rental deal with Dad, closed the bay doors, and locked the place up. This began an intensive retraining program for my brothers, brothers-in-law, and their hired men. I was the instructor. They were used to coming and going in the shop and all of a sudden it stopped. It was my fault and I became a very bad man, at least to one of the hired men. There were a few tense moments and a physical altercation before I got them properly trained. I was acquiring equipment and tools and didn't want the stuff ripped off. I had to lock the doors. Why not? I was paying rent. During this process, a phone got hung up prematurely. Click. But before I end this story and you start thinking that I've lost my touch in the fine art of switching stories in the middle of other stories, permit me to share another.

• •

Prior to the corn project I've been pursuing, I worked on developing a simple tire burner that was smokeless. I made great progress with the system, but was never 100% successful. One day I was up on a ladder checking temperatures. The wind blew a large, hot, metal baffle off the top of the unit. It struck me and then fell six feet or so. It landed on the backhoe bucket I had parked beside the burner. This was not a serious problem.

When the baffle hit me, I lost my balance and fell off the ladder. This also was not a serious problem. However, when I hit the ground, I ended up lying on the baffle with my arm in direct contact and all my weight resting on that arm.

Now this turned into a serious problem. My arm immediately started to sizzle. It took me a few seconds to shift my massive weight and get off the hot iron. I had just measured it while on the ladder. It was 1800 degrees Fahrenheit.

My arm was burned over a large area between my elbow and wrist. I jumped up and ran over to the shop water faucet. A 5-gallon bucket was under the tap, full of nice, cold water. I jammed my arm in the water and sat down on the concrete. I felt no pain because of the cool water. I sat in this position for an hour and a half.

When I pulled it out, it was scorched, but fine. I never had pain. I had no ill effects. What I did have was a burning testimony that the quicker you can get a burn in cold water and the longer you can keep it there, the better off you are. If I hadn't done the water thing, a nurse told me, after examining it, I would have had serious third-degree burns requiring a hospital stay and a whole lot of pain.

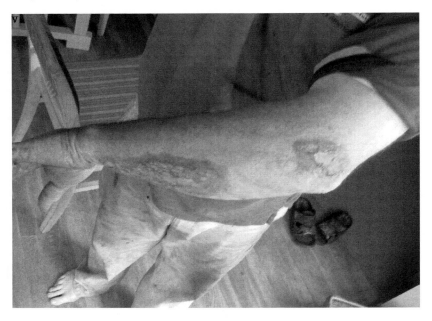

• •

So back to the sibling difference of opinion. One day we were on the phone and I heard a distinct and noticeable premature click on the other end.

Just to make a short story shorter, I got a little flustrated and in a moment of reciprocal impertinence I rented the spud shed and grain bins on a twelve year lease from my family. I had no idea of how I was going to utilize these facilities but I figured it would equalize the previous click. It ended up all turning out fine. My siblings and I, including the clicker, get along great. Maybe that hang-up was heaven-sent. Then again, maybe it was just a bad connection.

• •

And speaking of mixing it up with the siblings . . . when I was ten years old and Brad was six, we were out in the shed playing on the bed of Dad's truck. For some reason I pushed Brad and he fell off the truck and landed on his head on the concrete floor. It gave him a serious concussion, put him in bed, and made him delirious for a few days. I felt terrible. I remember lying on the top bunk bed and hanging over the side board looking at Brad in a long and deep sleep. I wondered if he was ever going to come out of his delirium. How I regretted the push and how badly I wanted him to wake up! He recovered, but struggled for several years after with lingering effects from the injury.

When I was in my teens, Brad got on my nerves one night. He was bugging my sisters and I told him to knock it off. He didn't so I decided I would knock him off. We had a little chase in the front room and after I caught up with him, I punched the back of his head with my fist. He went down, but quickly popped back up and reported the incident to Dad.

Dad gave me a lecture which I guess I had coming. The import of his talk didn't have much of an effect on me because I was concentrating more on the pain in my right hand. I ended up in the doctor's office with a broken hand, courtesy of Brad's hard head. The doctor's bill brought on more lecturing.

• •

The potato storage and grain bin facility had been idle and in disrepair for many years. I leased them for twelve years and then set to work making them usable. The first couple of years found me second-guessing myself because I was paying rent on them, but I had no tenants. Gradually things improved and, in the process, I hatched a plan to revolutionize the corn drying business.

I studied up on current technology and theorized that if I sectioned off a bin with layers of tubing, I could use natural air to dry corn much more efficiently. To make a very long story very short, I did it. There have been years of construction and years of destruction. New and expensive materials were installed and then those same materials became junk when I moved on and pulled them off.

My biggest problem is when I do a project, I go whole hog. Semi loads of materials get ordered. Instead of converting one bin, I converted five.

By the time the third year had rolled around, I knew my system worked, but I also knew the present design was not feasible. I had cut approximately 600, four-inch diameter holes in five bins for air tubes. By the end of the season, I had major problems. It took me a year to install the system. The corn dried, but the drying and shrinking process had put tremendous downward pressure on the bins, not to mention weakening from the holes.

One day as I walked by, I saw many sheared off bolt heads around the bottom of one 700-ton bin. As I looked closer, I could see the entire bin had dropped and sheared the bottom bolts between the bin wall and stiffeners. The stiffeners are the framework that gives the bin its strength. There was a large crease around the bin. The bolts had sheared and the bin had dropped and bulged out. Why that bin didn't collapse while full of corn, I'll never know.

We quickly reinforced the bin wall. Even with the reinforcement, we cross our fingers each time we walk by it.

So I knew the concept worked, but I also knew I had to make some major changes. So I made them. It's a great design if I do say so myself.

CHAPTER 45

SOMETHING OF A CIRCULAR LIFE

It is interesting how at the close of this book I realize that in the last couple of years I have had brushes with death, obvious miracles of protection, gone head-to-head with the law, sustained a minor maiming, and enjoyed a wonderful surprise. More interesting is that those things seem to comprise the carousel of my life, round and round, over and over, here we go again. Essentially this chapter, although the events it describes have all occurred in the last couple of years, seem to encapsulate the pattern of my life.

But before we get into all of that, as I finish up this recorded slice of my life, I must pay tribute to my wife. No two people are more different than Ben and Michele. It has been a marriage that has seen its share of turmoil. And yet, we have kept it together. Kids, religion, and covenants are the reasons we are still together. We are both very grateful we didn't quit.

• •

So who is Michele?

She is a mother who read every night to her children. Her personal interests always took second chair to our kids. She was the impetus behind the start of the Basin City Library. She has been in book clubs since arriving on these shores in the early 1980s. She's read hundreds of classics. The list is impressive. In contrast, I think I might have read one, about the time I was a sophomore. It was a February edition of *Mad* magazine. I read the entire masterpiece.

She's a pianist and fiddle player, giving music lessons to help those around her. On a monthly basis she rounds up her troops and they play music to older folks in facilities where not a lot of other entertainment occurs.

She's been the driving force behind all good things in each of our kids. Musical talents, spiritual heritage, family togetherness and limitless love are found in this one-of-a-kind lady. Without her, I would be hopping freight trains and sleeping on the rails.

Another thing about Mitch . . . oh, I've gotta tell a story. This was back in the day when my band practiced at our house that was attached to the tire shop in Utah. We were practicing in the middle of the day when Michele made me aware from the kitchen with a subtle gesture that she needed to talk to me. I told everybody that I needed to talk to my new bride and would be right back.

I have no idea what the subject was back then, but just a couple of months into the marriage and we were struggling. She whispered her problem to me and I presented a counter proposal. This went back and forth several times, escalating a bit each round. Finally when she got outside the line of what I thought was reasonable, I put my hand on her arm and in a soft and pleading voice said, "Mitch."

Her response was kind of a shocker to me since we were trying to keep the rest of the band in the other room uninformed of our difficulty. She recoiled and yelled, "Don't call me Mitch!!! Only my friends call me Mitch!!!"

Today it is kind of funny. Back then, it wasn't.

The room where my band was waiting fell into a hushed silence. I had no idea what to do so I slithered back to the friendlier confines and figured I would break the ice by saying, "Hey, guys. Sorry about the wait. Okay, let's hit it from the top."

• •

Okay, back to Mitch . . . oh, I've gotta tell another story. Years ago we took a trip to Boise, Idaho for a meeting of some sort. We arrived at the college early and with a couple hours to kill we figured we would walk around campus. We ended up in the auditorium where an orchestra was practicing. We walked down the steps, found a couple of seats, sat down, and listened.

I don't know what the tune was, but it was beautiful. I was struck by the music and shortly noticed that it had brought tears to my eyes. I wondered what Michele thought about the composition and turned to look at her. She turned at the same time and I could see that tears were filling her eyes also. It was a synergistic and bonding moment; rare, but welcome.

Okay, back to Mitch . . . I am whole because we are one. I need her. I love her. I couldn't have done better. We just might make it.

• •

A couple of years ago, I drove my Tundra down to work at the bins during corn season. A lady blew a stop sign along the way and pulled out from a cross street directly in front of me. I was doing 60 and heading for her driver's door. She was ripe for the funeral home. I swerved to miss her, but she kept proceeding. Her front end clipped my passenger side and tore my rear axle off. I went spinning and just about rolled. Everything in the back of my truck flew out, but it didn't roll and we both ended up okay. Both rigs were totaled. She was cited for no insurance and for not stopping. She didn't speak English and I just had liability insurance on my truck so I figured I was out a pickup.

The next day I visited her home. She came to the door. I asked if I could come in. She made a motion so I went in. I tried to communicate with her for a few minutes and then spoke with her English-speaking daughter on the phone. She asked how much my truck was worth and I estimated around five grand.

The next day I went to work. I was still installing my old drying system on the bins while unloading trucks. The current driver named Jorge had his 11-year-old son playing around without much oversight from his dad. I told Jorge he better watch his boy or he could get hurt. He had been there several times. The area was no place for kids. It made me really nervous, but I hated to get too nasty with the drivers.

The truck was dumping and I climbed a bin ladder to check moisture coming out of the exhaust holes in the bin. I usually never climbed this particular bin, but must have been inspired to do so on that day. Fans and augers and the elevator leg were running—lots of noise. I heard something and looked down. Normally I would not have been in this spot. Any other location and I never would have heard or seen anything. Junior was climbing through the corn in the pup trailer that was dumping.

I freaked. "Get him out of there!" I screamed. I hightailed it down the ladder as fast as I could. I ran over and climbed in the truck. Junior was gone. Just his fingertips on one hand were sticking out. He had been sucked into the corn as it siphoned out of the bottom of the truck. Senor Senior and I climbed in and grabbed his hands, but there was nothing we could do. It was like he was embedded in concrete. If we had attached his hands to a crane and lifted, we would have gotten two arms and no body.

We tried scooping the corn with our hands to get down to his head. It didn't work. The corn filled back in as soon as we scooped it out. We kept trying, but it was hopeless. The kid wasn't breathing. His fingers were turning blue.

I crawled out of the truck and ran over and shut the system down. I got back up in the container and we worked some more without a trace of progress. It was brutal. I jumped back out and got a scoop shovel. After climbing back in, I started shoveling. But it was useless. Jorge and I were both crying. At this point, it had probably been five minutes since Junior had taken a breath.

I sat back in the corn and started thinking about all the terrible ramifications of Senior not watching Junior. The poor kid was dead. That was the worst part, but there was more. Even though I had nothing to do with it, OSHA was going to swoop in and nail me for a half million dollars in fines. The lawyers would get to Senior and then we would be getting into some serious change. My world started turning black. I remember mentally clicking the off switch off, lying back in the corn, and giving up.

Just then, the following argument took place in my head:

"Pull the truck ahead! Dump the kid out!"

"No, I can't do that! It will bend him over backwards going through the hopper bottom or the trailer will run over him!"

"So what? He's dead anyway!"

Jorge was clinging to his son's hand. That's all he could do. I yelled at him to go get in the truck and pull ahead. He didn't move. I yelled again. He wouldn't let go. I screamed, "GET IN THE TRUCK AND PULL AHEAD!" My tone and volume scared him. He let go and headed for the cab. I jumped out and waited.

The truck pulled ahead. The hopper bottom trailer spilled a row of mounded corn on the concrete apron as it moved forward. Thirty feet down the driveway, Junior popped out, lifeless and mixed in with the corn. I ran to him and rolled him over. He was grey and dead. I cleaned the corn out that filled his mouth. I began mouth to mouth and chest compressions. Nothing. I kept it up.

I don't know where Jorge went, but he wasn't around. He was probably praying. A few minutes later, I saw an eyelid flicker. A couple breaths later he started choking. What a welcome miracle!

He was hurting. About then Jorge showed up. He was overcome with emotion. The kid started throwing up and was still lying in a slump. I started to call 911 because I didn't know what internal injuries the kid had. I figured he could use some oxygen.

For some reason, Jorge stopped me. He was adamant no authorities were called. I hung up. I then insisted he get his son to the hospital. I told him to take my truck. However, the keys were gone and I was shook up enough I didn't know where I'd put them. He bent over to pick up his son. I snapped a picture. He carried his son to his truck. They took off.

I sat down on an apple bin and tried to collect my wits. A couple minutes later, a deputy I knew pulled in. That was a surprise. We never see cops on Casper Lane because I always try to follow the letter of the law

He walked over, greeted me, and asked what was going on. I guess that he noticed a truckload of corn was lying on the driveway. I figured he was there because I had hung up on the 911 call.

I said, "You know what's going on, Gordon." He answered, "No, I don't." I asked why he was there. He replied that a lady that lived across the way had called the sheriff's department and reported that a man had forced his way into her home the day before and she was afraid he was going to beat her up. Deputy Thomasson informed me that they had information it was me.

Even though I had just been through a very traumatic experience, I had to laugh. I told him I thought she had invited me in. I was just trying to see if she was going to pay for my truck. He said he figured as much. He then asked about the corn in the driveway so I rehearsed the story.

He offered to take me home since, thanks to Jorge, corn harvest was over for the day and I couldn't find my keys. I took him up on the offer.

As we traveled toward Basin City, I mentioned we should go over and he could let the lady know I wasn't trying to harm her. He agreed. When we arrived, he got out and told me to stay in the car. He spoke with her on the back lawn for 15 minutes or so while her daughter translated over the phone. I figured everything was calmed down so I got out and walked over to their confab.

Just as I arrived, she pulled out a paper. I glanced over her shoulder at it and saw it was a Franklin County Small Claims Court Summons listing her as the plaintiff and me as the defendant. The claim was for $5,000. I went through the ceiling! (Remember, we were outside.) I had saved this lady's life by swerving away from her door a couple days earlier. Her actions had wrecked my ride. And now she wanted to sue me?

Deputy Gordon pointed at his car and yelled at me to get back in it. I retreated. They talked for another ten minutes. Then they walked over and Gordon filled me in. The lady wanted to pay me for my truck, but didn't speak English. She went to the courthouse, but they couldn't understand just what she was trying to say. They finally decided she was trying to sue me so they filled out the summons against me and charged her the filing fee.

This was welcome news for me. Two great things had happened to me in less than an hour. She paid me the five grand. Her name is Juana. She is a good lady in my book. And Junior was alive.

We got word later that day from the hospital that Jorge Jr. was fine. He was just sore on his sternum where I had done the chest compressions. The kid was without oxygen for a minimum of six minutes, and yet had no brain damage. My wife and I consider it a miracle.

That night I did some research on kids playing in truckloads of corn while the truck is dumping. It's kind of a fun activity. I did it when I was a kid. There have been many deaths under similar circumstances because after the kid gets sucked in, the dad and others shut things down and spend the next hour or two shoveling corn out of the truck. I understand completely why. When you are in the box (truck) and the emergency is on, it is very hard to think outside the box. All you can focus on is the kid that is covered in corn. This paradigm I have firsthand knowledge of.

I counted my blessings that day. I'm sure Jorge and his family did the same.

• •

Another journal post . . .

In the last week, I've had at least ten different times when I should have died from a grain bridge collapsing. The problem was that I didn't know I was on top of the void until last night. I thought an auger was plugged. I have been poking and prodding and pounding and yanking to no avail. I am in shock that it held together. If it had collapsed, I would have had no chance.

I was aware of the danger of grain bridges, but in the reality of the moment, getting the auger unplugged was my only thought. Feeling pretty stupid right now along with pretty lucky. Most of all, feeling blessed and watched over.

Two, little experiences from the last couple of days . . . I was heading down to the corn dryer last night at midnight doing 60 in our little Honda van. Half asleep and leaving my headlights on dim to save electricity, I suddenly saw 15 or 20 cows whiz by my left window. I had no time to react and didn't see them until I was past them. No kidding, they were less than six inches from my outside mirror. Amazing to me, they had the common courtesy to stay in the correct lane and not one of them was over the centerline. They must have all been sober. I have no doubt that with that many cows, my speed, and my "Made in Japan" roadster, I probably wouldn't have survived. I've shaken my head all day at the close call.

The other experience happened the night before last. I picked Michele up at the airport in Pasco after she spent two weeks in Phoenix with a new granddaughter. Coming home on Glade I saw a deputy parked at one of the spud sheds close to Pasco. I figured there would be no more speed traps the rest of the way home.

I was wrong. Coming into Merrill's Corner I noticed a little too late, two more cop cars lying in wait to ambush someone just like me. I hit the brakes, but it was too late. One of the black and whites turned on his red and blues so I pulled over. We shared the common conversation themes like "did I know how fast I was going?" and "why don't I have a current insurance card?" I tried to steer the conversation away from speeding so I focused on blaming my wife for not having a valid registration in the jockey box.

He said he would be right back. I knew I was toast. When he returned, he gave me my outdated paperwork and asked if I still had my seatbelt exemption. I was shocked! I didn't think I knew the guy. How would he know my personal trivia? I squinted my eyes and tried to get a better look in the dark, past the flashlight that was blinding me. I couldn't see who it was so I asked him. He said, "You don't recognize me, do you? I'm the guy you pulled up on a few years ago and read me the riot act."

Immediately I knew who he was. I won't go into the long story about what the problem had been, but let's just say that I was operating on misinformation and shouldn't have come unglued like I did in his presence. After our initial conversation in which I raised my voice, he and I both had a race to see who could call the undersheriff first. I won, but he came in a close second. Right after I unloaded on his superior, he said he had to go as this particular deputy was calling him.

Well, as future events unfolded and I was given some updated information, I realized that I could possibly have been mistaken. So about two weeks later as I was driving down the road, I saw a deputy parked off to the side. I made a quick U-turn and parked. After I got out, I saw that this indeed was the same guy from a couple of weeks previous. I think he tensed up and was getting ready for a bad experience, but after I spoke, he relaxed. I told him I may have been wrong and that I wanted to apologize. He seemed surprised which I don't understand because I have to apologize all the time.

He said that it took a big man to apologize and that he appreciated it. He then asked why I wasn't wearing my seatbelt, which I thought was a little strange, because who wears their seatbelt when they're standing in front of their pickup? I soon realized what he meant and showed him my seatbelt exemption.

Back to the other night, when he told me that he was the guy I had cussed out, I immediately reminded him that I had apologized soon after our first introduction. He said, "I know you did. That's why I'm not giving you a ticket for doing 46 in a 35." I then informed him that I would like to get out of my car and give him a big kiss. He told me that was against regulations, but that we could knock fists. We did.

I drove off ticketless and grateful that I don't have a hard time saying, "I'm sorry. I was wrong." It's been quite a week. This is just the tip of the iceberg.

• •

In February of 2015, I chopped my ring and middle fingers off at the first joint on my left hand with a brake press. I was working on my grain bin project. I had gloves on, but when I hit the pedal and put the press in motion, the poor quality gloves didn't help. The press stroked down, I felt the pain, and because the clearance was fairly tight, the bottom die pulled out of the press bed with my fingers and glove still attached. I was stuck. Lucky for me, Don was there. I yelled at him that I thought I had just cut my fingers off and he needed to bring me a hammer.

When the hammer arrived, I grabbed it and started beating on the bottom die. It soon released and I was set free. I pulled the glove off and the tips were hanging by threads of ligament. I figured these dangling phalanges constituted broken bones. They were the 26th and 27th broken bones I've had, from a running count that began back when I could remember all my injuries.

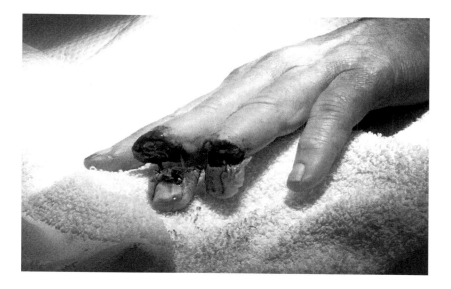

I told Don I was heading for the hospital. He said he would take me. We stood outside on the driveway and argued this point for a good five minutes. I didn't want him to miss out on production and he didn't want me to drive. I finally caved and he hauled me in. Halfway to the hospital, I started feeling "shocky" and was grateful that he had insisted on driving.

Michele came in to the hospital a little later and said that since I'd had this mishap, she'd better tell me that I would be gone the first week of March. On March 3ʳᵈ I would turn 60. Not gone as in dead, but gone as in gone from work. She wanted to prep me to make sure I was able to have all my work caught up.

A note from my journal:

> Went on an instantaneous diet and lost a little weight yesterday, probably just a few ounces. Typing skills, piano and guitar playing, sign language while driving, and nose picking—all no longer in my repertoire. Sheared part of my middle and ring fingers off. I'm already missing the little fellows. Farewell, my dear flanges. The doctor called it "revision of amputation," which probably means I didn't do it right. I must have been heavily sedated for the procedure. After the op I walked by my wife in the hall and didn't even know it. Two days later I went back to work as I had a lot of time-sensitive corn preservation to finish up on before we took off for my birthday trip.

The day came and we got on the plane and flew to Seattle. I had no idea where we were headed. When we got on the plane to Kauai, I figured out my surprise, or so I thought.

We just had carry-ons so I couldn't understand after we landed why my wife insisted we go out of our way and head for the baggage area. Arriving, I came around a corner and saw all these people with big signs and everybody taking pictures.

At first, I thought I was photo bombing a Mormon missionary homecoming and I started to get out of the way. When they yelled, "Surprise!" and started singing "Happy Birthday," I thought it was pretty cool that a missionary was coming home on his birthday. Finally I saw my six kids and their spouses, wondered why they were all there, and actually felt a little bummed that a missionary wasn't coming home on his birthday after all. The disappointment disappeared quickly, however, when I realized they were there for me.

We had a great week. I never thought I'd make it to 60. It was a memorable birthday. Thanks, Michele!

My son-in-law, Todd Holbrook, posted a video of the surprise on You Tube. It's titled, "Ben's Big Surprise."

• •

I saw a ditty on Facebook the other day describing creative people. I might have a sliver of that in me.

Creative people:

- *Easily bored*
- *Risk takers*
- *Color outside the lines*
- *Think with their heart*
- *Make lots of mistakes*
- *Hate the rules*
- *Work independently*
- *Change their mind a lot*
- *Have a reputation for eccentricity*
- *Dream big*

I've learned that my most important trait is never giving up. I've made a ton of mistakes. Everybody does. Those who say they haven't are making an even bigger mistake.

Scot Haws, Ben Casper, (Mom) Joan Casper, Brian Cook

CHAPTER 46

BATTING CLEANUP AT THE END OF THE ROAD

Dad used to tell me he played end and guard on the football team in high school. Then he got a little more detailed by specifying that he sat on the end of the bench and guarded the water bucket. I guess he wasn't a star player. In my book, at least in our later years, he was a star player in my game of life. He had character. At times I have been told I'm a character, so I'll take that as a compliment to mean I'm just like my dad.

A few random thoughts before I close this booklet. The cover picture was not my idea. I had plenty of wacky pics that normally go in my annual Christmas letter and that one happened to be in the mix. I asked Michele which one she liked and she picked my ugly mug. It was not a posed picture.

When my family surprised me on my 60th birthday in Hawaii, we visited some of the sights. I saw Derek's wife, Brianne, taking a shot of Kauai's Na Pali coast. I thought I'd spruce the scenery up and make it a bit more beautiful, so I jumped in front for the photo bomb.

Back in the 80s I played on our local church softball team with good friends. It gave me a lot of fun memories to think back on. We played in a church league and a city league. We also went to quite a few tournaments in the Tri-City, Othello, Spokane and Seattle areas. Some scattered memories include playing in the outfield and running up on a line drive that hadn't landed yet, losing it in the sun, getting smashed in the forehead, and having the sun fade from sight and stars replace it. I found myself flying backwards and landing flat on my back in the grass, realizing I probably wasn't ready for the big leagues.

Another memory was playing in a tournament in Kennewick. In the middle of the contest we played a tavern team made up of guys who were more "advanced" in the sport of softball than ourselves. I figured we were going to get our clocks cleaned.

However, in the first inning, one of their hot dogs hit a soft grounder to short. He knew he didn't stand a chance so he slammed his bat to the ground, yelled a few choice words and walked off the field. I think Vard Jenks was playing short, and after fielding the ball he threw it to first. The first baseman missed the catch and had to scramble to retrieve the ball and get back to tag the base.

The other team went nuts. If the batter had walked to first, he would have been safe. But because he had made no effort, he was out. His team started yelling at him and he responded in the same manner. It wasn't long before there was a brawl between the tavern team and the ousted batsman. We just stood and enjoyed the spectacle. The ump ejected the team and they forfeited the game to us. We advanced in the tournament after the five minute game.

We played for quite a few years during the 80s. During the last year, I was called to be coach. I don't have a lot of skill or strategy up my sleeve but we managed to have a winning season. Most coaches carefully select their batting order by the batting skill and speed of the different players. Me? I would just throw all the players' names in a hat and pull them out one by one. That was our batting order. It changed every game.

It worked. We won games, so it must have been a brilliant strategy. We played in a regional church tournament that year and won. This was mostly due, I think, to my competency in choosing the batting order.

Kent Mackay played in the outfield. He has an arm. On second thought, he has two arms. But one of his arms is worth talking about. He could throw the ball in from the outfield with great accuracy and speed. In high school, he set the record in the state tournament for the javelin by chucking it 219 feet 6 inches.

He also set and still holds another state record (over 40 years old now!) in the football arena. In his senior year he threw five interceptions in the state finals game. What an accomplishment! And yet, in all the years we've hung together, he has never once bragged about that feat.

In the 80s, Kent and I got together and planned a little surprise. I saw a cheap cruise advertised in the newspaper that went from Los Angeles to Ensenada, Mexico, and back. We lined up babysitters, surprised and loaded our wives into Mackay's Bronco at the last moment, and headed south. We drove all night before arriving at the cut rate boat dock. The boat didn't sink, but it wasn't the highest class vessel I've ever been on.

The first night after departing, the four of us were sitting in the dining room just getting ready to tear into some nice juicy steaks on our plates. The weather was getting rough and the boat was rocking. Silverware, plates and glasses were sliding off the tables at regular intervals. I thought it was kind of fun, but I was the only one. Cindy soon excused herself, followed by Michele, and then Kent. They all left with their faces tinted a pale green hue. It was memorable. That was the first dinner I've ever enjoyed while watching a live floor show of tumbling dinnerware, and people periodically jumping up, sliding around and running out. Having four steaks on my plate for the entrée was the highlight. There was no room for dessert.

While we're on the subject of the Mackays, several years ago they invited us to a concert in Spokane, followed by a night in their lake house. We didn't get to their house until after ten that evening. It was beautiful to be on a lake shore and see all the lights from the homes around the water.

Kent mentioned that one of his neighbors had brought in a big floating dock and anchored it in front of their beach property and home. It was against the rules of the community, and the guy had been asked to move it but refused. I could tell Kent was a little bugged, so I suggested we immediately relocate the offending edifice. He was surprised but agreed.

We grabbed a couple of Mackay's kayaks and told the womenfolk we would be back by two o'clock the next morning at the latest. We paddled out to the dock, soon had it disconnected from its moorings, hooked the kayaks up to it and started paddling. It was kind of romantic in the moonlight, with the sound of the water swooshing by as we silently paddled. On second thought, I guess it wasn't all that romantic with just Kent on board.

As we paddled, I noticed that my side of the dock kept getting ahead of Kent's. I wondered if he was a little sick, but I enjoyed the superior advantage of being able to stop paddling every little bit so he could catch up as I rested.

Finally, he verbalized what I had been wondering. He couldn't figure out why he couldn't keep his side of the dock up with mine. He announced that he had decided that I was using the j-stroke. I had no idea what the j-stroke was, but Kent explained that it was some kind of power stroke that veteran paddlers use when they really want to make their boat go. I think Kent was a little disappointed when he heard that I had no knowledge of j-strokes.

The next thing I knew, Kent wanted to trade sides, as he realized that the trouble was probably due to my side of the dock being more streamlined than his. We switched sides. His new side of the dock fell further back than his old side had. At his requests, we traded sides back and forth several more times. He never found his j-stroke.

I noticed water on his cheeks as we rowed. I don't know if some lake water got splashed up there or if they were tears of athletic disappointment, but I did feel kind of sorry for the guy. I slowed my pace from 80% to 30%. The dock stayed on an even track and Kent was happier the rest of the eve.

Other than the j-stroke thing, we had a great time that night. We rowed the dock around a bend in the lake and along a good distance of uninhabited shoreline. After a two or three mile trip, we found a large submerged log just off shore and attached the dock to it. We hopped in the kayaks and paddled home. I was careful not to use the j-stroke. I didn't want to lose Kent.

Kent informed me that a few months later the dock returned to its former and unwelcome spot. I guess we need to start looking for another concert in Spokane.

• •

Through my life, most of my time has been spent in Basin City. I've made a lot of errors in judgment and action. I have had to repent often and repeatedly ask others for forgiveness. I personally don't think this is a bad thing, as I learn and try to maintain friendship with those around me. Apologies and forgiveness are essential in relationships. Luckily, most of my friends have this same attitude. Unfortunately, I have noticed that a few would rather lie, deny, duck and dodge than keep an open, forgiving and honest relationship with others. These are they who can't truly be happy.

I would be remiss if I didn't say how much I appreciate the fact that I was raised in an LDS home. In spite of my slip-ups, I believe the LDS way of life has truly blessed my existence. The church has been a great help for Michele and I in raising our kids into the fine people they are today. Likewise, it is helping them raise their kids. I shudder to think where I, Michele or they would be without its influence.

As I think about my life in the Church, many fond memories come to mind. Much good was derived from the thousands of meetings I've attended in the Basin City LDS building. Two of them were similar because they both occurred on the stand behind the pulpit. One occurred when I was twelve years of age. Twelve and thirteen-year-old boys are called to be deacons in our church. One of the jobs deacons have each Sunday is to pass the sacrament to the congregation. We consider the sacrament to be a renewal of our baptismal covenants and a most important ordinance we can enjoy on a weekly basis.

One Sunday evening I was in the rank of deacons passing the trays of bread and then the trays containing small cups of water to the congregation. I was at the front of the line, which meant I was responsible to walk up and serve the bishop on the podium before the rest of the deacons left the sacrament table to serve everyone else.

As I started to walk up the steps at the front of the chapel, I tripped on the first step. I stumbled up the next two before regaining my balance. Before I got straightened out, however, the inertia of the water in the cups provided Bishop Vern Cook and Brother Don Montierth with a quick and wet shower. They were drenched. The congregation was surprised and intrigued as this scene was completely out of the ordinary. Usually the bishopric sat through the entire meeting in dry suits. But not this evening.

I was mortified. The people I passed the water to that night sipped water out of cups that had no more than an eighth of an inch of water in them. I remember being embarrassed the remainder of the evening.

The other event that comes to mind occurred more recently. A few years ago the Pasco Stake was divided and the Pasco North Stake was formed. The counselors in our bishopric were called into stake positions while

Bishop Rick Nielson continued as our bishop. In a series of memorable events, I was called to be the first counselor in the bishopric.

Normally this calling is not that big of a deal. But it was for me. I still shake my head at the miracle of me being called to serve in the bishopric. In spite of my personality and mistakes and history, Bishop Nielson told me that as soon as he was told that he was losing his two counselors to the stake, my name came to him as one he should call. I sincerely believe that if Rick had not been inspired, my name would have been the last one to pop into his head. It was a great experience and I thank Rick for his willingness and courage to follow the Spirit. I say courage because I'm sure it took some.

Not only do I shake my head at being called to the bishopric. I also shake my head at all the miracles, forgiveness, experiences and growth I have personally enjoyed while being a member of the Church. I wouldn't trade it for all the rice in China.

I will close. But first and most important, I want to thank my temporarily absent parents, eight siblings, one wife, six kids, eleven grandkids, one grandson on the way, hundreds of extended family, several ex-girlfriends and thousands of other good friends for being the great help and support to me they have always been. I'm sure the reader is one of them. If you're not, but want to be, send me ten bucks and I'll put you on my special friend list. You will stay there for one full calendar year from the postmark of your letter. Seriously, I consider myself lucky and blessed because of my friends.

I know my reality is just like everyone else's and doesn't square 100% with real reality or absolute truth. In this manuscript there may have been a few instances where I have thrown a curve ball on the outside corner of reality's strike zone just for effect. Add in legal and litigious considerations, my old age and resulting forgetfulness, dementia and confusion, and I guess I better state that this entire work is fiction and a figment of my imagination. Any stories that don't specifically name the actual people I have a personal relationship with are not real and their story is told for entertainment value only.

A couple of the major teachings in our church focus on two biggies. To be happier, we should all remember them—forgiveness and service.

I forgive everyone for their trespasses against me and I hope everyone else forgives the many various and sundry offenses I have piled up on them. As the great philosopher Rodney King once was rumored to have said, "Can't we all just get along?"

A prophet once stated: "I tell you these things that ye may learn wisdom; that ye may learn that when ye are in the service of your fellow beings ye are only in the service of your God." (Mosiah 2:17) I have been served constantly by those around me throughout my life. And in regards to all I've had experiences with through the years, both good and bad, thank you for the memories and education. I hold no hard feelings and feel much gratitude.

Thanks for reading. I hope it brightened your day. I know that serving and forgiving others and seeking God is what matters most and brings us the most happiness in the eternal scheme of things. I may be an idiot but I'm no dummy.